CULTURAL LEARNING IN HEALTHCARE

Recognizing & Navigating Differences

AMY K. DORE AND ALYSON B. EISENHARDT

NorthAmerican
Business Press
Atlanta – Seattle – South Florida – Toronto

Atlanta, Georgia
Seattle, Washington
South Florida
Toronto, Canada
Cultural Learning in Healthcare: Recognizing and Navigating Differences
ISBN: 9780991607143

Along with trade books for various business disciplines, the North American Business Press also publishes a variety of academic-peer reviewed journals.

Library of Congress Control Number: 2015938816

Library of Congress
Cataloging in Publication Division
101 Independence Ave., SE
Washington, DC 20540-4320

Printed in the United States of America

Table of Contents

Acknowledgements and Contributors

This book has been a journey encompassing three years plus many months of wishing and hoping, investigating, networking, researching, writing, proofing and editing. This endeavor would not have been possible without the help and support of many people. First, we would like to thank our families for their unfailing support and encouragement. As co-authors, we are extremely grateful to the many contributing authors who did not hesitate to commit to this project and help us achieve our goals. We thank you for your patience and for cheering us on and motivating us to "keep moving."

CO-AUTHORS:

Aly Eisenhardt, DHS
Associate Professor
Program Director, Health Care Management
Marymount University
Arlington, VA

Amy Dore, DHA
Associate Professor, Health Care Management
Department of Health Professions
Metropolitan State University of Denver
Denver, CO

CONTRIBUTORS:

Héctor Balcázar, PhD
Regional Dean and Professor
University of Texas Health Science Center-Houston
UTHealth, School of Public Health
El Paso Regional Campus
El Paso, Texas

Christye Brown, MPH, PhDc
Centers for Disease Control and Prevention
Atlanta, Georgia

Debasree DasGupta, PhD
Assistant Professor
Department of Kinesiology
University of Indianapolis
Indianapolis, Indiana

Jeffrey R. Helton, PhD
Assistant Professor, Health Care Management
Department of Health Professions
Metropolitan State University of Denver
Denver, Colorado

Holly E. Jacobson, PhD
Associate Professor
Department of Linguistics
University of New Mexico
Albuquerque, New Mexico

Uma Kelekar, PhD
Assistant Professor of Health Care Management
School of Business
Marymount University
Arlington, Virginia

Susanne Bruno Ninassi, J.D.
Associate Professor, Legal Studies
Department of Health Care Management
and Legal Administration
Marymount University
Arlington, Virginia

Dale Sanders, DO, MBA
Director, Health Care Administration
Assistant Professor, Business Administration &
Health Care Administration
Alma College
Alma, Michigan

Nancy Sayre, D.H.Ed.
Chair
Department of Health Professions
Metropolitan State University of Denver
Denver, Colorado

Erin Seedorf, MPH
Affiliate Faculty, Health Care Management
Department of Health Professions
Metropolitan State University of Denver
Denver, Colorado

Laurie Shanderson, PhD, MPA
Assistant Dean
School of Health Sciences
Stockton University
Galloway, New Jersey

Francisco Soto Mas, MD, PhD, MPH
Associate Professor of Public Health
Department of Family & Community Medicine
University of New Mexico School of Medicine
Albuquerque, New Mexico

Kevin D. Zeiler, JD, MBA
Assistant Professor, Health Care Management
Department of Health Professions
Metropolitan State University of Denver
Denver, Colorado

Chapter 1:

Defining Cultural Learning as a Continuum

Aly Eisenhardt and Amy Dore

KEY CONCEPTS:

Barriers to care
Culture
Cultural competency
Culturally competent
Culturally proficient
Cultural sensitivity
Ethnic
Ethnicity
Health
Health behaviors
Health belief model
Human genome project
Infant mortality
Mortality
Patient centeredness
Plurality nation
Race
Quality of care

CHAPTER OVERVIEW:

This chapter introduces the reader to the concept of cultural competency and the factors that help to formulate health concepts and beliefs. The content facilitates self-reflection and analysis of one's own culture and background. The chapter explains the link between culture, ethnicity, race and health. It proposes further exploration of this link and evaluates how key concepts and terms may be correlated.

WHY IS THIS IMPORTANT?

According to the United States Census Bureau (2013), the world population is expected to grow from 6 billion in 1999 to 9 billion by 2044, a 50 percent increase over the next three decades. By 2060, the U.S. population will be considered a **plurality nation** in which the non-Hispanic white population remains the largest single group, however no group will be the majority. The population will be more racially and ethnically diverse and significantly older (U.S. Census Bureau, 2012). These demographic and population changes are drivers for the need to understand and provide culturally competent healthcare to all populations and groups.

The process of cultural learning occurs along a continuum. Students, employees, and providers of healthcare must have a solid foundation in understanding the links between culture and health. This chapter provides the first stepping-stone in climbing the ladder towards cultural proficiency. In order to achieve cultural proficiency, an introduction to key concepts is necessary to understand how these concepts link to one another. This chapter draws on those links and provides a solid foundation for cultural learning.

CHAPTER EXPECTATIONS:

Upon reading this chapter, the reader will be able to:

- Define the terms: culture, ethnicity and race.
- Apply an understanding of these terms to: health risks, health outcomes, health behaviors, and health beliefs.
- Understand how cultural learning occurs along a continuum.
- Identify and evaluate where you are along the continuum of cultural proficiency.
- Identify and understand how to mitigate health risks and barriers to care, especially for minority populations.

WHAT YOU SHOULD KNOW:

Introduction to Health and Health Beliefs:

The World Health Organization (WHO, 2003) defines **health** as "a state of complete physical, mental and social well-being and not merely the absence of disease or infirmity." Definitions of health vary and thus, it is important to understand how you define health and understand how others around you may define health. In general, it is commonly believed that health is connected to a sense of "complete" wellbeing. How wellbeing is determined and assessed may vary based on individual perspective, background, and the current environment.

In his address to the WHO assembly, Dr. Derek Yach, former Executive Director for Non-communicable Diseases and Mental Health, discussed the topic of health in consideration of the following components: 1) the perception of health, 2) means of improving and maintaining health and, 3) the value and aim of health. In forming opinions and judgments about the definition of health, we consider all three components discussed by Dr. Yach (WHO, 2014). Ultimately, our thoughts about what health means is influenced by who we are, where we come from, and what we have been taught about health and illness. All of these factors help to mold our health beliefs.

Health beliefs are a system of beliefs that help to formulate individual perceptions about health and illness. The **Health Belief Model** (HBM) is used to understand and determine health behaviors. The Health Belief Model (Becker, 1974; Janz & Becker, 1984; Rosenstock,1966) is one of the first theories developed for understanding health behaviors and is still one of the most widely accepted today. The model is used to predict **health behavior** by examining factors of motivation that determine the effectiveness of health communication on an individual's attitude and beliefs. These motivational factors are: 1) perceived susceptibility, 2) perceived severity, 3) perceived benefit, 4) perceived barriers, 5) cues to action, and 6) self-efficacy (Brown, et al., 2011).

In the United States, the Health Belief Model has been used in programs targeting behaviors of minorities and specific ethnic groups. Flaer and colleagues (2010) applied the HBM to predict and change behaviors regarding dental health in underserved populations in the United States. Hispanic Americans were found to act on beliefs supported by those with whom they feel a connection rather than as an individual (Steers, et al., 1996). Structural barriers such as lack of transportation or health insurance were identified as the major factors attributing to low flu vaccination rates among Latinos. This group cited access and cost barriers more than any other ethnic group studied (Chen, et al., 2007).

The Health Belief Model has also been used to predict a patient's compliance with follow-up health care. Factors influencing the intent to keep initial appointments are different from those of keeping follow-up appointments. Subjects who perceived greater negative outcomes from failure to keep appointments were more likely to comply (Irwin, et al., 1993). By understanding and examining the factors that may determine health behavior, we can begin to change negative health behaviors into positive health behaviors.

It is important to understand that negative health behaviors may lead to negative health outcomes. For example, if a patient does not perceive Diabetes Type 2 as a "serious disease" and they do not believe they are susceptible to any of the health outcomes caused by the disease (e.g., stroke, blindness, loss of limb), then that patient may not perceive the benefits of taking a needle of insulin medication multiple times throughout the day. Consequently, that patient will not develop self-efficacy in preventing further disease and damage.

The HBM also addresses "perceived barriers" to healthcare. **Barriers to care** are obstacles that prevent the patient from seeking healthcare. They may be perceived or they may be actual barriers within the healthcare delivery system. For example, a person living in a rural environment may not have access to a healthcare facility within 120 miles of where they live. The person also may not have a reliable vehicle. Furthermore, it may be a financial hardship to spend the day off from work to seek healthcare. In this case, missing a day of work means missing a day of pay.

Introducing Race, Culture, and Ethnicity:

To understand and apply cultural competence, one must first understand the terms associated with this skill. Many of the definitions for culture, race, and ethnicity vary according to the discipline of study. Cultural learning is a process and these terms are at the core of that process.

Ethnicity, as defined by the Institute on Medicine (IOM), in a 1999 report edited by Haynes and Smedley (as noted by the National Center for Cultural Competence, 2013) is "how one sees oneself and how one is seen by others as part of a group on the basis of presumed ancestry and sharing a common destiny...". Factors of ethnicity may "tie" an individual to a specific group through a commonality in: skin color, religion, language, customs, ancestry, and/or geography. Persons belonging to the same ethnic group "may share a unique history different from that of other ethnic groups. Usually a combination of these features identifies an ethnic group" (National Center for Cultural Competence, 2013). The National Center for Cultural Competence (2013) defines the term **ethnic** as "....of or relating to large groups of people classed according to common racial, national, tribal, religious, linguistic, or cultural origin or background." Sharing a common link in ethnic and/racial background may lead to commonalities in health risks, health beliefs, and/or health outcomes.

According to the National Center for Cultural Competence (2013) there are many definitions for **race.** The Center points to the following as representative definitions:

- A tribe, people or nation belonging to the same stock; a division of humankind possessing traits that are transmissible by descent and sufficient to characterize it as a distinctive human type;
- A social construct used to separate the world's peoples. There is only one race, the human race, comprised of individuals with characteristics that are more or less similar to others;
- The IOM (Haynes & Smedley, eds., 1999) states that in all instances race is a social and cultural construct. Specifically a "construct of human variability based on perceived differences in biology, physical appearance, and behavior".

Recent literature demonstrates that the "traditional" concept of race is founded on a false premise that there are natural significant differences in biology and behavior that can be noted between groups. Furthermore, the National Center for Cultural Competence points out that the **Human Genome Project,** conducted by the National Institute of

Health, discovered there is a genetic code that exists for all human beings. This code is 99.9% identical across the human race. Thus, proving there are more differences within groups/races than there are differences across races (IOM, as noted by the National Center for Cultural Competence, 2013).

As noted by Edgede (2006) the US Department of Health and Human Services Office of Minority Health defines the term **culture** as "integrated patterns of human behavior that include the language, thoughts, communications, actions, customs, beliefs, values, and institutions of racial, ethnic, religious, or social groups." One's culture influences actions and behaviors to include health behaviors. Culture has a unique correlation with health and health behaviors. Culture may be indirectly or directly associated with the adoption of specific health beliefs and behaviors (Pasick, et al., 1994). The case example provides explanation of this connection.

Case Example: Connecting Culture and Health

During a public health campaign in Northern Peru, researchers noted that although it is common to practice eye health prevention behaviors in the US, behaviors such as wearing hats and sunglasses for eye health protection is not a common practice in Northern Peru (Eisenhardt & Kelekar, 2013, pending publication). Due to social barriers related to the belief that it is "snobbish" or "rude" to wear sunglasses and hats are often associated with the traditional cultures of Peru that may not seem "cool" to a younger population, the wearing of hats and sunglasses is not common. Thus, the prevalence of eye illnesses related to high UV exposure is common. To provide further analysis of this example, the use of home remedies, such as applying limejuice or honey to the eye is believed to alleviate certain eye conditions. This is one example of how culture and cultural beliefs may affect health and health behaviors.

This book considers culture in the context of health and health behaviors. In this way **culture** has been defined as "unique shared values, beliefs, and practices that are directly associated with a health-related behavior, indirectly associated with a behavior, or influence acceptance and adoption of the health education message" (Pasick, et al. 1994). These learned values and actions could transcend generations (Leniger, 1985, as noted by Edgede, 2006).

It may be obvious that since culture is correlated to health behaviors, healthcare professionals have an obligation to understand how one's culture in terms of health behaviors. However, it is essential for healthcare workers to not only understand, but to apply this understanding in the practice of healthcare. This is the difference between possessing **cultural sensitivity**, an understanding of culture and cultural differences, and being culturally competent. To be **culturally competent**, a healthcare professional must be able to apply the knowledge of cultural beliefs, behaviors, and needs to the context of health to ensure the most positive health outcomes (The Office of Minority Health, 2013). To go a step beyond being cultural competent, becoming **culturally proficient** allows one to be an advocate for the fulfillment of cultural needs and demands. What is important to remember is that cultural learning and application happens along a continuum, meaning that it requires continuous life-long effort on the part of the learner. Figure 1.1 below illustrates this continuum.

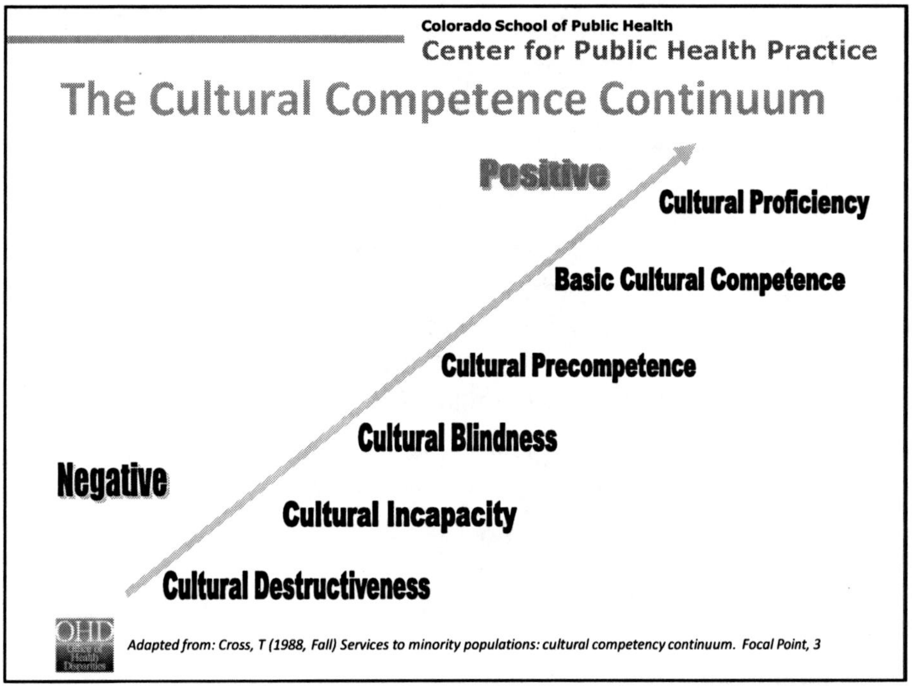

Figure 1. The Cultural Competence Continuum. Source: Cited by the Colorado Department of Public Health & Environment, Office of Health Disparities, Center for Public Health Practice, Colorado School of Public Health. (n.d.). Adapted from: *Cross, T. (1988, Fall) Services to minority populations: cultural competency continuum. Focal Point, 3.*

ACCULTURATION AND ASSIMILITATION:

Self-Assessment:

In order to evaluate and apply cultural competency and proficiency skills, one must first evaluate their own cultural beliefs and values. Since culture is inherently tied into one's world-view and perceptions, it is extremely important to assess one's own cultural perspective prior to evaluating and assessing the cultural perspectives of others. Below are some questions to be answered in assessing one's own culture and background (Adapted from Spector, R., 2009, Cultural Diversity in Health and Illness, Pearson Publishing):

1. What is your cultural heritage?
2. What major socio-cultural traditions and customs do you participate in? Or have participated in the past?
3. What religious or cultural practices do you or your family participate in?
4. How do you acquire economic assistance if needed?
5. What does health mean to you?
6. What does illness mean to you?
7. How do you stay healthy?
8. What traditional healing/illness protection practices have been passed down through the generations of your family?
9. How do you obtain healthcare services?
10. Who provides your healthcare? Do you ever seek assistance outside of the medical community for restoring or maintaining health?

By considering these questions and reflecting on your answers you are taking the first step in becoming culturally proficient. As you continue to explore other cultures be mindful that everyone has different answers for these questions and similar questions. Cultural belief systems are extremely complex and have multiple bonds to how we seek and use healthcare, maintain our health, and seek to become free of illness and/or injury.

Lack of Quality Care for Minorities:

According to the Kaiser Family Foundation (2013), "54% of people of color are projected to account for the majority of the U.S. population in 2050." Minority populations often are victim to healthcare disparities, inequities in quality of healthcare received, and optimal health outcomes. Although great strides have been taken to lessen the frequency and impact of healthcare disparities in the Nation, more work needs to be completed and the need among minority populations is greater than ever.

Social, cultural, and language barriers exist in the delivery and receipt of healthcare services. Differences in culture and language may affect communication, trust, and one's ability to properly use the healthcare system (Coleman-Miller, 2000; as noted by the Office of Minority Health, 2002).

In the Healthcare Disparities and Inequalities Report (2011), the CDC points to the following six broad domains relating to disparities in care:

1. Social Determinants of Health
2. Environmental Hazards
3. Healthcare Access and Preventive Health Services
4. Health Outcomes- Morbidity
5. Health Outcomes- Mortality
6. Health Outcomes- Behavioral Risk Factors

"People who live at a low socioeconomic level experience higher risk for mortality, morbidity, unhealthy behaviors, reduced access to healthcare, and inadequate quality of care" (CDC, 2011). Having a lower socioeconomic status is correlated to education and income level. If an individual is of lower income and lower education level that individual is at greater risk for experiencing poorer health outcomes over their more affluent counterpart. Persons living below the poverty level experience disparities in health and healthcare services, which leads to poorer health outcomes.

People living in unsafe homes are also at greater risk for experiencing diminished health. National efforts are being made to ensure that homes have safe ventilation systems, adequate waste-water and sewage, and proper smoke and carbon monoxide detectors. Although, the CDC acknowledges improvements in this area, "the disparity by race/ethnicity, socioeconomic status, and educational level is still substantial" (CDC, 2011). For example, non-Hispanic Blacks were the highest percentage of those living in "unhealthy" homes, followed by Hispanics and American Indians/Alaska Natives as noted in the Health Disparities Report (CDC, 2011).

Having health insurance is a strong indicator of health outcomes. In 2004 and 2008, nationally, there were more people between the ages of 18-34 who reported not having insurance versus older adults (CDC, 2011). Hispanics and non-Hispanic blacks also had higher rates of lacking health insurance (CDC, 2011). Without health insurance, people are more likely to delay needed healthcare and skip preventive care, such as screenings and exams. The uninsured also tend to not have primary care providers, thus seeking care through the emergency department, where care may be fragmented and not continuous and much more expensive.

Mortality is defined as the proportion of deaths to a population (Meriam-Webster). Causes of disproportionate mortality risks among racial/ethnic minorities include: homicide, suicide, motor vehicle related deaths, coronary heart disease and strokes (CDC, 2011). For example, in 2009, the African Americans population had the largest rates of death from cardiovascular disease and stroke as compared to other racial populations (CDC, 2013). The risk of death in all of these areas demonstrates a higher frequency of occurrence among minority populations. **Infant mortality** rates are commonly used to illustrate the overall health status of a population and for comparisons across societies. Infant mortality is calculated as "infant deaths per 1,000 live births" (LaVeist, 2005). In 2006, the overall infant mortality rate in the United States was 6.68 infant deaths per 1,000 births (CDC, 2011). The CDC (2011) noted considerable disparities among minority groups with the rate for non-Hispanic black women 2.4 times higher than for non-Hispanic white women.

Differences in the prevalence of morbidity, or the incidence of disease, also exist between minority populations and non-minority populations. In 2007, the incidence of preterm labor was 59% higher for non-Hispanic blacks and 49% higher for Hispanics than for non-Hispanic white women (CDC, 2011). Furthermore, the prevalence of obesity is higher among blacks than it is among whites (CDC, 2011). Unhealthy behaviors, such as the use of tobacco, are the highest among the Native American and Native Alaskan population (CDC, 2011). Through policy, education, and prevention, disparities in obesity and obesity-related diseases, such as Type 2 Diabetes, can be lessened. Population-based programs have been proven to be effective in this regard (CDC, 2011). Healthcare professionals have a responsibility to recognize and help avoid preventable diseases and inequities in healthcare. Culturally competent professionals can help mitigate the risk of healthcare disparities.

Linking Trends in Patient Centered Care:

The Institute of Medicine (2001) defines four essential components of **quality care**: safety, effectiveness, timeliness, and patient-centered care. At the core of these components is the assurance that care is provided by culturally competent providers at a culturally competent organization. All components are essential to the quality of care received.

"**Patient centeredness** refers to health care that establishes a partnership among practitioners, patients, and their families (when appropriate) to ensure that decisions respect patients' wants, needs, preferences, and the education and support patients' need to make decisions and participate in their own care" (IOM, 2001). A patient-centered focus considers the patient as a whole person, rather than just the disease or illness. Considering the patient within the context of the "whole," must include acquiring and applying cultural, racial, and ethnic knowledge that pertain to patient encounters (Office of Minority Health, 2002). Physicians must understand and apply the cultural influences on health behaviors and any alternative health treatments that may be incorporated in care (Office of Minority Health, 2002).

Central to patient-centered care is a system of open communication between the provider and the patient based on trust. Trust cannot occur without a mutual understanding of one another. Patients' mistrust of the healthcare system has been sited as a contributing factor to healthcare disparities (Office of Minority Health, 2002). Decades of inequality of health care provisions in the United States have created a sense of mistrust, primarily among minority populations and the poor. Additionally, certain populations hold belief systems that differ from the traditional Western medical practices. In order to reduce mistrust and build rapport amongst these populations, cultural beliefs, such as cultural/folklore, spirituality, and familial practices, must be acknowledged by healthcare providers. Furthermore, providers must practice "knowledge without judgment" and demonstrate openness to the patient's belief systems and practices related to his or her illness behaviors (Rose, 2013). Trust between patients and healthcare professionals should be reciprocal and built on a common understanding of one another, which includes culture.

In building a system of open communication and trust, providers must commit to the process cultural competence. This process requires self-reflection, experience, and a dedication to ongoing learning (Office of Minority Health, 2002). Providers must be active listeners when dealing with patients. Healthcare professional committed to the process of cultural competence help to ensure the delivery of quality care to all populations.

An Example of A Cultural "Collision":

In her novel, *The Spirit Catches and You Fall Down*, Anne Fadiman, tells the true story of Lia Lee, the daughter of refugee parents from Laos living in a small county in California. The family was from the Hmong culture common to their origins in Northeast Laos. Lia Lee, had a seizure disorder, which her family recognized as an act of the supernatural, "when the spirit and you fall down." Due to miscommunication and a "collision" of cultures between the American doctors and the Hmong family, an avoidable tragedy occurred and the young girl died.

Anne Fadiman discusses Harvard Medical Professor, Arthur Keinman's, set of cross-cultural medical questions developed to illicit an explanatory response from the patient (Fadiman, 1999). The author discusses the questions and explores Lia's parents' hypothetical responses. The purpose of exploring the possible responses by Lia's parents is to stress how their interpretation of Lia's condition might have assisted the medical staff in seeing the complete patient situation. Unfortunately, the medical staff never asked the parents. Below are the questions and responses that may have been given (Fadiman, 1997, p. 260):

1. What do you call the problem? *Quag dah peg; when the spirit catches you and you fall down.*
2. What do you think has caused the problem? *The loss of the soul.*
3. Why do you think it started when it did? *Lia's sister, Yer, slammed the door and Lia's soul was frightened out of her body.*
4. What do you think the sickness does? How does it work? *It makes Lia shake and fall down. It works because spirit called a dah is catching her.*
5. How severe is the sickness? Will it have a short or long term course? Why are you asking those questions? *If you are a good doctor, you should know the answers yourself.*
6. What kind of treatment do you think the patient should receive? What are the most important results that you hope she receives from this treatment? *You should give Lia some medicine for a week but no longer. After she is well, she should stop taking the medicine. You should not treat her by taking blood or fluid from her backbone. Lia should also be treated at home with our Hmong medicines and by sacrificing pigs and chickens. We hope Lia will be healthy, but we are not sure that we want her to stop shaking forever because it makes her noble in our culture, and when she grows up she might be a shaman.*
7. What are the chief problems that the sickness has caused? *It made us sad to see Lia hurt, and it make us angry at Yer.*
8. What do you fear most about the sickness? *That Lia's soul will not return.*

The questions and answers discussed above provide a clear view of the family's perceptions about Lia's illness. However, since this discussion between the doctors and the family did not occur, Lia's condition worsened and she died. Her death was the cause of miscommunication, mistrust, and misunderstandings between the American Western Medical Culture and the Northern Laos Medical Culture.

CONCLUSION:

This book is meant to be a tool to guide healthcare professionals through the process of understanding cultural competency and proficiency. Recognizing the diverse demographic composition of those living in the United States is one step towards understanding the need to provide high quality, culturally respectful health care. Chapter one introduced concepts such as cultural competency, cultural proficiency, cultural sensitivity, health behaviors, patient centeredness, and race. In order to be prepared for the demographic changes expected to occur in the United States over the next 30-40 years, healthcare professionals must be prepared to provide health services to a diverse population. With this come challenges in recognizing the differing health needs, approaches, and expectations of these differing populations. The first step is to understand how populations define "health" and the correlating cultural belief systems pertaining to personal wellness, prevention, health risks, and health outcomes. The belief that the same health model, the same treatment regime, and the same expected outcome is sufficient to meet all populations' needs will only reinforce culturally *incompetent* care that, ultimately, increase the barriers to care, health burdens, and mistrust of the healthcare system that is currently experienced by these underserved, minority populations. Taking the steps to increase cultural competency, proficiency, awareness, and patient centeredness as approaches to address the diverse needs of varying populations will promote the quality of healthcare provided, the patient's willingness to seek care, and the overall health outcomes.

CASE STUDIES:

Case #1:
Background:

The U.S. shares a 2,000-mile long border with Mexico that is easily crossed in both directions. The flow of people, goods, and ideas across it has a powerful impact on both countries. This is reflected in such facts as:

- Los Angeles has an extremely high urban Mexican population.
- Mexican Americans make up the majority of the largest non-English speaking population in the U.S.
- The Mexican American population is the fastest growing population in the U.S.
- The U.S. is the 6th ranking Spanish-speaking nation in the world. (CDC, The Hispanic Population, 2010)

Contrary to popular belief that most Mexicans live in rural areas, most live in urban locations. Mexicans are employed in all types of jobs, few however, have high paying or high status jobs in labor or management. The majority of the population works in factories, mines, and construction. Uninsured and uneducated rates are high.

You are heading a committee to establish a much needed community center along the border of Mexico and California (on the states' side). Your focus is to serve the large Hispanic population in this area, many of which may be in the U.S. illegally.

Step #1: Look closely at the population in your catchment area. Conduct research about Hispanics, who reside in California. Look at the demographic and health trends for this population. Gather the necessary information to make informed decisions about your new health care facility.

Step #2: Answer the below questions.

1. What type of facility will it be (community center, service specific, hospital, outpatient, ancillary care)?
2. What health care services do you want to offer? What services would you not offer? Why?
3. Who are the key staff members? Additional staff members?
4. What other community, state, or federal resources do you need to work in conjunction with to build quality and continuity in health care services?
5. What type of funding resources are available?
6. How would you go about advertising your facility?
7. How would you ensure that you are continuously meeting the changing needs of your population?
8. What would be the major focuses of the facility?
9. What would your payment system be?
10. What do you think the barriers would be to maintaining continuity of care for this population?
11. Any other issues you foresee in treating this population?
12. Would this facility alleviate some of the stressors on other local health care facility, which does not specialize in caring for this population? If so, why and how?

Think about the health risks, beliefs, and culture discussed during class to develop your scenario. Also, search the Internet for current community resources for Mexican Americans. Be sure to document your sources.

Case #2:
Background:

Health Disparities are a major issue for many minority populations. African Americans are no exception.

- The leading causes of death for this population group are:
  - Heart Disease
  - Cancer
  - Stroke
  - Unintentional Injuries
  - Diabetes
  - Homicide
  - Chronic lower respiratory disease
  - Nephritis
  - HIV/AIDS
  - Septicemia
  - African Americans make up 13% of the US population
- The African American population is represented throughout the country, with the greatest concentrations in the Southeast and mid-Atlantic regions, especially Louisiana, Mississippi, Alabama, Georgia, South Carolina, and Maryland.
- A large percentage of the African American population is represented in the South, as such many of the counties inhabited by the African American population are non-metropolitan areas. Other high prevalence health issues include: Hypertension, infant mortality, and TB (CDC, Black and African American Populations, 2013)

Step #1: You are heading a committee to establish a community health center in a rural Southern county (within a state and area of your choice). Your focus is on disease prevention and population education. The demographics of your catchment area are primarily African American. Your goal is to serve those who are underserved in this area. How might this be accomplished?

Step #2: Look closely at the population in your catchment area. Research African Americans in the South. Look at the demographic and health trends for this population. Gather the necessary information to make informed decisions about your new health care facility. What are some of the considerations you will need to include when establishing a community health center in this type of area and for this population?

Case #3:
Background:

American Indians and Alaska Natives (AI/ANs) are people having origins in any of the original peoples of North and South America (including Central America), and who maintain tribal affiliation or community attachment. There are 569 federally recognized AI/AN tribes, plus an number of unknown tribes that are not federally recognized. Each tribe has its own culture, beliefs, and practices. Many of these tribes are served by the United States Public Health Service/Indian Health Service for their healthcare needs. However, many tribes are located in extremely isolated and rural geographic regions with the nearest facility over 50 miles away from their homes.

- According to the 2000 U.S. Census, those who identify only as AI/AN constitute 0.9 percent of the United States population, or approximately 2.5 million individuals.
- The greatest concentrations of AI/AN populations are in the West, Southwest, and Midwest, especially in Alaska, Arizona, Montana, New Mexico, Oklahoma, and South Dakota.
- Geographic isolation, economic factors, and tendency towards traditional spiritual beliefs are some of the reasons why health among this population is poorer than other groups.
- Among this group there are high incidence of obesity, sudden infant death syndrome (SIDS), mental health issues, and substance abuse. (CDC, American Indian and Alaska Native Populations, 2013)

Step #1: You are heading a committee to establish a community health center in a rural South Dakota county. Your focus is on disease prevention and population education. Your goal is to treat the tribes in this area. First, look closely at the population in your catchment area. Research Native Americans in South Dakota. What tribes may be located out there?

Step #2: Look at the demographic and health trends for this population. Gather the necessary information to make informed decisions about your new health care facility. What information did you find?

Movie and Discussion:
In-Class view the movie Sicko, by Director Michael Moore

Discussion Questions:

1. Whose story made the biggest impression on you? Why?
2. What are the issues facing the uninsured and underinsured in America?
3. How can these issues be resolved? Do you think the Nation is improving this situation? Why or why not?
4. What can you, as future healthcare professionals due to improve disparities among the uninsured and underinsured in America?

Classroom Discussion Opportunity:

Explain the difference between generalizations and stereotypes. Ask students if they think it could be beneficial to make generalizations, discuss why or why not? Ask students to give examples about how generalizations may be helpful in healthcare, but why it is important to ask questions, consider the patient as a whole, and not to make assumptions.

Classroom Activity:

Activity Adapted from "Building Bridges," A Peace Corps Classroom Guide to Cultural Understanding (n.d.)

Objective: Understanding how cultural norms and values influence perception and behavior.

Instructions:

1. Remove the furniture from the center of the classroom to allow space to move around freely.
2. Split the class into two groups. Half of the group will receive nametags with the word "Pandya" printed on them. The other half will receive nametags with the word "Chispa" printed on it.
3. Have the groups go to each side of the room. Provide each group member with the list of cultural norms below that pertain to their assigned group. All Chispas will have the cultural norms for Chispas and all Pandyas will have the cultural norms for Pandyas.

4. Discuss separately with each group their cultural norms and stress the importance of staying in character and abiding by these norms when interacting.
5. Announce that there are two nations invited to a party. Each person is from the nation they have been assigned.
6. Have the two groups socialize with one another for about 10 – 15 minutes. While the groups are interacting the instructor should walk around and observe.

Pandya Cultural Norms:

- Pandyas prefer to interact with members of their own culture.
- Pandyas do not initiate conversation. They speak only when spoken to.
- Pandyas have very formal speech patterns. For example, they always use "sir" and "ma'am."
- Among Pandyas, women have more status than men. Men are chaperoned by Pandya women.
- Pandya men avoid eye contact with women from other cultures.
- Pandya men do not talk directly to women from other cultures. They respond through their chaperones.
- Pandya men can talk to men from other cultures. They can maintain eye contact with men from other cultures.

Chispa Cultural Norms:

- Chispas are informal and friendly.
- Among Chispas, there are no gender roles. Men and women behave the same way.
- Chispas are outgoing. They love to make contact with people from other cultures.
- Chispa contacts are brief and casual.
- Chispas are democratic and call everyone by his or her first name.

Discussion Questions after Exercise:

1. How did you the norms of your group make you feel? How did the norms of the other group make you feel?
2. Did your group members respect the norms of the other group? Of your own group?
3. What did you observe about the other culture?
4. How do you think this might relate to real-world cross-cultural interactions?

Role Play Activities:

Scenario 1:

Student 1: You are a Chinese man who has been hospitalized with a fractured hip. Post surgery, your doctor has prescribed pain medication three times a day. Each time the nurse comes in you refuse the medication.

Student 2: You are the nurse assigned to the man. Following the doctor's instructions you offer the patient his medication each time as scheduled. The patient refuses to take his medication each time. You are becoming extremely frustrated with the patient. You feel that the patient is just being stubborn. It is obvious that he is in extreme pain. What do you do?

Notes for Instructor: In the Chinese culture stoicism is a common attitude. Pain is accepted as part of suffering and enduring. The patient may also not want to bother the nurse, as she may be busy with other patients. Using a pain scale to assess pain and asking the patient again if he would like medication would be appropriate.

Scenario 2:

Student 1: You are a Vietnamese mother, who has just recently delivered your first baby. You do not look at the baby or show any interest and affection to the child nor does your husband, the baby's father.

Student 2: You are the nurse assigned to a new mother. You are shock and upset at the lack of interest the new parents show in their newborn. The couple seems to have minimal physical contact with the child. They do not cuddle or fuss over the child at anytime. You feel extremely bad for the child and are concerned the parents may neglect the child when they go home. What do you do?

Notes for Instructor: There is a Vietnamese belief that showing newborn babies a lot of attention and appreciate invites evil spirits. Parents will not draw a lot of attention to the baby and will say the opposite of the baby is "cute or pretty."

Scenario 3:

Student 1: You are a 65 year-old Cuban woman, whose 66-year-old Cuban male spouse is hospitalized for chest pain. He has hypertension and chronic cardiac disease. Doctors alter his medication regiment and give him a strict low sodium, low fat die and low impact exercise to follow. The nurse educator has been working with him to ensure he will understand and follow this new medical regime. The nurse speaks only to your husband when providing information and she expects that he will take care of himself.

Student 2: You are the nurse assigned to a 66-year-old Cuban male hospitalized for chest pain. He has hypertension and chronic cardiac disease. You note that every time you enter his hospital room his wife is feeding him, bathing him, or otherwise tending to his every personal need. You have repeatedly stressed the patient is able to and should care for himself in order to keep up his strength and wellbeing. On the last day prior to discharge you are working diligently to review the medication and diet with the couple. You become extremely frustrated when the man appears to pay no attention to your instructions and is visibly ignoring you, while the wife is being very attentive and even taking notes. You assume that the patient has no interest in his own health. What do you do?

Instructor's notes: It is common in man Hispanic cultures for woman to take care of men. A "machismo" attitude, where women are caregivers and men are providers is often accepted and does not have a negative connotation.

Culture as and Iceberg Exercise:

Discussion:

Culture has often been described as an Iceberg with factors above the waterline that are visible to the outside observer; dress, language, food, customs, etc. and those factors (accounting for a larger portion of culture) that are not visible below the waterline; body language, concepts of time, values, attitudes, etc.

Instructions:

In groups, have the students draw Icebergs and begin to identify and provide examples for each component of culture that might be "above the waterline" or easily visible versus those components of culture that might be "below the waterline" or not easily visible.

Have each group present their iceberg.

Ask students how making assumptions based on what is "visible culture" might be detrimental? How might this apply to a healthcare setting?

Are there factors that are easily changeable?

Discussion Questions:

1. Discuss the concept of acculturation, when members of one group take on the beliefs or values of another group.
2. Discuss the concept of assimilation, the process whereby a minority group blends with the majority. Ask students for examples. Ask if this is positive or negative?

Suggested Assignments and Papers:

Following APA format, write a 5 to 7 page double spaced paper on a minority population of your choice. Concisely and accurately discuss all of the following topics:

I. The general demographics of the population
- numbers
- where they live
- socio economic status (SES)

II. Background Information
- Where did they originate?
- What is the background and history on this population?
- Outline significant historical events that may be relevant to the current state of this group.

III. Health Risks/Biological
- What are the prevalence incidences of specific diseases?
- Top leading causes of morbidity and mortality?

IV. Cultural Issues
- Cultural practices
- Methods of healing

V. Health Concerns and Disparities
- Why are they more prone to certain diseases?
- What are the reasons for disparities (access to care, barriers, cultural concerns, environmental issues, etc.)

VI. Community Resources
- What are some of the community resources that are available to this group either within the state or nationally?

VII. Conclusion
- Summarize what you found in your research?

REFERENCES:

Center for Disease Control. (2011). Health Disparities and Inequalities Report. Retrieved from http://www.cdc.gov/minorityhealth/reports/CHDIR11/ExecutiveSummary.pdf

Center for Disease Control (2010). The Hispanic Population. Retrieved from http://www.census.gov/prod/cen2010/briefs/c2010br-04.pdf

Center for Disease Control (2013). Black or African American Populations. Retrieved from http://www.cdc.gov/minorityhealth/populations/REMP/black.html#Disparities

Center for Disease Control (2013). American Indian and Alaska Native Populations. Retrieved From http://www.cdc.gov/minorityhealth/populations/REMP/aian.html

Chen, J. Y., Fox, S. A., Cantrell, C. H., Stockdale, S. E., & Kagawa-Singer, M. (2007). Health disparities and prevention: racial/ethnic barriers to flu vaccinations. *Journal of Community Health*, 32(1), 5-20.

Colorado Department of Public Health & Environment, Office of Health Disparities, Center for Public Health Practice, Colorado School of Public Health. (n.d.). Adapted from: *Cross, T. (1988, Fall) Services to minority populations: cultural competency continuum. Focal Point, 3*

Edgede, L. (2006). Race, Ethnicity, Culture, and Disparities in Health Care. *Journal of General Internal Medicine*. June: 21(6): 667-669.

Eisenhardt, A., and Kelekar, U. (2013). Peru Eye Health Project Survey and Focus Group Reports, Unpublished.

Flaer, P., Younis, M., Benjamin, P., & Al Hajeri, M.. (2010, October). A Psychosocial Approach to Dentistry for the Underserved: Incorporating Theory into Practice. *Journal of Health Care Finance*, 37(1), 101-108.

Hazavehei, S.M.M., Sharifirad, Mohabi, S. (2007). The Effect of Educational Program Based on Health Belief Model on Diabetic Foot Care. *The International Journal of Diabetes in Developing Countries*, Volume 27, Issue 1, p18-23.

Irwin Jr., C. E., Millstein, S. G., & Ellen, J. M. (1993). Appointment-Keeping Behavior in Adolescents: Factors Associated With Follow-up Appointment-Keeping. *Pediatrics*, 92(1), 20.

Janz, N. & Becker, M. (1984). The Health Belief Model: A Decade Later. *Health Education Quarterly*, 11, 1-47.

Kaiser Family Foundation. (2013). Electronically retrieved from http://kff.org/disparities-policy/

Leininger MM. (1985) Transcultural care diversity and universality: a theory of nursing. *Nursing Health Care* ;6:208–12.

LaVeist, T.A. (2005). *Minority populations and health: An introduction to health disparities in the United States.* San Francisco, CA: Jossey-Bass.

National Center for Cultural Competence. (2013). Georgetown University, Center for Child and Human Development. Retrieved from http://www.nccccurricula.info/glossary.html

Office of Health and Human Services (2013), Administration of Aging. Retrieved from http://www.aoa.gov/AoARoot/Aging_Statistics/future_growth/future_growth.aspx

Pasick, RJ, D'Onofrio CN, and Otero-Sabogal R. (1994). Similarities and differences across cultures: questions to inform a third generation for health promotion research. *Health Education Quaterly*. V23: S142-61.

Rose, P.R. (2013). *Cultural competency for the health professional.* Burlington, MA: Jones & Bartlett Learning.

Steers, W., Elliott, E., Nemiro, J., Ditman, D., & Oskamp, S. (1996). Health Beliefs as Predictors of HIV-Preventive Behavior and Ethnic Differences in Prediction. *Journal of Social Psychology*, 136(1), 99-110.

The Office of Minority Health, 2013. Retrieved from http://minorityhealth.hhs.gov/templates/browse.aspx?1v1=2&lvlID=11

The Office of Minority Health, US Department of Health and Human Services. (2002). Teaching Cultural Competence in Health Care: A Review of Current Concepts, Policies, and Practices.

The Institute of Medicine (2001). Envisioning the National Healthcare Quality Report: Committee on the National Quality on Health Care Delivery. Retrieved from The National Academy Press at http://books.nap.edu/openbook.php?record_id=10073&page=R1

United States Census Bureau. (2013, December 19). *International Programs.* Retrieved from http://www.census.gov/population/international/data/idb/worldpopgraph.php

United States Census Bureau. (2012, December 12). *U.S. Census Bureau Projections Show a Slower Growing, Older, More Diverse Nation a Half Century from Now.* Retrieved from http://www.census.gov/newsroom/releases/archives/population/cb12-243.html

World Health Organization, WHO, Definition of Health (2003). Retrieved at http://who.int/about/definition/en/print.html

Yach, D. (2004). Health and illness: The definition of the World Health Organization. Retrieved March 6, 2014 from http://www.medizinethik.ch/publik/health_illness.htm

Chapter 2:

An Introduction to Overcoming Access and Utilization Barriers To Health Care

Laurie Shanderson and Dale Sanders

KEY CONCEPTS:

Access to care/services
Accessibility
Affordability
Barriers to care/services
Emergency Medical Treatment & Labor Act (EMTALA)
Medically indigent
Patient Protection Affordable Care Act (PPACA)
Policy implementation
Public health
Social determinants of health

CHAPTER OVERVIEW:

There are many factors that influence individual and population access to and utilization of healthcare services. Barriers that prevent or impede care-seeking behaviors include, but are not limited to: economic, social, and quasi-economic challenges. The unfortunate outcome of these barriers is the marginalized health status of certain individuals. This chapter explores the reasons why the health care system has eluded various groups (segments of the United States population) and why disparities exist. Additionally, an exploration of the Patient Protection and Affordable Care Act (PPACA) and measures to minimize barriers to utilization will be considered.

WHY IS THIS IMPORTANT?

According to research, access to care, in its various forms, is the single most salient impediment to one's ability to enter into the healthcare system. For certain populations (vulnerable) access to care can ultimately determine the quality of one's life. The inability to access care and determine a usual source of care is a main reason why people go without and/or delay seeking medical care. While current literature and research discusses many issues that significantly impact vulnerable populations (e.g., language, affordability, race/ethnicity, and gender), significant gaps still exist. Understanding the factors

> FAQ: The United States spends more money on health care than any other country (2010 = $2.6 trillion/17.9% of GDP. No other country spends over 12% of their GDP (Davidson, 2013).

that impede access for vulnerable populations is key in addressing health disparities and maximizing health for all.

CHAPTER EXPECTATIONS:

Upon reading this chapter, the student will be able to:

- Explain the concept and understand the nature of "access to care" issues.
- Understand the barriers to care for defined populations.
- Contrast and explain economic, non-economic and quasi-economic barriers to care.
- Identify utilization, barriers to care, and the groups impacted by barriers to care.
- Appreciate how access to care impacts utilization for all, including vulnerable populations.
- Recognize the importance of the Patient Protection and Affordable Care Act (PPACA) as it relates to access for vulnerable populations.
- Understand the key considerations necessary to minimize access and utilization barriers to care.

INTRODUCTION:

The reasons why a person may not be able to seek regular or even emergency care are still widely underappreciated. The Agency for Healthcare Research and Quality (AHRQ) completes extensive research each year leading to an annual *National Healthcare Disparities Report* (NHDR) and *National Healthcare Quality Report* (NHQR). This research has repeatedly shown that uninsured individuals were less likely to receive suggested care for disease prevention measures, such as: cancer screenings, dental care, diet and exercise counseling, flu vaccination, and recommendations for disease management (example: diabetes care management) (AHRQ, 2014).

While many people might argue that unpopular policy implementation has threated or prevented access to healthcare services, the truth is that for certain segments of the population healthcare provision has a history of being elusive. It is a fact that not having health insurance or having only limited health insurance is a major obstacle relative to receiving healthcare services. However, with regard to underserved and disparaged groups, we also recognize that socioeconomic status (SES), geographic location, and race are part of the equation. For example, even with insurance, individuals living in rural or inner cities do not have the same access to providers, facilities, or comprehensive hospitals as their counterparts in urban and suburban areas.

Stephen Davidson (2013) suggests utilizing a two-pronged approach when researching the problems facing our health system – the individual perspective and the aggregate perspective. The *individual perspective* considers three possible reasons why Americans lack access to needed services:

1. The location of where a person resides has an inadequate supply of doctors, hospitals, and other health professionals and facilities.
2. Lack of health insurance or lack of adequate health insurance.
3. For those insured, high out-of-pocket costs, e.g., cost sharing – the amounts not covered by insurance.

The *aggregate perspective* takes into consideration the collection or the "whole" (vulnerable population) instead of individual health care needs. For example, many individuals view their health care issues on the individual level and, therefore, do not feel the issues are important enough for corrective public policy changes. When the issues are viewed in the aggregate perspective the "whole" suddenly becomes more apparent. Understanding this and other barriers that contribute to limited access and prevent utilization of healthcare services is an important step in preventing health issues and reducing disparities in the United States.

HISTORICAL CONTEXT:

Access, when related to health care, refers to ones ability to obtain care when needed and/or desired (Shi & Singh, 2015). There are many obstacles that might impede one's ability to seek care and for some, these obstacles may be compounded. For example, an older person with limited mobility and no transportation living in a rural area. This person may find it difficult to get to the only clinic in town that operates during standard office hours.

According to Kovner and Knickman (2011), "Factors determining ease of access also include availability of health care facilities, transportation to them and reasonable hours of operation." These factors may also be known as **barriers to care**.

The following list further illustrates reasons why individuals may not be able to access care. Note that some may overlap.

Barriers to Accessing Healthcare Services:

- Lack of or inadequate health insurance
- Availability of health care facilities
- Geographic barriers (location of residence)
- Lack of transportation
- Reasonable hours of operation
- Irregular source of care
- Legal obstacles
- Language barriers, and
- Age (Kovner and Knickman, 2011; Mandal, 2014)

Access to health care is measured through:

- Structural measures of the absence or presence of particular resources that facilitate health care, i.e., having health insurance and/or a usual source of care,
- Evaluations from patients of how easily they can gain access to health care, and
- Utilization measures such as the successful receipt of needed medical services. (AHRQ, 2014)

The scope of how health care services are used refers to **utilization**. Furthermore, utilization "refers to the consumption of health care services and the extent to which health care services are used" (Shi & Singh, 2015). For many reasons, it is important to measure utilization. Imagine how useful it would be for a local public health department to know how many children in an inner city low-income catchment area are utilizing free physicals or immunization services? Additionally, understanding why women seek medical treatments more than men is important in understanding women's health issues.

Along with barriers to care, there are many factors that influence utilization of medical services including:

- Type of insurance coverage
- Health status
- Availability of health care facilities and health care providers
- New markets generated by the development of new treatments or medical procedures
- Differing provider practice patterns and standards of care

While research on recent healthcare reform shows an overall decrease in hospital admissions and average length of stay, utilization of outpatient visits has more than doubled. Similarly, visits to specialty healthcare services have increased more than 40 percent. It may not be a surprise that the utilization of prescription drugs has also increased (HCCI, 2013). However, the overall rate of growth as measured by the National Health Expenditure shows a general decrease in annual growth in overall healthcare spending per insured individual (particularly for years 2009, 2010, and 2011), which is the lowest rate since reporting began in 1960 (U.S. GPO, "Reducing Costs And Improving The Quality Of Health Care," n.d.).

Many assumptions may be made about the relationships between decreasing hospital admissions and average length of stay corresponding to the increases in specified utilization rates. Intuitively, this pattern may be linked to the fact that as a greater number of Americans become insured, they will be more likely to use outpatient healthcare services. Thus, it is less likely they will be admitted to the hospital. Consequently, they also are more likely to receive needed specialty care referrals. Following this pattern, the overall spending per insured individual would decrease, since these patients will be more likely to receive needed services, which would have a lower dollar cost than an extended hospital stay.

It is important to consider the changes that healthcare reform has put into place. A few of the changes indicated in the PPACA includes: 1) efficiencies in hospital spending, 2) the incorporation of healthcare information management systems, and 3) better coordination of care. These changes and others in the new healthcare law improve healthcare spending, as well as, the overall value of healthcare. The changes are also an attempt at "leveling the playing field" for all Americans with regard to healthcare service access and utilization. It is important to consider healthcare value from multiple stakeholder perspectives to include the patient, the payer, and the providers. All stakeholders must work together to ensure the value and quality of healthcare services is equally and fairly distributed and received (White House, "The Affordable Care Act and Trends in Health Care Spending," n.d.).

WHAT YOU SHOULD KNOW:

For many individuals, the health care system they utilize is defined in large measure by the insurance plans or entitlement programs to which they may access (Williams & Torrens, 2008). In order to understand the effects of the changes occurring within the nation's healthcare delivery system, it is important to first gain a historical perspective of the system's critical successes and failures. Overall, mortality in the United States continues to decline as our successes in disease prevention and intervention mount. Although the total mortality rates continue to drop while life expectancy continues to increase, these macro trends mask concerns involving specific illnesses, diseases, injuries, and population groups (Williams & Torrens, 2008). Low-income population groups, particularly those in inner city and rural areas, certain minority groups, and individuals with economic challenges are among those with the greatest barriers. Barrier to access for these population groups are broad based and include financial resources, insurance plans and entitlement programs; serious access limitations including physical access to care, transportation, the availability of specialty and primary care services; and effective patient flow and referral system(s) (Williams & Torrens, 2008). According to Shi and Stevens (2010) vulnerability to poor health is determined by a convergence of predisposing, enabling, and need characteristics at both the individual and ecological levels.

Social determinants of health care inequalities are comprised of major factors that influence health outcomes for lower socioeconomic populations and minorities. The field of public health has documented the trends of lower quality health care provided to these populations. These disadvantaged populations are impacted by lower quality health care across a wide range of diseases and medical services. Several examples include:

- Minorities and lower socioeconomic individuals on a watchful protocol receive disproportionally low medical monitoring visits and procedures. These disparities cannot be explained by the characteristics of the disease or socio-demographics characteristics (Mandelblatt, Yabroff, & Kerner, n.d.).
- Minorities and lower socioeconomic individuals are less likely to be recommended for "coronary artery bypass grafting" (CABG) (a surgery that improves blood flow to the heart) (Mandelblatt, Yabroff, & Kerner, n.d.).
- Minorities and lower socioeconomic individuals are over diagnosed with schizophrenia at five times the rate of whites (O. O., C. F., & N. I., 2001).
- Minorities and lower socioeconomic individuals are more likely to experience difficulties obtaining insurance authorization when accessing emergency care (Mandelblatt, Yabroff, & Kerner, n.d.).

As previously stated, the presence of health insurance is the main factor allowing individuals access to the health care system and, as a result, alleviating and minimizing negative health outcomes such as the above examples. The burden of lack of access not only impacts health status, but is also connected to financial instability for individuals. In 2014, one in five American adults struggled to pay medical bills (LaMontagne, 2014). The inability to pay medical bills is the leading cause of personal bankruptcy. This dismal information is apparent in the following:

- In 2013, approximately 56 million Americans under 65 experienced trouble paying medical bills.
- An estimated 16 million children live in households that struggle with medical bills.
- Even with the presence of medical insurance, approximately 10 million Americans ages 19-64 face medical bills in which they are unable to pay.
- Approximately 17 million Americans live in households that will declare bankruptcy as a result of the inability to pay medical bills.
- California, Illinois, and Florida account for a quarter of those living in medical-related bankruptcy.
- As a method to save expenses, approximately 25 million adults ages 19-64 will either not take their prescription medications, take less than the prescribed amount, or delay refilling prescription medications to save costs (LaMontagne, 2014).

Being uninsured for a prolonged period of time results in a person's reduced health status and stability, bringing with it risks of suboptimal health care and health status for the individual and the population as a whole (AHQR, 2014). The implementation of the Patient Protection Affordable Care Act is aimed at reducing these barriers with an increase in availability of health insurance and services.

Changing Availability:

To deal with the problem of lack of access to health care; a major component of the Patient Protection Affordable Care Act (PPACA), passed in 2010, aimed at increasing the number of Americans with health insurance. The

Congressional Budget Office (2013) predicts the ACA will extend insurance coverage to approximately 25 million additional people by 2019. The Kaiser Family Foundation (2010) explains the Act seeks to accomplish this goal through the following mandates and programs:

1. Individual mandate: As of 2014, all individuals are required to have health insurance or pay a penalty. The penalty is being phased in from 2014-2016. There are some exceptions to this requirement that include financial hardship, religious objections, and for American Indians.
2. Expansion of public programs: States will have the options to increase Medicaid to cover those up to 133% of the federal poverty level. In 2009, that level would have been $14,404 for an individual and $29,327 for a family of four. This expansion will create a national uniform eligibility standard across the states. The federal government will pay for much of the expansion.
3. American Health Benefit Exchanges: People who do not receive employer-sponsored insurance and who make more than 133% of the federal poverty level, health insurance will be available through the new American Health Benefit Exchange created by states.
4. Changes to private insurance: Health insurance regulations will change the way insurers operate. Insurers will:
    a. Not be able to deny coverage to people because of their health status (i.e., preexisting conditions),
    b. Not be able to charge people more because of health status or gender,
    c. Will provide comprehensive coverage that includes a minimum set of services, caps out-of-pocket spending, does not impose cost sharing for preventive services, and does not impose annual or lifetime limits on coverage,
    d. Will allow young adults to remain on their parents' health insurance up until the age of 26, and
    e. Will limit waiting periods to no longer than 90 days.
5. Employer requirements: There is no employer mandate to offer health insurance to employees, but employers with fifty or more employees will be assessed a fee of $2,000 per full-time employee (in excess of 30 employees) if they do not offer coverage and if they have at least one employee who receives a premium credit through an exchange. Employers with 50+ employees who do offer health insurance, but have at least one employee who receives a premium credit through an exchange will be required to pay the lesser of $3,000 per employee who receives a premium credit of $2,000 per employee (in excess of 30 employees). If employers offer coverage and have workers who do not sign up for the plan or do not opt out of a plan, the employer must automatically enroll employees in the lowest cost premium plan. In addition, if employers offer coverage to employees with income less than 400% of the federal poverty level and the employee's share of the premium is between 8% and 9.8% of their income, then employers will be required to provide vouchers so employees can enroll in a plan in an exchange (Henry J. Kaiser Family Foundation, 2010).

Accessibility

With a plethora of different means of gaining access to health care services, access has been and continues to be a major health issue in the United States. Health insurance coverage and the generosity of coverage are major determinants of access of health care. According to Adams, Kirzinger, and Martinez (2013), the following are examples of how accessibility of health care and health outcomes correlates:

- Approximately 25.9 million persons (8%) delayed seeking medical care in 2012 year due to cost, and 19.2 million (6%) did not receive needed care due to the cost.
- Adults aged 18-44 and 45-64 were more likely than older adults and children to delay seeking or not receiving medical care due to cost.
- Persons with the least education were approximately three times as likely as persons with the most education to have not received needed medical care due to cost, and they were more likely to have delayed seeking care for this reason.
- Persons in the lowest income group were about 10 times as likely as persons in the highest income group to not receive needed medical care due to cost and more than six times as likely to delay seeking medical care.
- Persons under the age 65 who were uninsured were about three times as likely as persons who had Medicaid and persons who had other insurance to delay seeking or not receive needed medical care due to cost.
- Persons who were in fair or poor health were about three to four times as likely as persons who were in excellent or very good health to delay seeking or not receive needed medical care due to cost.

Affordability:

According to Zelman, McCue and Glick (2009) many factors have led to rising health care costs, which have increased faster than general inflation over the past decade. Although the average life expectancy of the general population has risen by only approximately three years over this time period, the cost to keep people healthy has approximately doubled. Factors that contributed to the higher cost of health care are: payment system, technology, aging population, prescription drugs cost, chronic diseases, litigation, and the number uninsured/underinsured.

Interestingly enough, the uninsured do not lack emergency care because no one needing such care will be turned away from any emergency department as provided under the **Emergency Medical Treatment & Labor (EMTALA)**. According to Pozgar (2012) hospital emergency room is subject to two principal obligations, commonly referred to as (1) the appropriate medical screening requirement and (2) the stabilization requirement. The appropriate medical treatment is to screen any individual in order to determine whether the individual has an emergency medical condition. If an emergency medical condition exists, the hospital is required to provide stabilization treatment before transferring the individual.

However, the uninsured usually do not have access to primary care, such as checkups, screenings for chronic illnesses, and prenatal care. Those who are unable to receive medical care because they cannot afford it are termed "medically indigent." The **medically indigent population** in America includes people and families with income above the poverty level who are thus ineligible for Medicaid, or government health insurance for the poor, but who are unable to afford health care or health insurance. It is worth noting that eight out of ten uninsured or underinsured persons are members of working families (McKenzie, Pinger, & Kotecki, 2012).

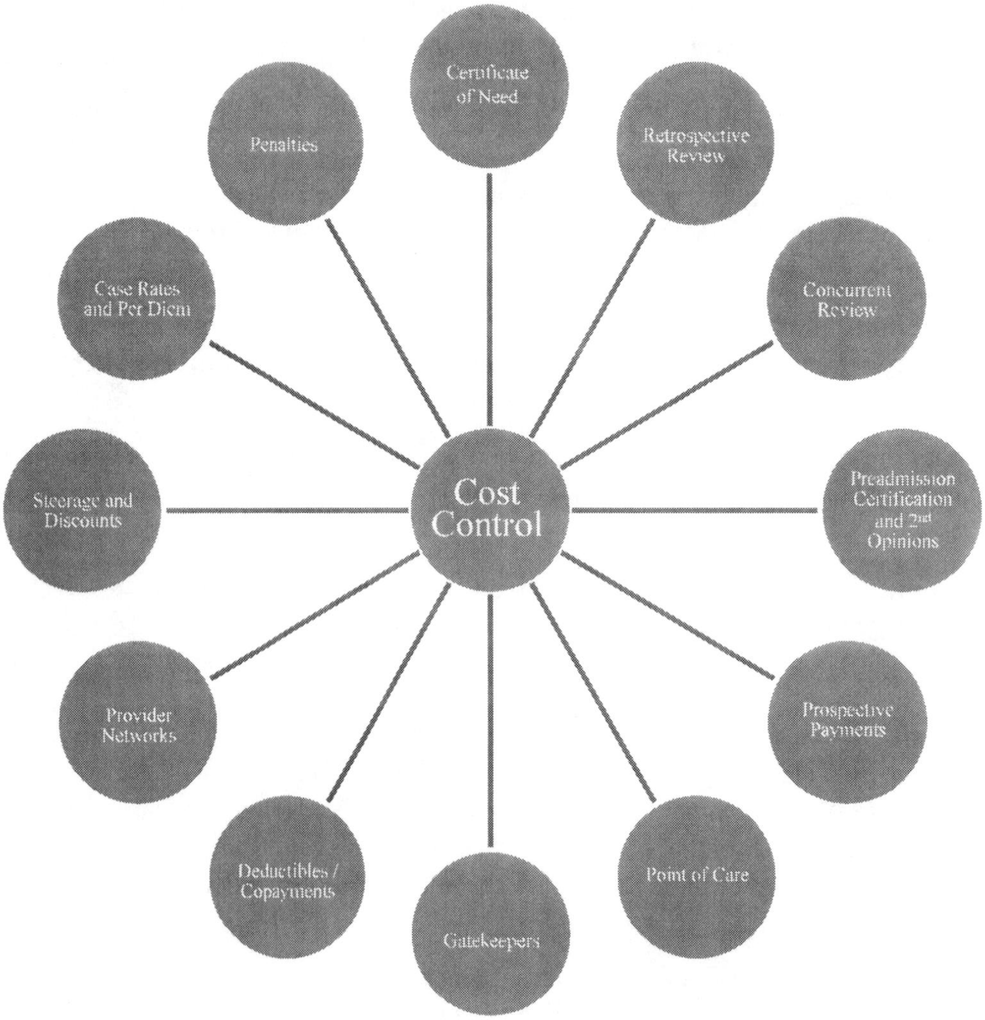

Figure 1. Factors that Contribute to the Cost of Healthcare (Zelma, McCue, & Glick, 2009).

As illustrated in the Figure 1 above, the United States has imposed a number of methods to control cost. Methodologies that worked for a number of years have limitations when it comes to individuals who are employed, but are unable to afford health insurance. It is estimated there are more than 30 million working poor in the United States. Others may be uninsured because individual health policies are expensive and may be unavailable. Historically, young adults often lost their eligibility under their parents' policy when they turned 19 or graduate from college. In the past and moving towards the future, health care in the United States is closely tied to having insurance.

Higher health insurance premiums have caused corporations that previously offered traditional health insurance to their employees to either stop providing traditional health insurance for their employees or to offer them high deductible health plans. Another reason for offering high deductible plans is that consumers can decide how to use their medical dollars and, in turn, shop around for less costly medical care as well as reduce their consumption of health care. With a high deductible health plan, employers pay lower premiums to the health plan for the insurance coverage. Because they are high deductible plans, employees may be required to set aside funds to pay for deductibles and any other copayments or non-covered medical expenses, such as prescriptions drugs, dental visits, or vision services (Wolper, 2011). As a result of increased employer spending, such costs may be passed off to the employee through lower wages.

WRAP-UP:

This chapter explored access, barriers and utilization of healthcare. While the future of healthcare looks to new policy implementation, it is important to know the Affordable Care Act (ACA) will not solve all of the health care problems of our nation. The following are just a few of the challenges that we will need to address:

1. The continued income inequality will produce barriers for low-income families when trying to access medical care.
2. The continued education inequality will produce barriers for low-income families when trying to access medical care.
3. Navigating the online system will remain a major challenge for many.
4. Many will feel intimidated and helpless because of their infrequent past interactions with the health care system.
5. Are there enough medical providers who will accept public insurance?
6. Continued financial burden of health care costs – high premiums and out-of-pocket payments.
7. Patient understanding of the need for preventive care.

As previously mentioned, reduced access to health care is not an individual problem, but also a societal problem. The more people with illness and disease, the greater the chance of the spread of disease and illness to others. This results in an increased burden of disease for society as a whole – necessitating the need for increased societal awareness through public health efforts. **Public health**, as described by Derose, Gresenz, & Ringel, 2011, is what society collectively does to assure people can lead healthy lives. The authors propose a public health framework that includes increased efforts in assurance, assessment, policy development, and increased visibility of local health departments in the planning, developing, and implementation of health care reform.

It is important for future health care administrators to acknowledge that access to care is impacted by both financial and nonfinancial barriers that are deeply rooted in the fibers of our nation. With systematic changes continuously evolving in the administration and delivery of health care, administrators and providers need to understand the benefits of accessing ever-changing policies and solutions.

DISCUSSION QUESTIONS:

1. Identify strategies that a health care center can implement to improve health outcomes for vulnerable populations.
2. Describe some of the barriers to health that U.S. populations will encounter with the Affordable Care Act.
3. What are the biggest challenges to maintaining a healthy U.S. population? Consider financial and non-financial barriers.
4. What barriers might a single mother of two, who earns minimum wage, face with regard to accessing health services for herself and her family?
5. Describe the relationship between access and utilization. Does having access guarantee utilization? Explain your response.

RESOURCES:

Access to Health Care–CDC
http://www.cdc.gov/nchs/fastats/access-to-health-care.htm

Access to Health Care–AHRQ
http://www.ahrq.gov/research/findings/nhqrdr/nhqr11/chap9.html

Access to Health Care –The RAND Corporation
http://www.rand.org/about.html

Access to Health Services – Healthy People 2020
http://www.healthypeople.gov/2020/topicsobjectives2020/overview.aspx?topicid=1

Financial Barriers to Health Care Access–AMA
http://www.ama-assn.org/ama/pub/physician-resources/medical-ethics/code-medical-ethics/opinion90651.page

Kaiser Family Foundation – ACA
http://kff.org/health-reform/fact-sheet/summary-of-the-affordable-care-act/

ACTIVITY:

This activity illustrates the various and unique barriers which impact groups and individuals in a community and helps students to explore possible health outcomes.

1. Divide the classroom into random groups of no more than five students each.
2. Assign a city–Explore the major urban city closest to you. (Using the closest city may represent one with which they are most familiar but you may choose any city as long as all are assigned to the same one.)
3. On a sheet of paper the students will note the city and a series of concentric circles with a uniform distance (i.e. 5 mile radius, 10 miles, 15 miles) to plot health outcomes.
4. Instruct each group to consider the differences in housing, transportation, access to health facilities, etc., as they consider those further from the city.
5. Items to ponder:
    a. Geographic location will greatly impact access to public transportation.
    b. Geographic location will greatly impact types of housing.
    c. Geographic location will greatly impact access to some services.
    d. What challenges might each group face?
    e. What other considerations need to be addressed that might affect the stated population? (e.g. social, economic, education, etc.)
    f. Why might some in this population perimeter have better outcomes than others?

REFERENCES:

Adams, P. F., Kirzinger, W. K., & Martinez, M. E. (2013). *Summary Health Statistics for U.S. Populations: National Health Interview Survey, 2012.* Hyattsville: U.S. Department of Health and Human Services.

Congressional Budget Office. (2013, February). *Effects of the Affordable Care Act on Health Insurance Coverage.* Washington, DC. Retrieved from http://www.cbo.gov/publication/43900

Davidson, Stephen M. (2013). *A New Era in U.S. Health Care.* Stanford, CA: Stanford University Press.

Derose, K., Gresenz, C. & Ringel, J. (2011, October). Understanding Disparities in Health Care Access – And Reducing Them – Through a Focus on Public Health. *Health Affairs,* (30)10, 1844-1851. Retrieved from http://www.abcardio.org/graphics11/2.pdf

Health Care Cost Institute. (2013). *Utilization Fact Sheet.* Retrieved from http://www.healthcostinstitute.org/fact-sheets

Henry J. Kaiser Family Foundation. (2010, April). *Focus on Health Reform.* Retrieved from Henry J. Kaiser Family Foundation Web Site: http://kff.org/health-reform/fact-sheet/summary-of-new-health-reform-law/

Kovner, A. R., & Knickman, J. R. *Health Care Delivery in the United States* (10th Edition ed.). New York, NY, USA: Springer Publishing Company.

LaMontagne, C. (2014, March 26). *NerdWallet Health Finds Medical Bankruptcy Accounts for Majority of Personal Bankruptcies.* [Blog]. Retrieved from http://www.nerdwallet.com/blog/health/2014/03/26/medical-bankruptcy/

Mandal, A. (2014). Disparities in Access to Health Care. *Medical News.* Retrieved from http://www.news-medical.net/health/Disparities-in-Access-to-Health-Care.aspx

Mandelblatt, J., Yabroff, K., & Kerner, J. (n.d.). *Access to Quality Cancer Care: Evaluating and Ensuring Equitable Services, Quality of Life, and Survival.*

McKenzie, J. F., Pinger, R. R., & Kotecki, J. E. (2012). *An Introduction to Community Health.* Sudbury: Jones & Bartlett Learning.

National Healthcare Disparities Report, 2013: Chapter 10. Access to Health Care. May 2014. Agency for Healthcare Research and Quality, Rockville, MD. http://www.ahrq.gov/research/findings/nhqrdr/nhdr13/chap10.html

Pozgar, G. D. (2012). *Legal Aspects of Health Care Administration .* Sudbury: Jones & Bartlett Learning.

Shi, L., & Singh, D. A. (2015). *Delivering Health Care in America: A Systems Approach.* Burlington, MA, USA: Jones & Bartlett.

Shi, L., & Stevens, G. D. (2010). Vulnerable Populations in the United States. In L. Shi, & G. D. Stevens, *Vulnerable Populations in the United States* (pp. 18-19). Hobokeen: Jossey-Bass.

(US), O. O., (US), C. F., & (US), N. I. (2001 Aug). *Office of the Surgeon General (US); Center for Mental Health Services (US); National Institute of Mental Health (US). Mental Health: Culture, Race, and Ethnicity: A Supplement to Mental Health: A Report of the Surgeon General.* Rockville: Substance Abuse and Mental Health Services Administration (US).

United States Government Printing Office. (n.d.). *Reducing Costs And Improving The Quality Of Health Care* (Ch 5). Retrieved From http://www.gpo.gov/fdsys/pkg/ERP-2013/pdf/ERP-2013-chapter5.pdf

White House. (n.d.). *The Affordable Care Act and Trends in Health Care Spending.* Retrieved from http://www.whitehouse.gov/sites/default/files/docs/fact_sheet_ implementing_the_affordable_care_act_from_the_erp_2013_final1.pdf

Williams, S. J., & Torrens, P. R. (2008). *Introduction to Health Services.* Clifton Park: Delmar Cengage Learning.

Wolper, L. F. (2011). *Health Care Administration.* Sudbury : Jones & Bartlett.

Zelma, W. M., McCue, M. J., & Glick, N. D. (2009). Financial Management of Health Care Organizations: An Introduction to Fundamentals Tools, Concepts, and Applications. In W. M. Zelma, M. J. McCue, & N. D. Glick, Financial Management of Health Care Organizations: An Introduction to Fundamentals Tools, Concepts, and Applications (p. 13). San Francisco: Jossey-Bass. Copyright @ 2009 by John Wiley & Sons, Inc. All rights reserved.

Chapter 3:

Exploring Social Determinants of Health

Amy Dore

KEY CONCEPTS:

Access
Determinants of health
Education
Equity
Health
Health behaviors
Health disparities
Health equity
Income
Measure
Objective
Occupation
Race
Risk factors
Social determinants of health
Socioeconomic status
Social class
Wealth

CHAPTER OVERVIEW:

This chapter introduces the student to the concept of social determinants of health and the correlating factors impacting a person's health status and health outcomes. Understanding the differences between health inequalities and inequities between populations will be explored. Special attention will be paid to current initiatives created with the goal of improving health for all through research and comprehension of the types and differences of health inequalities and inequities. This chapter offers the opportunity to take an in-depth look at the components of the social determinants of health and the five determinants typically researched by scientists and researchers in trying to understand the health differences between populations. Lastly, socioeconomic status will be investigated to understand the impact it has on varying populations with differing educational, income, and occupational levels.

WHY IS THIS IMPORTANT?

Social determinants of health are the framework for the circumstances facing differing populations and the health inequities resulting from these differences. Social determinants of health are widely impacted by societal forces–economically, politically, and socially. Research will show you these health inequities are avoidable and preventable when proper actions are taken to reduce the risk of illness by improving environmental, societal and political conditions in which populations live. Learning, recognizing, and taking action to improve social determinants of health is the roadmap to health equality for all populations.

CHAPTER EXPECTATIONS:

Upon reading this chapter, the reader will be able to:

- Appreciate the historical context underlying the concept of social determinants of health.
- Understand social determinants of health and its correlating factors impacting the health status and health outcomes of differing populations.
- Contrast and explain the differences between health, health disparities, health inequalities, and health inequities.
- Describe the meaning and differences between determinants of health and social determinants of health.
- Explain the five determinants of health in which scientists typically view the health of a population.
- Identify the role socioeconomic status plays in relationship to the social determinants of health.
- Analyze possible causes of and linkages between the varying determinants.

INTRODUCTION:

Understanding the conditions in which a person is born, lives, works, and their cultural identity, race, gender, ethnicity, and age all influence health beliefs, health status and the ability to access health services. These conditions and identifiers combined are quite complex and are also heavily influenced by external factors such as the social and physical environment, socioeconomic factors, and biological factors. Remembering the domino effect of these differences can shed light on the importance of the social determinants of health. For example, a person with a low income more than likely has fewer educational opportunities, lives in an underserved area with little access to nutritious food and food sources highly concentrated on fast food or convenience groceries, fewer recreational areas in which to exercise, and less access to quality health services. The causes of health inequalities are the foundation and reason for understanding the social determinants of health.

HISTORICAL CONTEXT:

Healthy People is an initiative created by the U.S. Department of Health and Human Services to provide science-based, measurable objectives for improving the health and achieving health equity of all Americans. Healthy People's mission is to established benchmarks to monitor over time and is considered a comprehensive national health effort to investigate, promote and encourage the prevention of disease. In the past three decades (1990, 2000, 2010), Healthy People has served as an agenda for public health goals and actions and, as a result, has served as a public health roadmap (Koh, 2010).

Healthy People 2020 has approximately 600 objectives and more than 1,300 measures. Each **objective** has three components: 1) a reliable data source, 2) a baseline measure, and 3) a target for defined improvements to be achieved by the year 2020 (Healthy People "Objective Development and Selection Process," 2011). As part of the Healthy People 2020 criteria, the objectives should be **measurable** using valid, reliable, and nationally representative data and data systems (Healthy People "Objective Selection Criteria," 2009). A majority of the objectives are quite narrow and focus on interventions created to reduce or eliminate illness, disability and premature death among individuals and within communities. Other objectives are quite broad and focus on eliminating health disparities, addressing social determinants of health, improving access to health services, improving the dissemination of health information, and strengthening public health services (Healthy People "Objective Development and Selection Process," 2011). Among the 600 objectives are a number of new topics of focus including adolescent health, dementia, global health, LGBT (lesbian, gay bisexual and transgender) health, just to mention a few (Koh, 2010).

The importance of addressing the social determinants of health is recognized by the overarching goals for Healthy People 2020:

- Attain high-quality, longer lives free of preventable disease, disability, injury, and premature death.
- Achieve health equity, eliminate disparities, and improve the health of all groups.
- Create social and physical environments that promote good health for all.
- Promote quality of life, healthy development, and healthy behaviors across all life stages (Healthy People "Introducing Healthy People," 2012).

Social Determinants of Health, as established by Healthy People 2020, focuses on five general areas. The main goal of this initiative is to recognize and create social and physical environments that promote good health for all. The focus areas for the Social Determinants of Health are:

- Neighborhood and built environment
- Health and health care
- Social and Community Context
- Education
- Economic stability (Healthy People "Social Determinants of Health," 2013).

In 2005, the World Health Organization created the Commission on Social Determinants of Health to research and advocate for dissemination of evidence on what can be done to promote health equity and foster a global campaign to achieve it. The Commission's overarching goals and principles of action are shown in Figure 1.

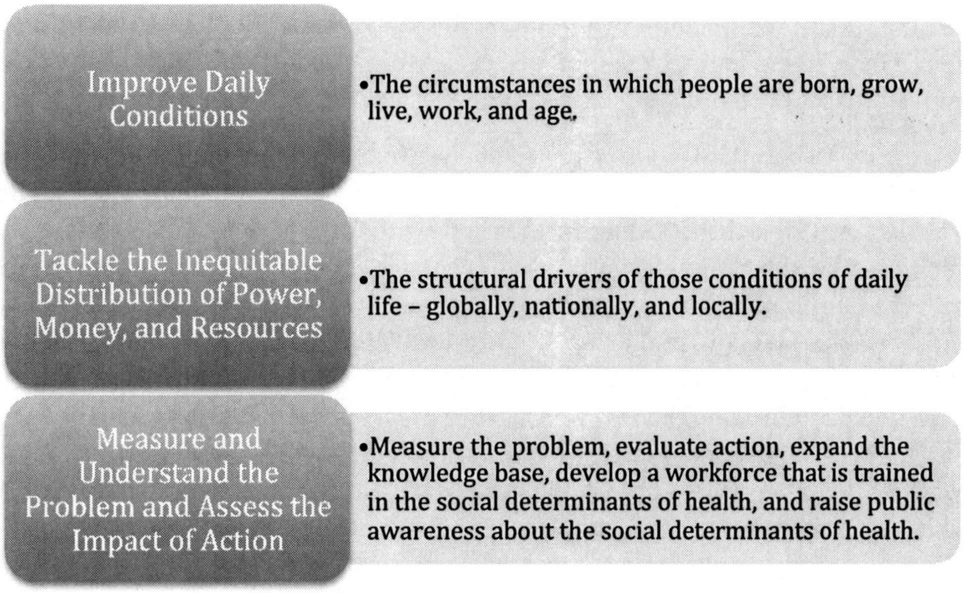

Figure 1. Overarching Recommendations. Adapted from: Word Health Organization, (2008). *Commission on Social Determinants of Health.* Retrieved from http://www.who.int/social_determinants/thecommission/en/

These two efforts demonstrate the context in which health disparities and disease prevention are currently approached. However, efforts to improve health outcomes in communities are not new endeavors. History shows community health measures relating back thousands of years in areas such as the concern of transmittable diseases, good quality and adequate supply of water, and the provision of appropriate medical care. Archeologists have found ruins of a bathroom dating back thousands of years to the Middle Kingdom (2100-1700 B.C.) in Egypt. Elaborate ruins of sewage systems and baths note the public health achievements of the Inca Empire (early 13th century) (Rosen, 1958). Early U.S. history shows us the importance of public and community health in areas such as life expectancy at birth and catastrophic illnesses such as tuberculosis, smallpox, cholera, and dysentery. Early founders of the United States (George and Martha Washington, Abigail and John Adams, Benjamin Franklin, and Thomas Jefferson as examples) often, out of necessity, educated themselves about health and medical treatments. These early founders can also be credited for advocating some of the first government-sponsored public health programs. Benjamin Franklin, as an example, is an iconic figure in American history who was exceedingly versatile and a visionary in his ability to be a skilled diplomat, effective businessman, scientist, and an essential participant in the development of medicine in early America. Franklin's unique skills allowed him to create his own medical theories, conduct experiments and disseminate medical information to a wide American audience (Abrams, 2013).

As medical discoveries and interventions have improved over time we can view the progress and achievements in the advancement of medical diagnoses, treatments, and prevention techniques. Despite these improvements in medical technology, the United States continues to struggle with limitations in health equality, health equity for all, and the delicate balance between social responsibility and individual rights (Abrams, 2013).

WHAT YOU SHOULD KNOW:

Living a long, healthy, happy life free of illness, disease or chronic conditions is a reasonable goal and expectation of people living in the United States and countries throughout our world. But why is this goal not reachable for some people? When considering reasons why people differ in their ability to maintain favorable health status we must consider several factors. The Merriam-Webster dictionary defines **health** as "the condition of being well or free of disease" (2014). Using this as a basic explanation of health is limiting when we do not acknowledge that the concept of *health* differs between cultures. As an example, the term *obese* has different connotations depending on the culture. In many cultures throughout the world the term obese equates to material well-being and, particularly for women, fertility and maternal capability. Therefore, defining health in only this sort of bio-medical character discounts the varying context of the term (Edberg, 2012).

Health disparities are defined as the differences in health outcomes and their determinants between segments of the population defined by attributes such as social, demographic, environmental, and geographic characteristics (Truman, et al., 2011). Dreachslin, Gilbert, and Malone (2103) define **equity** in health care as equal quality of care based solely on need and clinical factors. Health inequalities and health inequities are terms sometimes used interchangeably. **Health inequalities**, which are oftentimes very similar to health disparities, explore the health status of differing populations and patterns of health within these populations. It is a term utilized to designate differences, variations, and disparities in the health achievements of individuals and groups (Kawachi, Subramanian, & Almeida-Filho, 2002). **Health inequities** are a subset of health inequalities associated with social disadvantage and are considered preventable, unfair, and unjust and involve a value judgment (Truman, et al., 2011; Kawachi, Subramanian, & Almeida-Filho, 2002). As a side note, the term *heath disparity* is almost exclusively used in the United States while globally the terms *health inequalities* and *health inequities* are more common (Isaac, 2013).

Examples of health inequalities:

- A higher incidence (rate) of disease type X in group A as compared to group B of population P (Kawachi, Subramanian, & Almeida-Filho, 2002).
- Differences in mobility between elderly people and younger populations (WHO, 2014).
- Differences in infant mortality and educational attainment.

Examples of health inequities include:

- Infant mortality rate is higher in population *A* versus population *B*.
- Life expectancy at birth for men in urban city *A* is 23 years higher than that of men in rural city *B*, within the same state.
- The difference in smoking rates and the incidence (rate) of cancer among upper and lower income individuals (Andress, n.d.).
- Rates of obesity between low versus higher income families.

Unequal access to health services, lack of education, poverty, racism and stigma are all social determinants of health that contribute to health inequities. Achieving health equity for all populations would mean that each person has the opportunity to reach their optimal health status and social position and the combined related circumstances would no longer dictate the ability to reach this optimal level of health status (CDC "Social Determinants FAQ," 2013).

Determinants of Health:

To better understand social determinants of health it is also important to understand the concept of **determinants of health.** What is the difference? One is based on specific social aspects of health (social determinants of health) and the other is connected to broader circumstances such as biological, socioeconomic, psychosocial, behavioral, or social characteristics (determinants of health) (CDC "Definitions," 2013).

Determinants of health, as defined by the Centers for Disease Control and Prevention (CDC), take into account the factors contributing to a person's current state of health (2013). These factors can be recognized as biological in nature, psychosocial, social, behavioral, or socioeconomic. The CDC further explains the five determinants of health in which scientists typically view health of a population:

1. Biology and genetics (gender and age)
2. Behavior (individual)
3. Environment (physical)
4. Environment (social)
5. Access (to health services)

Social Determinants of Health:

According to the World Health Organization (2014), the **social determinants of health** are defined as the conditions in which people are born, grow, live, work and age ("Social determinants of health," n.d.). The CDC (2013) defines the social determinants of health in a similar manner, but expands the definition by including the systems put in place to deal with illness. These social determinants of health play a role in health inequities. They also help scientists and researchers explain how a person defines health and illness; how an individual utilizes the health care system in seeking care; and other health-seeking behaviors such as self-treatment of health conditions.

Environmental Determinants (Social and Physical):

Environmental factors include physical surroundings such as neighborhoods, places of employment, towns, and cities and built environments. *Social relationships* include position in social hierarchy, racism and differential treatment of social groups, and social networks (Davis, Cohen, & Rodriguez, 2009).

Examples of Physical Determinants:

- Weather conditions and the natural environment
- Built environment: sidewalks, bike lanes, roads, buildings
- Settings such as worksites, schools, recreational settings
- Physical barriers (people with disabilities)
- Exposure to toxic elements, substances and physical hazards

Examples of Social Determinants:

- Available resources (food, medical, safe housing)
- Educational, economic and job opportunities
- Access to health services
- Public safety and transportation
- Social norms and attitudes (racism, discrimination, distrust of government and healthcare providers)
- Exposure to violence, crime and other social disorder
- Socioeconomic conditions
- Language and literacy
- Culture (CDC "Understanding Social Determinants of Health," 2013).

When considering the health status of a population it is important to recognize the factors involved in being considered a healthy individual versus someone in poor health. Health status can improve or worsen based on a person's surroundings. Davis, Cohen and Rodriguez (2009) explain that poor health directly affects the entire population of a community whose health status is worsened by the poor health status of its least healthy members. Poor health is a burden to those directly impacted and to the entire community by placing a disproportionate strain on the health care system.

Where a person lives, works, and their ability to participate in wellness-seeking behaviors and activities directly influence overall health status. As stated by Rivlin and McClellan (2013), having a nurturing childhood, eating nutritious food, exercising in a safe neighborhood, and avoiding violence and drug abuse have far more to do with health than health care. In addition, all of these factors are closely related to where a person lives. A person's ZIP code can be an indicator as to how long and how well a person lives. Research shows a person living in a neighborhood where the median household income is less than $25,000 a year has a life expectancy 14 years shorter than someone living in a neighborhood where the median annual household income is greater than $53,000 (Rivlin & McClellan, 2013). For most people, home represents shelter, safety and security. A person's home is typically their single largest expenditure, representing their greatest source of wealth. Housing influences health in several ways, including the conditions within the home, neighborhood conditions, and housing affordability (Braveman, Dekker, Egerter, Sadegh-Nobari, & Pollack, 2011).

Why is housing considered one of most important physical determinants of health? As stated above, the impact housing has on a person's health is significant. Substandard housing increases the risk for injury, illness, and overall health status. Populations disproportionately impacted by substandard health and housing experience relatively higher frequencies of childhood lead poisoning, injuries, respiratory diseases, and quality of life issues. More than 6 million substandard housing units, nationwide, are impacted by these conditions. Additionally, the risk for fire, exposure to toxins, injuries from falls, rodent bites, and combustible gases increase in substandard housing. The availability of healthy, safe, affordable, accessible and environmentally friendly housing are all recommendations for decreasing these health disparities (CDC "Healthy Homes," 2012).

In addition to housing, a person's place of employment can affect their health. According to the U.S. Bureau of Labor Statistics, the average person between the ages of 24-54 with children under the age of 18 spends approximately 8.8 hours working (within a 24 hour period). This is the largest segment of time spent each day other than sleeping (average 7.7 hours/day) (BLS, 2013). Combined, these two activities leave little time for external activities such as leisure and sports that might promote positive health. Furthermore, where we work, how we work, and the nature of the work we do can affect our physical and mental health.

The Bureau of Labor Statistics reported in 2012:

- 375 workers were killed in shootings on the job,
- 4,383 suffered fatal injuries while on the job, and
- 112 cases per 10,000 full-time workers involved non-fatal occupational injury and illness requiring days away from work (BLS, 2013).

Hazardous work conditions not only stem from workplace violence, but also exposure to conditions that are hazardous to one's health. For example, inadequate ventilation and temperature in a workplace can impact health conditions such as asthma. As shown in Figure 2, physical aspects of the workplace coincide with psychosocial and work-related resources and opportunities. Differences in the level of control a person feels they have over their workplace environment impacts both physical and mental health. Reducing work-related stress can have positive implications on health for the workers and their families as well. Lastly, work-related opportunities and resources impact health through the ability for a person to use their earnings to take advantage of and make decisions regarding how they live, types and availability of leisure activities, schooling opportunities, etc. Additional work-related benefits include the ability to obtain health insurance, paid time off for sick and personal leave, workplace wellness programs, retirement benefits and child and elder care resources (An, Braveman, Dekker, Egerter, Grossman-Kahn, 2011). According to the Robert Wood Johnson Foundation, "healthy workers and their families are likely to incur lower medical costs and be more productive, while those with chronic health conditions generate higher costs in terms of health care use, absenteeism, disability and overall reduced productivity" (An, et al., 2011).

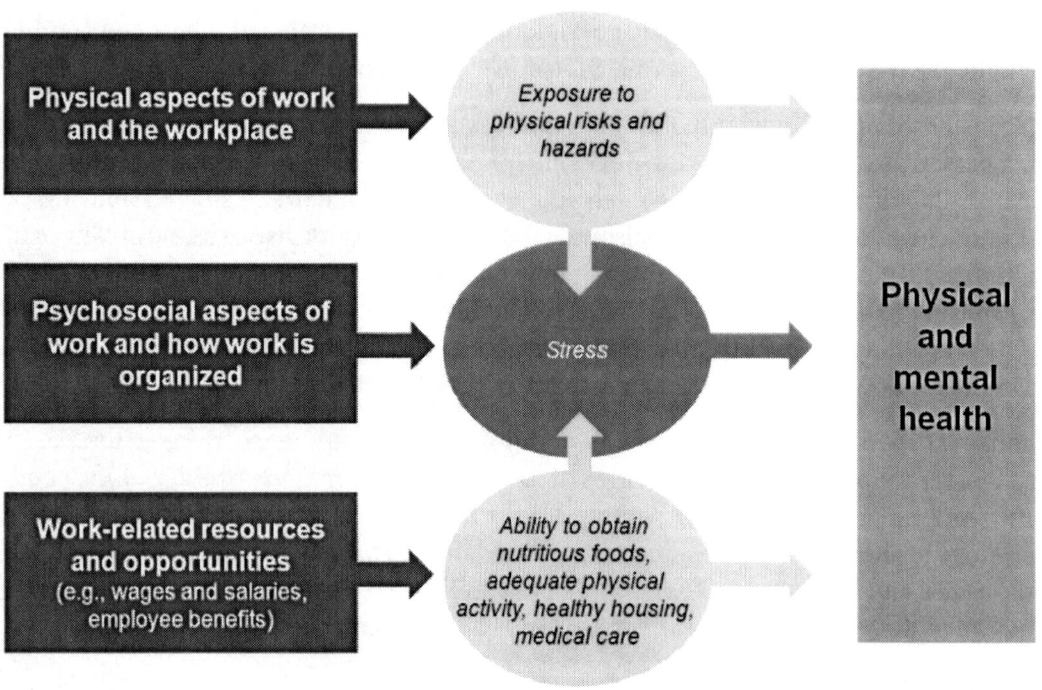

Figure 2. How work shapes health for workers and their families. Adapted from: An, J., Braveman, P., Dekker, M., Egerter, S., & Grossman-Kahn, R. (2011, May). The links between health and the physical aspects of work. *Exploring the Social Determinants of Health Issue Brief*, series (#9). Robert Wood Johnson Foundation. Retrieved from http://www.rwjf.org/content/dam/farm/reports/issue_briefs/2011/rwjf70459. Copyright 2011. Robert Wood Johnson Foundation. Used with permission from the Robert Wood Johnson Foundation.

Understanding physical and social environmental determinants of health contributes to the understanding of why health disparities and inequities exist, the impact they have on populations, and identifying opportunities to reduce or eliminate the disparities.

Socioeconomic Status:

Stephen Bezruchka (2010) noted that on average, people in the United States die much younger, experience worse health, and tolerate serious societal dysfunction when compared to people in other rich nations. A person's personal actions and health behaviors are oftentimes explained as the reason for such outcomes. However, we cannot avoid the fact that as one of the richest and most powerful nations in world history, persons living in the United States also experience a substantially shorter duration of life in comparison to other rich nations (Bezruchka, 2010). Why is this the case? Inequalities within societies have been shown to be strong determinants of health and other measures of societal function (Wilkinson & Pickett, 2009). Examinations of socioeconomic status often reveal inequities in access to resources, in addition to issues related to privilege, power, and control (APA "Socioeconomic Status," 2014). In defining socioeconomic Status (SES) it is important to acknowledge that there is no true consensus or agreement on the definition. An Internet search will provide many resources, definitions, and recommendations. The CDC defines **socioeconomic status** as a composite measure that typically incorporates economic, social, and work status. Economic status is measured by income. Social status is measured by education. Work status is measured by occupation (CDC "Definitions," 2013). The American Psychological Association (APA) explains SES is typically measured as a combination of education, income, and occupation. Conceptually, SES is oftentimes viewed as the social standing or class of an indivdiual or group. When viewed in this manner it is easy to see how social class, privilege, power, and control can become the main focus. As explained by the APA, when viewing SES as a gradient or continuous variable, the inequities in access and distribution of resources are more obvious (APA "Ethnic and Racial Minorities & Socioeconomic Status, 2014).

LeVeist (2005) explains that "SES is a method of stratification whereby individuals are categorized in a hierarchy along varying dimensions of social class. **Social class** represents groupings of individuals based on their association to the economy. The concept of social class has origins found in the writings of Karl Marx (1818-1883). Marx considered social classes as a grouping of individuals who played similar roles in the economic system of a society. Max Weber (1864-1920) expanded Marx's ideas of social class by viewing classes as groupings of individuals who have similar life chances. He considered a person's opportunities in life as a result of multiple stratification dimensions such as religious affiliation, education, occupation, birthrights, and privilege" (LaVeist, 2005).

The take-away point to understand is that SES has many dimensions including a variety of measures that are typically utlized as indicators of a person's personal SES. Combining the measures allows us to form a composite picture of a person's position within a society's social stratification system and to better understand the complex variables that define a person's health status (LaVeist, 2005).

Why does SES matter?

From the above definitions it should be easier to see the impact SES has on society and its various populations. Understanding SES and how it is measured allows us to recognize the level of inequalities within and between societies. Without these measures it becomes difficult to address the inequalities and advocate for change. Furthermore, without valid measurement of SES it is difficult to understand the correlation between intergenerational change of social status over time and the relationship between health and life outcomes (Oakes, n.d.).

Adverse health behaviors and higher rates of morbidity and mortality are strongly tied to lower socioeconomic status. However even with this knowledge, the mechanisms responsible for these connections are not well understood. Socioeconomic status and health equity go hand in hand when considering the differences in population health that can be traced to unequal economic and social conditions (Adler & Newman, 2002; APA "Ethnic and Racial Minorities and Socioeconomic Status", 2014). Socioeconomic status has proven to be a consistent predictor of health status. For example, persons with low SES typically have poorer health outcomes than persons with higher a SES. When considering differences between populations it is important to remember that even though there are considerable differences in SES by race/ethnicity, it is not always the case that racial/ethnic differences are the results of differences in SES (LaVeist, 2005).

Measures of SES:

Socioeconomic status is measured by a variety of components including education, income (wealth), and occupation. Utilizing a singular measure without consideration of the other components runs the risk of inaccurate conclusions and biased results (LaVeist, 2005; Adler & Newman, 2002). According to Adler and Newman (2002), **education** is considered as the most basic SES component since it shapes future occupational opportunities and earning potential. Education also allows for life skills that permit better-educated persons to gain access to information and resources to promote health and a lifestyle conducive to good health (Adler & Newman 2002; LaVeist, 2005). Poor academic performance typically results in lower educational attainment, which decreases upward mobility impacting a person's health status. Research shows persons with increased educational attainment have lower morbidity from the most common acute and chronic diseases such as stroke, hypertension, high cholesterol, diabetes, and asthma (Telfair & Shelton, 2012). This is credited, in part, to the fact that the level of educational attainment and achievement plays a role in determining the type of job or career a person has, which directly correlates with one's financial or socioeconomic status. Educational status shapes occupational opportunities and earning potential (2012). This, in turn, increases the type and amount of resources available to promote positive health behaviors and the opportunity to seek care when

> **FAQ:** Students from low-SES schools entered high school 3.3 grade levels behind students from higher SES schools (Palardy, 2008).

needed. Inadequate education and increased dropout rates affect academic achievement, which perpetuates the low-SES and corresponding community. Improving school systems and early intervention programs can help reduce these risk factors and help researchers identify strategies to alleviate these disparities at the individual and societal level (APA "Education & Socioeconomic Status," 2014).

Income is defined as money earned from sources such as work, investments, and business transactions ("Income," 2014). Income provides the means for purchasing health care and higher incomes provide the means for better housing, schooling, nutrition, and recreation (Adler & Newman, 2002). **Wealth** refers to the accumulated value of all assets, typically income-generating assets. Examples include home equity, stocks and mutual funds, retirement accounts, vehicles, businesses, and rental properties (LaVeist, 2005).

According to the Bureau of Labor Statistics (2013), the term **occupation** refers to categories based on work performed, skills, education, training, and credentials. Workers are classified into occupational categories based on the above areas. Some occupations are connected to specific industries, such as the healthcare industry. Other occupations can be found within a variety of industries. For example, janitors can be found in the healthcare industry as well as the manufacturing industry. Job status and job prestige impact a person's SES, as higher job status and prestige typically equates to higher income (LaVeist, 2005). And, as we have determined, higher income equates to increased opportunities to purchase health services.

FAQ: According to the BLS, as of May 2012, several newly defined occupations earned high wages relative to the U.S annual mean of $45,790. Nurse anesthetists had an annual mean wage of $154,390, nurse practitioners, $91,450 and nurse midwives, $91,070 (BLS, 2013).

Research tells us that measuring SES is a complex endeavor in regards to the validity when using education, income (wealth), and occupation as measures. Education tends to be viewed as the most stable measurement and vigorous indicator of SES. However, the education measure has its limitations in that educational achievement does not necessarily guarantee a higher income or job stability as the relationship between income and education varies by race or ethnicity (LaVeist, 2005; Williams & Collins, 2013). Using income as a measure can be problematic due to the sensitivity involved in collecting information related to income and wealth. Additionally, analyses utilizing the measurement of income can be prone to reverse causation arguments. For example, decreased health can lead to a decline in income such that the association between low income and health status can be a cause rather than a consequence of poor health (Williams & Collins, 2013). Lastly, occupational status as a measurement varies depending on one's theoretical perspective regarding the significance of various aspects of work life (Adler & Newman, 2002).

Behavior as a Determinant:

We have previously established that while the U.S. spends more per person on health care than any other nation, Americans die sooner and experience poorer health than residents living in comparable high-income countries. For the past thirty years, the U.S. has been falling behind in terms of life expectancy and overall health over a lifespan. The blame for these outcomes cannot fully be placed on a singular political administration or social reform policies. Americans have an established pattern of poorer health consistent and pervasive over a lifetime starting at birth, throughout childhood and adolescence, young adulthood, middle-age, and for older adults (IOM "U.S. Health ...," 2013). **Health behaviors** are the combined knowledge, practices, and attitudes that motivate the actions we take pertaining to our health. These actions can be purposeful to promote or protect health, they can be thoughtless actions without concern of potential health risks, or conscious, even defiant actions, without regard of the consequences to health (Last, 1988; Bouwman, 2011). Health behaviors involve certain **risks factors** that increase a person's likelihood of negative health outcomes. The World Health Organization (WHO) (2014) defines a risk factor as "any attribute, characteristic or exposure of an individual that increases the likelihood of developing a disease or injury." Examples of important risk factors, as detailed by WHO, include underweight, unsafe sex, high blood pressure, alcohol and tobacco consumption, and unsafe water, sanitation, and hygiene (WHO "Risk Factors," 2014). Health behaviors are vital determinants of health. Unhealthy behaviors accounts for approximately half of the annual deaths in the U.S. whereas 20% of deaths are due to environmental factors, 20% to genetics, and 10% to inadequate medical care (Williams & Collins, 2013). Approximately half of premature mortalities can be connected to behavioral factors and the greatest behavioral risk factor for premature mortality is smoking. Adler and Newman (2002) observe that those with less education and less income are more likely to smoke. On the other hand, Americans smoke less and drink alcohol less heavily when compared to peer countries. The comparisons shift though when we take into consideration that Americans consume the most calories per person, have higher rates of drug abuse, are less likely to use seat belts, are involved in more traffic accidents involving alcohol, and are more likely to use firearms in acts of violence (IOM "U.S. Health ...," 2013).

FAQ: Cigarette smoking harms almost every organ of the body, causes over 440,000 deaths in the U.S. each year, increases the risk of coronary heart disease by 2-4 times, and increases the risk for preterm delivery and stillbirth death (CDC, 2013).

Considering the varying types of illness and injury, when compared with the average of peer countries, Americans as a group fare worse in nine areas of health:

1. Adverse birth outcomes such as infant mortality and low birth weight
2. Injuries and homicides
3. Adolescent pregnancy and sexually transmitted infections
4. Heart disease
5. Chronic lung disease
6. HIV and AIDS
7. Drug-related deaths
8. Obesity and diabetes
9. Disabilities such as arthritis and activity limitations (IOM "U.S. Health...," 2013; McHaney, 2013).

As one might expect, SES plays a large role in behaviors and health outcomes. No matter how SES is measured it can be linked to several health issues including cardiovascular disease, hypertension, low birth weight, cancer, diabetes, and arthritis (Adler & Newman, 2002). SES is connected to health behaviors, stress, and how we age, all of which have correlating consequences. SES impacts how we function, not only concerning overall health, but also our mental health. Differences in SES and its effects can be observed across one's lifespan (APA, "Age & SES, 2014). Access, use, and quality of health care vary by SES; all of which have received a great deal of attention from policy makers and political leaders. Low SES has been associated with more sedentary lifestyle and lower consumption of fiber and healthy foods, including fresh vegetables and fruits. Limited education can be connected to less exposure of information and preventive measures regarding risky health behaviors. Health promotion efforts offer an opportunity for communities and populations to learn about resources available. Without these efforts, the disparities and differences in SES are likely to increase (Adler & Newman, 2002).

Risky health activities or poor health behaviors (cigarette usage, poor nutrition, alcohol usage, etc.) are typically the main focus when considering negative health status. However, additional behaviors such as a sedentary lifestyle, risky sexual activity, and general overall wellness also impact health. According to the Institute of Medicine of the National Academies (2013), communities in the U.S. and surrounding built environments are more likely than comparable peer countries to be designed around automobiles, therefore, discouraging physical activity which contributes to higher obesity rates. The American Heart Association notes the following consequences of physical inactivity:

- Sixty-eight percent of adults are obese or overweight.
- Creating an active lifestyle is more difficult today due, in large part, to technology and better mass transit.
- Jobs have changed. Physically active jobs comprise only approximately 25% of our workforce. Since 1950, sedentary jobs have increased 83 percent.
- Our workweek is longer. Americans work on average 164 more hours per year (47 hours a week) than 20 years ago.
- Obesity is costly. American companies spend approximately $225 billion per year in health-related productivity losses.
- Employees who are obese costs employers on average an additional $460 to $2,500 in medical cost and sick days per year. (The American Heart Association, 2013)

Sullivan (2013) connects the changes employees have experienced in the workplace to increased technological capabilities and the ramifications of a struggling economy. Government data from 2011 finds that 35 percent of people work on weekends, an average of five hours, and often without compensation. Employees are competing for fewer jobs resulting in the tendency to work beyond defined workplace hours as a method of proving worth as a valued employee. Technology has assisted employees in the feeling of needing to work and to be available to their employer at all times. Smartphone users check for messages an average of 150 times per day. As stated by Sullivan, "it took labor unions 150 years to fight for nights and weekends off, while smartphones took them away in about three years" (Sullivan, 2013). As a consequence, rather than being more productive, employees are oftentimes exhausted, stressed, and resentful.

The health of residents living in the U.S. will more than likely continue to fall behind that of other peer nations if current trends are not reversed. Furthermore, the economic consequences of people living shorter lives and poorer health in the U.S. will, in the long run harm the nation's economy as health care costs continue to rise and the workforce remains less healthy. While the U.S. has fallen behind other high-income countries on most measures of health, it is important to note that the United States does experience a few health advantages in comparison to peer countries such as lower cancer death rates, better control of blood pressure and cholesterol, and higher life expectancy for Americans who reach the age of seventy-five (IOM "U.S. Health...," 2013).

Access as a Determinant:

Populations utilize health services in differing manners. The causes of the differences in how racial/ethnic groups are able to access and utilize services can be viewed as a disparity (possibly caused by an injustice) or a dissimilarity in which patient choice or cultural preferences play a role in how health services are accessed and utilized (LaVeist, 2005).

The RAND Corporation defines access to health care as, "the ease with which an individual can obtain needed medical services" (RAND, 2013). The Agency for Healthcare Research (AHRQ), explains access to health care as, "the timely use of personal health services to achieve the best health outcomes" (as cited by the IOM, 1993). The AHRQ identifies three distinct steps required in attaining good access to health care:

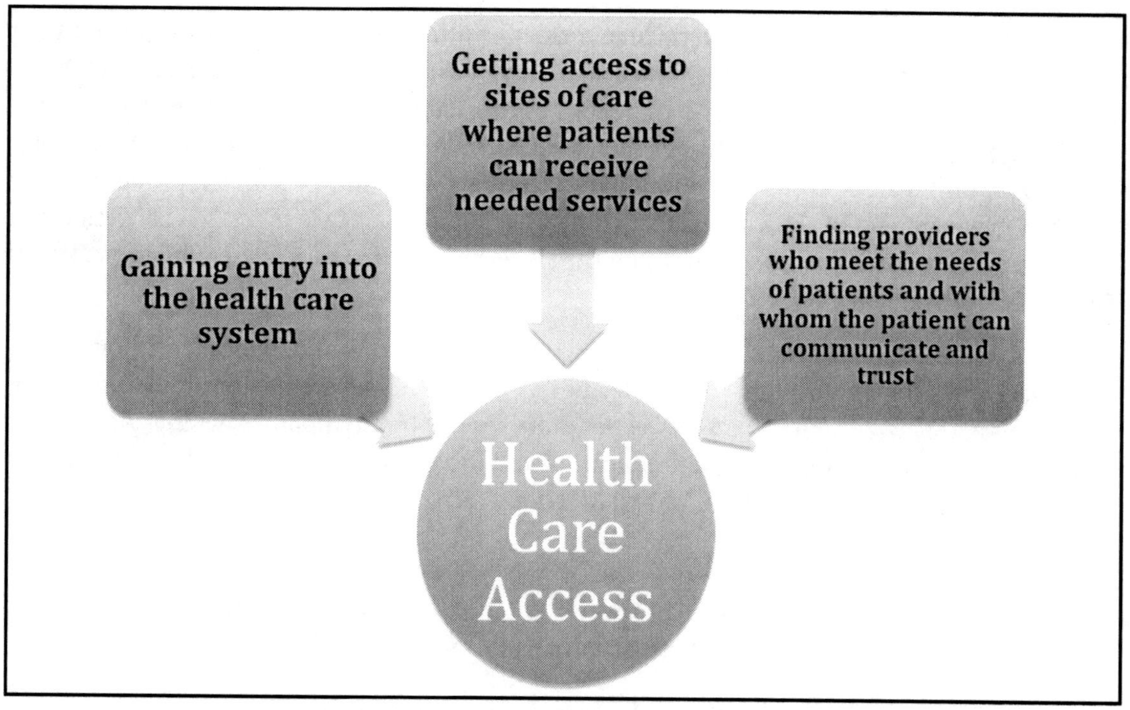

Figure 3. Components of Health Care Access. Adapted From: *Agency for Healthcare Research and Quality.* (2013). Rockville, MD. Retrieved from http://www.ahrq.gov/research/findings/nhqrdr/nhqr12/chap9.html

According to Healthy People (2013), access to health care impacts:

- Physical, social, and mental health status
- Prevention of disease and disability
- Detection and treatment of health conditions
- Quality of life
- Preventable death
- Life expectancy

> **FAQ:** Research shows that even when access to health care is equal, ethnic/racial minorities experience lower-quality of care (LaVeist, 2005).

Most Americans are fortunate to have good access to health services. However, racial and ethnic minorities and people with lower SES are disproportionately represented among those with access issues (AHRQ, 2013). Differences in access to health services impact individuals and society. A person's quality of life is highly dependent on their ability to access health care services. Barriers to service include lack of availability, high cost, and lack of insurance coverage (Healthy People "Access to Health Services, 2013). The ability for a person to obtain health insurance has been identified as a main contributor to health outcomes. Low-income individuals and people of color are at a disproportionate risk of being uninsured, relative to whites and those with higher incomes. And, as mentioned earlier in this chapter, where an individual lives impacts his or her likelihood of having coverage. Rates of those who are uninsured vary greatly across states (4% in Massachusetts to 24% in Texas) (Kaiser Family Foundation "Focus on Health Care Disparities," 2012).

In 2005, approximately 34% of Americans failed to receive necessary health care services. In 2009, this number dropped to 30%–a slight improvement in the quality and availability of care received by Americans. However, research shows the opposite is true for access to care. In 2002, approximately 24% of Americans encountered difficulties accessing heath care. In 2009, this number increased to 26% of Americans (National Healthcare Disparities Report, 2012). Furthermore, research shows that individuals with limited English proficiency are less likely to seek care even when insured showing us that vulnerable populations face increased barriers when accessing care and even receive poorer quality of care when care is received (Kaiser Family Foundation "Focus on Health Care Disparities," 2012).

As previously mentioned, the U.S. spends more on health care than other nations and, typically without better outcomes. And with this comes the assumption that minorities or those with severe health problems are the cause of the elevated spending patterns. However, this is not quite true as research shows us that Americans with health insurance and those who have the highest education and income levels fall behind in comparison to other comparable countries (IOM "U.S. Health...," 2013; McHaney, 2013).

Health care access is measured by:

- Structural measures of the absence or presence of specific resources that facilitate health care. Examples include having health insurance or a usual source of care.
- Assessments by patients of how easily they can gain access to health care services.
- Utilization measures of the essential outcomes of good access to care (i.e., the patient's success in obtaining needed services). (AHRQ, 2013)

Measuring health care access allows us to recognize and address the barriers associated with access issues. Ultimately, poor access to health care comes at a personal and societal cost, which increases the burden of disease for the individual and for society as a whole. Barriers to accessing health care services lead to unmet health needs, delays in receiving timely and appropriate care, inability to obtain preventive services, and avoidable hospitalizations (AHRQ, 2013; Healthy People "Access to Health Services," 2013).

According to the Centers for Disease Control (CDC), the issues surrounding lack of access to health care will be greatly reduced through the Accountable Care Act (ACA), which is expected to extend insurance coverage to an additional 32 million people by 2019 (CDC "Health Care: See Why Being Insured Matters," 2010). Insurance coverage is one step toward health equality by enabling individuals to secure a usual and continual source of care. Overall, people with a usual source of care (primary care provider) experience improved health outcomes, fewer disparities, and fewer costs associated with receiving health care services. Consequently, as more people gain access to health insurance through the ACA starting in 2014, our already strained U.S. health care system will see a large influx of patients. As 32 million additional Americans obtain health insurance and seek much-needed health care services, the creation of new strategies to handle a lack of access stemming from this influx will be required (Healthy People "Access to Health Services," 2013).

Biology and Genetics as Determinants:

Discussions regarding biology and genetics as determinants of health are quite varied and call into question the validity of attributing differences in disease risk across populations solely on genetic disadvantage. While there has been success in linking single genes to disorders connected to specific populations (i.e., sickle cell disease among African Americans and Mediterranean groups, cystic fibrosis among white persons of European heritage), many genes require interaction with the environment in order to be clearly expressed (Dreachslin, Gilbert, & Malone, 2013). Advances in genomic science have shown that the widely held belief that there are biological differences between race groups is incorrect. The belief that race has some biological relevance is still supported by some scientists, but this belief is losing ground and viewed as unsustainable because genetics alone can not explain variances across varying disorders. It is important to acknowledge the role race plays as a determinant of health status and health care quality (LaVeist, 2005; Dreachslin, Gilbert, & Malone, 2013; LaVeist, 2013).

The concept of **race** can be difficult to define due to varying opinions amongst researchers and the transition of the concept over time. Authors Dreachslin, Gilbert & Malone (2013), refer to race as a commonly used word to differentiate groups of people. Sociologist Dalton Conley explains race as primarily unitary in that a person can only have one race. However, a person can claim more than one ethnic affiliation. Conley further states that, "the fundamental difference is that race is socially imposed and hierarchical" (California News Reel "Race," 2003).

As future research on genetic risk factors evolves, the ability to understand race as a social construct that has a large impact on biological mechanisms and health status will become clearer (LaVeist & Isaac, 2013). Biological anthropologist C. Loring Brace explains, "Race is a social construct derived mainly from perceptions conditioned by events of recorded history, and it has no basic biological reality" (Hotz, 1995). The advances in science and genetics have shown a greater variation among people of the same race than between those of different races, bringing forth the need to explore the variations (LaVeist & Isaac, 2013). Furthermore, recognizing the lack of biological racial significances between groups of people should not undermine political (affirmative action) and medical (health status and outcomes) ideas, which may be based on cultural differences stemming from how groups have been treated historically and differences in behaviors between groups (Hotz, 1995; LaVeist, 2005).

When considering social determinants of health, some populations are affected by biological and genetic factors more than others. Healthy People (2012) provides the following examples of biological and genetic social determinants of health:

- Age
- Sex
- HIV status
- Inherited conditions (sickle-cell anemia, hemophilia, and cystic fibrosis)
- Carrying the BRCA1 or BRCA2 gene (increases ovarian and breast cancer risk)
- Heart disease (family history)

The World Health Organization (2014) recognizes genetics in terms of inheritance, which plays a role in determining lifespan, healthiness and the likelihood of developing particular illnesses. In midst of the debates regarding biology and genetics as determinants, tackling disease disparities by addressing poverty, education, personal behavior, coping skills, lifestyle factors, and access to health services are most certainly a positive investment in overcoming these challenges.

WRAP-UP:

This chapter explored the social determinants of health and the correlating concepts including the basic determinants of health, health disparities, health inequalities and inequities, and socioeconomic status. As the demographic composition of our country continues to change, understanding these factors and how they affect the health of individuals, populations, and communities is vital to reaching the overall goal of access and quality health care for all.

DISCUSSION QUESTIONS:

1. In your opinion, which do you view as more important: 1) health inequalities or 2) health inequities? Explain.
2. Compare and contrast the differences between a person in good health versus a person considered to be in ill health. What factors contribute to a person's health status?
3. Consider the ZIP code in which you currently reside. How does the ZIP code impact your personal health? Do you feel your individual behaviors and overall health status reflects your ZIP code?
4. Of the three components of socioeconomic status (education, income, occupation), which do you feel is most important to your overall health status? Why?
5. Consider your own race and ethnicity. How would you define each concept? Do you relate better to your race or your ethnicity?
6. Which of the five determinants typically researched by scientists and researchers in trying to understand the health differences between populations do view as most important? Why?

RESOURCES:

National Partnership for Action
http://minorityhealth.hhs.gov/npa/

National Prevention Council
http://www.surgeongeneral.gov/initiatives/prevention/about/index.html

RACE – The Power of an Illusion (Video Series)
http://www.pbs.org/race/000_General/000_00-Home.htm

World Health Organization Commission on Social Determinants of Health Final Report
http://whqlibdoc.who.int/publications/2008/9789241563703_eng.pdf

World Health Organization video:
http://video.who.int/streaming/csdh/WHA65_film_sdh.wmv

Youth Risk Behavior Surveillance System (YRBSS)
http://www.cdc.gov/HealthyYouth/yrbs/index.htm

ACTIVITY:

This activity illustrates the impact socioeconomic status (SES) has on an individual, family and community.

1. Divide the classroom into three random groups (A,B,C).
    a. No matter the actual size of the group, each group will represent a family of four.
    b. The groups are allowed to decide the ages and genders of the group members.
2. Distribute $100 in play money to each group.
3. Provide Group A with the following instructions:
    a. Double the $100 and multiple by 1,000 (Total will be $200,000)
    b. This total dollar amount represents the total annual income for the family.
4. Provide Group B with the following instructions:
    a. Double the $100 and multiple by 350 (Total will be $70,000)
    b. This total dollar amount represents the total annual income for the family.
5. Provide Group C with the following instructions:
    a. Double the $100 and multiple by 125 (Total will be $25,000)
    b. This total dollar amount represents the total annual income for the family.
6. Each group much use their money to purchase the following:
    a. Insurance
        i. Health = Mandatory, 3.5% of total dollars
        ii. Car = Mandatory 2% of total dollars
        iii. Coverage is for 2 of the 4 family members.
    b. Shelter (Housing)
    c. Transportation
    d. Food
    e. Education
    f. Entertainment
    g. Miscellaneous
7. Instruct each group to work together to come to a consensus in how the above items are budgeted.
8. Items to ponder:
    h. Geographic location will greatly impact how far the money goes.
    i. Demographic information will impact how far the money goes (age, gender, etc.)
    j. What challenges did each group face? For example, where might Group A reside compared to Group B? What types of foods can Groups A and B afford to purchase compared to Group C? Does each group have an equal chance of seeking the same type of educational opportunities?
    k. Have each group discuss the resources available for their "family" based on their total income.

REFERENCES:

2012 National Healthcare Disparities Report. June 2013. Agency for Healthcare Research and Quality, Rockville, MD. http://www.ahrq.gov/research/findings /nhqrdr/nhdr12/index.html

Abrams, J.E. (2013). *Revolutionary medicine: The founding fathers and mothers in sickness and in health.* New York, NY: University Press.

Adler, N.E. & Newman, K. (2002). Socioeconomic disparities in health: Pathways and policies. *Health Affairs*, 21(2), 60-76.

Agency for Healthcare Quality (2013). *National Healthcare Quality Report*, Components of Health Care Access. Retrieved from http://www.ahrq.gov/research/findings/nhqrdr/nhqr12/chap9.html

American Heart Association. (2013). *The Price of Inactivity.* Retrieved from: http://www.heart.org/HEARTORG/GettingHealthy/PhysicalActivity/StartWalking/The-Price-of-Inactivity_UCM_307974_Article.jsp

American Psychological Association. (2014). *Age & Socioeconomic Status.* Retrieved from http://www.apa.org/pi/ses/resources/publications/factsheet-age.aspx

American Psychological Association. (2014). *Education & Socioeconomic Status.* Retrieved from http://www.apa.org/pi/ses/resources/publications/factsheet-education.aspx

American Psychological Association. (2014). *Ethnic and Racial Minorities & Socioeconomic Status.* Retrieved from http://www.apa.org/pi/ses/resources/ publications/factsheet-erm.aspx

American Psychological Association. (2014). *Topics: Socioeconomic Status.* Retrieved from http://apa.org/topics/socioeconomic-status/index.aspx

An, J., Braveman, P., Dekker, M., Egerter, S., & Grossman-Kahn, R. (2011, May). The links between health and the physical aspects of work. *Exploring the Social Determinants of Health Issue Brief*, series (#9). Robert Wood Johnson Foundation. Retrieved from http://www.rwjf.org/content/dam/farm/reports/issue_briefs/2011/rwjf70459. Copyright 2011. Robert Wood Johnson Foundation. Used with permission from the Robert Wood Johnson Foundation.

Andress, L. (n.d.). *Health Disparities And Health Inequities: How the Two Concepts Work.* Retrieved from http://www.bridgingthehealth-gap.com/uploads/louisville _what_is_health_equity.pdf

Anglin, T., DeCoster, E., Roper, A., & Tebo, G. (2013). *Using a Social DeterminantsFramework to Promote Sustainability* [PowerPoint slides]. Retrieved from http://www.hhs.gov/ash/oah-initiatives/teen_pregnancy/training/Assests/social_determinants_framwork.pdf

Bezruchka, S. (2010). Health equity in the USA. *Social Alternatives*, 29 (2), pp 50-56. http://depts.washington.edu/eqhlth/pages/BezruchkaUSHealthInequality10Cor.pdf

Bouwman, L. (2011). Behavior. *Oxford University Press.* Retrieved from http://www.oxfordbibliographies.com/view/document/obo-9780199756797/obo-9780199756797-0006.xml?rskey=CRm7Gq&result=1&q=

Braveman, P., Dekker, M., Egerter, S., Sadegh-Nobari, T., & Pollack, C. (2011). Exploring the social determinants of health: Housing and health. *Robert Wood Johnson Foundation.* Retrieved from http://www.rwjf.org/en/research-publications/find-rwjf-research/2011/05/housing-and-health.html

Bureau of Labor Statistics. (2013, October). *Charts from the American Time Use Survey.* Retrieved from http://www.bls.gov/tus/charts/

Bureau of Labor Statistics. (2013). *Injuries, Illnesses, and Fatalities.* Retrieved from http://www.bls.gov/iif/

Bureau of Labor Statistics. (2013). *Occupational Employment and Wages News Release.* Retrieved from http://www.bls.gov/news.release/ocwage.htm

California Newsreel. (Producer). (2003). Race- The power of an illusion [Video file]. Retrieved from http://www.pbs.org/race/000_General/000_00-Home.htm

Centers for Disease Control and Prevention. (2013). *Definitions.* Retrieved fromhttp://www.cdc.gov/socialdeterminants/Definitions.html

Centers for Disease Control and Prevention. (2013). *Determinants of Health.* Retrieved from http://www.cdc.gov/socialdeterminants/Definitions.html

Centers for Disease Control and Prevention. (2010). *Health Care: See Why Being Insured Matters.* Retrieved from http://www.cdc.gov/features/vitalsigns/HealthcareAccess/

Centers for Disease Control and Prevention. (2013). *Health Effects of Cigarette Smoking.* Retrieved from http://www.cdc.gov/tobacco/data_statistics/fact_sheets /health_effects/effects_cig_smoking/

Centers for Disease Control and Prevention. (2012). *Healthy Homes.* Retrieved from http://www.cdc.gov/healthyplaces/newhealthyhomes.htm

Centers for Disease Control and Prevention. (2013). *Why is Addressing the Role of Social Determinants of Health Important?* Retrieved from http://www.cdc.gov/ socialdeterminants/FAQ.html

Commission on Social Determinants of Health (2008). *Closing the gap in a generation: health equity through action on the social determinants of health. Final Report of the Commission on Social Determinants of Health.* Geneva, World Health Organization.

Davis, R., Cohen, L., & Rodriguez, S. (2009). Toward health equity: A prevention framework for reducing health and safety disparities. In B. J. Healey & R.S. Zimmerman (Eds.), *The new world of health promotion: New program development, implementation, and evaluation* (pp. 163-194). Sudbury, MA: Jones & Bartlett.

Dreachslin, J.L., Gilbert, M.J., & Malone, B. (2013). *Diversity and cultural competence in health care: A systems approach.* San Francisco, CA: Jossey-Bass.

Edberg, M. (2013). *Essentials of health, culture, and diversity: Understanding people, reducing disparities.* Burlington, MA: Jossey-Bass.

Health. (2014). Merriam-Webster Dictionary. Retrieved from http://www.merriam-webster.com/dictionary/health*Health Care Access.* 2013). RAND Corporation: Topics. Retrieved from http://www.rand.org/topics/health-care-access.html

Health inequality and inequity. (2014). World Health Organization: Glossary of terms. Retrieved from http://www.who.int/hia/about/glos/en/index1.html

Healthy People 2010. (2013). *Access to Health Services.* Retrieved from http://www.healthypeople.gov/2020/topicsobjectives2020/overview.aspx?topicid=1

Healthy People 2020. (2012). *Biology and Genetics.* Retrieved from http://www.healthypeople.gov/2020/about/DOHAbout.aspx#biology

Healthy People 2020. (2012). *Introducing Healthy People 2020, Overarching Goals.* Retrieved from http://www.healthypeople.gov/2020/about/default.aspx

Healthy People 2020. (2011). *Objective Development and Selection Process.* Retrieved from http://www.healthypeople.gov/2020/about/objectiveDevelopment.aspx

Healthy People 2020. (2009). *Objective Selection Criteria.* Retrieved from http://www.healthypeople.gov/2010/hp2020/objectives/selectioncriteria.aspx

Healthy People 2020. (2013). *Social Determinants of Health.* Retrieved from http://www.healthypeople.gov/2020/topicsobjectives2020/overview.aspx?topicid=39

Healthy People 2020. (2013). *Understanding Social Determinants of Health.* Retrieved from http://www.healthypeople.gov/2020/about/DOHAbout.aspx#socialfactors

Hotz, R.L. (1995, February 20). Scientists say race has no biological basis. *Los Angeles Times.* Retrieved from http://articles.latimes.com/1995-02-20/news/mn-34098_1_biological-basis *Income.* (2014). Merriam-Webster Dictionary. Retrieved from http://www.merriam- webster.com/dictionary/income

Isaac, L. (2013). Defining health and health care disparities and examining disparities across the life span. In T.A. LeVeist & L.A. Isaac (Eds.), *Race, ethnicity, and health: A public health reader* (pp. 11-31). San Francisco, CA: Jossey-Bass.

Kaiser Family Foundation. (2012, December). *Focus on Health Care Disparities: Key Facts.* Retrieved from http://kaiserfamilyfoundation.files.wordpress.com/ 2013/01/8396.pdf

Kawachi, I., Subramanian, S.V., & Almeida-Filho, N. (2002). A glossary for health inequalities. *J Epidemiol Community Health* 2002; 56:647-652. Retrieved from http://jech.bmj.com/content/56/9/647.full.pdf+html

Koh, H.K. (2010, December 03). Health People 2020: A Roadmap for Health. *Let's Move Blog.* Message posted to http://www.letsmove.gov/blog/2010/12/02/healthy-people-2020-roadmap-health

Last, J.M. (1988). *A dictionary of epidemiology* (2nd ed.). New York: Oxford University Press.

LaVeist, T.A. (2005). *Minority populations and health: An introduction to health disparities in the United States.* San Francisco, CA: Jossey-Bass.

LaVeist, T.A. (2013). The ethnic demographic transition. In T.A. LaVeist & L.A. Isaac (Eds.), *Race, ethnicity, and health: A public health reader* (p. 7). San Francisco, CA: Jossey-Bass.

McHaney, S. (2013, January). Americans far less healthy, die younger than global peers, study finds. *PBS News Hour.* Retrieved from http://pbs.org/newshour/rundown /2013/01/report-americans-less-healthy-die-younger-than-global-peers.html

Oakes, M. (n.d.). Measuring socioeconomic status [e-source]. *National Institutes of Health Office of Behavioral & Social Sciences Research.* Retrieved from http://www.esourceresearch.org/eSourceBook/MeasuringSocioeconomicStatus/1LearningObjectives/tabid/767/Default.aspx

Palardy, G. J. (2008). Differential school effects among low, middle, and high social class composition schools: A multiple group, multilevel latent growth curve analysis. *School Effectiveness and School Improvement, 19,* 21-49.

Rivlin, A. & McClellan, M. (2014, January 13). How to take on health equity in America. *Chicago Tribune.* Retrieved from http://articles.chicagotribune.com/2014-01-13/opinion/ t-oped-health-0113-20140113_1_health-care-health-rankings-health-inequality

Robert Wood Johnson. (2013). *Social Determinants of Health.* Retrieved from http://www.cdc.gov/socialdeterminants/Definitions.html

Rosen, G. (1958). *A history of public health.* New York, NY: MD Publications, Inc.

Sullivan, B. (2013, May). How the smartphone killed the three-day weekend. *NBC News.* Retrieved from http://www.nbcnews.com/technology/how-smartphone-killed-three-day-weekend-6C10071237

Truman, B.I., Smith, C.K., Roy, K., Chen, Z., Moonesinghe, R., Zhu, J., Crawford, C.G., & Zaza, S. (2011). Rationale for regular reporting on health disparities and inequalities – United States. In CDC health disparities and inequalities report — United States, 2011, *Morbidity and Mortality Weekly Report, Vol 60.* Retrieved from http://www.cdc.gov/mmwr/pdf/other/su6001.pdf

U.S. health in international perspective: Shorter lives, poorer health. (2013, January). Institute of Medicine of the National Academies [report brief]. Retrieved from http://www.iom.edu/~/media/Files/Report%20Files/2013/US-Health-International-Perspective/USHealth_Intl_PerspectiveRB.pdf

Wilkinson, R., & Pickett, K.E. (2009). *The spirit level: Why greater equality makes societies stronger.* New York: Bloomsbury.

Williams, D.R. & Collins, C. (2013). U.S. socioeconomic and racial differences in health: Patterns and explanations. In T.A. LaVeist & L.A. Isaac (Eds.), *Race, ethnicity, and health: A public health reader* (pp. 355-3). San Francisco, CA: Jossey-Bass.

Woolf SH, & Aron LY. The US Health Disadvantage Relative to Other High-Income Countries: Findings From a National Research Council/Institute of Medicine Report. *JAMA.* 2013;309(8):771-772. doi:10.1001/jama.2013.91.

World Health Organization. (2014). *Health Impact Assessment: The Determinants of Health.* Retrieved from http://www.who.int/hia/evidence/doh/en/index.html

World Health Organization. (2014). *Social Determinants of Health.* Retrieved from http://www.who.int/topics/social_determinants/en/

Chapter 4:

Defining and Exploring the Differences Between Race, Ethnicity, and Culture

Erin Seedorf and Amy Dore

KEY CONCEPTS:

American Indian or Alaskan Native
Analytic cognitive style
Asian or Pacific Islander
Baby boomers
Bergmann's rule
Black
Black codes
Civil Rights Act of 1964
Culture
Cultural humility
Cultural proficiency
Cultural sensitivity
Directive 15
Ethnicity
Fifteenth Amendment
Fourteenth Amendment
Holistic cognitive style
Independent social style
Indian Removal Act
Interdependent style
Japanese-American internment
Jim Crow
Natural decrease
Nineteenth Amendment
Office of Management and Budget (OMB)
Office of Minority Health (OMH)
Physical anthropologists
Race
Sickle Cell Anemia
Slavery
Tay-Sachs Disease
Thirteenth Amendment
United States Census Bureau
Voting Rights Act of 1964

CHAPTER OVERVIEW:

Heighten attention in the effort to define and explore the differences between race, ethnicity, and culture are the result of the shifting demographic composition of our country. The attention given to the concepts of race, ethnicity, and culture have also brought with it the need to understand how the differences between these concepts impact a person's health and health outcomes. Being culturally sensitive, competent, and proficient requires an awareness of the fundamental basis of: how human beings are classified, how these classifications create diversity between groups, social behaviors stemming from the classifications, and how these behaviors are connected to health. This chapter will explore the historical context of defining and classifying the human population, including the distinctions created over time based on geographic location. A brief account of U.S. history pertaining to racism and segregation will be introduced. The basis of race and ethnic categories will be considered by utilizing the Office of Management and Budget and the U.S. Census Bureau's guidelines. Lastly, a closer look at the concept of culture will be considered including an introduction to the concepts of the cultural proficiency framework and cultural and linguistic competence.

WHY IS THIS IMPORTANT?

Census data shows a long-term shift in the demographic composition of the United States in which non-Hispanic white Americans are predicted to become a minority group over the next three decades, specifically the time period of 2012-2060. These population projections, based on the 2010 Census, point to a noticeably older and more racially and ethnically diverse population by 2060 (U.S. Census Bureau, 2012). The trends point to a markedly different United States from what we currently recognize and understand. According to former (retired) Deputy Director of the U.S. Census Bureau, Thomas L. Mesenbourg reported, "the next half century marks key points in continuing trends – the U.S. will become a plurality nation where the non-Hispanic white population remains the largest single group, but no group is the majority" (U.S. Census Bureau, 2012).

Contributing to the population trends are the **Baby Boomers**, those born between 1946 and 1964. This group numbered 76.4 million in 2012 and accounted for approximately one-quarter of the population. Projections estimate the population group age 65 and older will more than double between 2012 and 2060 – from 43.1 million to 92.0 million. And, the "oldest old"–those 85 and older are expected to triple from 5.9 million to 18.2 million, approximately 4.3 percent of the total population. However, by 2060 the youngest of the baby boomers will be 96 years old and will represent 2.4 million, or 0.6 percent of the total population, resulting in a dramatic drop in overall population (U.S. Census Bureau, 2012).

Author Hope Yen (2013) summed up the Census data by reporting that, for the first time in more than a century, the number of deaths now exceeds births among white Americans. Known as **natural decrease**, this phenomenon occurred before the government's original projected time period and is a sign of the white population decline that is soon to arrive (Yen, 2013). Historically, births have always exceeded deaths in the United States with the exception of some rural areas of the United States in which deaths have exceeded births for decades. Johnson (2011) explains that *natural decrease* occurs when more deaths than births occur in an area or a given year. The primary cause of natural decrease is an age structure distorted by young adult outmigration and aging in place (and at a higher risk of mortality) (Johnson, 2011).

The group that best represents the demographic changes is the Millennial Generation with birth dates ranging from the early 1980s to the early 2000s. This group is the most racially diverse generation in the history of our country, partially due to the influx of Hispanic and Asian immigrants. Approximately 43% of Millennial adults are non-white and about half of babies born today are non-white (Pew Research, 2014). The Millennial Generation represents the "new normal" for our country and represents the profound demographic shift currently taking place. In order to provide proper, timely, and culturally sensitive care, managers and providers working in the healthcare industry must recognize how race, ethnicity, and culture are connected to health for each population group.

CHAPTER EXPECTATIONS:

Upon reading this chapter, the student will be able to:

- Define the concepts of race, ethnicity, and culture
- Recognize the differences between race, ethnicity, and culture
- Understand how race, ethnicity, and culture play a role in health
- Identify examples of genetic diseases related to a person's race and ethnicity
- Acknowledge the need for cultural proficient care, sensitive to the needs of differing populations

HISTORICAL CONTEXT:

We will begin by expanding the previously defined classification and concept of race. From a basic sense, races have traditionally been identified chiefly on the basis of the most easily observable anatomical traits. Evidence of basic racial classification has been identified within cave drawings and art from early human civilizations, primarily based on skin color and other basic physical features. However, we are challenged today by the notion of classifying people according to biological or social constructs, and yet, we can see that health of the population has not been equally distributed, and we must look to understand the basis of those differences.

The difficultly of placing humans into biologically distinct categories is that we operate in a genetically open system, which means that regardless of physical type, humans can mate or interbred with other "types" of humans (Marger, 2011). Therefore, when we look to define people based on their genetic make-up, there are infinite possibilities. However, that has not stopped us from continuously trying to classify our population.

Defining the human population has been a difficult and yet important task since the dawn of man. The Age of Discovery led Europe to unexplored areas of the world, and previously unknown populations of people (Smith, 2008). As they continued to encounter these new groups, there was a perceived need to classify people into racial classifications or categories. These early classifications were based on three primary aspects: skin color, religion, and place of origin or nationality. The historical concept of race dates back to a few biologically based definitions. One such definition is derived from Carolous Linnaeus, a Swedish botanist, physician, and taxonomist (Jandt, 2012). Linnaeus wrote, in 1755, that humans should be classified into four types: Africanus, Americanus, Asiaticus, and Europeaeus. In that same year, a German physiologist and anthropologist Johann Friedrich Blumenbach presented a five-point classification of the humans: Caucasian or White, Mongolian or Yellow, Malayan or Brown, Negro or Black, and American or Red (LaVeist, 2005). This classification system was widely accepted through the 18th Century, beginning the trend to consider race as biologically occurring and natural, and should be based on physical characteristics such as skin color and other facial and bodily features.

INTERESTING POINT: Race and Geography

We can explore the biological idea of race through the interactions of humans with our environment. Physical anthropologists study the adaptation of populations to their environment. Our bodies have adapted to certain environmental conditions that human populations have faced in different geographic locations and climates. The distribution of different skin tones can be historically tied to climate and location. Darker skin tones are found more often in tropical areas where exposure to more constant sunlight developed the need to protect the skin from damage, developing the adaptation of darker pigmentation. Lighter skin tones have been tied to geographic areas with less sun exposure. Generations of this exposure have developed skin pigment adaptations that are characteristic of their region, and are the basis for many race and ethnicity classifications.

Within this area of study, Bergmann's Rule specifies that warm-blooded species in colder regions of the world have stockier bodies for the purpose of retaining body heat more efficiently.

Source: Smith, Cameron (2008). Anthropology for Dummies, John Wiley & Sons Inc.

However, given the hierarchical structure of European culture, we began to see the placement of racial categories, again associated with skin color, where lighter skinned people (Europeans) were placed at the top of the scale in society and darker-skinned people were placed below (Smith, 2008). In the developing United States, where Europeans were now mixing with new native populations, we see the origins of racism, and effects it has had on the infrastructure of the country.

A Brief View of US History- Policies of Racism and Segregation

1830- Indian Removal Act: Signed into law by President Andrew Jackson, the act allowed the forcible removal of the 5 identified "Civilized Tribes" and their relocation to reservations in the Oklahoma Territory. This period of US history is referred to as the "Trail of Tears."

1640- 1863- Period of Slavery: The most commonly recognized and cited date for the arrival of Africans to the United States was in August of 1619. From this date until President Abraham Lincoln's Emancipation Proclamation of 1863, the African populations in the US were classified as slaves. The Emancipation Proclamation only freed the African groups living in states that had succeeded from the confederacy. The "Period of Slavery" lasted for approximately 244 years.

1863-1865- Reconstruction and Jim Crow: A period where federal law, or "black codes" regulated racial and ethnic minorities to second-class citizens. Jim Crow laws created societal segregation, where minority groups were limited in their rights as individuals, such as the right to vote and the right to access to equal community resources like schools and medical care facilities.

1865- Ratification of the Thirteenth Amendment: Outlawed slavery in the United States and all territories.

1868- Ratification of the Fourteenth Amendment: Gave citizenship to all persons born in the US or naturalized.

1870- Ratification of the Fifteenth Amendment: Barred any state from prohibiting the right of any male citizen from voting.

1920- Ratification of the Nineteenth Amendment: Gave the right to vote to all female US citizens.

1942- Japanese-American Internment: During World War II, President Roosevelt signed an executive order for the relocation of all Americans of Japanese ancestry to concentration camps in the US. This policy was based on a fear that Japanese Americans would remain loyal to their ancestral land and were feared as national security risk. During this time over 127,000 US citizens were imprisoned.

1964- Civil Rights Act: Prohibited discrimination in public accommodations such as mass transportation, restaurants, and hotels on the basis of race, color, religion, or national origin.

1964- The Voting Rights Act- Eliminated discriminatory election practices like literacy tests, established new and more equitable voting procedure, and very specifically prohibited the denial or abridgement of the right to vote based on race or color.

Sources: Adapted from LaVeist, Thomas (2005). Minority Populations and Health: An Introduction to Health Disparities in the United States, Jossey-Bass and "Japanese American Internment." New World Encyclopedia, www.newworldencyclopedia.org

Today, race and ethnicity continue to be one of most studied concepts in the medical and public health literature. However, the definition and use of these concepts are also heavily disputed, questioning the validity of such categories to separate our world population. In 1942 a publication entitled *Man's Most Dangerous Myth: The Fallacy of Race*, publicly criticized the validity of using the classifications of race (LaVeist, 2005). By the 1970's, the majority of scientific investigators questioned the biologic basis of race, and de-valued its power in explaining the differences in the human species. However, in 1994, two prominent scientists, Richard J. Herrnstien and Charles Murray, published one of the most famous publications on the subject of genetic determination. *The Bell Curve* argued that intelligence is a better predictor of human behavior and separated the "cognitive elite" from those considered average or below average. In 1996, *Time Magazine* ran a cover story on the topic of genetic determination, and a leading scientist behind the Human Genetic Diversity Project, Luca Cavalli-Sforza, challenged "The Bell Curve" concept (Duster, 2003). In a conference presentation, Calli-Sforza stated:

> *If you take differences between two random individuals of the same population, they are about 85% of the differences you would find if you took two individuals at random from the whole world. This means two things: 1) the differences between individuals are the bulk of variation, and 2) the differences among populations, races and continents are very small* (Smith & Sapp, 1997, pg. 53).

This scientific conversation and disagreement still occurs today. However, it does not lessen the importance of studying the health of the population, exploring the differences and disparities in health outcomes, and evaluation of how we can identify and address the identified health concerns.

WHAT YOU SHOULD KNOW:

Concepts of Race and Ethnicity:

When discussing issues of race, ethnicity, and culture it is important to evaluate and understand how these terms are being defined. Webster-Merriam dictionary (2014) defines the concept of **race** as a category of humankind that shares distinctive physical traits. The concept of **ethnicity** is defined as a particular ethnic affiliation or group. However, the challenges with these definitions are two-fold. First, and particularly with the concept of race, we see an emphasis on the biological features of humans and less weight on the impact of a shared experiences or culture. Second, we are faced with the challenge of who defines the identified affiliation or "shared experience."

Authors Ford and Harawa (2010), in their paper A New Conceptualization of Ethnicity for Social Epidemiological and Health Equity Research, state that the terms race and ethnicity have imposed a socially-constructed segregation of the US population, assigning people to one of five major subpopulations established hundreds of years ago. And while the terms of race and ethnicity have been incorrectly and at times synonymously used, they pose the concepts as critical to exploring our population, our social constructs, and our health outcomes. Their challenge is to expand the definition of such terms, acknowledging and evaluating the complex social experiences and constructs that influence an individual's personal identify and group social relations. History illustrates the disparities of health and health outcomes for different populations, and presents the continuing challenge of investigating these differences.

Two Identified Genetic Diseases Connected to Racial/Ethnic Groups

Tay-Sachs Disease: A life-threatening disease of the nervous system passed down through families. This disease is due to a defective gene in chromosome 15, where an inability of the body to break down a chemical found in nerve tissue causing a build up in brain cells. When both parents carry the defective Tay-Sachs gene, a child has a 25% chance of developing the disease. Although anyone can be a carrier of the Tay-Sachs gene, the disease is most common among the Ashkenazi Jewish population. About 1 in every 27 members of this population carries the Tay-Sachs gene.

Sickle Cell Anemia: A disease passed down through families where the body's red blood cells, normally shaped like a disc, take on a sickle or crescent shape. This unusual shape affects the red blood cell's ability to carry oxygen throughout the body. This disease is inherited from both parents, and those that inherit from only one parent are considered to have "sickle cell trait", but do not present with the symptoms of sickle cell anemia. Sickle cell disease is found to be much more common in people of African or Mediterranean descent, but also can be seen in populations from South and Central America, the Caribbean, and the Middle East.

Sources: *Medline Plus [Internet]. Bethesda (MD): National Library of Medicine (US); [updated 2015 April 24]. Sickle Cell Anemia; [updated 2014 February 24]; Available from: http://www.nlm.nih.gov/medlineplus/ency/ article/000527.htm Medline Plus [Internet]. Bethesda (MD): National Library of Medicine (US); [updated 2015 April 24]. Tay-Sachs disease; [updated 2012 November 2]; Available from: http://www.nlm.nih.gov/medlineplus/ency/article/ 001417.htm*

Establishing the Collection of Racial and Ethnic Information

The **Office of Management and Budget (OMB)**, the largest office within the Executive Office of the President of the United States, is charged with the primary function of assisting the President in preparing the federal budget. In the 1970's the OMB went through a multi-year process, including many studies and hearings, to determine a set of categories to classify the population of the United States. In 1977, the OMB established the **Directive 15**, which standardized the collection of racial and ethnic information among federal agencies, and to include data on persons of Hispanic origins, as required by Congress (White House, Office of Management and Budget, 1994, June 9). The purpose of this directive is to keep national data consistent, providing researchers, business, and industry with common categories of the US population. A new version, Version 2, of the directive was issued in 1997 (White House, Office of Management and Budget, 1997, October 30). However, there is much discussion around the validity of these categories, and whether or not the categories accurately capture the diversity of the U.S. population.

The basic racial and ethnic categories for Federal statistics and program administrative reporting are defined as follows:

American Indian or Alaskan Native: A person having origins in any of the original peoples of North America, and who maintains cultural identification through tribal affiliation or community recognition.

Asian or Pacific Islander: A person having origins in any of the original peoples of the Far East, Southeast Asia, the Indian subcontinent, or the Pacific Islands. This area includes, for example, China, India, Japan, Korea, the Philippine Islands, and Samoa.

Black: A person having origins in any of the black racial groups of Africa.

White: A person having origins in any of the original peoples of Europe, North Africa, or the Middle East.

To provide flexibility, it is preferable to collect data on race and ethnicity separately. If separate race and ethnic categories are used, the minimum designations are:

Race:

- American Indian or Alaskan Native
- Asian or Pacific Islander
- Black
- White

Ethnicity:

- Hispanic origin
- Not of Hispanic origin

When race and ethnicity are collected separately, the number of White and Black persons who are Hispanic must be identifiable, and capable of being reported in that category. If a combined format is used to collect racial and ethnic data, the minimum acceptable categories are:

- American Indian or Alaskan Native
- Asian or Pacific Islander
- Black, not of Hispanic origin
- Hispanic
- White, not of Hispanic origin.

(Office of Management and Budget, 1994, http://www.whitehouse.gov/omb/fedreg_notice_15)

The **United States Census Bureau** was established through Title 13 and Title 26 of the U.S. Code, and serves as the national agency to collect data on the U.S. population and economy. The Census Bureau's full mission statement is, "...to serve as the leading source of quality data about the nation's people and economy. We honor privacy, protect confidentiality, share our expertise globally, and conduct our work openly. We are guided on this mission by scientific objectivity, our strong and capable workforce, our devotion to research-based innovation, and our abiding commitment to our customers" (United State Census Bureau, 2012, August 27).

US Census Bureau- About Us

Types of Data Collected & When:

- Population & Housing Census- Every 10 years
- Economic Census- Every 5 years
- Census of Governments- Every 5 years
- American Community Survey- Annually
- Economic Indicators- Each indicator is released on a specific schedule, see the Economic Indicator Calendar for more information
- Other Surveys- Periodic, both Demographic & Economic

How Data is Used:

To determine the distribution of Congressional seats to states:

- mandated by the U.S. Constitution
- used to apportion seats in the U.S. House of Representatives
- used to define legislature districts, school district assignment areas and other important functional areas of government.

To make decisions about what community services to provide Changes in your community are crucial to many planning decisions, such as where to:

- provide services for the elderly
- where to build new roads and schools
- or where to locate job training centers

To distribute more than $400 billion in federal funds to local, state and tribal governments each year Census data affects how funding is allocated to communities for:

- neighborhood improvements
- public health
- education
- transportation
- and much more

To provide age search information for:

- Qualifying for Social Security and other retirement benefits
- Passport applications
- Proving relationship in settling estates
- Researching family history or a historical topic

Adapted from: United States Census Bureau (2012), "About Us." Retrieved from www.census.gov/aboutus/

FAQ:

The 23rd federal census (Census 2010) used the following questions to classify and individual's identification of race and ethnicity for the 2010 Census survey:

Is the person of Hispanic, Latino, or Spanish origin?

a. No, not of Hispanic, Latino, or Spanish origin

b. Yes, Mexican, Mexican Am., Chicano

c. Yes, Puerto Rican

d. Yes, Cuban

e. Yes, another Hispanic, Latino, or Spanish origin — Print origin, for example, Argentinean, Colombian, Dominican, Nicaraguan, Salvadoran, Spaniard, and so on.

What is the person's race?

- White
- Black or African American
- American Indian or Alaska Native — Print name of enrolled or principal tribe.
- Asian Indian
- Chinese
- Filipino
- Other Asian — Print race, for example, Hmong, Laotian, Thai, Pakistani, Cambodian, and so on.
- Japanese
- Korean
- Vietnamese
- Native Hawaiian
- Guamanian or Chamorro
- Samoan
- Other Pacific Islander (Example: Fijian, Tongan)
- Some other race — (Example: Write in the race specified by the individual)

NOTE: This census acknowledged that "race categories include both racial and national-origin groups.

Adapted from: United State Census Bureau (2012), "About Us." Retrieved from https://www.census.gov

The Concept of Culture:

Scientists interested in the study of culture define the concept of **culture** as a shared knowledge and mutual expectations produced, disseminated and reproduced among a group of interacting individuals (Grossman & Na, 2014). As researcher Shweder (1991) points out, it is difficult or even impossible to explore or define culture within and individual or group without acknowledging the shared experience, background, and psychological processes within that culture.

Hotstede (1994) classified **culture** into four categories: symbols, rituals, values, and heroes:

1. *Symbols*- verbal and nonverbal language,
2. *Rituals*- the socially essential collective activities within a culture,
3. *Values*- the feelings not open for discussion within a culture about what is good or bad, beautiful or ugly, normal or abnormal, which are present in a majority of the members of a culture, or at least in those who occupy pivotal positions, and
4. *Heroes*- the real or imaginary people who serve as behavior models within a culture. Heroes are expressed in the culture's myths.

Grossman & Na (2014) discuss two concepts from the last two decades of research on culture: 1) independent vs. interdependent social style, and 2) holistic vs. analytic cognitive style. An **independent social style** is focused on the individual, acting on one's own person values and beliefs, compared to an **interdependent style** focused on a culture's socially shared norms and values. **Analytic cognitive style** focuses on a single dimension and is driven by a use of rule-based categorization of objects, whereas a **holistic cognitive style** focus on multiple layers of contextual information, and is driven by relation-focused categorization of objects.

Health Disparity, Health Equity Research

Research into health disparities and health equity continues to demonstrate the differences in health outcomes among different ethnically defined groups (Ford & Harawa, 2010). This pushes the need to build our knowledge and understanding of the fundamental basis of such differences.

The Office of Minority Health (OMH) was created in 1986, and based on outcomes from the *1985 Secretary's Task Force Report on Black and Minority Health* (OMH, 2013). This office is charged with the responsibility of improving the health of racial and ethnic minorities in the U.S. OMH is responsible for the administration of health policies and programs that will help eliminate disparities. They work in partnership with national and local organizations, and provide funding to: state offices of minority health, multicultural health, and health equity; community faith-based organizations; institutions of higher education; tribes or tribal organizations; and other organizations with the mission of improving health outcomes for disparate populations.

Health Care and Cultural Competence

It is essential for health care professionals to understand how cultural aspects of our population and the relationship to health, health outcomes, and health behaviors. To do this, health care practice must take on practices that promote cultural awareness, sensitivity, and an acknowledgement of cultural differences.

There is a growing body of study that feels we should go beyond the concept of being culturally competent, and instead move toward cultural proficiency. **Cultural proficiency** allows one to move beyond pure understanding of cultural differences, to a place of application, where one advocates for the fulfillment of cultural needs. This new approach illustrates the process of proficiency as a continuous process, where the learning is constantly seeking and applying knowledge gained about culture and cultural differences. Dr. Kikanza Nuri-Robins, a researcher for equitable education, created a framework to describe this learning progression of cultural proficiency.

Cultural Proficiency Continuum					
The Continuum provides language for describing situations and events.					
DESTRUCTION	**INTOLERANCE**	**REDUCTIONISM**	**PRECOMPETENCE**	**COMPETENCE**	**PROFICIENCY**
Destroy differences Judge differences among people as wrong and seek to eliminate them.	***Demean differences*** Accept that differences exist, but regard some as superior to others.	***Discount differences*** Act as if there are no differences. Treat everyone equally, regardless of their differences.	***Embrace differences*** Begin to make changes, some of which may be inadequate, or incorrect because of limited understanding.	***Engage with differences*** Use the essential elements as standards for individual behavior and organizational practices	***Esteem and learn from differences*** Interact equitably in a variety of cultural environments; advocate for others.

(Source: The Cultural Proficiency Framework. Nuri-Robins and Bundy. (Work in Progress). The Cultural Proficiency Framework. *Fish Out of Water*. Thousand Oaks, CA: Corwin.)

Another approach to the study of culture is that of cultural humility. Cultural humility proceeds to the next step from proficiency, moving individuals to gain a better understanding of one's own world-view and the cultural implications of one's own identity group membership (Cohen, et al., 2007). Chavez, et al. in their book chapter *Community Organizing for Health and Social Justice* define **cultural humility** as a life-long commitment to self-evaluation and self-critique to redress power and imbalances and to develop and maintain mutually respectful dynamic partnerships based on mutual trust (Chavez, et al., Ed. Cohen, et al., 2007).

Along the same lines is the concept of **cultural sensitivity** in which health care providers, administrators, and those in the healthcare industry have a general awareness of a patient's cultural background, beliefs, and values. Respect comes from this awareness and proficiency is enhanced. As an end result, patient compliance is increased through treatment plans that are mutually agreed upon between patient and provider (Rose, 2013). Regardless of approach, we can see that in order to truly address issues of health and health outcomes in health care, we must not only be aware of differences in race, ethnicity and culture, but we must take it on ourselves to pursue of life-long process of cultural study, reflection, and application.

CONCLUSIONS/WRAP-UP:

This chapter provides a glimpse of the varying definitions and the historical contexts surrounding how race, ethnicity, and culture impacts health. In a society that functions by placing people in pre-defined categories, understanding these categories will prepare us for the expected changes our country will face over this next half century. Whether comparing a group, population, or generation, each brings varying expectations, beliefs, and behaviors regarding their health. Even with all of the advances in medicine and improvements in access to care, these advances are not a "one size fits all" solution. Additionally, our changing health care system brings with it another layer in which racial, ethnic, and cultural differences will, once again, remind us that health outcomes are not guaranteed.

RESOURCES:

White House, Office of Management and Budget
http://www.whitehouse.gov/omb

United State Census Bureau
https://www.census.gov

U.S. Department of Health and Human Services, Office of Minority Health
http://minorityhealth.hhs.gov

The Rise and Fall of Jim Crow
http://www.pbs.org/wnet/jimcrow/

The DNA Files
http://www.dnafiles.org

All of Us are Related, Each of Us is Unique
http://allrelated.syr.edu/index.html

Race – Are We So Different?
http://www.understandingrace.org

Discussion Questions:

1. When considering health, in your opinion, which is more important: race, ethnicity, or culture? Why?
2. How do generational differences impact health?
3. Why is it important to place people into categories or assign people to a specific race?
4. What is the most common method of defining a person's race?
5. List and explain the racial and ethnic categories created by the Office of Management and Budget.
6. How does cultural play a role in a person's behaviors and beliefs about health.
7. Which do you feel is more important: cultural competency, humility, sensitivity, or proficiency? Explain your answer.

Classroom Activities:

Activity #1:
Who am I?

Step 1: Each student in the class has 60 seconds to describe him or herself. This can be a list of words, descriptors, or characteristics.

Step 2: Once time is up, have the class pair up in groups.

Step 3: Have the groups compare their list. Are there commonalities? Differences?

Step 4: Complete a few rotations of groups to allow for a broader perspective and comparisons.

Step 5: Ask the class how many "lists" included descriptors or characteristics related to race, ethnicity, or culture. Discuss the outcomes and the importance of the items listed.

Activity #2:
Guess Who? The Cost of Racial "Color Blindness"

Step 1: Play the game as instructed in the *Guess Who* article and video:

http://hbr.org/2013/07/the-costs-of-racial-color-blindness/ar/1

Step 2: Follow up by watching the entire video. What are the results of the class groups?

(Adapted from: Michael I. Norton and Evan P. Apfelbaum)

Case Study:

Background:

The elderly account for nearly 12% of the population in the U.S. and one third of all hospital stays. The aging baby boomers are major consumers of all healthcare services. This growing number of older adults places increasing demands on the public health system and on medical and social services.

- In some states, a quarter of the population will be aged 65 and older.
- The cost of providing health care for an older American is three to five times greater than the cost for someone younger than 65.
- By 2030, the nation's health care spending is projected to increase by 25% due to demographic shifts unless improving and preserving the health of older adults is more actively addressed.
- Due to the issue of ageism, many elderly adults are denied treatment, surgery, and state of the art, quality care.
- Proper preventative screenings and continuous quality care measures can help reduce many chronic disease issues and frequent hospital stays. (Office of Health and Human Services, 2013)

Step #1: You are heading a committee to establish an elderly community health center in South Florida. Your focus is on disease prevention and population education. Your goal is to treat the elderly in this area. Identify the top items you will need to consider in order to effectively treat this population.

Step #2: Look closely at the population in your catchment area. Look at the demographic and health trends for this population. Gather the necessary information to make informed decisions about your new health care facility. What information did you find?

In-Class Ice Breakers:

1. Have students define race, ethnicity, and culture. In groups have them draw a Venn diagram. Using the diagram have students write each term within each of the three circles of the venn diagram. Explain briefly that the factors related to each term may overlap in certain areas.
2. Have the students discuss the components/factors related to race, ethnicity, and culture. Instruct them to illustrate the overlapping factors on the diagram.
3. Have students stand up and change their seats to sit next to someone they do not know (or do not know well). Have each student make assumptions about the other student's race, ethnicity, culture and background. Discuss the assumptions made and why these assumptions may have been made. Explain the importance of asking questions and applying the knowledge gained about race, ethnicity, and culture to health.

REFERENCES:

Chavez, V., et al. (2007). "Community Organizing for Health and Social Justice," Prevention is Primary, Ed. Cohen, L., et al., *Jossey-Bass, A Wiley Imprint,* ISBN: 978-0-7879-8318-9.

Cohen, L., et al. (2007). Prevention is Primary, Jossey-*Bass, A Wiley Imprint,* ISBN: 978-0-7879-8318-9.

Duster, T. (2003). "Buried Alive: The Concept of Race in Science," Genetic Nature and Culture: Anthropology and Science Beyond the Two-Culture Divide, Ed. Goodman et al., *University of California Press,* 13: 258-277, ISBN: 0-520-23792-7.

Ford, C., Harawa, N., (April, 2010). A New Conceptualization of Ethnicity for Social Epidemiologic and Health Equity Research, *Social Science and Medicine.* Retrieved from http://www.elsevier.com/locate/socscimed

Grossman, I., Na, J., (2014). Research in Culture and Psychology: Past Lessons and Future Challenges, *WIREs Cognitive Science.* Retrieved from http://onlinelibrary.wiley.com/doi/10.1002/wcs.1267/full

Jandt, F. (2013). An Introduction to Intercultural Communication: Identities in a Global Community, *Sage Publications INC.*, ISBN: 978-1-4129-9287-9.

"Japanese American Internment." New World Encyclopedia, www.newworldencyclopedia.org, Page Update: May 2, 2014.

Johnson, K.M. (2011, Spring). Natural Decrease in America, More Coffins than Cradles, *CarseyInstitute* (Issue Brief No. 30). Retrieved from http://www.carseyinstitute.unh.edu/publications /IB-Johnson-Natural-Decrease.pdf

LaVeist, T. & Issac, L. (2013). Race, Ethnicity, and Health: A Public Health Reader, *John Wiley & Sons Inc.*, ISBN: 978-1-118-08698-8.

LaVeist, T. (2005). Minority Populations and Health: An Introduction to Health Disparities in the United States, *Jossey-Bass, A Wiley Imprint,* ISBN: 0-7879-6413-1.

Maldistribution. (2014). Merriam-Webster Dictionary. http://www.merriam-webster.com/dictionary/maldistribution

Marger, M. (2012). Race and Ethnic Relations: American and Global Perspectives, *Wadsworth,Cengage Learning,* ISBN: 978-1-111-18638-8.

Medline Plus [Internet]. Bethesda (MD): National Library of Medicine (US); [updated 2015 April 24]. Sickle Cell Anemia; [updated 2014 February 24]; Available from: http://www.nlm.nih.gov/medlineplus/ency/ article/000527.htm

Medline Plus [Internet]. Bethesda (MD): National Library of Medicine (US); [updated 2015 April 24]. Tay-Sachs disease; [updated 2012 November 2]; Available from: http://www.nlm.nih.gov/medlineplus/ency/article/ 001417.htm

Nuri-Robins and Bundy. (Work in Progress). The Cultural Proficiency Framework. *Fish out of Water.* Thousand Oaks, CA: Corwin.

Pew Research: Social and Demographic Trends. (2014, March 7). *Millennials in adulthood: Detached from institutions, networked with friends.* Retrieved from http://www.pewsocialtrends.org/2014/03/07/millennials-in-adulthood/

Rose, P.R. (2013). *Cultural competency for the health professional.* Burlington, MA: Jones & Bartlett.

Shweder, R. (1991). Thinking Through Cultures: Expectations in Cultural Psychology, *Harvard University Press,* ISBN: 0-674-88416-7.

Smith, C. (2008). Anthropology for Dummies, *John-Wiley & Sons, INC,* ISBN: 978-0-470-27966-3.

Smith, E. (1997). Plain Talk about the Human Genome Project: A Tuskegee University Conference on Its Promise and Perils... and Matters of Race, *Tuskegee University,* ISBN: 978-1-891-19601-0.

United States Census Bureau. (August 27, 2012). *About Us.* Retrieved from https://www.census.gov/aboutus/

United States Census Bureau. (August 27, 2012). *Exploring the Form.* Retrieved from https://www.census.gov/2010census/about/interactive-form.php

United States Census Bureau. (2012, December 12). *U.S. Census Bureau Projections Show a Slower Growing, Older, More Diverse Nation a Half Century from Now.* Retrieved from http://www.census.gov/newsroom/releases/archives/population/cb12-243.html

U.S. Department of Health and Human Services, Office of Minority Health. (December 24,2013), *About OMH.* Retrieved from http://minorityhealth.hhs.gov/templates /browse.aspx?lvl=1&lvlID=7

U.S. Department of Health and Human Services, Office of Minority Health. (2013, May 9). *What is Cultural Competency?* Retrieved from http://minorityhealth. hhs.gov/templates/browse.aspx?lvl=2&lvlID=11

White House, Office of Management and Budget, (June 9, 1994). *Standards for the Classification of Federal Data on Race and Ethnicity.* Retrieved from http://www.whitehouse.gov/omb/fedreg_notice_15

White House, Office of Management and Budget, (1997, October 30). *Revisions to the Standards for the Classification of Federal Data on Race and Ethnicity.* Retrieved from http://www.whitehouse.gov/omb/fedreg_1997standards/

Yen, H. (2013, June 13). Census: White majority in U.S. gone by 2043. *U.S. News NBC News.*Retrieved from http://usnews.nbcnews.com/_news/2013/06/13/18934111-census-white-majority-in-us-gone-by-2043?lite

Chapter 5:

Understanding the Role Demographics Play in Health and Healthcare

Christye Brown

KEY CONCEPTS:

Acculturation
Acculturation Complexity Model
Demography
Demographic survey data
Disease prevalence
Fertility
Gender
Health demography
Maternal and child health
Mortality
Migration
Neighborhoods
Risk behaviors
Sarcopenia
Successful aging
Youth Risk Behavior Surveillance System

CHAPTER OVERVIEW:

The study of populations allows for an in-depth examination of factors as they relate to health and healthcare. This chapter will explore age, employment and income, gender, and geographical location. More specifically, it will discuss the risk behaviors and chronic diseases commonly associated with these various demographics. Finally, this chapter will discuss urban barriers to healthcare services, including mental health treatment.

WHY IS THIS IMPORTANT?

As you study the various populations in our society, it is important to understand how demographics and behavioral risk factors can influence the health and disease status of individuals and communities. Learning these factors will increase one's cultural proficiency and provide a comprehensive perspective on health and healthcare in these various populations. While the literature suggests there are varied viewpoints and theories on demographics and causal factors of specific conditions, this chapter will present the general philosophies of thought surrounding the role of demographics in health and healthcare.

CHAPTER EXPECTATIONS:

Upon reading this chapter, the student will be able to describe:

- Demographics and their bidirectional influences on health
- Risk behaviors and chronic disease prevalence in various populations
- Geographic barriers to healthcare
- Culturally-related barriers to accessing mental health treatment

WHAT YOU SHOULD KNOW:

Demography is the study of human populations including: the size, the distribution, and the composition of populations. In 2010, the total US population was 309 million with projections of 439 million by 2050 (U.S. Census Bureau, 2011). This projection is accompanied by the expectation of significant changes specific to age, race, and ethnicity (American Medical Association, 2012).

Population trends in health and illness are evident through decades of demographic research. The study of health in demography surrounds how factors (e.g. age, marital status, and income) influence both health status and health behavior of populations and how health-related occurrences affect demographic attributes (Pol & Thomas, 2001). In essence, there is a bidirectional relationship between health and demographic factors; these relationships are often assessed and evaluated through survey data.

In surveys designed to assess the health of persons from various racial/ethnic groups in the US, participants are asked to evaluate their own health status (McGee, Liao, Cao, & Cooper, 1999). Findings from many US cohorts (First National Health and Nutrition Examination Survey, Longitudinal Study of Aging, MacArthur Field Study of Successful Aging, and Human Population Laboratory Cohort) show that self-reported health status is related to subsequent mortality among various racial/ethnic and national groups, and those reporting poorer health have a higher mortality rate than do those reporting better health (McGee et al., 1999).

Collectively, **demographic survey data** is the platform for the analysis of factors that can inform health policy, clinical interventions and community-based health education efforts. The next section will present a discussion on several demographic factors and associated behavioral risk factors and disease prevalence.

Gender

According to the World Health Organization (Women, Gender and Health, 2013), **gender** refers to the socially constructed roles, behaviors, activities, and attributes that a given society considers appropriate for men and women; the distinct roles and behaviors of men and women in a given culture, dictated by that culture's gender norms and values, give rise to gender differences.

Reminder! – Key Determinants of Health

- Neighborhoods are the synthesis of combinations of social, economic, demographic, structural and geographic conditions, all of which affect the health of individuals in that setting (Weden, Bird, Escarce, & Lurie, 2010).
- Socioeconomic status represents the position of an individual or household in the social stratification (Stronks, Van De Mheen, Van Den Bos, & Mackenbach, 1997) and is usually measured by education, occupation, employment, income and wealth (Pampel, Krueger, & Denney, 2010).

Risk behaviors

- Individual behavior, biology and genetics, health services, and social factors are all known as determinants of health (HealthyPeople 2020, 2012). Social and economic conditions and their effects on people's lives determine their: 1) risk of illness, 2) actions taken to prevent becoming ill, and 3) actions taken to treat illness when it occurs (World Health Organization, 2013). These actions, known as individual behavior determinants of health, can increase the risk of disease or illness. Biological factors such as age and gender can disproportionately affect certain populations while access and quality to health services also impact health (HealthyPeople 2020, 2012).
- Behavioral determinants of health include diet, exercise, and smoking. Each of these factors plays a role in the health status of an individual and can also be further influenced by biological factors. Research has shown that diet, exercise and smoking are all behavioral determinants of health that contribute importantly to SES differences in health and mortality (Lantz, Golberstien, House, & Morenoff, 2010). It is also important to note that the manner in which people seek health information on diet and physical activity has also been examined. Findings revealed the most common Internet health information seekers were younger, female, and of higher income and education; newspaper information seekers were older, of higher education, and non-White; and television health information seekers were non-White (Beaudoin & Hong, 2011).

Maternal and child health

Fertility in demography refers to the number of live births–not the ability to have children. The level of fertility throughout the world depends on culture, social and economic conditions, as well as by individual characteristics such as age, however, the proximate determinants of behavior and biology mediate these factors (Frank, 2012). In general, the more developed the society, the lower the levels of fertility.

FAQ: Understanding racial-ethnic differences in fertility is important for understanding American fertility more broadly since the majority of births in the U.S. are to non-White women (Hartnett, 2014).

Maternal and child health (MCH) is a field that defines its focus by the growth and developmental stages of the individual; children have unique vulnerabilities that may relate to their growth and development (Dallo, Archer, & Misra, 2014). MCH can be viewed from a life cycle perspective that has interdependent components, including reproductive health, prenatal health and children's health (Kotch, 2013). This intricately woven life cycle involves demographics that affect the health and health status of both mother and child along their life course. As such, demographic considerations in maternal and child health are complex.

MCH studies show a "disconnect" between diet and health among low-income women (Dammann & Smith, 2009), a high prevalence of postpartum depression at nine months in a largely ethnic, low-income population (Gress-Smith, Luecken, Lemery-Chalfant, & Howe, 2012). Furthermore, low income women and children generally have worse outcomes than do high-income women and children, and those living in rural areas generally have worse outcomes than do those in urban areas (Boerma, Bryce, Kinfu, Axelson, & Victora, 2008).

According to the Millennium Development Goals (4 and 5) adopted by the United Nations member states, the overall goals in MCH are to reduce the mortality rate by 66% in children younger than 5 years and to reduce maternal mortality by 75%, both between 1990 and 2015 (Lozano, Wang, Foreman, et al., 2011). **Mortality** can be defined as deaths as a component of population change (Filippin, Teixeira, da Silva, Miraglia, & da Silva, 2014) .

To make progress in the wide inequities in coverage for key interventions as it relates to demographic factors, global and national efforts must focus on reaching the poorest and other vulnerable sub-groups of the population (Countdown to 2015, 2013). One effort to track progress was illustrated in a collaboration known as Countdown to 2015, a "global, multi-disciplinary, multi-institutional collaboration of academics, governments, international agencies, health-care professional associations, donors, and nongovernmental organizations" (Countdown to 2015, n.d.). As international efforts are shaped to address and improve MCH, demographic factors in the U.S. will continue to impact the child's health well into their adolescent and adult years.

Migration and Acculturation

When compared to those who involuntarily leave their country of origin (e.g., refugees) and have little support or resources, individuals and families who migrate to the new country by choice typically bring with them economic and educational resources as well as varying environmental and familial resources (Iwamasa, Regan, Subica, & Yamada, 2013). Acknowledging these migration differences is paramount to providing culturally appropriate and culturally sensitive care. In a study of depression and anxiety among first-generation immigrant Latino youth (Potochnick & Perreira, 2010), **migration** supports such as family, teacher support, and personal-motivation were found to minimize the stressors of migration and documentation status was found to play a significant role in the adaptation of the acculturation process.

Children and Adolescents

In a study by Stingone and colleagues, researchers reported co-morbidity was most prevalent in males, Latinos and children in low-income households (Stingone, Ramirez, & Svensson, 2011). In a study by Stingone et al. (2011), researchers reported co-morbidity was most prevalent in males, Latinos and children in low-income households. In the National Health and Nutrition Examination Surveys (NHA NES), findings independent of race/ethnicity revealed that 6- to 17-year-olds from low-income families have higher prevalence of obesity, sedentary behavior, and tobacco exposure (Ali, McKeever, Beckles, Stevens, Barker, & Narayan, 2011).

> **What is comorbidity?** The presence of more than one disease or condition in the same person at the same time.
>
> Example: The CDC Arthritis Program examines comorbidities in the following two ways: 1) **Comorbidities among people with arthritis.** Everyone in this group has arthritis, plus at least one additional condition. 2) **Arthritis among people with other chronic conditions.** A subset of people with other chronic conditions who also have arthritis (NCCDPHP, Division of Population Health, 2014).

From a mental health perspective in children, psychotropic prescription use showed marked increase in boys, white children and those without private health insurance (Chirdkiatgumchai, Xiao, Fredstrom, Adams, & Epstein, 2013). In a study to examine mental health service use in adolescents, data from the National Survey on Drug Use and Health indicated that Blacks, Hispanics and Asians who received any treatment for major depression were significantly lower than non-Hispanic whites and were significantly less likely than non-Hispanic whites to receive treatment and prescription medication for major depression and to receive any mental health treatment in an outpatient setting–independent of family income and insurance status (Cummings & Druss, 2011).

The **Youth Risk Behavior Surveillance System** (YRBSS) monitors priority health-risk behaviors among youth, including behaviors that contribute to unintentional injuries and violence, tobacco use, alcohol and other drug use, sexual behaviors that contribute to unintended pregnancy and sexually transmitted diseases (STDs) – including human immunodeficiency virus (HIV) infection – unhealthy dietary behaviors, physical inactivity, and prevalence of obesity and asthma (Eaton, Kann, Kinchen, Shanklin, Flint, & Hawkins, 2012). The YRBSS findings showed that male high school students were more likely to engage in tobacco use, alcohol and other drug use, and sexual behaviors related to unintentional pregnancy and STDs, including HIV infection. Female high school students were more likely than males to engage in suicide-related behaviors, been physically inactive, engaged in unhealthy weight control behaviors (Eaton, et al., 2012). Findings related to race and ethnicity were as follows:

- White high school students were more likely to have used tobacco.
- Black students were most likely to have engaged in risky sexual behaviors, be physically inactive and obese.
- Hispanic high school students were most likely to have felt sad or hopeless, had their first drink of alcohol before age 13 years, had not used any method to prevent pregnancy during last sexual intercourse, and to have ever used cocaine, inhalants, and ecstasy. (Eaton, et al., 2012)

The YRBSS (2012) 20-year trends show a decrease in prevalence of current sexual activity and current frequent tobacco use, obesity increased during this same period and suicide attempts increased over the two-year period (2009-2011) (Eaton, et al., 2012).

Adults and Elderly

Recent studies suggest that obesity significantly shapes mortality levels in the United States, making it a primary concern for public health action (Masters, Reither, Powers, Yang, Burger, & Link, 2013) (Weden, Bird, Escarce, & Lurie, 2010). We have also learned that chronic diseases often occur in multiples and, on average, affect individuals differently based on age, sex, ethnicity, and other demographic factors (Ward & Schiller, 2013). Chronic diseases are long lasting conditions that cannot be cured and are the nations leading causes of disability and death (National Center for Chronic Disease Prevention and Health Promotion, 2014). The US Census predicts life expectancy will reach 79.5 years by 2020, and while older adults can carry a heavy burden of disease and disability, studies on optimal health in later life is limited (McLaughlin, Connell, Heeringa, Li, & Roberts, 2010).

Sarcopenia: defined as both low muscle mass and poor muscle strength, are highly prevalent and important risk factors for disability and increased mortality in individuals as they age (Filippin, Teixeira, da Silva, Miraglia, & da Silva, 2014).

According to the National Institute on Aging (2012), many older adults can be well and active into their advancing years although aging presents a greater risk for health issues. "**Successful aging,**" a concept that defines healthy aging, is characterized as the avoidance of disease and disability, the maintenance of high physical and cognitive function, and sustained engagement in social and productive activities (Rowe & Kahn, 1997). For the purposes of our discussion on demographics, we will briefly examine and compare survey findings that estimated the prevalence of successful aging in a national and regional elderly population sample.

In an Alameda County, California study of 867 participants aged 65–99 years (Strawbridge, Wallhagen, & Cohen, 2002), researchers found 18.8% aging successfully according to the successful aging measure; higher percentages were observed among those with higher education, women, younger older adults, and White compared to Black race. Using data from the Health and Retirement Study, researchers analyzed a sample size of over 9110 adults aged 65 years and older at four time points (1998, 2000 2002, 2004) and found the prevalence of successful aging was higher in all years for those with higher education, income, men than women, and White than Black or Hispanic; no greater than 11.9% of older adults were aging successfully in any year (McLaughlin, Connell, Heeringa, Li, & Roberts, 2010).

While the large majority of individuals in both studies do not qualify as "aging successfully" as defined by Rowe and Khan, self-reported measures of successful aging in general depict contrasting statistics. In an Alameda County Study, the percentage of those rating themselves as aging successfully was 50.3% (Strawbridge, Wallhagen, & Cohen, 2002), and many with chronic conditions and functional difficulty also rated themselves as aging successfully. Furthermore, in a demographic assessment of current health, functional status, and chronic disease in an inner city Houston neighborhood, adults aged 60 and older were interviewed at their homes. Banerjee and colleagues found that residents with low literacy levels, low household income, and a high prevalence of frequently reported chronic disease also reported non-participation in community and social-natured activities. Blacks reported worse health outcomes on all indicators than other sub-groups and women reported poorer health and greater structural barriers in community involvement (Banerjee, Perry, Tran, & Arafat, 2010).

McLaughlin et al. (2010) have highlighted the fact that successful aging has informed many studies although there has been debate and commentary over the past decade concerning its conceptualization. Even so, without research doctrine to guide health demography studies in the elderly population, it is important to attain a broad perspective of demographic variations in different communities throughout the US.

WRAP-UP:

The discussion on the role of demographics in health and health care has provided a snapshot of statistical findings related to age, SES, gender, residential settings and associated behavioral risk factors and disease prevalence. We have learned that higher behavioral risk factors may contribute to–but not necessarily serve as a complete explanation for–the higher risk of mortality.

Additionally, since studies may vary in their measurement and analysis of demographic factors and associations between risk behaviors and eventual mortality, our ability to generalize findings over similar populations can be limited. However, in subsequent studies, researchers are able to contribute to the literature and advance the body of knowledge through comparative assessments and continued analysis of risk behaviors and socio-demographic variables.

Finally, it is expected that the reader highlight the health implications and behaviors amenable to intervention in an effort to affect change at the individual, population and policy levels as appropriate.

RESOURCES:

HealthyPeople 2020:
http://healthypeople.gov/2020/default.aspx

Child Statistics
www.childstats.gov

Countdown to 2015 Maternal, Newborn and Child Survival
http://www.countdown2015mnch.org/

Think Cultural Health – Office of Minority Health
https://www.thinkculturalhealth.hhs.gov/index.asp

CLASSROOM ACTIVITIES:

Think Cultural Health

This activity is a practical way to examine your cultural competency in a time of crisis.

In small groups of 3-4, review the worksheet together and determine a mock disaster scene. Take 5-10 minutes to think and formulate responses and exchange dialogue, serving as health worker and patient.

https://www.thinkculturalhealth.hhs.gov/pdfs/DisasterPreparednessRespondTool.pdf

MEASURE DHS: Demographic and Health Surveys

The **Demographic and Health Surveys** (DHS) program collects, analyzes and disseminates data on the health of populations through nationally-representative household surveys in over 90 countries (ICF International).

Go to www.measuredhs.com, briefly review the website to gain a general overview of MEASURE DHS and then follow the following steps:

- Select and click "What We Do" at the top of the webpage.
- Select and click "Survey Search" under Resources and Tools.
- Under Select Survey Status, click "Completed" and leave all other fields as is.
- Click "Start Search" and review the list of countries to select a survey with a completed survey dataset.
- Review the Country's final report to answer the following questions:
    - Describe the characteristics of the population (survey respondents)
    - Highlight one demographic (women, children, elderly) and describe any health trends in chronic diseases and risk factors associated with this demographic

REFERENCES:

Ahs, A., Burell, G., & Westerling. (2012). Care or Not Care-that is the Question: Predictors of Healthcare Utilisation in Relation to Employment Status. *International Journal of Behavioral Medicine*, 29-38.

Ali, M., McKeever, B. K., Beckles, G., Stevens, M., Barker, L., Narayan, V., et al. (2011). Household income and cardiovascular disease risks in U.S. children and young adults: analyses from NHANES 1999-2008. *Diabetes Care*, 1998-2004.

American Medical Association. (2012). Demographics and the health status of the U.S. Population Trends worth watching.

Artazcoz, L., Borrell, C., Benach, J., Cortes, I., & Rohlfs, I. (2004). Women, family demands and health: the importance of employment status and socio-economic position. *Social Science & Medicine*, 263-274.

Banerjee, D., Perry, M., Tran, D., & Arafat, R. (2010). Self-reported Health, Functional Status and Chronic Disease in Community Dwelling Older Adults: Untangling the Role of Demographics. *Journal of Community Health*, 135-141.

Beaudoin, C. E., & Hong, T. (2011). Health Information seeking, diet and physical activity: An empirical assessment by medium and critical demographics. *International Journal of Medical Informatics*, 586-595.

Boerma, J., Bryce, J., Kinfu, Y., Axelson, H., & Victora, C. (2008). Mind the gap: equity and trends in coverage of maternal, newborn, and child health services in 54 Countdown countries. *Lancet*, 1259-1267.

Chen, Y., Briesacher, B. A., Field, T. S., Tjia, J., Lau, D. T., & Gurwitz, J. H. (2010). Unexplained Variation Across US Nursing Homes in Antipsychotic Prescribing Rates. *Archives of Internal Medicine*, 89-95.

Chirdkiatgumchai, V., Xiao, H., Fredstrom, B. K., Adams, R. E., & Epstein, J. N. (2013). National Trends in Psychotropic Mediciation Use in Young Children: 1994-2009. *Pediatrics*, 615-623.

Chirdkiatgumchai, V., Xiao, H., Fredstrom, B. K., Adams, R. E., & Epstein, J. N. (2013). National Trends in Psychotropic Mediciation Use in Young Children: 1994-2009. *Pediatrics*, 615-623.

Countdown to 2015. (2013). *Accountability Report Accountability for Maternal, Newborn & Child Survival: The 2013 Update.* Retrieved September 30, 2013, from Countdown to 2015: http://www.countdown2015mnch.org/reports-and-articles/2013-report

Countdown to 2015. (n.d.). *Structure and Governance.* Retrieved September 28, 2013, from Countdown to 2015 Maternal, Newborn and Child Survivor: http://www.countdown2015mnch.org/structure

CSDH. (2008). *Closing the gap in a generation: health equity through action on the social determinants of health. Final Report of the Commission on Social Determinants of Health.* Geneva: World Health Organization.

Cummings, J. R., & Druss, B. G. (2011). Racial/Ethnic Differences in Mental Health Services Use Among Adolescents With Major Depression. *Journal of the American Academy of Child & Adolescent Psychiatry*, 160-170.

Cummings, J. R., Ponce, N. A., & Mays, V. M. (2010). Comparing Racial/Ethnic Differences in Mental Health Service Use Among High-Need Subpopulations Across Clinical and School-Based Settings. *Journal of Adolescent Health*, 603-606.

Dallo, F. J., Archer, C., & Misra, D. P. (2014). Maternal and Child Health. *Biopsychosocial Perspectives on Arab Americans* , 325-346 .

Dammann, K. W., & Smith, C. (2009). Factors Affecting Low-income Women's Food Choices and the Perceived Impact of Dietary Intake and Socioeconomic Status on Their Health and Weight . *Journal of Nutrition Education and Behavior*, 242-253.

Eaton, D. K., Kann, L., Kinchen, S., Shanklin, S., Flint, H, K., et al. (2012). *Morbidity and Mortality Weekly Report.* Atlanta: Centers for Disease Control and Prevention.

Filippin, L. I., Teixeira, V. N., da Silva, M. P., Miraglia, F., & da Silva, F. S. (2014). Sarcopenia: a predictor of mortality and the need for early diagnosis and intervention. *Aging clinical and experimental research.*

Frank, O. (2012, August 17). *The Demography of Fertility and Infertility*. Retrieved November 24, 2014, from WHO Collaborating Centre in Education and Research in Human Reproduction: http://www.gfmer.ch/Books/Reproductive_health/The_demography_of_fertility_and_infertility.html

Gress-Smith, J. L., Luecken, L. J., Lemery-Chalfant, K., & Howe, R. (2012). Postpartum Depression Prevalence and Impact on Infant Health, Weight, and Sleep in Low-Income and Ethnic Minority Women and Infants. *Maternal Child Health*, 887-893.

Hartnett, C. S. (2014). White-Hispanic differences in meeting lifetime fertility intentions in the U.S. *Demographic Research*, 1245-1276. http://www.prb.org/Publications/Lesson-Plans/Glossary.aspx. (2014). *Glossary of Demographic Terms.* Retrieved November 24, 2014, from Population Reference Bureau: http://www.prb.org/Publications/Lesson-Plans/Glossary.aspx

ICF International. (n.d.). *What's New at MEASURE DHS*. Retrieved June 10, 2013, from MEASURE DHS: http://www.measuredhs.com/

Iwamasa, G. Y., Regan, S. M., Subica, A., & Yamada, A.-M. (2013). Nativity and Migration: Considering Acculturation in the Assessment and Treatment of Mental Disorders. In G. Y. Iwamasa, *Handbook of Multicultural Mental Health* (p. 167).

Kotch, J. B. (2013). *Maternal and Child Health Programs, Problems and Policy in Public Health Third Edition*. Burlington: Jones and Bartlett Learning.

Lantz, P. M., Golberstien, E., House, J. S., & Morenoff, J. (2010). Socioeconomic and behavioral risk factors for mortality in a national 19-year prosepective study of U.S. adults. *Social Science & Medicine*, 1558-1566.

Lozano, R., Wang, H., Foreman, K., & al., e. (2011). Progress towards Millennium Development Goals 4 and 5 on maternal and child mortality: an updated systematic analysis. *Lancet*, 1139.

Masters, R. K., Reither, E., Powers, D. A., Yang, Y. C., Burger, A. E., & Link, B. G. (2013). The Impact of Obesity on US Mortality Levels: The Importance of Age and Cohort Factors in Population Estimates. *American Journal of Public Health*, 1895-1901.

McGee, D. L., Liao, Y., Cao, G., & Cooper, R. S. (1999). Self-reported Health Status and Mortality in a Multiethnic US Cohort. *American Journal of Epidemiology*, 41-46.

McLaughlin, S. J., Connell, C. M., Heeringa, S. G., Li, L. W., & Roberts, J. S. (2010). Successful Aging in the United States: Prevalence Estimates From a National Sample of Older Adults. *Journal of Gerontology: Social Sciences*, 216-226.

Merikangas, K. R., He, J.-p., Burstein, M., Swendsen, J., Avenevoli, S., Case, B., et al. (2011). Service Utilization for Lifetime Mental Disorders in U.S. Adolescents: Results of the National Comorbidity Survey-Adolescent Supplement. *Journal of the American Academy of Child & Adolescent Psychiatry*, 32-45.

National Center for Chronic Disease Prevention and Health Promotion. (2014, November 18). *Chronic Disease Prevention and Health Promotion*. Retrieved November 26, 2014, from Centers for Disease Control and Prevention: http://www.cdc.gov/chronicdisease/

National Institute on Aging. (2012, February). *Can We Prevent Aging? Tips from the National Institute on Aging*. Retrieved July 30, 2013, from National Institute on Aging: http://www.nia.nih.gov/health/publication/can-we-prevent-aging

NCCDPHP, Division of Population Health. (2014, March 13). *Comorbidities*. Retrieved November 25, 2014, from Centers for Disease Control and Prevention: http://www.cdc.gov/arthritis/data_statistics/comorbidities.htm

Pampel, F. C., Krueger, P. M., & Denney, J. T. (2010). Socioeconomic Disparities in Health Behaviors. *Annual Review in Sociology*, 349-370.

Pol, L. G., & Thomas, R. K. (2001). *The Demography of Health and Health Care*. New York: Springer.

Potochnick, S. R., & Perreira, K. M. (2010). Depression and Anxiety among First Generation Immigrant Latino Youth: Key Correlates and Implications for Future Research. *Journal of Nervous and Mental Disorders*, 470-477.

Rowe, J. W., & Kahn, R. L. (1997). Successful Aging. *The Gerontologist*, 433-440.

Smith, J. H. (2006). Sex, Gender, and Health. Baltimore, Maryland, USA.

Stingone, J. A., Ramirez, O. F., & Svensson, K. C. (2011). Prevalence, Demographics, and Health Outcomes of Comorbid Asthma and Overweight in Urban Children. *Journal of Asthma*, 876-885.

Strawbridge, W. J., Wallhagen, M. I., & Cohen, R. D. (2002). Successful Aging and Well-Being. *The Gerontologist*, 727-733.

Stronks, K., Van de Mheen, H., Van Den Bos, J., & Mackenbach, J. (1997). The Interrelationship between Income, Health and Employment Status. *International Journal of Epidemiology*, 592-600.

Stronks, K., Van De Mheen, H., Van Den Bos, J., & Mackenbach, J. P. (1997). The Interrelationship between Income, Health and Employment Status. *International Journal of Epidemiology*, 592-600.

Tadmor, C. T., & Tetlock, P. E. (2006). Biculturalism: A Model of the Effects of Second-Culture Exposure on Acculturation and Integrative Complexity. *Journal of Cross-Cultural Psychology*, 1-19.

Telzer, E. H., & Fuligni, A. J. (2013). Positive Daily Family Interactions Eliminate Gender Differences in Internalizing Symptoms Among Adolescents. *Journal of Youth and Adolescence*, 1498-1511.

Trived, M. H., & al., e. (2013). Clinical and sociodemographic characteristics associated with suicidal ideation in depressed outpatients. *Canadian Journal of Psychiatry*, 2011-20132.

U.S. Census Bureau. (2011). Demographic Analysis. Retrieved April 18, 2015, from http://www.census.gov/popest/research/demo-analysis.html

U.S. Department of Health and Human Services. (2012, September 20). *Determinants of Health.* Retrieved July 5, 2013, from HealthyPeople.gov: http://healthypeople.gov/2020/about/DOHAbout.aspx

University of Michigan. (2011, December 31). *What is Chronic Disease?* Retrieved November 25, 2014, from Center for Managing Chronic Disease: http://cmcd.sph.umich.edu/what-is-chronic-disease.html

Ward, B. W., & Schiller, J. S. (2013). Prevalence of Multiple Chronic Conditions Aong US Adults: Estimates From the National Health Interview Survey, 2010. *Prevention of Chronic Diseases.*

Weden, M. M., Bird, C. E., Escarce, J. J., & Lurie, N. (2010). Neighborhood archetypes for population health reserach: Is there no place like home? *Health & Place,* 289-299.

Wilper, A. P., Woolhandler, S., Lasser, K. E., McCormick, D., Bor, D. H., & Himmelstein, D. U. (2009). Health Insurance and Mortality in US Adults. *American Journal of Public Health,* 2289-2295.

World Health Organization. (2013). *Social Determinants of Health.* Retrieved July 5, 2013, from World Health Organization: http://www.who.int/social_determinants/thecommission/finalreport/key_concepts/en/

World Health Organization. (2013). *Women, Gender and Health.* Retrieved August 10, 2013, from World Health Organization: http://www.who.int/gender/whatisgender/en/index.html

Chapter 6:

Health Literacy in Minority Populations

Francisco Soto Mas, Holly E. Jacobson, & Héctor Balcázar

KEY CONCEPTS:

Adult learning theory
American sign language
Communicative health literacy
Critical health literacy
Culture
Cultural Competence
Education and health
Ethnic group
Functional health literacy
Health Belief Model
Health communication
Health literacy
Health outcomes
Healthcare access
Hearing loss and deafness
Inter-sectorial approach
Language access
LGBT
Limited English proficiency
Limited health literacy
Linguistic competence
Literacy
Literacy demands
Minority
Minority group
Minority populations
National Action Plan
Numeracy
Patient-provider communication
Plain language
Quality of life
Racial group
Rapid estimate of adult literacy in medicine
Self-efficacy
Social cognitive theory
Stereotyping
System-based barriers
Test of functional health literacy in adults

CHAPTER OVERVIEW:

What is health literacy? Why is health literacy important to individual and community health? What do we need to know about health literacy and minority populations? How can the health literacy level of minority groups be improved? This chapter addresses all these questions by presenting an up-to-date comprehensive overview of health literacy, and how it relates to the health and well-being of minority populations. In addition to presenting definitions and basic health literacy concepts, the chapter discusses practice and research issues relevant for addressing low health literacy in minority populations.

WHY THIS IS IMPORTANT:

Health literacy has become an increasingly popular area of study in both medicine and public health. Functional health literacy has been linked to health disparities and associated with mortality, access to care, health outcomes, health behavior, and healthcare costs. Certain population groups are more likely to experience **limited health literacy**. These include racial/ethnic groups other than Whites, recent refugees and immigrants, non-native speakers of English, and the deaf community. This is due to the fact that health literacy is influenced by language and communication skills, socioeconomic status, cultural background, and past experiences (e.g. with the health care system). This chapter provides the background to understand and address health literacy issues in minority populations.

CHAPTER EXPECTATIONS:

Upon reading this chapter, students will be able to:

- Contrast the different paradigms commonly used to define health literacy
- Identify population groups that are more affected by low health literacy
- Describe the connection between health literacy and health disparities
- Discuss practice and research approaches currently used to address low health literacy
- Critically discuss the limitations of current approaches to improving health literacy
- Describe the need for advancing health literacy research and practice with minority populations

WHAT IS HEALTH LITERACY?

Paradigms and Definitions – Functional, Communicative, Critical Health Literacy

Since its introduction (Simonds, 1974) the term "health literacy" has no single, accepted definition. This may be because the language used to describe health literacy reflects the unique approach of a distinctive field or discipline. It may also be due to its relatively recent adoption by the health field, from education. The fact is that health literacy has gained momentum in health research, policy and practice (Sorensen & Brand, 2013) both at the national and international level. According to a report by the United Nations Educational, Scientific and Cultural Organization (UNESCO), literacy has taken a broader focus from the individual to include a contextual and societal transformation in terms of linking health literacy to socio-cultural and political change and to economic growth (UNESCO, 2005).

Health literacy has been defined as the ability to apply skills to health situations at home, work, and the community. Related to healthcare, health literacy includes tasks such as accessing services, overcoming structural barriers to health, navigating institutions, and advocating for self and family (Kickbusch, 1997). This definition implies that health literacy interventions must include intrapersonal and interpersonal aspects as well as social skills (Berkman, Davis, & McCormack, 2010), while ultimately promoting self-efficacy and empowerment (Nutbeam, 2000).

A popular definition of health literacy, adopted by the National Library of Medicine and the U.S. Department of Health and Human Services was presented by Ratzan and Parker in 2000: "*The degree to which individuals have the capacity to obtain, process, and understand basic health information and services needed to make appropriate health decisions.*"

Nutbeam (2000) defines health literacy as, "*The personal, cognitive and social skills which determine the ability of individuals to gain access to, understand, and use information to promote and maintain good health.*" Nutbeam divides health literacy into three sequential levels:

- Level I, Functional Health Literacy,
- Level II, Communicative/Interactive Health Literacy, and
- Level III, Critical Health Literacy.

Level I, **Functional Health Literacy**, refers to basic reading, writing and literacy skills as well as health knowledge, which is the intended outcome of traditional health education interventions. Low functional health literacy is seen as a potential risk factor, which is managed within the clinical care process and system. Level II, **Communicative/Interactive Health Literacy** includes communication and social skills, which are used to derive meaning from various communication techniques and to apply new information to changing environments (Nutbeam, 2000). Health literacy education, in concept, is directed to the development of the personal capacity, motivation and confidence (self-efficacy) to change health-related behavior. Level III, **Critical Health Literacy** is the higher level social and cognitive skills needed to critically analyze information and the use of these skills to gain greater control over life events through individual and collective action. Integral to critical health literacy is the need to raise awareness of the social, economic and environmental determinants of health and to promote individual and collective actions to modify these determinants. In this way, health literacy is not just individually beneficial but has great societal benefit through the development of community action and social capital (Nutbeam, 1998), it is also about "rights, access, and transparency." It includes a political right to understand the determinants of individual, community, national, and global health in a way that can be easily and broadly accessed (Kickbusch, 2009).

Health Literacy Demands

Beyond general literacy skills, health literacy requires additional health-related knowledge and skill such as conceptual knowledge of health and illness, basic health-related vocabulary, and familiarity with how the healthcare system operates. Thus, health literacy encompasses all the general literacy skills as well as health-related skills necessary to navigate an increasingly complex healthcare context commonly experienced as fast paced, high tech, and intimidating (Liechty, 2011). This is particularly true now when healthcare is gradually moving toward self-direction and self-management. Within this shifting paradigm there is an expectation that consumers take a more active role in decisions about their health (Eysenbach & Kohler, 2002). For consumers to function effectively, they require a set of skills to seek, understand, and use health information – the concept referred to as health literacy (Simonds, 1974; Nutbeam, 1998).

From this perspective, there seems to be an implicit obligation on the part of individuals to search for information themselves, to understand rights and responsibilities, and to make decisions on health issues (Nielsen-Bohlman, Panzer, & Kindig, 2004). This is illustrated by a growing recognition of the need to account for the demands of the public health and healthcare systems when measuring health literacy at the individual level (Baker, 2006). Thus, the expectations about consumers' roles and responsibilities as active participants in their health are ever-expanding (McCormack, Trieman, Peinado, & Alexander, 2009). These expectations include taking proactive steps, such as obtaining recommended preventive health services, eating a healthy diet and getting regular physical activity, recognizing signs of illness and disease, self- managing chronic illnesses, and navigating the health insurance system (Hibbard, n.d.). These real-world expectations assume consumers will use valid and often complex information to support these behaviors. This expanded role for consumers may raise parameters for what constitutes health literacy.

HEALTH LITERACY AND PUBLIC HEALTH:

Epidemiology of Healthcare Literacy: Healthcare Access, Quality, Health Outcomes, Quality of Life

Health literacy has become a relevant topic in medicine. This is due to the fact that research has shown that low health literacy is related to poor health care quality and health outcomes. Fortunately, public health has also become highly involved in health literacy. *Healthy People 2010* identified limited health literacy as a public health problem, and *Healthy People 2020* included several health literacy objectives. The important point is to keep in mind that health literacy is socially constructed. Health literacy should not be treated, as it often has been, as a biomedical issue with social roots. Rather, it is a social issue with biomedical implications.

Limited English Proficiency	Individuals who do not speak English as their primary language and who have a limited ability to read, speak, write, or understand English
Culture	Attitudes and behaviors that are characteristic of a group or community
Cultural Competence	A set of congruent behaviors, attitudes, and policies that come together in a system, agency, or among professionals that enables effective work in cross-cultural situations
Linguistic Competence	The capacity to communicate effectively and convey information in a manner that is easily understood by diverse audiences
Plain Language	Writing that is clear and to the point, which helps to improve communication and takes less time to read and understand

Table 1. Related definitions

Limited health literacy has been negatively associated with the use of preventive services (e.g., mammograms, flu shots), management of chronic conditions (e.g., diabetes, high blood pressure, asthma), hospital admissions, and mortality. Economic studies have estimated the direct cost of limited health literacy at \$1.6 – \$3.6 trillion; this is without including added indirect costs, such as more chronic illness and disability, lost wages, and a poorer quality of life. Unfortunately, only 12% of English-speaking adults in the U.S. have proficient health literacy skills. Approximately 30 million Americans are unable to perform basic literacy tasks, such as reading instructions. These adults, who are not literate in English, are more likely to report their health as poor and are more likely to lack health insurance compared to adults with "proficient" health literacy (Berkman, Sheridan, Donahue, Halpern, Viera, Crotty, & Viswanathan, 2011; Kutner, Greenberg, Jin, & Paulsen, 2006; Nielsen-Bohlman, Panzer, & Kindig, 2004; Rudd, Anderson, Oppenheimer, & Nath, 2007). The U.S. government, federal agencies, and professional organizations have highlighted the relevance of health literacy.

The National Action Plan to Improve Health Literacy seeks to engage organizations, professionals, policymakers, communities, individuals, and families in a linked, multi-sector effort to improve health literacy. The plan is based on the principles that: (1) everyone has the right to health information that helps them make informed decisions and (2) health services should be delivered in ways that are understandable and beneficial to health, longevity, and quality of life. The vision informing this plan is of a society that:

- Provides everyone with access to accurate and actionable health information
- Delivers person-centered health information and services
- Supports lifelong learning and skills to promote good health

The report contains seven goals that will improve health literacy and suggests strategies for achieving them:

1. Develop and disseminate health and safety information that is accurate, accessible, and actionable
2. Promote changes in the health care system that improve health information, communication, informed decision making, and access to health services
3. Incorporate accurate, standards-based, and developmentally appropriate health and science information and curricula in child care and education through the university level
4. Support and expand local efforts to provide adult education, English language instruction, and culturally and linguistically appropriate health information services in the community
5. Build partnerships, develop guidance, and change policies
6. Increase basic research and the development, implementation, and evaluation of practices and interventions to improve health literacy
7. Increase the dissemination and use of evidence-based health literacy practices and interventions

Table 2. National Action Plan to Improve Health Literacy
Source: U.S. Department of Health and Human Services. http://www.health.gov/communication/hlactionplan/

Policy and Organizational Actions on Health Literacy

The **National Action Plan to Improve Health Literacy** identified highest priority strategies that will promote a health literate society. Similarly, the need for advancing health literacy – related research and practice is a recognized priority. The Affordable Care Act includes requirements for agencies, health plans, and providers to communicate clearly and effectively, and the Plain Writing Act of 2010 mandates that federal agencies write information clearly enough so people can understand and use it. The National Institutes of Health (NIH) and Agency for Healthcare Research & Quality (AHRQ) support health literacy research. Numerous health professional organizations – such as the Institute of Medicine (IOM), American College of Physicians, the American Dental Association, the American Medical Association, the American Academy of Pediatrics, and the Association for Clinicians for the Underserved – have made health literacy a priority issue for their members. Accreditation organizations have developed standards for health care organizations to assess their performance in improving health literacy. Audit tools – such as the Pharmacy Health Literacy Assessment Guide (AHRQ) and the Health Literacy Environment of Hospitals and Health Centers (National Center for the Study of Adult Literacy and Learning) allow organizations to assess their own performance in addressing health literacy-related barriers.

Global Health Literacy

Internationally, the World Health Organization (WHO) introduced the concept of health literacy in its glossary of health promotion terms in 1998. The International Union for Health Promotion and Education has established a Global Working Group on Health Literacy. The United Nations has agreed on a goal of improving health literacy, and stated that *"health literacy is an important factor in ensuring significant health outcomes and in this regard call for the development of appropriate action plans to promote health literacy"* (UNESCO, 2009).

In Canada, the interest in the relationship between literacy and health began in the late '80s, due in part to the availability of new data that showed an unexpected low literacy level among the general population. In 1994, the Canadian Public Health Association (CPHA) established the National Literacy and Health Program with the aim of raising awareness among health professionals about the link between literacy and health and advancing health literacy research. In 2006, the Health and Learning Knowledge Centre of the Canadian Council on Learning funded CPHA to establish an Expert Panel on Health Literacy to assess health literacy in Canada and make recommendations on future research, policy and programming initiatives (Rootman & Gordon-El-Bihbety, 2008).

Health literacy is becoming more relevant in Europe. The European Health Literacy (HLS-EU) Project, co-financed by the European Commission, was launched in 2009 by a consortium of nine academic and research institutions with the aims of: 1) measuring health literacy in eight European countries; 2) establishing a network of professionals who can take on the challenge of advancing health literacy in Europe; and 3) organizing national initiatives to promote health literacy at national levels. The project was completed in 2011, and developed regional-specific instruments and documented the diverse ways health literacy is operationalized in various national contexts. It also explored the overall social and political impact of health literacy in Europe (HLS-EU Consortium, 2012).

Despite the national and international interest in health literacy, and the abundance of data and information indicating not only the overall poor health literacy level of adults, but also the negatively associated health outcomes, strategies for effectively improving health literacy are scarce. This may be due to the fact that low health literacy is not a disease state, and does not have the clearly defined boundaries we typically expect from a medical condition. As such, the prevalence of low health literacy is a moving target, dependent on the definition and measurement tool used by any given study. A study that defines low health literacy as "below average" may yield a high prevalence of health literacy (Rudd, 2007), whereas the use of functional rather than relative standards can yield different results (Kutner, Greenberg, Jin, & Paulsen, 2006). Health literacy, like socio-economic status, may be best viewed as a continuum, such that every incremental improvement in health literacy yields an associated incremental improvement in overall health (Kutner, Greenberg, Jin, & Paulsen, 2006; Marmot, 2006).

However, studies of health literacy and outcomes show the effects of health literacy appear most strongly for those with low health literacy (Berkman, Sheridan, Donahue, Halpern, Viera, Crotty, & Viswanathan, 2011; DeWalt & Hink, 2009). Across different instruments and different systems of categorization, "low health literacy" may be roughly construed to indicate the bottom quartile of literacy ability (Kutner, Greenberg, Jin, & Paulsen, 2006; Parker, Ratzan, & Lurie, 2003; Eichler, Wieser, & Brugger, 2009; Paasche-Orlow, Parker, Gazmararian, Nielsen-Bohlman, & Rudd, 2005). This group is prioritized in interventions, not because low health literacy is a disease state, but because it is a disparity and a mediator of disparities, and a social justice perspective indicates a focus on the group with the greatest need (Nutbeam, 2000).

Health and Literacy

Functional health literacy has been linked to many health outcomes, including adherence to treatment, health status, mortality, healthcare use, and healthcare costs (Wolf, Wilson, Rapp, Waite, Bocchini, Davis, & Rudd, 2009). However, the importance of health literacy has not been matched by evidence demonstrating the effectiveness of health literacy interventions in improving health (Ross, Culbert, Gasper, & Kimmey, 2009). Similarly, empirical evidence of the causal relationship between health literacy and health outcomes is very limited.

EDUCATION AND HEALTH:

The Role of Education in Health

Education is an important determinant of health, and some have suggested that general knowledge is more relevant than health-specific knowledge (Cutler & Lleras-Muney, 2010). The fact is that people with more years of education tend to have better health and well-being and live longer. For instance, in 1990, a 25 year-old male college graduate could expect to live another 54 years while a high school dropout of the same age could expect to live 46 years (Richards & Barry, 1998).

Education supports and promotes human development, human relationships and family and community well-being (OECD, 2006). At the individual level, the impact of education is significant, at it reduces the need for health care and its associated economic and human suffering costs. More specifically, studies have shown that individuals with high educational attainment are less likely than those with low levels of education to have diabetes and heart ailments, they are less likely to be overweight and to smoke cigarettes, and they are more likely to abstain from illegal drugs and excess alcohol (Kolata, 2007; Ross & Wu, 1995).

Health Literacy and Education

Although people with strong literacy skills may have trouble obtaining, understanding, and using health information, research has shown educational attainment plays a predictably strong role in health literacy. The 2003 National Assessment of Adult Literacy found higher health literacy levels among adults who had taken some graduate classes or completed a graduate degree, compared to those with lower levels of education (Kutner, Greenberg, Jin, & Paulsen, 2006).

Despite the empirical evidence of the positive role of education in health literacy, there are signifiant barriers to the integration of education and health. According to the 2004 IOM report on health literacy, the lack of consistent health curricula across grades K–12 may reduce student health literacy (Neilsen-Bohlman, Panzar, & Kindig, 2004). Programs aimed at improving health at individual and community levels must include educational interventions. The National Action Plan to Improve Health Literacy recommends incorporating age-appropriate health information and curricula, starting with child care and continuing through the university level.

Providing more education opportunities may be a key in improving health literacy in adults, particularly among certain minority groups. Observational studies have shown that Hispanic college students have higher health literacy levels than the general Hispanic population; and that adult education programs improve health literacy among Hispanic adults even without health-specific content (Soto Mas, Jacobson, & Dong, 2014; McDermott, Soto Mas, Olivárez, Mein, Muro, & Quiroz, 2009; Soto Mas, Ji, Fuentes, & Tinajero, 2015).

Minority group	A subordinate group whose members have significantly less control or power over their own lives than members of the dominant or majority group have over theirs
Racial group	A group that is set apart from others because of physical differences that have taken on social significance. Race as a biological category does not exist. The social construction of race is based in part on physical characteristics, but also on historical, cultural, and economic factors
Ethnic groups	A group that is set apart from others primarily because of their national origin or distinctive cultural patterns
Stereotyping	Assuming, unfairly, that all people or things with a particular characteristic are the same. Often used to justify unequal access to resources

Table 3. Minority definitions

HEALTH LITERACY IN MINORITY POPULATIONS:

Who is a Minority?

Minority is a term that refers to a distinctive social group whose members experience various disadvantages because of the systems and structures facilitated by another social group (Vander Zanden, 1972). These disadvantages are generally caused by an unequal access to power, goods and services and, in general, less control over their lives compared to the members of the dominant or majority group. As a result, many minority groups experience socioeconomic disparities (differences), including disparities in education, health care and health status.

Although the term minority is often related to racial and ethnic categories, it goes beyond people of color and culturally distinctive groups. For instance, disparities in health care and health status have been identified by gender, income, education, disability, geographic location, sexual orientation, and race and ethnicity (Soto Mas, Allensworth, & Jones, 2010). Recent research has identified health literacy as one critical factor contributing to health disparities (Paasche-Orlow, & Wolf, 2010).

Health Literacy in Minority Groups: LGBT and the Deaf Community

Health literacy is most crucial for individuals of minority groups, as they generally have culturally and linguistically specific needs that may not be addressed by "standard" approaches and programs. Communication does not take place in a vacuum, and health literacy must be viewed in the context of language and culture (Ratzan, & Parker, 2000). Language and cultural barriers often compromise communication, and racial/ethnic immigrants can have more difficulties understanding health information related to services and benefits, which adversely influences their ability to access health care (Gee, 2000; Becker & Lhajoui, 2004).

According to the 2003 National Assessment of Adult Literacy, adults age 65+ had lower health literacy levels than those in the younger age groups. Health literacy increased with educational attainment. Similarly, adults living below the poverty level had lower average health literacy than those living above the poverty threshold (Kutner, Greenberg, Jin, & Paulsen, 2006).

One minority group that has not yet been included in the health literacy research and practice agenda includes people who are **lesbian, gay, bisexual, or transgender** (LGBT). According to the Centers for Disease Control and Prevention (CDC), LGBT *"are diverse, come from all walks of life, and include people of all races and ethnicities, all ages, all socioeconomic statuses, and from all parts of the country. The perspectives and needs of LGBT people should be routinely considered in public health efforts to improve the overall health of every person and eliminate health disparities"* (CDC, 2011).

Members of the LGBT community are at increased risk for a number of health threats when compared to their heterosexual peers (Mayer, Bradford, Makadon, Stall, Goldhammer & Landers, 2008; Wolitski, Stall, & Valdiserri, 2008; Clements, Marx, Guzman, & Katz, 2001; Meyer & Northridge, 2007; Solarz, 1999). Although differences in sexual behavior account for some of these disparities, others are associated with the stigma and discrimination often experienced by the LGBT population (CDC, 2011).

Social and structural inequality is often associated with poorer health status. For instance a study in Chicago found that, when compared to heterosexual youth, LGBT youth were more likely to report depression and depressive symptoms, previous suicide attempts, and non-suicidal self-injury; more likely to be underweight and to report vomiting to lose weight; more likely to report sex risk behaviors, and in female-born youth, were more likely to report pregnancy (Mustanski, Clifford, Bigelow, Andrews, Birkett, Ashbeck, & Fisher, 2012).

Health literacy is important because people who have high literacy have a lower risk of developing preventable mental and/or physical health conditions. According to the CDC, improving health literacy may be key in reducing LGBT health disparities. *Healthy People 2010* addressed the health literacy and communication needs of LGBT, including improving the health literacy of people with inadequate or marginal literacy skills. Similarly, a goal of *Healthy People 2020* is to improve the health, safety, and well-being of LGBT individuals.

Numerous barriers often prevent effective communication of LGBT-specific health promotion and disease prevention messages. Additionally, inadequate communication between health care providers and LGBT patients can increase LGBT health disparities. Future health communication efforts should focus on increasing access to health information resources. Specific strategies may include: involving LGBT professionals in the development of appropriate health communication campaigns and materials; enhancing media literacy among LGBT individuals; supporting LGBT-focused research and evaluation of health communication activities; and ensuring that health care providers possess the knowledge, skills, and competency to communicate effectively with LGBT consumers (HealthyPeople.gov, 2013).

Another minority group that is underrepresented in health literacy research and practice is the deaf community. People in the U.S. with **hearing loss and deafness** have faced significant challenges in meeting their health information and communication needs. Although insufficient knowledge of health-related vocabulary is not limited to deaf adult sign language users with low educational attainment (McEwen & Anton-Culver, 1988; Pollard & Barnett, 2009), deaf people who use **American Sign Language** (ASL) are medically underserved and often excluded from health research and surveillance. They are at particular risk for low health literacy, due in part to the likelihood of low English literacy if they are born deaf or lose their hearing in early childhood and ASL is their first language.

In the U.S., an estimated 100,000 to 1 million people use ASL as their primary language. Although measures of health literacy have not been validated or developed with deaf adults, data indicate that many adults deaf since birth or early childhood have low health literacy. This low health literacy results from a lifetime of limited access to information that is often considered common knowledge among hearing persons (Pollard, 1998). For example, many adults deaf since birth or early childhood do not know their own family medical history, having never overheard their hearing parents discussing this with their doctor (Barnett, 1999). Family history is a risk factor for some chronic diseases, including diabetes and heart disease.

Even when well-educated, many deaf people who use sign language face significant health literacy barriers. Studies with young adults indicate that deaf and hard of hearing people may be at higher risk for suicide behaviors (O'Hearn, 2009). A study with young adolescents found that those with lower English proficiency were least likely to report access and receipt of preventive services and a usual source of primary care. Deaf older adolescents face significant barriers to care, and those with low English proficiency have the least access (Finigan, 2007).

Deaf adolescents confront many communication and social barriers to accessing, understanding, and applying health information, such as lack of confidence, insufficient access to visual information, and mistrust of hearing people. As a result, many deaf adolescents appear not to be exposed to experiences that might prompt them to recognize their health literacy skills and undertake actions to overcome such challenges (Smith, 2011).

RACIAL/ETHNIC MINORITIES AND HEALTH LITERACY:

Population-Specific Data

Health literacy is influenced by socioeconomic status, past experiences (e.g. with the health care system), cultural and language background, and communication skills (U.S. Department of Health and Human Services, 2010). Therefore, population groups that experience social, economic, cultural and language barriers are particularly vulnerable to the adverse consequences of low health literacy. This is confirmed by data, African Americans, American Indians and Hispanics experience lower health literacy levels compared to other population groups. For instance, the 2003 National Assessment of Adult Literacy (NAAL) found that White and Asian/Pacific Islander adults had higher average health literacy than Black, Hispanic, and American Indian/Alaska Native (Kutner, Greenberg, Jin, & Paulsen, 2006). The data are consistent with the fact that many African Americans and Native Americans experience educational and socioeconomic disadvantages. Most Hispanic immigrants must deal with a new culture and language when coming to the U.S. Therefore, these groups are particularly at risk of having limited health literacy.

African Americans in the U.S. have lower health literacy than their Caucasian counterparts (Kutner, Greenberg, Jin, & Paulsen, 2006; Shea, Beers, McDonald, Quistberg, Ravenell, & Asch, 2004). A recent study found evident ethnic differences in health literacy: American Indians and African Americans had lower scores than Whites (Kirk, Grzywacz, Arcury, Ip, Nguyen, Bell, Saldana, & Quandt, 2012). A local study that assessed oral health literacy (OHL) in adults found differences between racial groups, with Whites scoring significantly higher than African-Americans and American Indians (Lee, Divaris, Baker, Rozier, Lee, & Vann, 2011). A clinical study with non-Hispanic White, African American and American Indian older adult diabetes patients found that American Indian participants had the lowest levels of health literacy of the three ethnic groups (Nguyen, Kirk, Arcury, Ip, Grzywacz, Saldana, Bell, & Quandt, 2013).

National data indicate Hispanic adults had lower average health literacy than adults in any other racial/ethnic group. Similarly, adults who spoke only English before starting school had higher average health literacy than adults who spoke other languages alone or other languages and English (Kutner, Greenberg, Jin, & Paulsen, 2006). A cautionary note is necessary, however, with respect to language acquisition, there is evidence that bilingualism and multilingualism have positive cognitive effects on learning and literacy in children. In addition, there are many confounding variables to consider when exploring the links between health literacy and language development and acquisition, which must be considered in future research.

HEALTH LITERACY, CULTURE, PRIMARY LANGUAGE, AND ENGLISH PROFICIENCY:

Health Literacy and Communication

Culture affects how people communicate, understand, and respond to health information. Language is a primary expression of culture. In the U.S., for many individuals with a primary language other than English the inability to communicate is a major barrier to accessing health information and services. In the U.S. the language of the health care system is English. However, most foreign-born minorities in the U.S. have difficulties with English (Kaestle, Campbell, Finn, Johnson, & Mikulecky, 2001). Research has shown English proficiency is a much better predictor of the impact of language barriers on health and health care than primary language (Flores, Abreu, & Tomany-Korman, 2005). The IOM has identified language as an important component of health literacy (Nielsen-Bohlman, Panzer, & Kindig, 2004). It has been suggested that in the U.S. limited English proficiency may constitute a greater health-related risk than low health literacy among ethnic groups with a primary language other than English (Sentell & Braun, 2012).

Health Literacy in Language Minorities

Despite the fact that disparities in health literacy levels have been identified and reported since 2005, a recent systematic review sponsored by AHRQ indicated that there are no national data on the health literacy skills in native languages of populations in the U.S. with limited or no English language skills (Berkman, Sheridan, Donahue, Halpern, Viera, Crotty, & Viswanathan, 2011). This is an important research limitation that must be properly addressed should we be serious about improving health literacy and eliminating health disparities.

HEALTH LITERACY AND THEORY:

Intrapersonal and Interpersonal Level Theories

There is a need for interventions that effectively improve health literacy, particularly among minority adults. An efficient strategy to improve health literacy includes multi-level interventions that engage partnerships with individuals, families, educators, community stakeholders, health providers, and policy-makers at the local, state, and federal level (Noar & Zimmerman, 2005). Health literacy initiatives that incorporate behavioral theory are more open to acceptance by the population of interest and are more likely to be linked with positive behavioral change (Doak, Doak, Leonard, & Root, 1996). Social Cognitive Theory (Bandura, 1977), the Health Belief Model (Becker, 1974), and the Theory of Planned Behavior (Ajzen, 1991) are some of the behavioral theories that have been applied in health literacy projects.

Social Cognitive Theory, formally known as Social Learning Theory, postulates that human behavior can be described as triadic reciprocal causation including environment, person, and behavior. In other words, this theory can explain human behavior by looking at the interaction between the angles of environment, behavior, and personal factors (such as biological events, affect, and cognitions). The application of this theory can be used as the basis for intervention strategies. An example of this application is illustrated at the Saint Louis Christian Chinese Community Service Center where the development and delivery of linguistically and culturally sensitive materials are helping older adults and recent immigrants improve their health literacy skills (Ross, Culbert, Gasper, & Kimmey, 2009).

Self-efficacy is another theoretical construct that has been related to health literacy. According to Henk and Melnick (1995), **self-efficacy** is defined as a person's judgment of their ability to successfully participate in an activity and the effect this perception has on future activities. A person's perception about their abilities influences their thought patterns and how they behave (Bandura, 1984). Self-efficacy is action-specific and performs a central role in behavior change (Sharma & Romas, 2012).

Self-efficacy may be a determinant of self-management behaviors among populations with low health literacy skills. In studies that involve the relationship of health literacy with the management of diabetes, there is evidence that suggests that self-efficacy may have a role in the behavior of self-management (Paasche-Orlow & Wolf, 2007). Self-efficacy is a construct that affects motivation and can inhibit or promote learning (Evans, 1989). People form beliefs on what they can and cannot do and this affects their motivation (Bandura, 1993). For example in a self-management intervention, patients with low health literacy who receive reinforcement show similar or better self-management skills than patients with adequate health literacy (Kim, Love, Quistberg, & Shea, 2004).

Self-efficacy is a construct in the **Health Belief Model** (HBM) (Becker, 1974). Self-efficacy, in the HBM, applies particularly to the performance of recurrent or habitual behaviors (Glanz, Lewis, & Rimer, 2008). According to this model, health behavior is more likely to be adapted if an individual believes he or she can successfully perform the desired behavior. HBM is based on the concept that people act on value and expectancy beliefs. In other words, individuals are more apt to engage in a health behavior when they think it will reduce a likely threat that has serious consequences. An application of this model that is related to health literacy would be to identify and reduce barriers through reassurance, incentives, and assistance. An example of this application is demonstrated at the Missouri Health Literacy Enhancement Center where neighborhood health literacy programs are helping people understand nutrition and prescription labels (Ross, Culbert, Gasper, & Kimmey, 2009).

Another example of a behavior theory that has been employed in health literacy projects is the Theory of Planned Behavior (Ajzen, 1991). The significant feature of this model is that behavioral intention is the most important determinant of behavior (Sharma & Romas, 2012). According to this theory, behavior is steered by three beliefs: beliefs about the likely outcomes of the behavior and the evaluations of these outcomes, beliefs about the normative expectations of others and the motivation to yield to these expectations, and beliefs about the presence of factors that may impede or facilitate performance of the behavior and the perceived power of these factors (Ajzen, 1991). Even though the Theory of Planned Behavior does not necessarily explain behavior change, this model has been used to predict behavioral intention and behavior. A recent study involving Mexican-American women with low literacy used the TBP as part of its theoretical framework. The study concluded that TBP may constitute an essential tool in developing instruments that can aid and benefit patients with low literacy as well as their healthcare providers (Lopez-McKee, 2011).

In addition to behavior theories, education and learning theories must be considered when addressing low health literacy in adults. One such theory is **Adult Learning Theory**, which embraces a different set of assumptions about how adults learn and was developed in the 1970's by Malcolm Knowles. The model uses approaches to learning that are problem-based and collaborative rather than didactic (Knowles, 1980). An example where Adult Learning Theory is applied in health literacy is the Health Literacy and ESL (English as a Second Language) Curriculum, developed by a multidisciplinary team of researchers and practitioners. To meet the specific language and health literacy needs of adult Hispanic immigrants, the curriculum incorporates health literacy within an English as a second language program (Soto Mas, Fuentes, Arnal, Mein, & Tinajero, 2013; Soto Mas, Mein, Fuentes, Thatcher, & Balcázar, 2013). The Health Literacy and ESL Curriculum has shown to be effective in improving both health literacy and English proficiency among Spanish-speaking adults (Soto Mas, Ji, Fuentes, & Tinajero, 2015).

Ecological Theory

Viable solutions to health literacy should include an ecological approach, as the problem is multi-causal and includes individual and system-based barriers. Individual barriers that affect health literacy include: a) having low levels of formal education; b) lack of knowledge and skills about health and health care systems; c) speaking a language other than that of the dominant group; d) living with disabilities and degenerative processes associated with aging; and e) social stigma and discrimination.

System-based barriers to health literacy include: a) lack of opportunities for quality education among children, youth and adults; b) education disparities and income inequalities; c) lack of adult education opportunities for minorities and second language learners; c) confusing and conflicting health information and messages; d) increasing digital divide; e) complexity of the health care system; f) increasing demand on patients to manage their chronic diseases and share in decisions. Although there is consensus on the important role that these individual and systematic barriers play on health literacy, ecological solutions are still to be implemented and evaluated.

MEASURING HEALTH LITERACY:

Popular Instruments

There have been a number of instruments developed and used to measure health literacy. The most extensively used and oldest instruments are those that measure individual functional health literacy such as the **Rapid Estimate of Adult Literacy in Medicine** (REALM) or the **Test of Functional Health Literacy in Adults** (TOHFLA). These measure reading ability or print literacy and some also include numeracy. Other functional measures were created to screen patients for low literacy in clinical settings (e.g. Newest Vital Sign); or to measure health literacy in non-English speaking populations (e.g. Short Assessment of Health Literacy-Spanish and English (SAHL-S&E).

Public health experts have extended the concept of health literacy to include domains beyond individual competence and medical context (Sorensen,Van den Broucke, Fullam, Doyle, Pelikan, Slonka, & Brand, 2012). The most commonly used model for this broader concept is Nutbeam's critical health literacy (Nutbeam, 2000; Sorensen, et al., 2012). Researchers have identified the need to create measures that encompass this fuller range of skills and knowledge associated with critical health literacy and the full spectrum of critical health literacy materials and processes (Baker, 2006; Mancuso, 2009; Jordan, Osborne, & Buchbinder, 2011; McCormack, et al., 2010). Recent publications are reporting on preliminary studies of measures that attempt to do this (e.g. Health Literacy Skills Instrument (HLSI) (Bann, McCormack, Berkman, & Squiers, 2012).

Group-Specific Instruments

Regarding minority populations, finding appropriate instruments to assess health literacy in certain groups may be challenging, particularly for language minorities. In the U.S., health literacy is generally assessed in English, which may constitute a relevant confounding factor for people who are not proficient in the language of the test. In other words, the test may not be accurately measuring health literacy as takers would have difficulties reading and comprehending the questions.

There is a need for group-specific instruments for Native Americans in general, and for Native Americans who only speak a language other than English. Similarly, some studies have found that the Spanish TOFHLA, one of the most popular health literacy instruments, might be relatively easy for someone even with a basic level of education and might not produce reliable results (Soto Mas, Jacobson, & Dong, 2014). Other studies with Hispanics have found that using different instruments result in very different health literacy levels within the same participants (Quiroz, Soto Mas, Olivárez, Mein, Muro, & McDermott, 2009; Soto Mas, McDermott, Mein, Olivárez, Quiroz, & Muro, 2010).

PROGRAMS THAT WORK:

Health Literacy, Health Promotion, and Disease Prevention

Health literacy interventions have become a popular strategy for health promotion and disease prevention at the health care and community levels. The rationale behind the use of health literacy interventions to improve health and decrease disease relates to the fact that literacy-related skills are needed for better health. **Literacy** is defined as a set of reading, writing, basic math, speech, and comprehension skills. **Numeracy**, which is part of literacy, implies a *"facility with basic probability and numerical concepts"* (Schwartz, Woloshin, Black, & Welch, 1997). Studies in education and adult literacy showed that literacy influences a person's ability to access information, use print materials, and function in society (Rudd, Moeykens, & Colton, 2000). These are abilities someone would need to read a nutrition label, get a flu shot, or manage a health condition. Similarly, general literacy facilitates communication, which is also a relevant factor related to understanding health-related information and interacting with health care providers.

Health Literacy and Health Disparities

Health literacy constitutes today an important venue for addressing health disparities in minority populations. Health disparities are highly correlated with higher levels of poverty and lower levels of education, which lead to low health literacy. From a health care seeking perspective, minority adults from immigrant and non-immigrant communities are faced with many barriers to confront the complex and predominantly English-based U.S. health system. These challenges may be addressed through health literacy interventions that are audience-centered, use existing community systems, and take a comprehensive approach that addresses more than one factor influencing health literacy.

Health Literacy Interventions for Minorities

It is important to realize that the literature lacks examples of interventions that have effectively improved health literacy at the population level. In the U.S., federal funding for understanding and advancing health literacy has generally supported research on how to measure health literacy, and clinical-based, disease-specific approaches directed toward "mitigating" low health literacy by simplifying written materials and artificially directing communicative interactions (e.g. readability tests, plain language, teach back, storytelling). For the most part, these efforts have not provided evidence of the specific design features that effectively improve health outcomes related to differences in health literacy levels (Berkman, Sheridan, Donahue, Halpern, Viera, Crotty, & Viswanathan, 2011), nor have they translated into more literate and healthy communities. This is even truer when considering minorities. There exists a pressing demand for interventions that address the health and literacy needs of minority communities.

The literature includes examples of small-scale interventions and programs that have effectively addressed low health literacy in racial/ethnic minority groups:

- Howard-Pitney and colleagues published the Stanford Nutrition Program, a randomized study to test a classroom-based intervention that aimed to reduce low fat intake in an ethnically diverse adult population with low literacy skills in San Jose California (Howard-Pitney, Winkleby, Albright, Bruce, & Fortmann, 1997). The intervention utilized a combination of class-based instruction and a maintenance component totaling 18 weeks total for both components. The curriculum emphasized interactive learning. The literacy level was assessed among participants and it was shown to be at the eight-grade level. Changes in nutrition-related outcomes (i.e. knowledge, attitudes, self-efficacy, dietary habits) were assessed as well as clinical outcomes such as BMI, and blood cholesterol. Positive results were observed for those participants of the intervention arm (newly developed curriculum, versus controls who received an existing general curriculum that focused on general nutrition), in terms of achieving greater nutrition knowledge, attitudes and self-efficacy and fat-related nutritional changes.

- Health literacy interventions have been implemented to address the high prevalence of risk factors for chronic disease among minority populations such as Hispanics (De Heer, Balcazar, Morera, Lapeyrouse, Heyman, Salinas, & Zambrana, 2013). A strategy with recent immigrants is to integrate English language skills with health-specific content. Studies have documented that Hispanics seek opportunities to improve their English proficiency to access the workforce and American society. In fact, data indicate that Hispanics are overrepresented in English as a Second Language (ESL) instruction. This constitutes a unique opportunity to implement strategies that contribute to improving the health and literacy skills of Hispanic immigrants. Federal agencies recognize this opportunity, and the National Action Plan to Improve Health Literacy recommends: a) supporting and expanding local efforts to provide adult education, English language instruction; b) building community partnerships for addressing health literacy issues; c) increasing basic research and the development, implementation, and evaluation of practices and interventions to improve health literacy; and d) increasing the dissemination and use of evidence-based health literacy practices and interventions.
- Elder and colleagues (Elder, Candelaria, Woodruff, Criqui, Talavera, & Rupp, 2000) implemented the program *Language for Health*, a nutrition education intervention that was incorporated into an English as a second language (ESL) class. A two-group repeated measures research design was used in which the intervention received the nutrition/health education ESL and the control group received same quantity of education in the area of stress management. The results were satisfactory for the intervention group as compared to the control group in terms of outcomes such as HDL ratio, systolic blood pressure, self-reported avoidance and nutrition knowledge. The authors acknowledge that effects shown at posttest disappeared at follow-up and some positive effects in terms of health changes were shown in the control group at posttest, making the program modestly effective. The authors recommended that, based on the results of this study, ESL classes consider incorporating health not only as a component of ESL but as part of vocational classes.
- Recently, Soto Mas and colleagues developed a health literacy and ESL curriculum for Hispanic immigrants that showed to be effective in improving both health literacy and English proficiency (Soto Mas, Fuentes, Arnal, Mein, & Tinajero, 2013; Soto Mas, Ji, Fuentes, & Tinajero, 2015; Soto Mas, Mein, Fuentes, Thatcher, & Balcázar, 2013). The curriculum integrates health behavior, adult education, and communication theory. An important component of the curriculum are educational materials and activities adopted from Salud para su Corazón, a National Heart, Lung, and Blood Institute (NHLBI) program that addresses Hispanic cultural values through "fotonovelas" and audiovisual materials that reflect the family-oriented structure that is common in the Hispanic culture (Balcazar, Alvarado, Luna-Hollen, Gonzalez-Cruz, & Pedregon, 2005; Balcazar, Byrd, Ortiz, Sumanth, & Chavez, 2009). A similar integration of ESL and health-related information as it relates to physical activity has been published for Chinese immigrants (Taylor, Cripe, Acorda, The, Coronado, Do, Woodall, & Hislop, 2008).
- Health literacy interventions for minority groups including African Americans and Hispanics have also been explored for people with low income and low health literacy living with HIV/AIDs. Kalichman and colleagues (2005) reported a pilot testing of a brief nurse-delivered antiretroviral treatment adherence intervention for a primarily African American low literacy skill group living with HIV. This pilot intervention was guided by the theory of health behavior change and health education principles. The intervention consisted of two adherence improvement sessions and one booster session. The results showed that for the 30 HIV-positive low-literacy men and women who received the intervention,

positive findings were observed in terms of increased HIV/AIDS knowledge, intentions to improve adherence, and self-efficacy for adhering to medication (Kalichman, Cherry, & Cain, 2005).

- Servellen and colleagues reported another pilot study to evaluate the acceptability and effectiveness of the program "Es Por La Vida" to enhance health literacy in low-income monolingual Latinos utilizing a quasi experimental design. "Es Por la Vida" consisted of a 5-week instructional support modular program with a 6-month follow-up nurse case-management component. Data was collected for 41 intervention participants and 40 comparison group patients (who received standard clinical care). Program participants showed significant improvement as compared to controls in terms of greater knowledge with respect to HIV/AIDS treatment, greater levels of recognition and understanding of HIV terms. There were no differences associated with the understanding of instructions on medical prescriptions. The authors conclude that "Es Por La Vida" program was able to enable and empower participants to more fully participate in their care for their HIV condition (Servellen, Carpio, Lopez, Garcia-Teague, Herrera, Monterrosa, Gomez, & Lombardi, 2003).
- New methodologies for applying concepts of health literacy in order to improve communication and education among low literacy groups (majority African Americans) with type 2 diabetes have been reported using multimedia computer-based modules (Kandula, Nsiah-Kumi, Makoul, Sager, Zei, Glass, Stephens, & Baker, 2009). Results of the multimedia computer intervention consisting of two modules lasting five minutes each (modules combined graphics, animation, spoken audio and on-screen text) showed that patients across all literacy levels had significant increases in knowledge scores after viewing the intervention. However patients with inadequate literacy learned significantly less as compared to those with adequate literacy.

While the U.S. has generally supported small-scale, clinical-based health literacy studies, comprehensive approaches have been proposed in places like Europe and Canada. The European Health Literacy Project, sponsored by the European Union, proposed that actions to improve health literacy in Europe must facilitate enhanced individual life competencies at school, work, the market place, and the political level. This requires collaborative efforts from a variety of stakeholders, such as governments, the private sector, and the civil society. Canada has proposed an inter-sectorial approach for improving health literacy that is illustrated in Figure 1. These comprehensive approaches are more complex and difficult to implement, but they are also more likely to result in improved health literacy at the population level.

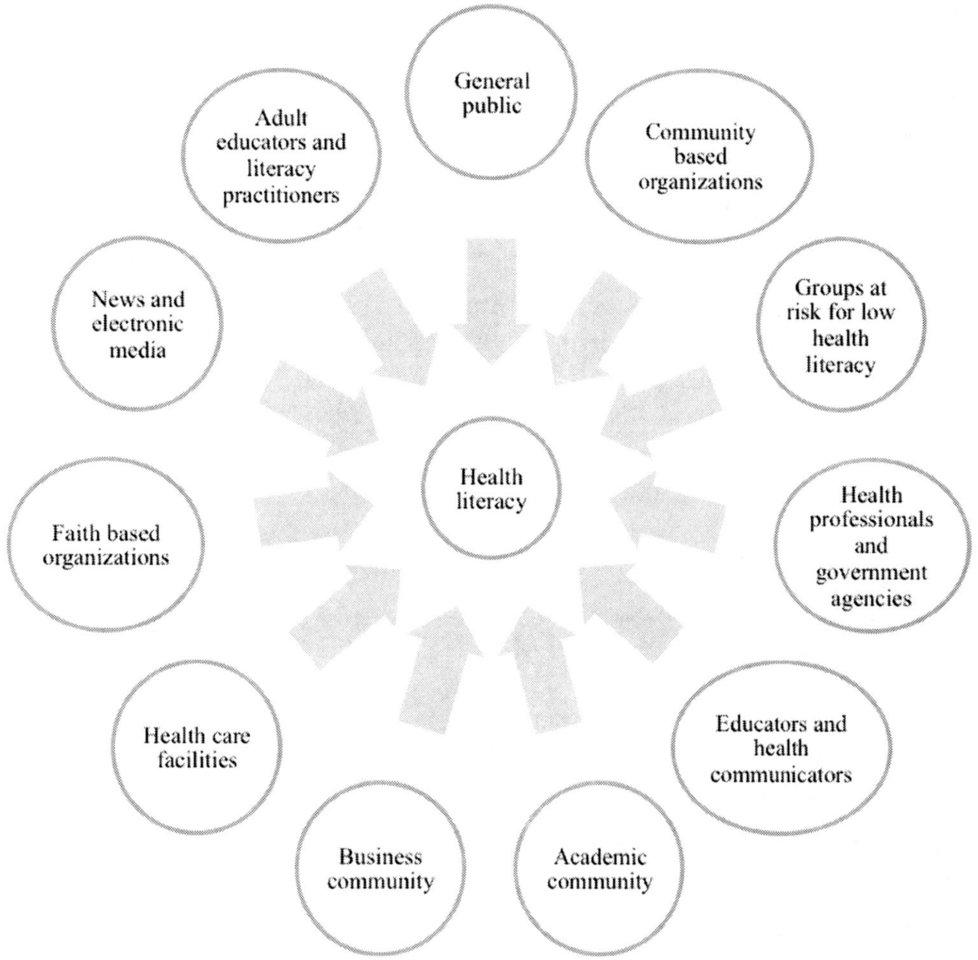

Figure 1. An inter-sectorial approach for improving health literacy *(Source: Mitic, & Rootman, 2012. An Inter-sectorial Approach for Improving Health Literacy for Canadians: A Discussion Paper. Public Health Association of BC, 2012. Available at: http://www.phabc.org/userfiles/file/IntersectoralApproachforHealthLiteracy-FINAL.pdf)*

POLICY:

Health Literacy: An Opportunity for Policy Action

Health agencies have acknowledged that health literacy is a determinant of health and well-being, which offers a unique opportunity for policy action. Similarly, the fact that there is evidence of low health literacy being systematically more prevalent among certain social groups indicates that targeted initiatives can strengthen health literacy among vulnerable populations and can help address health inequities. International, national, regional or local governments can provide supportive environments that foster the commitment to health literacy. According to the WHO, health literacy is a public health imperative and a key dimension of health citizenship. Strengthening health literacy not only improves health, but also builds resilience to help individuals and communities navigate their way to health-sustaining resources and actions. Therefore, health literacy must be addressed from an inter-sectorial perspective, and policy must support this comprehensive perspective.

The Inter-Sectorial Approach

When proposing policy action, we must first consider the role of society in health literacy. Creating social environments that support social justice, promote equity, and minimize disparities is essential to an educated and healthy society. From this perspective, the WHO recommends policy action "*championing and leading for health literacy across society, aligning with the values and principles of the public good, advocating to put health literacy on the public policy agenda, strengthening the evidence base of health literacy through support for research and monitoring, building adequate capacity for action and finding effective ways to work together for health literacy*" (WHO, 2013).

The **inter-sectorial approach** must include, at a minimum education, health systems, and health care providers. Education is essential to health outcomes and literacy. Education is an essential determinant of health, and people who have higher educational attainment have higher health literacy compared to their less educated counterparts. How health systems and providers relate to and interact with patients is also key in the health literacy equation. From this inter-sectorial perspective, a policy analysis on health literacy conducted by a group of researchers and supported by Pfizer Inc., proposed recommendations for health insurers, federal policymakers and the government, and health professions education and training programs (Vernon, Trujillo, Rosenbaum, & DeBuono, n.d.). The recommendations are included in Table 4.

1. Incentivize health insurers and healthcare professionals to identify and address health literacy-related issues
2. Build health literacy-related costs, such as translation and interpreter services and easy to understand oral instructions and written materials, into payment systems
3. Increase federal funding for health literacy research, particularly with populations at elevated risk for health disparities
4. Establish health literacy centers of excellence to promote research and the adoption of best practices, and support activities by state and local health agencies that work with high risk populations
5. Make health literacy skills a basic component of federally supported health professions education and training programs, particularly programs that train minority students

Table 4. Policy recommendations: *Adapted from: Vernon JA, Trujillo A, Rosenbaum S, DeBuono B, n.d. Available at:* Available at *http://www.pfizerhealthliteracy.com/physicians-providers/LowHealthLiteracy.aspx*

In the U.S., specific policy actions have mostly been limited to communication issues. There is an urgent need to address the gap between the health information currently available and the skills people have to understand and use this information to make life-altering decisions. Examples of such policies include:

The Americans with Disabilities Act, which dictates that communication needs of patients who are deaf and hard-of-hearing are to be met in health care. This means health care service providers are to provide American Sign Language interpretation in a timely manner to patients who request it, either through an in-person interpreter or video remote interpretation, at no cost to the patient.

The Affordable Care Act, the health care reform law passed in 2010. It includes requirements for agencies, health plans, and providers to communicate clearly and effectively.

The National Action Plan to Improve Health Literacy, which is based on the belief that all people have a right to health information that helps them make informed decisions. The plan is based on the principles that (1) everyone has the right to health information that helps them make informed decisions; and (2) health services should be delivered in ways that are understandable and beneficial to health, longevity, and quality of life. The vision informing this plan is of a society that provides everyone with access to accurate and actionable health information; delivers person-centered health information and services; and supports lifelong learning and skills to promote good health.

The Plain Writing Act of 2010. It mandates federal agencies write information clearly enough so people can understand and use it. President Obama signed the Plain Writing Act of 2010. The law requires that federal agencies use *"clear Government communication that the public can understand and use."* On January 18, 2011, he issued a new Executive Order, "E.O. 13563–Improving Regulation and Regulatory Review. It states that "[*our regulatory system*] *must ensure that regulations are accessible, consistent, written in plain language, and easy to understand.*" While the Act does not cover regulations, two separate Executive Orders emphasize the need for plain language. E.O. 12866 says that regulations must be *"simple and easy to understand, with the goal of minimizing uncertainty and litigation..."* (Sec. 1, Par. (b)(12)) and E.O. 12988 says that each regulation must specify its effect *"in clear language"* (Sec. 3 Par. (b)(2).

Others have proposed policy to address health literacy in specific population groups. For instance, a recent published paper (Barnett, McKee, Smith, & Pearson, 2011) made recommendations for the deaf community that included: 1) public health entities must work together with deaf sign language users to address inequities in health information access; 2) include deaf people in surveillance and health research; 3) collect new data, and analyze existing data, in ways that allow us to learn about actual deaf populations; 4) encourage deaf sign language users to participate in public health; 5) encourage deaf sign language users to pursue careers in public health, health research, and health care; and 6) advocate for funding to support communication access costs for public health programs and research.

Regarding the urgent need to address the gap between the health information currently available and the skills people have to understand and use this information, the U.S. Department of Health and Human Services proposes the approaches for policymakers, health care administrators, educators, and health care and public health professionals to consider (See Table 5).

Promote universal access to health information. These may include:
Setting guidelines about information access and design. Just as there is universal access to buildings (e.g., ramps) and the telecommunications infrastructure (e.g., closed captioning), information can be designed to be more accessible, even universally accessible. Guidelines that define what constitutes accessible health information could be developed and widely disseminated. Adherence to guidelines could be tied to funding decisions by public and private organizations.
Change the way health information is designed and delivered. Simply designating a reading grade level for print materials is not effective. Materials must be redesigned using best practices to reduce health literacy demands and match consumer preferences. Periodic testing of materials with the intended consumers is essential.
Encourage professional health care provider organizations to distribute understandable materials for their members to use with their patients and families. Even in the Internet age, providers remain a critical source of health information and should disseminate reliable information that is accessible to all of their patients.
Address health literacy as part of disparities initiatives. Health literacy improvement should be a high priority in disparities initiatives, and cultural and linguistic competence should be addressed when developing health materials.
Encourage public insurers to model improvements and innovations. Public insurers could develop accessible materials and processes for communicating with persons with limited health literacy. Using the most effective ways to present and deliver health information and services would help Medicare and Medicaid beneficiaries and would provide models for private insurers and employers.
Promote health education and health professional standards. National standards designed to improve primary and high school students' health literacy skills have not been widely adopted. Most professional schools do not require proficient communication skills for graduation or licensure. Improving the skills of both the population and health professionals can help patients and providers "speak the same language.

Table 5. Recommended approaches for policymakers, health care administrators, educators, and health care and public health professionals
Source: U.S. Department of Health and Human Services. Available at: http://www.health.gov/communication/literacy/issuebrief/

WRAP UP:

In summary, the success of health system reform will depend in large part on the capacity of individuals, families and communities to make informed decisions about their health. Health literacy is lowest among the more vulnerable members of our communities—those with lower education levels, racial/ethnic minorities, the uninsured and publicly insured, and the elderly. Innovative approaches, as well as application of existing best practices to developing and disseminating health information, are necessary if we are going to increase the likelihood that people will make healthy choices, successfully manage their own health, and make the best use of limited health care resources.

Policymakers, health care administrators, educators, and health care and public health professionals can take advantage of the many options at their disposal to create a society that is sensitive to the health literacy needs of its population and provides accessible health information that matches the health literacy skills of the public.

This chapter presents a review of issues that are important for understanding and addressing health literacy in minority populations. Therefore, these issues are relevant to both research and practice. As a relatively new topic, health literacy remains a fertile ground for exploration of concepts and frameworks, and how they determine health literacy and the lives of people on a daily basis.

Health literacy in minority populations is a fertile area of study that requires more rigorous research and practical approaches. The mechanism by which health literacy affects minority populations is multi-causal, and effective solutions must address a variety of factors at the individual, interpersonal, organizational, community, and public policy levels. This perspective presents many challenges, as there is still a need to identify contextual factors affecting minority communities such as culture, language usage, place of birth, and acculturation level; develop culturally and linguistically acceptable instruments; explore group-specific causal pathways between health literacy and health outcomes; and propose models that successfully promote policy actions for a more literate society.

Similarly, a comprehensive approach to improve health literacy at the population level provides a unique opportunity to contribute to society. Such as approach must include, at minimum, coordinated education and health actions. Education and health outcomes are critically important for social welfare and economic growth. Education is considered the most basic component of socioeconomic status, and positively affects life expectancy. These associations are true across countries, in blacks and whites, and men and women. Policies that impact educational attainment could have an enormous effect on social disparities, and ultimately on population health.

It is in the context of these challenges and opportunities that this chapter offers guidance for better understanding the role health literacy in minority health, and practical suggestions for addressing health literacy and improving the health and well-being of minorities.

EXERCISES, SCENARIOS, AND CASE STUDIES:

1. Using reliable sources of data and information, address the following:
    - What is the distribution of health literacy among U.S. adults?
    - What is the relationship between health literacy and the social and personal characteristics of individuals? (e.g. do different age or language minority groups manifest different skill levels? do males and females perform differently? how do adults who have completed different levels of education perform?)
    - What is the relationship between health literacy and health outcomes (e.g. healthcare utilization, morbidity and mortality indicators)?
    - What is the relationship between health literacy and health disparities?
2. In 2003, Dr. Richard H. Carmona, Surgeon General of the US, delivered the statement "The Obesity Crisis in America" before the Subcommittee on Education Reform, Committee on Education and the Workforce, United States House of Representatives. One of the solutions he proposed to end the "epidemic" of obesity among children was to increase health literacy.
    - How does obesity distribute among population groups, including minority groups?
    - How might obesity in minority groups relate to health literacy?
    - How does health literacy relate to healthy choices (e.g. food and physical activity)?
    - How does health literacy relate to health communication (e.g. reading food labels, understanding health information)?
    - How can health literacy be improved among minority parents and children?
3. System related barriers affect health literacy. These include: challenges in implementing quality school health programs; lack of accessible English as a Second Language programs for immigrants and community-based adult education programs; confusing and unreliable health information; complex healthcare systems; demanding self-care management; and lack of awareness and knowledge about health literacy among healthcare providers and educators.
    - What are the approaches or models that have been proposed to improve health literacy at the population level?
    - Identify a minority group and discuss evidence-based programs that have been shown to be effective in improving health literacy in that group.
    - Identify and discuss policies that may contribute to improving health literacy among minority populations.
4. Identify a health literacy program or intervention that includes a minority population. Assess whether the program/intervention includes culturally and/or linguistically appropriate approaches and materials, such as personnel, researchers, designs, procedures, and instruments. Does the program or intervention use a specific definition of health literacy (e.g. functional or critical health literacy)? Is the program or intervention multilevel or address just one specific levels of influence (e.g. intrapersonal or interpersonal)? What about policy? Does the program or intervention include policy activities that relate to the participating minority group or groups?

5. Assume you are an educator working with a specific ethnic/racial minority community. The leaders are concerned about the level of education and the health status of the community, a concern that is confirmed by reliable education and health data. You are asked to outline a solution. What steps would you take to respond to the request? If you proposed a health literacy intervention, what definition, approaches, instruments, and policy activities would you include?

6. Assume you are a public health/health educator practitioner working in a clinic or hospital serving one language minority group with demonstrated low health literacy level (e.g. Hispanic). The administrators are concerned about access, and you are asked to intervene. What are system-based situations that may constitute a barrier for accessing available services? (Think about a complete process, from making an appointment to check out and follow-up). How might these situations be influenced by health literacy? What individual-level health literacy-related interventions would you propose to address the problem? (Consider not only patients, but also providers and administrators). What system-based interventions and policies would you recommend?

LEARNING TOOLS:

- Health Literacy From A to Z. Second Edition: Practical Ways to Communicate your Health Message. Helen Osborne, 2011.
    - *Health Literacy from A to Z, Second Edition* includes updated and new health literacy topics, strategies, resources, and stories. There are even checklists about how to use this book in practice, in teaching, and with patients.
- Advancing Health Literacy: A Framework for Understanding and Action. Christina Zarcadoolas, Andrew Pleasant, David S. Greer, 2006.
    - *Advancing Health Literacy* addresses the crisis in health literacy in the United States and around the world. This book thoroughly examines the critical role of literacy in public health and outlines a practical, effective model that bridges the gap between health education, health promotion, and health communication. Step by step, the authors outline the theory and practice of health literacy from a public health perspective.
- Measures of Health Literacy: Workshop Summary. Lyla M. Hernandez. Roundtable on Health Literacy; Institute of Medicine. National Academies Press. 2009.
    - Discusses the current status of measures of health literacy, including those used in the health care setting; possible surrogate measures that might be used to assess health literacy; and ways in which health literacy measures can be used to assess patient-centered approaches to care.
- Health Literacy: A Prescription to End Confusion. Lynn Nielsen-Bohlman, Allison M. Panzer, David A. Kindig, Committee on Health Literacy. National Academies Press, 2004. Makes recommendations for health care systems to reduce the negative effects of limited health literacy and emphasizes the importance of incorporating knowledge and skills into the existing curricula of kindergarten through 12th grade classes, as well as into adult education and community programs. Furthermore, the authors recommend that programs to promote health literacy, health education, and health promotion be developed with involvement from the people who will use them. And all such efforts must be sensitive to cultural and language preferences.

- Proceedings of the Surgeon General's Workshop on Improving Health Literacy. Office of the Surgeon General (US); Office of Disease Prevention and Health Promotion (US). Rockville (MD): Office of the Surgeon General (US), 2006. Available at http://www.ncbi.nlm.nih.gov/books/NBK44257/

Resources for Faculty and Students:

Government Resources

- National Network of Libraries of Medicine. Health Literacy (http://nnlm.gov/outreach/consumer/hlthlit.html)
    - The site includes information on the economic impact of low health literacy, research, and links to additional resources.
- MedlinePlus: How to Write Easy-to-Read (http://www.nlm.nih.gov/medlineplus/etr.html)
    - MedlinePlus, the National Library of Medicine's website for patients and their families and friends includes easy-to-read health information, and a resource page with tips on how to write easy-to-read.
- National Action Plan for Health Literacy (http://www.health.gov/communication/HLActionPlan/)
    - The National Action Plan seeks to engage organizations, professionals, policymakers, communities, individuals, and families in a linked, multi-sector effort to improve health literacy.
- PlainLanguage.gov, Improving Communication from the Federal Government to the Public (http://www.plainlanguage.gov/)
    - Plain language is the law. Discover tips and tools to start and plan a plain language program. The site includes the Federal Plain Language Guidelines.
- Health.gov. Health Literacy (http://www.health.gov/communication/literacy/)
    - Includes tools, resources and research.
- Agency for Healthcare Research and Quality
    - Pharmacy Health Literacy Center (http://www.ahrq.gov/professionals/quality-patient-safety/pharmhealthlit/index.html)
        - This site provides pharmacists with recently released health literacy tools and other resources from the Agency for Healthcare Research and Quality (AHRQ).
    - Health IT Literacy Guide (http://healthit.ahrq.gov/health-it-tools-and-resources/health-it-literacy-guide)
        - This guide and checklist provide a structure, strategies, and other resources for the development of technologies for populations with limited literacy.
    - CAHPS Item Set for Addressing Health Literacy (https://cahps.ahrq.gov/surveys-guidance/item-sets/literacy/index.html)
        - The Item Set for Addressing Health Literacy focuses on assessing providers' activities to foster and improve the health literacy of patients.
    - Universal Precautions Toolkit (http://www.ahrq.gov/professionals/quality-patient-safety/quality-resources/tools/literacy-toolkit/index.html)
        - The AHRQ Universal Precautions Toolkit offers primary care practice a way to assess services for health literacy considerations, raise awareness of the entire staff, and work on specific areas.

- Questions Are the Answer (http://www.ahrq.gov/patients-consumers/patient-involvement/ask-your-doctor/index.html)
    - The AHRQ Questions Are the Answer encourages patients to ask questions at health visits, because health depends on good communication. The site includes a question builder and short videos of patients and providers sharing the importance of asking questions.
- Centers for Disease Control and Prevention
    - CDC Health Literacy: Accurate, Accessible and Actionable Health Information for All (http://www.cdc.gov/healthliteracy/)
        - Provides information and tools to improve health literacy and public health. These resources are for all organizations that interact and communicate with people about health, including public health departments, healthcare providers and facilities, health plans, government agencies, non-profit/community and advocacy organizations, childcare and schools, the media, and health-related industries.
    - Health Literacy, Health Communication and e-Health (http://health.gov/communication/literacy/)
        - Provides an overview of health literacy, tools, reports/research and related resources.
    - Improving Health Literacy for Older Adults (http://health.gov/communication/literacy/)
        - Expert Panel Report with a practitioner and researcher highlighting each component of the Healthy People 2010 definition of health literacy.
    - Simply Put, A Guide for Creating Easy-to-Understand Materials(http://www.cdc.gov/healthliteracy/pdf/Simply_Put.pdf)
        - This Simply Put Guide teaches how to create easy-to-read materials using effective communication and design.
    - CDC Gateway to Health Communication & Social Marketing Practice (http://www.cdc.gov/healthcommunication/)
        - Gateway to access many resources to help build health communication or social marketing campaigns and programs.
- Health Resources and Services Administration
    - Free Health Communication training course (http://www.hrsa.gov/publichealth/healthliteracy/)
        - Effective Communication Tools for Healthcare Professionals (formerly Unified Health Communication) is free, on-line, go-at-your-own-pace training that has helped more than 4,000 health care professionals and students improve patient-provider communication.
- National Center for Education Statistics
    - National Assessment of Adult Literacy (NAAL) (https://nces.ed.gov/naal/health.asp)
        - Provides information on the status of health literacy of American Adults
    - Adult Literacy and Lifeskills (ALL) Survey (http://nces.ed.gov/surveys/all/)
        - Provides information about the literacy skills of adult populations (international)

American Medical Association (AMA)

- Health Literacy (http://www.ama-assn.org/ama/pub/about-ama/ama-foundation/our-programs/public-health/health-literacy-program.page) HL kits and multimedia resources.

Canadian Public Health Association

- Health Literacy Portal (http://www.cpha.ca/en/portals/h-l.aspx). Internet portal designed to provide easy access to key information about health literacy for health professionals, researchers and interested individuals. It features the Expert Panel on Health Literacy's final report as well as links to other key Canadian and international health literacy resources.

REFERENCES:

Ajzen, I. (1991). The theory of planned behavior. *Organizational Behavior and Human Decision Processes*, 50(2), 179-211.

Baker, D. W. (2006). The meaning and the measure of health literacy. *Journal of General Internal Medicine*, 21(8), 878-883.

Balcazar, H., Alvarado, M., Luna Hollen, M. Gonzalez-Cruz, Y. & Pedregon, V. (2005) Evaluation of Salud Para su Corazon (Health for your Heart)-National Council of La Raza Promotora Outreach Program. *Preventing Chronic Disease*, 2(3):A09.

Balcazar, H., Byrd, T., Ortiz, M., Sumanth, R., & Chavez, M. (2009). A randomized community intervention to improve hypertension control among Mexican Americans: using the promotoras de salud community outreach model. *Journal of Health Care for the Poor and Underserved*, 20, 1079-1094.

Bandura, A. (1977). *Social Learning Theory*. Englewood Cliffs, NJ: Prentice Hall.

Bandura, A. (1984). Recycling misconceptions of perceived self-efficacy. *Cognitive Therapy and Research*, 8(3), 231-255.

Bandura, A. (1993). Perceived self-efficacy in cognitive development and functioning. *Educational Psychologist*, 28(2), 117-148.

Bann, C. M., McCormack, L. A., Berkman, N. D., & Squiers, L. B. (2012). The Health Literacy Skills Instrument: a 10-item short form. Journal of Health Communication, 17(Suppl. 3), 191-202.

Barnett, S. (1999). Clinical and cultural issues in caring for deaf people. *Family Medicine*, 31(1), 17-22.

Barnett, S., McKee, M., Smith, S. R., & Pearson, T. A. (2011). Deaf sign language users, health inequities and public health: opportunity for social justice. *Preventing Chronic Disease*, 8(2), A45.

Becker, M. H. (Ed.). (1974). The health belief model and personal health behavior. *Health Education Monographs*, 2, 324–508.

Bekker, M. H., & Lhajoui, M. (2004). Health and literacy in first- and second-generation Moroccan Berber women in the Netherlands: Ill Literacy? *International Journal for Equity in Health*, 3(8), 11-23.

Berkman, N. D., Davis, T. C., & McCormack, L. (2010). Health literacy: what is it? *Journal of Health Communication*, 15(2), 9-19.

Berkman, N. D., Sheridan, S. L., Donahue, K. E., Halpern, D. J., Viera, A., Crotty, K., . . . Viswanathan, M. (2011). *Health Literacy Interventions and Outcomes: An Updated Systematic Review*. Rockville, MD: Agency for Healthcare Research and Quality.

CDC. (2011). *About LGBT Health*. National Center for HIV/AIDS, Viral Hepatitis, STD, and TB Prevention, Centers for Disease Control and Prevention. Available at: http://www.cdc.gov/lgbthealth/about.htm. Accessed December 5, 2013.

Clements, N. K., Marx, R., Guzman, R., & Katz, M. (2001). HIV prevalence, risk behaviors, health care use, and mental health status of transgender persons: implications for public health interventions. *American Journal of Public Health*, 91, 915-921.

Cutler, D. M., & Lleras-Muney, A. (2010). Understanding differences in health behaviors by education. *Journal of Health Economics*, 29(1), 1-28.

De Heer, H., Balcazar, H., Morera, O., Lapeyrouse, L., Heyman, J., Salinas, J., & Zambrana, L. (2013). Barriers to care and co-morbidities along the U.S.-Mexico border. *Public Health Reports*, 128(6), 480-488.

DeWalt, D. A., & Hink, A. (2009). Health literacy and child health outcomes: a systematic review of the literature. *Pediatrics*, 124(Suppl. 3), S265-S274.

Doak, L., Doak, C., Leonard, C., & Root, J. (1996). *Applying theory in practice in teaching patients with low literacy skills*. Philadelphia: J.B. Lippincott.

Eichler, K., Wieser, S., & Brugger, U. (2009). The costs of limited health literacy: a systematic review. *International Journal of Public Health*, 54(5), 313-324.

Elder, J.P., Candelaria, J.I., Woodruff, S. I., Criqui, M.H., Talavera, G.A., & Rupp, J.W. (2000). Results of language for health: cardiovascular disease nutrition education for Latino English-as-a-second-language students. *Health Education & Behavior*, 27(1), 50-63.

Evans, R. (1989). *Albert Bandura: the man and his ideas-a dialogue*. New York: Praeger.

Eysenbach, G., & Kohler, C. (2002). How do consumers search for and appraise health information on the world wide web? Qualitative study using focus groups, usability tests, and in-depth interviews. *British Medical Journal*, (324), 573-577.

Finigan, E.G. (2007). *Deaf older adolescents: health care access disparities in an understudied Population*. Presented at American Public Health Association 135th Annual Meeting, Washington, DC.

Flores, G., Abreu, M., & Tomany-Korman, S. C. (2005). Limited English proficiency, primary language at home, and disparities in children's health care: how language barriers are measured matters. *Public Health Reports*, 120(4), 418-430.

Gee, G. C. (2000). A multilevel analysis of the relationship between institutional and individual racial discrimination and health status. *American Journal of Public Health*, 92(4), 615-623.

Glanz, K., Lewis, F., & Rimer, B. (2008). *Health Behavior and Health Education: Theory and Practice* (4th ed.). San Francisco: Jossey-Bass.

HealthyPeople.gov. (2013). Lesbian, Gay, Bisexual, and Transgender Health. Available at: http://healthypeople.gov/2020/topicsobjectives2020/overview.aspx?topicId=25. Accessed December 5, 2013.

Henk, W., & Melnick, S. (1995). The reader self-perception scale (RSPS): a new tool for measuring how children feel about themselves as readers. *The Reading Teacher*, 48(6), 470-482.

Hibbard, J. (n.d.). *Consumers in a Complex and Dynamic Health Care Environment*. Available at: http://www.neahin.org/health-literacy/hibbard-paper.pdf. Accessed December 5, 2013.

HLS-EU Consortium. (2012). *Comparative Report of Health Literacy in Eight EU Member States. The European Health Literacy Survey HLS-EU*. Available at http://ec.europa.eu/eahc/news/news162.html. Accessed December 5, 2013.

Howard-Pitney, B., Winkleby, M. A. Albright, C. L., Bruce, B., & Fortmann, P. (1997). The Stanford nutrition action program: a dietary fat intervention for low-literacy adults. *American Journal of Public Health*, 87(12), 1971-1976.

Jordan, J., Osborne, R. H., & Buchbinder, R. (2011). Critical appraisal of health literacy indices revealed variable underlying constructs, narrow content and psychometric weaknesses. *Journal of Clinical Epidemiology*, 64(4), 366-379.

Kaestle, C. F., Campbell, A., Finn, J. D., Johnson, S. T., & Mikulecky, L. J. (2001). *Adult Literacy and Education in America: Four Studies Based on the National Adult Literacy Survey*. National Center for Education Statistics. (NCES 2001–534).

Kalichman, S. C., Cherry, J., & Cain, D. (2005). Nurse-delivered antiretroviral treatment adherence intervention for people with low literacy skills and living with HIV/AIDS. *Journal of the Association of Nurses in Aids Care*, 16(5), 3-15.

Kandula, N. R., Nsiah-Kumi, P. A., Makoul, G., Sager, J., Zei, C. P., Glass, S., Stephens, Q., & Baker, D. (2009). The relationship between health literacy and knowledge improvement after a multimedia type 2 diabetes education program. *Patient Education and Counseling*, 75(3), 321-327.

Kickbusch, I. (1997). Think health: what makes the difference? *Health Promotion International*, 12(3), 265-272.

Kickbush, I. (2009). Health Literacy:engaging in a political debate. *Internal Journal of Public Health*, 54, 131-132.

Kim, S., Love, F., Quistberg, A., & Shea, J. (2004). Association of health literacy with self-management behavior in patients with diabetes. *Diabetes Care*, 27(12), 2980-2982.

Kirk, J. K., Grzywacz, J. G., Arcury, T. A., Ip, E. H., Nguyen, H. T., Bell, R. A., Saldana, S., & Quandt, S. A. (2012). Performance of health literacy tests among older adults with diabetes. *Journal of General Internal Medicine*, 27(5), 534-540.

Knowles, M. (1980). *The Modern Practice of Adult Education: From Pedagogy to Andragogy*. Englewood Cliffs, NJ: Cambridge Adult Education, Prentice Hall Regents.

Kolata, G. (2007). *A Surprising Secret to a Long Life: Stay in School*. New York Times, January 3, 2007.

Kutner, M., Greenberg, E., Jin, Y., & Paulsen, C. (2006). *The Health Literacy of America's Adults: Results from the 2003 National Assessment of Adult Literacy*. Washington D. C.: U. S. Department of Education National Center for Education.

Lee, J. Y., Divaris, K., Baker, A. D., Rozier, R. G., Lee, S. Y., & Vann, W. F. Jr. (2011). Oral health literacy levels among a low-income WIC population. *Journal of Public Health Dentistry*, 71(2), 152-160.

Liechty, J. M. (2011). Health literacy: Critical opportunities for social work leadership in health care and research. *Health and Social Work*, 36(2), 99-107.

Lopez-McKee, G. (2010). Development of the mammography beliefs and attitudes questionnaire for low health literacy Mexican-American women. *The Online Journal of Issues in Nursing*, 16(1).

Mancuso, J. (2009). Assessment and measurement of health literacy: an integrative review of the literature. *Nursing & Health Sciences*, 11(1), 77-89.

Marmot, M. G. (2006). Status syndrome: a challenge to medicine. *JAMA*, 295(11), 1304-1307.

Mayer, K. H., Bradford, J. B., Makadon, H. J., Stall, R., Goldhammer, H., & Landers, S. (2008). Sexual and gender minority health: What we know and what needs to be done. *American Journal of Public Health*, 98(6), 989-995.

McCormack, l., Bann, C., Squiers, L., Berkman, N., Squire, C., Schillinger, D., . . . Hibbard, J. (2010). Measuring health literacy: a pilot study of a new skills-based instrument. *Journal of Health Communication*, 15(S2), 51-71.

McCormack, L., Trieman, K., Peinado, S., & Alexander, J. (2009). *Environmental Scan of Patient Roles and Responsibilities: Recommendations for a Communication Initiative*. Triangle Park, NC: RTI International.

McDermott, B., Soto Mas, F., Olivárez, A., Mein, E., Muro, A., & Quiroz, T. (2009). Evaluating the use of health literacy assessment tools with Spanish-speaking adults. Presented at Society for Public Health Education 60th Annual Meeting, Philadelphia, Pennsylvania.

McEwen, E., & Anton-Culver, H. (1988). The medical communication of deaf patients. *Journal of Family Practice*, 26(3), 289-291.

Meyer, I. L., Northridge, M. E. (Eds.). (2007). *The Health of Sexual Minorities: Public Health* Perspectives on Lesbian, Gay, Bisexual and Transgender Populations. New York: Springer.

Mitic, W., & Rootman, I. (Eds.). (2012). *An Inter-sectorial Approach for Improving Health Literacy for Canadians: A Discussion Paper.* Victoria, BC: Public Health Association of BC.

Mustanski, B.S., Clifford, A., Bigelow, L., Andrews, K., Birkett, M.A., Ashbeck, A., & Fisher, K. (2012). *A Healthy Chicago for LGBT Youth: An IMPACT Program White Paper on Health Disparities in Chicago's LGBT Youth*. Chicago, IL: The IMPACT Program at Northwestern University. Available at: http://www.impactprogram.org/youth/whitepaper. Accessed December 5, 2013.

Nguyen, H. T., Kirk, J. K., Arcury, T. A., Ip, E. H., Grzywacz, J. G., Saldana, S. J., Bell, R. A., & Quandt, S. A. (2013). Cognitive function is a risk for health literacy in older adults with diabetes. *Diabetes Research and Clinical Practice*, 101(2), 141-147.

Nielsen-Bohlman, I., Panzer, A. M., & Kindig, D. A. (2004). *Health Literacy: A Prescription to End Confusion*. Washington, DC: The National Academic Press.

Noar, S., & Zimmerman, R. (2005). Health behavior theory and cumulative knowledge regarding health behaviors: Are we moving in the right direction? *Health Education Research*, 20(3), 275-290.

Nutbeam, D. (1998). Health promotion glossary. *Health Promotion International*, 13(4), 349-364.

Nutbeam, D. (2000). Health literacy as a public health goal: a challenge for contemporary health education and communication strategies into the 21st century. *Health Promotion International*, 15(3), 259-267.

OECD. (2006). *Measuring the Effect of Education on Health and Civic Engagement: Proceedings of the Copenhagen Symposium.* Organisation for Economic Co-operation and Development.

O'Hearn, A. (2009). *Odds of self-reported suicide behaviors in deaf and hard of hearing college entering adults.* Presented at American Public Health Association 137th Annual Meeting, Philadelphia, Pennsylvania.

Paasche-Orlow, M. K., Parker, R. M., Gazmararian, J. A., Nielsen-Bohlman, L. T., & Rudd, R. R. (2005). The prevalence of limited health literacy. *Journal of General Internal Medicine*, 20(2), 175-184.

Paasche-Orlow, M., & Wolf, M. (2007). The causal pathways linking health literacy to health outcomes. *American Journal of Health Behavior*, 31(1), S19-S26.

Paasche-Orlow, M. K., & Wolf, M. (2010). Promoting health literacy research to reduce health disparities. *Journal of Health Communication*, 15(Suppl. 2), 34-41.

Parker, R. M., Ratzan, S. C., & Lurie, N. (2003). Health literacy: a policy challenge for advancing high-quality health care. *Health Affairs*, 22(4), 147-153.

Pollard, R. Q. (1998). Psychopathology. In: M. Marschark, & D. Clark. (Eds). *Psychological Perspectives on Deafness* (Volume 2). Mahwah (NJ): Lawrence Erlbaum, Inc., p. 171-197.

Pollard, R. Q., & Barnett, S. (2009). Health-related vocabulary knowledge among deaf adults. *Rehabilitation Psychology*, 54(2), 182-185.

Quiroz, T. G., Soto Mas, F., Olivárez, A., Mein E., Muro, A., & McDermott, V. B. (2009). *Evaluating the use of health literacy assessment tools with Spanish-speaking adults.* Presented at Society for Public Health Education 60th Annual Meeting, Philadelphia, Pennsylvania.

Ratzan, S. C., & Parker, R. M. (2000). Introduction. In: *National Library of Medicine Current Bibliographies in Medicine: Health Literacy.* NLM Pub. No. CBM 2000-1.

Richards, H., & Barry, R. (1998). U.S. life tables for 1990 by sex, race, and education. *Journal of Forensic Economics, 11*(1), 9-26.

Rootman, I., & Gordon-El-Bihbety, D. (2008). *A Vision for a Health Literate Canada: Report of the Expert Panel on Health Literacy.* Canadian Public Health Association.

Ross, C. E., & Wu, C. (1995). The links between education and health. *American Sociological Review*, 60(5), 719-745.

Ross, W., Culbert, A., Gasper, C., & Kimmey, J. (2009). *A Theory-Based Approach to Improving Health Literacy.* St. Louis: Missouri Health Foundation. Available at: http://www.inter-disciplinary.net/wp-content/uploads/2009/06/ross-paper.pdf. Accessed December 5, 2013.

Rudd, R. E. (2007). Health literacy skills of U.S. adults. *American Journal of Health Behavior*, 31(Suppl. 1), S8-S18.

Rudd, R. E., Anderson, J. E., Oppenheimer, S., & Nath, C. (2007). Health literacy: an update of public health and medical literature. In: J. P. Comings, B. Garner, C. Smith. (Eds). *Review of Adult Learning and Literacy* (Volume 7). Mahway NJ: Lawrence Erlbaum Associates, pp 175-204.

Rudd, R., Moeykens, B. A., & Colton, T. C. (2000). Health and literacy: a review of the medical and public health literature. In: J. Comings, B. Gerners, & C. Smith (eds.). *Annual Review of Adult Learning and Literacy.* New York: Jossey-Bass.

Schwartz, L. M., Woloshin, S., Black, W. C., & Welch, H. G. (1997). The role of numeracy in understanding the benefit of screening mammography. *Annals of Internal Medicine*, 127(11), 966–972.

Sentell, T., & Braun, K. L. (2012). Low health literacy, limited English proficiency, and health status in Asians, Latinos, and other racial/ethnic groups in California. *Journal of Health Communication*, 17(Suppl. 3), 82-99.

Servellen, G. V., Carpio, F., Lopez, M., Garcia-Teague, L., Herrera, G., Monterrosa, F., Gomez, R., & Lombardi, E. (2003). Program to enhance health literacy and treatment adherence in low-income HI-infected Latino men and women. *Aids Patient care and STDs*, 17(11), 581-594.

Sharma, M., & Romas, J. (2012). *Theoretical Foundations of Health Education and Health Promotion* (2nd ed.). Sudbury: Jones & Bartlett Learning.

Shea, J. A., Beers, B. B., McDonald, V. J., Quistberg, D. A., Ravenel,l K. L., & Asch, D. A. (2004). Assessing health literacy in African American and Caucasian adults: disparities in rapid estimate of adult literacy in medicine (REALM) scores. *Family Medicine*, 36(8), 575-581.

Simonds, S. (1974). Health education as social policy. *Health Education Monographs*, 2(Suppl. 1), 1-10.

Smith, S. R. (2011). *Health Knowledge and Literacy of Deaf Adolescents Who Use Sign Language: Formative research Findings.* Department of Community and Preventive Medicine University of Rochester, Rochester, NY. Available at ttp://www.bumc.bu.edu/healthliteracyconference/files/2011/07/Scott-Smith.pdf. Accessed December 5, 2013.

Solarz, A. L. (Ed.). (1999). *Lesbian Health: Current Assessment and Directions for the Future.* Washington, DC: National Academy Press.

Sorensen, K., & Brand, H. (2013). Health literacy lost in translations? Introducing the European Health Literacy Glossary. *Health Promotion International*, 29(4), 634-44.

Sorensen, K., Van den Broucke, S., Fullam, J., Doyle, G., Pelikan, J., Slonka, Z., & Brand, H. (2012). Health literacy and public health: a systematic review and integration of definitions and models. *BMC Public Health*, 12(80), 1-13.

Soto Mas, F., Allensworth, D., & Jones, C. (2010). Health promotion programs designed to eliminate health disparities. In: C. Fertman, D. Allensworth (Eds.). *Health Promotion Programs: From Theory to Practice.* San Francisco, CA: Jossey-Bass, pp 29-55.

Soto Mas, F., Fuentes, B. O., Arnal, P., Mein, E., & Tinajero, J. (2013). *Health literacy & ESL Curriculum.* MedEdPORTAL. Available at: https://www.mededportal.org/publication/9420. Accessed December 5, 2013.

Soto Mas, F., Jacobson, H., & Dong, Y. (2014). Health literacy level of Hispanic college students. *Southern Medical Journal*, 107(2), 61-65.

Soto Mas, F., Ji, M., Fuentes, B., & Tinajero, J. The health literacy & ESL study: a community-based intervention for Spanish speaking adults. *Journal of Health Communication*, 2015, 20 1-8. doi:10.1080/10810730.2014.965368. [Epub ahead of print].

Soto Mas, F., McDermott, B., Mein, E., Olivárez, A., Quiroz, T., & Muro, A. (2010). *A comparative analysis of Spanish health literacy tools: S-TOFHLA & NVS.* Presented at American Public Health Association 138th Annual Meeting, Denver, Colorado.

Soto Mas, F., Mein, E., Fuentes, B., Thatcher, B., & Balcázar, H. (2013). Integrating health literacy and ESL: an interdisciplinary curriculum for Hispanic immigrants. *Health Promotion Practice*, 14(2), 263-273.

Taylor, V. M., Cripe, S. M., Acorda, E., The, C., Coronado, G., Do, H., Woodall, E., & Hislop, G.T. (2008). Development of an ESL curriculum to educate Chinese immigrants about physical activity. *Journal of Immigrant Minority Health*, 10(4), 379-387.

UNESCO. (2005). Education for all. Literacy for life. *EFA Global Monitoring Report 2006*. United Nations Economic and Social Council. Paris, France: Graphoprint.

UNESCO. (2009). Draft ministerial declaration of the 2009 high-level segment of the Economic and Social Council: Implementing the internationally agreed goals and commitments in regards to global public health. United Nations Economic and Social Council. Geneva, Switzerland.

U.S. Department of Health and Human Services. (2010). *National Action Plan to Improve Health Literacy*. Office of Disease Prevention and Health Promotion. Washington, DC: Author.

Vander Zanden, J. (1972). *American Minority Relations* (3rd ed). New York: Rondal

Vernon, J. A., Trujillo, A., Rosenbaum, S., & DeBuono, B. (n.d.). *Low Health Literacy: Implications for National Health Policy*. Available at http://www.pfizerhealthliteracy.com/physicians-providers/LowHealthLiteracy.aspx. Accessed December 5, 2013.

WHO. (2013). *The Solid Facts: Health Literacy*. I. Kickbusch, J. M. Pelikan, F. Apfel & A. D. Tsouros. (Eds.). Regional Office for Europe, World health Organization.

Wolf, M. S., Wilson, E. A., Rapp, D. N., R.Waite, K., Bocchini, M. V., Davis, T. C., & Rudd, R. E. (2009). Literacy and learning in health care. *Pediatrics*, 124(Suppl. 3), S275-S281.

Wolitski, R. J., Stall, R., & Valdiserri, R. O. (Eds.). (2008). *Unequal Opportunity: Health Disparities Affecting Gay and Bisexual Men in the United States*. New York: Oxford University Press.

Chapter 7:

Disparities and Diversity In Sexual Orientation

Aly Eisenhardt and Susanne Ninassi

KEY CONCEPTS:

Antigay
Biological sex
Bisexual
Cisgender
Cross-dressing
Gay
Gender affirmation
Gender expression
Gender identity
Gender reassignment
LGBT
Heterosexist
Heterosexual
Homophobia
Homophobic
Homosexual
Lesbian
Reparative therapy
Sexual orientation
Social gender roles
Transgender
Transsexual

CHAPTER OVERVIEW:

The lesbian, gay, bisexual and transgender (**LGBT**) community is comprised of all races, ethnicities, ages, religions, and social classes (Healthy People 2020, 2015). The community has unique health needs and demands that practitioners and healthcare managers alike must understand and respond appropriately to, regardless of circumstance. Culturally proficient healthcare professionals have the ability to facilitate and ensure that the highest quality of care is provided to the LGBT community. This chapter will introduce the reader to the LGBT community. The chapter will outline specific health needs and concerns, and present activities and scenarios to enhance cultural competency and mastery pertaining to this population.

CHAPTER EXPECTATIONS:

Upon reading this chapter, the reader will be able to:

- Become familiar with terms and identifiers used to describe the LGBT community.
- Gain an understanding and be able to apply general knowledge about the LGBT community's unique health needs.
- Respond appropriately to a multitude of scenarios and case examples confronting the issues of health and health disparities faced by the LGBT community.
- Integrate the knowledge gained through this chapter in defining their role within the healthcare community to ensure the delivery of quality health care for LGBT individuals.

INTRODUCTION:

According to the American Psychological Association ("Sexual Orientation, Homosexuality, and Bisexuality," 2008), "**sexual orientation** refers to an enduring pattern of emotional, romantic, and/or sexual attractions to men, women, or both sexes. Sexual orientation also refers to a person's sense of identity based on those attractions, related behaviors, and membership in a community of others who share those attractions." Gender and sexual orientation do not only have biological and physiological components, but also have a strong cultural component (American Psychological Association, "Sexual Orientation, Homosexuality, and Bisexuality," 2008). Much of a person's identity is linked to these components. It is important to recognize how these factors relate to culture and, in turn, how they relate to health status and outcomes.

WHAT YOU SHOULD KNOW:

Healthcare professionals should understand and be able to appropriately apply the terms "sexual orientation" and "gender identity," and understand the unique differences between the terms. Sexual orientation is separate from other components of sex and gender. However, considerations of culture, health, and all other components should be understood. **Biological sex** is the anatomical, physiological, and genetic characteristics associated with being male or female. **Cisgender** (Oxford Dictionaries) is a person whose self-identity conforms to the gender that matches their biological sex, i.e., their sex matches their birth certificate. **Gender identity** is the psychological sense of being male or female. **Social gender roles** are the cultural norms that define feminine and masculine behaviors (American Psychological Association, "Sexual Orientation, Homosexuality, and Bisexuality," 2008).

Sexual orientation is defined with consideration to relationships with others. People express sexual orientation through their behaviors with others of the same or opposite sex. Sexual orientation is closely tied to the intimate personal relationships that meet a person's needs for love, attachment, and intimacy (American Psychological Association, "Sexual Orientation, Homosexuality, and Bisexuality," 2008). Additionally, these relationships may include nonsexual physical affection, common goals and values, mutual support, and an ongoing commitment. Thus, sexual orientation is not only a personal trait, but it also may define the group or community one may often associate with and from which one seeks satisfying relationships (American Psychological Association, "Sexual Orientation, Homosexuality, and Bisexuality," 2008).

Sexual orientation is not linear, but rather, it ranges along a continuum from exclusive attraction to the other sex–to exclusive attraction to the same sex. Various cultures identify and describe the range of sexual orientation and attraction behaviors in a variety of ways. Many cultures around the world use labels to identify sexual orientation behaviors and attractions. However, in the U.S., sexual orientation may be discussed in terms of the following three main categories:

- **heterosexual**, or having emotional, romantic, or sexual attractions to members of the other sex,
- **gay** or lesbian, or having emotional, romantic, or sexual attractions to members of one's own sex, (also referred to as **homosexual**)
  - **lesbian** refers to a female who experiences romantic love or sexual attraction to other females.
- **bisexual**, or having emotional, romantic, or sexual attractions to both men and women (American Psychological Association, "Sexual Orientation, Homosexuality, and Bisexuality," 2008).

This population as a whole is recognized as the Lesbian, Gay, Bisexual, and Transgender, or LGBT community.

To fully comprehend sexual orientation one must also understand gender and gender identity. **Gender identity** refers to a person's "internal sense" of being either male or female, or in some instances, something else. One's **gender expression** is the way in which an individual communicates his or her gender identity to the outside world. Gender expression can be communicated through behavior, clothing, hairstyles, voice, or body characteristics (American Psychological Association, "Sexuality and Transgender," 2013). It is one way that we, as individuals, express who we are as persons.

The term **transgender** is used to describe persons whose gender identity, gender expression, or behavior does not conform to that typically associated with the sex to which he or she was assigned at birth (American Psychological Association, "Sexuality and Transgender," 2013). While transgender is generally the term used, not everyone whose appearance or behavior is "gender-nonconforming" will identify himself or herself as a transgender person. The world's perception of transgender persons is constantly changing, as represented in pop culture, academia, the media, and mainstream society.

Transsexual refers to people whose gender identity is different from their assigned sex at birth. Often, transsexuals seek to alter their bodies through hormones, surgery, and other means. The intent is to make their bodies as congruent as possible with the gender in which they most identify. The process of transitioning through medical intervention is often referred to as **gender reassignment**. More recently it is also referred to as **gender affirmation** (American Psychological Association, "Sexuality and Transgender", 2013). It is not uncommon in the healthcare setting to interact with a patient who is seeking gender affirmation. As such, healthcare professionals should understand and react to the specific and unique population needs. It should be noted that some individuals who transition from one gender to another prefer to be referred to as a man or woman, rather than transgender.

While being transgender is tied to the physical alteration of one's gender, some LGBT community members choose to cross-dress. **Cross-dressing** is the behavior of wearing clothing that is traditionally or stereotypically worn by another gender (American Psychological Association, "Sexuality and Transgender," 2013). Similar to sexual orientation, cross-dressing also occurs across a continuum. Individuals who choose to cross-dress may vary from wearing one piece of clothing to fully dressing as a different gender. In contrast to transgender individuals, those who cross-dress are usually comfortable with their assigned sex and do not seek to change it (American Psychological Association, "Sexuality and Transgender," 2013). Cross-dressing is a form of gender expression, and this is not indicative of sexual orientation.

The terms defined and discussed above will be used throughout the content of this chapter. The terms and identifiers may be used in a professional healthcare setting as appropriate. It should be noted, however, that some individuals within the LGBT community might choose to use different terms or none at all to identify themselves. Healthcare professionals should not attempt to "label" patients according to sexual behavior and orientation, but rather should apply an understanding of the community's unique health needs and demands.

Understanding the Culture of the Community

Like all people in the U.S., the LGBT community is diverse in terms of education, race, age, ethnicity, income, and residence. The degree to which sexual orientation or gender identity is the focus of one's self-definition, the level of affiliation with other LGBT people, and the rejection or acceptance of societal stereotypes and prejudice vary greatly among individuals, as is the case with most minority groups (American Psychological Association, "Guidelines", 2008). Determining the number of LGBT people in the U.S. is difficult since federal census questions do not include questions regarding sexual orientation (Gates, 2011). However, based upon studies of various population-based surveys, it is estimated that 3.4% of women, 3.6 % of men in the U.S. classify themselves as lesbian or gay or bisexual and 0.3% classify themselves as transgender (Gates, 2011).

The large range is because all data is self-reported. It should be noted that many members of the community live in urban areas. The number of urban dwellers among this community is disproportionate to that of rural residents.

Health Risks

One of the main goals of Healthy People 2020 is to "improve the health, safety, and well-being of lesbian, gay, bi-sexual, and transgender individuals." The LGBT community, like all vulnerable populations, is at risk for experiencing healthcare disparities. The LGBT community, as a sexual minority population, experiences unique healthcare disparities and are prone to specific health risks (Institute of Medicine, 2001).

Literature notes that LGBT individuals face health disparities that are often linked to social stigma, discrimination, and denial of civil and human rights (Healthy People 2020, 2013). Such discrimination has been associated with a high incidence of psychiatric disorders, substance abuse, and suicide (Healthy People 2020, 2013). Healthcare professionals, who may be reluctant to recognize signs and risks, must take such issues very seriously. Violence and victimization experiences among LGBT community members are too frequent and have long-term effects on the community and individuals (Healthy People 2020, 2013). Acceptance (personal, family, and social) is the key to mitigating the physical and mental health issues endured by LGBT individuals.

Another specific need of this population is addressing specific diseases, such as human immunodeficiency virus (HIV) and acquired immune deficiency syndrome (AIDS). Since 1981, it is estimated that more than 702,000 Americans have been diagnosed with AIDS. Out of these 702,000 individuals, 54% are homosexual men (Centers for Disease Control and Prevention, "Diagnosis of HIV Infection," 2011). Minority men are the majority (38%) of this percentage (Centers for Disease Control and Prevention, "Diagnosis of HIV Infection," 2011). Minorities are becoming infected in greater numbers and at younger ages. The LGBT community is also at a higher risk for Hepatitis B. The population experiences a high incidence of the disease, however, a low incidence of vaccination (Centers for Disease Control and Prevention, "Gay and Bisexual Health," 2010).

Research indicates that LGBT persons are more likely to use alcohol and drugs than the general population (Center for Substance Abuse Treatments, "Provider's Introduction to Substance Abuse," 2012). It has been reported that approximately 20-25% of gay men and lesbians are "heavy" alcohol users as compared to 3-10% of the heterosexual population (Center for Substance Abuse Treatments, "Provider's Introduction to Substance Abuse," 2012). These are serious health risks and concerns. Healthcare professionals must recognize the need to facilitate the mitigation of mental health, preventable diseases, and substance abuse issues among the LGBT community.

Substance Abuse among LGBT Individuals

Some LGBT individuals self-medicate with drugs and alcohol as a way to cope with or numb negative feelings, such as isolation, fear, depression, anxiety, anger, and mistrust that are associated with heterosexism (Leible,

2013). Others in the gay community may use mind-altering substances as a way to cope with stressors caused by the tensions of living under the stigma of marginalization. In fact, substance use is a large part of the social life of many in the LGBT community. The gay bar scene is regarded as a risk factor for substance abuse among the gay community. But these bars have often been the only places where LGBT community members can socialize and feel free from the prevailing oppression that is experienced everyday in a strongly heterosexist society. The LGBT individual who has experienced rejection from his or her biological family may find in the gay bar that one opportunity for identity affirmation and acceptance (Cheng, 2003, as noted by Leible, 2013).

Heterosexism also causes many LGBT individuals stress (Leible, 2013). LGBT individuals may be forced to conform to societal norms in order to have successful and thriving lives. However, this attempt to "fit in" may cause major stress and emotional turmoil. For these reasons, substance abuse may be an alternative to ease their problems.

Barriers to Care

Throughout the decades, attitudes and beliefs about homosexuality and chemical abuse have progressed. At one time scientists believed there was a causal relationship between homosexuality and alcoholism. This idea stemmed from the belief that suppressed homosexual tendencies actually triggered chemical abuse and dependency (Leible, 2013). However, this myth has been dispelled by research that indicates there are societal factors attributed to the higher incidence of substance abuse and alcoholism rates among the LGBT community.

Up until the mid-1970's, homosexuality was defined as a mental illness by the American Psychiatric Association. For years, people outside of the LGBT community stressed the need for **reparative therapy**. Reparative therapy is the use of a range of treatments that aim to change sexual orientation from homosexual to heterosexual. Acting on the belief that homosexuality is an immoral "choice" that can be altered, the practice attempts to change homosexuals into heterosexuals. Reparative therapy is still used by some people today. Although the LGBT minority group continues to strive for equality and anti-discrimination, stigmas associated with gender preferences are still a very real threat to the health of this population. **Homophobic** and **antigay** are terms commonly used to describe negative attitudes toward lesbians and gay men.

A **heterosexist** refers to characteristics of an ideological system that denies, denigrates, and stigmatizes any non-heterosexual form of behavior, identity, relationship, or community (Pride Institute, 2013). Examples of heterosexism are negative messages about the gay and lesbian lifestyle or incidents of hate in the form of threats, acts of humiliation, emotional abuse, and even murder (Pride Institute, 2013). Additional examples of heterosexism may include rejection by family, friends, or peers, loss of employment or lack of promotion, and making heterosexist remarks (Selvidge, 2000, as noted by the Pride Institute, 2013). Heterosexism can result in internalized shame and a negative self-concept. Heterosexism plays a part in the LGBT individual's inability to access health services. Healthcare providers often are not able to meet the needs of this special population (Pride Institute, 2013).

Despite the recent movement of tolerance and acceptance over the past two decades, many Americans view homosexuality as morally wrong, in the same category as adultery. The consequences of these beliefs echo throughout society, as well as the healthcare policy and delivery system. Insurance companies, government, hospitals, and health facilities often fail to recognize committed lesbian and gay relationships, and deny gay and lesbian partners the privileges and rights granted to married heterosexual couples. The denial of such rights may interfere with the proper execution and delivery of healthcare services.

Many LGBT rejected by or uncomfortable with their families, lose traditional social support after disclosure of their sexual identity. The effects of stigmas are often traumatic and long lasting. They may include isolation, violence, and stress. These issues are all associated with greater health risks. Consequently, mental health issues, such as suicide, depression, substance abuse, and eating disorders, are also risks faced by the community.

Like all other minority groups, the LGBT community experiences cultural and personal barriers to quality medical treatment, care, and outcomes. **Homophobia**, or prejudice against lesbian and gay men, plays a significant role in inadequate treatment, prevention, and medical assessment. Individuals may be subject to discrimination and bias in medical encounters or in gaining health system access. This puts the individual at greater risk of having poor health outcomes.

Providers may not be knowledgeable to the specific health risks and concerns of the LGBT community. They may also be uncomfortable asking patients about specific health concerns having to do with sexual orientation and gender. In fact, as noted by one study, 40% of physicians indicated they were sometimes or often uncomfortable providing care to lesbian or gay patients (Dionne, 2002). Furthermore, 67% of gay and lesbian providers believed gay and lesbian patients receive substandard care due to their sexual orientation (Schatz and O'Hanlan, 1994). Contributing to this statistic is the fact that many gays and lesbians feel providers are not knowledgeable and/or sensitive to their specific health concerns and issues. Whether perceived or not, this factor is a true threat to the provider-patient relationship. Any previous negative experiences may delay care and alter health outcomes.

The medical education system as a whole has not effectively been trained to be culturally proficient when addressing the needs of the LGBT community. Sadly, many transgender and LGBT individuals may delay or entirely avoid seeing a medical provider because of fear of discrimination, humiliation, or the risk of being misunderstood. One large study of transgender people found that 28% had postponed necessary medical care when sick or injured, and 33% delayed or did not try to get preventive health care due to discrimination by health care providers (Grant, et. al., 2011). There is also a scarcity of health professionals trained in transgender medical and behavioral health care. Fifty percent of transgender individuals report having to teach their doctors about transgender healthcare issues (Grant, et. al., 2011). As healthcare professionals, we are all responsible for closing the gap on these issues.

According to a survey conducted by the Gay and Lesbian Medical Association (1994) "52% of physicians surveyed observed the denial of care or the provision of suboptimal care to lesbian and gay clients. Furthermore, 88% of these physicians overheard colleagues make disparaging remarks about lesbian and gay patients." However, the majority of physicians surveyed agreed that it is important for patients to admit their sexual orientation (Gay and Lesbian Medical Association, 1994). The participants surveyed also noted that the risk of LGBT patients for receiving substandard care is higher than those of their heterosexual counterparts (Substance Abuse and Mental Health Services Administration, 2012).

Contributing to a reluctance to address sexuality and sexual health issues among clinicians are biases, stigmas, and a lack of cultural sensitivity and knowledge. Whether these biases and stigmas are unconscious or conscious, they may hamper the quality of care. Patients may choose to remain silent about important health issues they fear may lead to stigmatization.

Patients may also be reluctant to seek health care, which may result in delayed diagnoses, lack of prevention, and poor health outcomes (Substance Abuse and Mental Health Services Administration, 2012). Biases from health care professionals and perception of such bias have been identified as personal and cultural barriers to care, leading to reduction in seeking treatment and quality of care.

As a result, many LGBT individuals, particularly those who are transgender, are often unwilling to use mainstream health care services. Thus, the community, as a whole is underserved. However, the result of recent policy and advocacy efforts has led to changes in mainstream professional medical organizations (Substance

Abuse and Mental Health Services Administration, 2012). Policy statements addressing the needs of LGBT community have now begun to transform the current environment. Although it is important to recognize these changes and the effects of establishing ethical guidelines for appropriate care, many healthcare providers remain uncomfortable with sexual diversity and continue to discriminate against LGBT patients (Substance Abuse and Mental Health Services Administration, 2012).

Due to perceived insensitivity and lack of knowledge of the provider, patients may be uncomfortable with disclosing certain information necessary for the medical provider to make a comprehensive health assessment. Lack of communication either on the part of the provider or on the part of the patient is likely to result in the patient receiving substandard care. Although, it may be uncomfortable to disclose or discuss personal information, disclosure is crucial when it comes to health and healthcare. The provider-patient relationship, like all relationships, requires clear lines of communication and understanding. Failure on either end to establish clear communication will often lead to poor health outcomes.

In addition to a shortage of LGBT culturally competent providers, the LGBT community faces "legal discrimination in access to health insurance, employment, housing, marriage, adoption, and retirement benefits" (Healthy People 2020, 2015). Some of these areas are being highlighted in new federal and state laws, but the nation is making slow progress. Healthcare professionals should be aware of the detrimental effects these issues may have on LGBT individuals and their family members.

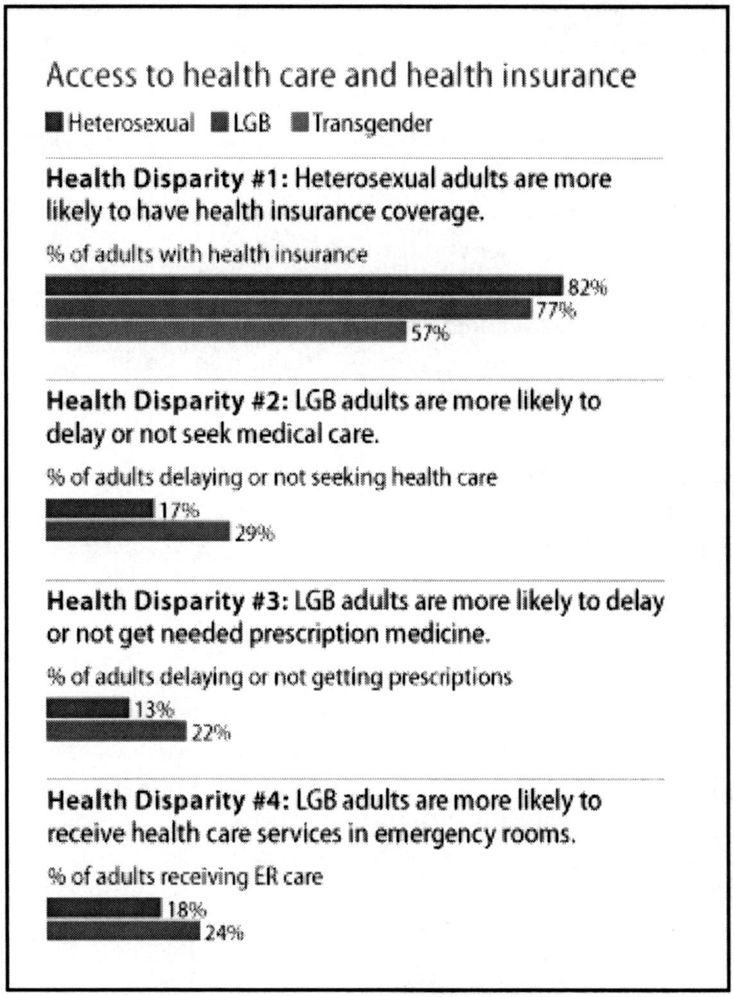

Table 1: Access to health care and health insurance. (2014). "How to Close the LGBT Healthcare Gap." *Center for American Progress.* Retrieved from http://www.americanprogress.org/issues/lgbt/report/2009/12/21/7048/how-to-close-the-lgbt-health-disparities-gap/

The LGBT community is at a higher risk for mental health issues, substance abuse, attempted suicide, HIV and other STDs, obesity, tobacco and alcohol use, victimization and isolation (Healthy People 2020, 2015). Yet, this population is also less likely to have health insurance, due to legal discrimination against same-sex partnerships. In the past decade, the LGBT population has made significant progress in advancing their equal rights.

There are several reasons that LGBT people lack health insurance. First, due workplace discrimination and harassment, LGBT people are more likely to quit or lose their jobs or to not get hired at all. In the U.S., the insurance system is largely employer based. Thus, due to the high cost of purchasing private health insurance and the barriers of accessing insurance coverage, many people in this community go without coverage (Center for American Progress, 2014). Secondly, many employers do not recognize same-sex partnerships and therefore, will not offer insurance to a gay or lesbian domestic partner (Center for American

Progress, 2014). Thirdly, insurance plans are exclusive and therefore do not cover the specific care that may be needed for a LGBT patient (Center for American Progress, 2014). Contributing to the disparities, discrimination among healthcare providers ultimately leads LGBT people to forgo preventative treatments. Additionally, without insurance people are less likely to be able to afford screening and prevention for illness and disease. Ultimately, the result is delay of treatment. More focus must be placed on the development and implementation of anti-discrimination public policy, healthcare research, and cultural competency training among healthcare professionals (Center for American Progress, 2014). See Table 1 for rates comparing access to care of LGBT and heterosexuals.

Transgender Individuals and Access to Care

It should be noted that the literature concerning health care provider attitudes towards transgender people is quite limited, as this group is not frequently broken out within the LGBT community. However, from the existing literature, one can clearly note the barriers to care and apparent inequities. For example, a study conducted with transgender participants noted that 33% delayed or did not attempt to get preventative care due to discrimination by healthcare providers (Grant, et. al., 2011). Transgender discrimination should not be underestimated as a barrier to care (Norton and Herek, 2012, as noted by Poteat, et al., 2013). Norton and Herek found that attitudes toward transgender people are significantly less favorable than toward LGB people (Norton and Herek, 2012, as noted by Poteat, et al., 2013).

Even when transgender people are able to access health care, the care they receive is often far from high quality. A statewide needs-assessment conducted in Virginia (Xavier, Hannold, Bradford, & Simmons, 2007) found that 46% of transgender respondents had to educate their regular doctors about their health care needs. The National Transgender Discrimination Survey (NTDS) of over 6,000 transgender and gender non-conforming individuals throughout the U.S. found that 50% of respondents reported having to teach their medical providers about transgender care (Grant, et. al., 2011). Beyond this lack of clinical competence, some transgender people experience outright mistreatment from medical providers. Lambda Legal (2009) found that 20.9% of transgender respondents had been subjected to harsh language, and 20.3% of them reported being blamed for their own health problems. Fifteen percent reported that health care professionals refused to touch them or used excessive precautions, and 7.8% experienced physically rough or abusive treatment by a medical provider (Lambda Legal, 2009). The prevalence of mistreatment among transgender respondents was twice that of lesbian, gay, and bisexual respondents (Poteat, et al., 2013).

WRAP-UP:

It is imperative that students and professionals alike consider the health risks and specific needs of the LGBT community when dealing with its members in a healthcare setting. Through the process of becoming culturally proficient, one begins to understand and apply what he/she has learned about LGBT individuals. It is up to healthcare professionals to ensure that discrimination does not occur. Thus, it is your job to ensure quality healthcare for all individuals, regardless of gender and sexual orientation.

CLASSROOM CASE STUDY

Real-Life Case Discussion: Interview with Jody Huckaby, Executive Director of PFLAG Organization conducted October 2, 2013

Interview Introductions:

Parents, Families, and Friends or Lesbians and Gays (PFLAG), is a national non-profit organization that is over 40 years old. A straight mother of a gay son who had come out to his parents founded the organization. His parents were extremely supportive. The son was attacked at a rally in New York City. His mother decided that something needed to be done to bring an end to the harassment of gays. In 1972, she began to gather support from other parents and friends, and eventually she founded PFLAG with the intent to support the LGBT community, educate people regarding LGBT issues, and to advocate. Today there are 350 chapters of this organization with over 200,000 supporters. The mission of the national organization is three fold: support branches and LGBT individuals, educate communities, and advocate for legislative change. (See more at: www.PFLAG.org)

Interview Content and Answers:

What are the components that may work into acceptance for young members of the LGBT community?

Acceptance has multiple layers and must happen on multiple levels. It must occur with families, friends, classmates, colleagues, etc. Acceptance begins at home with families. For LGBT youth, acceptance at schools is extremely important. In order to combat issues that plague LGBT youth: suicide, drug and alcohol abuse, depression, etc. schools must take a lead in anti-bullying policies, enforcement, and monitoring. Acceptance is a big part of mental health!

What can healthcare students do to educate themselves on the topic?

Students should stay abreast of current topics and trends. Students should stay educated and get a head start on being LGBT culturally competent prior to entering the field of healthcare. Once working in the field they should make an effort to grow this competency level and stay on top of issues concerning the LGBT community. Staying current means knowing what is happening at the U.S. congressional level in healthcare and reform that may have an impact on the community. Don't be afraid to have dialogue with community members about what is appropriate. Whether you are a provider or not, you can do your part to facilitate equitable and quality care in a welcoming environment. Be open and accepting!

What do you see as the biggest barriers to quality healthcare being provided to the LGBT community?

The biggest barrier is inequality. There is not civil equality for LGBT community members. There currently is no foundation for this community and its protection against disparities in the legislation. This is an enormous issue and something that should be examined and corrected on a national scale.

Another huge contributing factor is the lack of education. There are too many people who do not understand the unique issues facing the LGBT community. Furthermore, there is little concern for the community at large. There is need for a cultural change when it comes to acceptance of the community and a willingness to confront these issues.

What can healthcare organizations do to lessen the discrimination and minimize barriers to quality care? What can government do? What can individuals do?

There has not been enough research conducted between the connection of mental issues and the frequency of substance abuse and depression among the LGBT community. Efforts need to be expanded and supported.

More research will lead to better education on the topic, greater awareness, and eventually a lowered incidence of depression and substance abuse among the community, where it currently runs rampant.

Dr. Caitlyn Ryan has published research on the topic of parental acceptance of Y (Youth) LGBT and likelihood of mental health risks. Further research will have an impact on lessening the negative image and social stigma that follows LGBT and particularly YLGBT, who are facing coming out in their home life and in their schools.

If you had one message to give to healthcare students about this topic and its importance, what would it be?

Do your part and keep yourself current and educated. Don't be afraid to be an advocate!

What is PFLAG 's role in the education healthcare professionals?

PFLAG aims to lay the foundation for open communication pathways between healthcare providers and the LGBT community. We seek to build relationships and understanding from both sides. This means helping organizations analyze their own culture and attitudes of acceptance. For example, does the healthcare organization have a non-discrimination policy? Do the intake forms include LGBT categories and demographic options? If not, what message are we sending? If I can't be "out", I will edit my information to the provider?

Furthermore, it is important to understand if the organization is training healthcare professionals to be thoughtful. An open and accepting healthcare environment begins at the first point of contact with the patient. For example, the front desk person asks personal questions aloud that should be asked privately. This small example could set the stage in creating barriers. Questions that may be perceived to be personal should be asked in private and the questioning should be appropriate. It is the responsibility of the organization to create an open culture, to train providers, and to influence change on a larger level. All change begins with education and advocacy. This is PFLAG's focus.

We encourage advocacy on all levels. Healthcare professions can act locally to advocate for the LGBT community. PFLAG seeks to make education and training materials accessible and relevant. We attempt to make our presence known in the medical community through conference exhibits, local and national education sessions, and the distribution of materials for streamlining and ensuring the delivery of quality healthcare services to the LGBT community.

In an environment where quality drives the healthcare world, PFLAG attempts to help healthcare organizations and providers understand the impact that disparities may have on an organization's productivity and reimbursement. In appealing to a competitively driven workforce, we help organizations and providers understand that inclusion is fundamental to being the best.

There is the Straight for Equality in Healthcare Website. What is the role of the program and is it working?

Straight For Equality is a start. It skims the surface. The purpose is to make the connection and spark interest. We aim to create the relevancy around what providers may be interested and then we appeal to the issues of the LGBT community. This creates an appeal to why healthcare professionals should pay attention to these issues. PFLAG aims to educate and change the culture of a healthcare environment that lacks acceptance and education. We want to change that culture from the inside. The site is a conversation starter for this agenda. It appeals to providers' sense of altruism and connects it with lessening disparities while increasing quality care and provider performance. The same holds true for making the connection with students of healthcare. I encourage them to think about why they are choosing healthcare as a profession. Somewhere in the answer to that, it is common for people to say that they want to help people. This should include helping ALL people.

Congress is currently working on the Federal law: Health Disparities in LGBT Americans Act. What are your thoughts about this moving forward?

There is a lot of hope in Affordable Care Act's ability to address some of the barriers and disparities. However, the disparities cannot be minimized through legislation alone. Education needs to be consistent and constant. This means educating families, communities, and medical organizations and providers. Commitments should be made from legislators, family members, activists, teachers, and individuals to ensure equality.

The LGBT community itself needs to be more actively engaged in the issues around equality. There is a lack of engagement and advocacy work on the part of LGBT community members. Only a small number are willing to speak out and get involved. This may be due to stigma and the threat of not being socially accepted.

Section 1557 is the civil rights provision of the Patient Protection and Affordable Care Act. PFLAG is currently working with the Office of Health and Human Services (HHS) to ensure affordable and equitable quality care is provided for everyone. PFLAG is helping to push this Act through and to make it as effective as possible in combating disparities. Federal legislation will impact and improve access to care.

CLASSROOM ACTIVITIES:

The following activities include discussions, scenarios and exercises that can be utilized during or outside of class.

Activity 1: Practice Brochure

a. Design a LGBT practice brochure:
   You are a practice administrator for a Primary Care Clinic in downtown San Francisco. The market area location of the clinic has a high percentage of LGBT healthcare consumers.

b. Develop 3-5 objectives for becoming a LGBT competent and friendly community practice.

c. Design a functional practice website that will attract potential LGBT patients.

d. In-class discussion:
   Explain your design in both the brochure and the website and why/how it will help to attract this patient population. How will it help the practice achieve the objectives set?

Activity 2: Scenario and discussion questions

You are a young gay professional, who recently has relocated to (Oklahoma, Utah, Kansas, Kentucky, South Carolina, or Nebraska).

Find each of the following in your community:

- A community center offering support groups
- A gay church, social network or club
- A community health resource
- A dental health resource

Activity 3: The Gender Identity Continuum

Have all individuals in the group stand up. Have one person from the group step out. Tell this person that they need to put the group in order across a continuum from "most masculine" to "most feminine."

After the group is in line ask if the students agree with the placement. Would they have placed themselves differently? Why or why not? What does this tell us about gender identity perceptions and assumptions?

Activity 4: Case Suggestion and/or Role-play (In class exercise)

A transgender patient comes into the medical office. The patient, who is named Stacey, is dressed as a female but is male. Dr. Barnes, the clinician assigned to the patient tells you, the administrator, that he is not comfortable seeing a transgender patient. He asks you to change his schedule and assign this patient to his team member, Dr. Han. As the administrator, would you follow through on his request? Why or why not?

Students may be assigned a role to play in this scenario. In groups of four, they may play the part of the administrator, Stacey, Dr. Han, Dr. Barnes.

Activity 5: Discussion Question

As a healthcare manager, what do you see as your role in facilitating quality care for LGBT individuals? How do you plan to fulfill this role?

Activity 6: Exploration of Topics

Students may choose to explore the following topics further through literature review and additional research: access to health services, Healthy People 2020 agenda for the LGBT community, LGBT adolescent health concerns, HIV and AIDS, mental health and mental disorders, substance abuse issues of the LGBT community, and reparative and restorative therapy.

Activity 7: Website Exploration I

In groups or individually, students will explore the Straight for Equality Website at www.straightforequality.org

Step 1: Discuss two to three resources found within the website. Navigate the site for the class. Explain to the class why the links/resources you found are useful; what recommendations do you have for the class for using the resources found on the site? Were there other areas within the site that were interesting to you and/or your group? What are they and why?

Step 2: Why is it important to address the health disparities of this group?

What are some key ways that these issues may be addressed from a government standpoint, organizational, community, and individual? What efforts would be made by each stakeholder and why?

Activity 8: Website Exploration II

In groups or individually, students will explore the following website: Council for Responsible at the Council for Responsible Genetics. http://www.councilforresponsiblegenetics.org

Present to the class a brief summary of one of the topics of interest explored within the website. What relevancy does the topic explored have on the LGBT community? What can be learned from this issue/topic? What recommendations do you have in addressing the issues presented?

Activity 9: Website Exploration

We All Count at Queercensus.org

Explore the above website and respond to the following discussion. What impact does census inclusion have on the LGBT community? Do you think this affects the healthcare issues discussed in this chapter? Why or why not?

Activity 10: Bullying

Research has also shown that up to 78% of transgender individuals were harassed in school, with 50% being rejected by their families (Grant, et. al., 2011). One can only imagine the mental stress of such emotional turmoil.

You are a recently hired school principal who is addressing the issue of bullying in school. Develop a plan for an anti-bullying campaign that includes gay, lesbian, and transgender youth.

Activity 11: Healthcare Organization Ranking

Review The Healthcare Equality Index, which ranks healthcare organizations regarding LGBT care issues. Present to the class a healthcare organization in your geographic area that was ranked high on the index. Explore the organization's website and comment on the ability to provide equitable care. Additional ideas: Interview someone from this organization on the issues of equality at their organization.

Activity 12: Coming Out Letter

Explore the following resources below. Then write a letter as a LGBT youth to a family member stating your feelings about "coming out." OR write a letter from a bully apologizing for victimizing a LGBT youth at school. In a brief summary explain how writing this letter made you feel.

Research led primarily by Caitlyn Ryan, PhD, ACSW through the Family Acceptance Project at familyproject.sfsu.edu

Of particular note are the following:

"Family Rejection as a Predictor of Negative Health Outcomes in White and Latino Lesbian, Gay, and Bisexual Young Adults" in Pediatrics, Volume 123, No. 1, January 1, 2009

"Family Acceptance in Adolescence and the Health of LGBT Young Adults" at www.familyproject.sfsu.edu in the Journal of Child and Adolescent Psychiatric Nursing, Volume 23, Number 4, November 2010

"Lesbian, Gay, Bisexual and Transgender Adolescent School Victimization: Implications for Young Adult Health and Adjustment" at Familyproject.sfsu.edu

Catherine Tuerk, MA. R.N., C.S. and Edgardo Menvielle, M.D. and James de Jesus "If You Are Concerned About Your Child's Gender Behaviors: A Guide for Parents" at www.childrensnational.org

Gender and Sexuality Psychosocial Programs at Children's National Medical Center at www.childrensnational.org

Dr. Menvielle's and Catherine Tuerk's published work at www.childrensnational.org

In 2012, Catherine Tuerk published "Mom Knows: Reflections on Love, Gay Pride and Taking Action at www.catherinetuerk.com

Activity 13: Policy Letter

Explore the below resources. Write a letter to either your Congressman about current public policy issues that should analyzed in support of the LGBT community equity effort OR write a letter to the president of an organization, which does not provide equitable healthcare services to the LGBT community based on organizational and cultural beliefs. Your letter should be an appeal for equity.

The project, Out2Enroll at www.sellersdorseyfoundation.org has been created to educate the LGBT community about healthcare coverage options under the ACA and the projected impact on LGBT healthcare.

Joint statement by the Center for American Progress, the Sellers Dorsey Foundation and the Federal Agencies Project on Out2Enroll. September 12, 2013 at www.americanprogress.org

The Joint Commission's "Advancing Effective Communication, Cultural Competence, and Patient-and Family-Centered Care" at www.jointcommission.org

RESOURCES:

LGBT Health Websites:

Gay and Lesbian Medical Association
http://www.glma.org

National Coalition for LGBT Health
http://lgbthealth.webolutionary.com/home

National Gay and Lesbian Task Force
http://www.thetaskforce.org

Centers for Disease Control and Prevention – Lesbian Gay Bisexual and Transgender Health
http://www.cdc.gov/lgbthealth/

Human Rights Campaign
http://www.hrc.org

The Williams Institute
http://williamsinstitute.law.ucla.edu

The Mautner Project: The National Lesbian Health Organization
http://mautnerproject.org

Cultural Competency:

Ard K, and Makadon H. Improving the Health Care of Lesbian, Gay, Bisexual and Transgender (LGBT) People: Understanding and Eliminating Health Disparities. The Fenway Institute, Fenway Health, 2012. http://www.lgbthealtheducation.org/publications/lgbt-health-resources/

Advancing Effective Communication, Cultural Competence, and Patient- and Family-Centered Care for the Lesbian, Gay, Bisexual, and Transgender (LGBT) Community: A Field Guide. (The Joint Commission) http://www.jointcommission.org/assets/1/18/LGBTFieldGuide.pdf

Guidelines for the care of Lesbian, Gay, Bisexual, and Transgender Patients (Gay and Lesbian Medical Association) http://safezone.sdes.ucf.edu/docs/glma-guidelines.pdf

A Provider's Handbook on Culturally Competent Care: Lesbian, Gay, Bisexual and Transgendered Population (Kaiser Permanente National Diversity Council) http://kphci.org/downloads/KP.PHandbook.LGBT.2nd.2004.pdf

Bonvicini KA, Perlin MJ. The Same but Different: Clinician-Patient Communication with Gay and Lesbian Patients. Patient Education and Counseling. 2003; 51:115-122.

Engaging with Men Who Have Sex with Men in the Clinical Setting: A Primer for Physicians, Nurses, and other Health Care Providers (Global Forum on MSM & HIV)

Reaching Out to Other Special Populations: Providing Services to Gay, Lesbian, Bisexual and Transgender Patients (National Association of Community Health Centers. Special Population Series' Information Bulletin #11) http://www.lgbthealtheducation.org/publications/lgbt-health-resources/

Providing Services to LGBT Patients (National Association of Community Health Centers) http://www.nachc.com/ProvidingServicestoLGBTPatients.cfm

Garnero, TL. Providing Culturally Sensitive Diabetes Care and Education for the Lesbian, Gay, Bisexual, and Transgender (LGBT) Community. Diabetes Spectrum. 2010; 23(3).

Top Health Issues for LGBT Populations Information & Resource Kit. Substance Abuse and Mental Health Services Administration, 2012. http://store.samhsa.gov/shin/content/SMA12-4684/SMA12-4684.pdf

Posters promoting GLBT health care access; brochures on cancer and GLBT people (GLBT Health Access Project) http://www.glbthealth.org/HAPMaterials.htm

Sample Non-Discrimination Policies (Human Rights Campaign) http://www.hrc.org/resources/entry/sample-employment-non-discrimination-policies

Self-Assessment Checklist for Personnel Providing Services and Supports to LGBTQ Youth and Their Families. National Center for Cultural Competence, Georgetown University Center for Child and Human Development, 2012. http://nccc.georgetown.edu/documents/Final%20LGBTQ%20Checklist.pdf

National Healthcare Disparities Report 2013. http://www.ahrq.gov/research/findings/nhqrdr/nhdr13/2013nhdr.pdf

When Health Care Isn't Caring. Results from Lambda Legal's Health Care Fairness Survey. Lamda Legal, 2009. http://www.lambdalegal.org/sites/default/files/publications/downloads/whcic-report_when-health-care-isnt-caring_1.pdf

Grant JM, Mottet LA, Tanis J. Injustice at Every Turn: A Report of the National Transgender Discrimination Survey. National Center for Transgender Equality and the National Gay and Lesbian Task Force, 2011. http://www.thetaskforce.org/static_html/downloads/reports/reports/ntds_full.pdf

REFERENCES:

American Psychological Association (2013). Sexuality and Transgender. Retrieved from http://apa.org/topics/sexuality/transgender.aspx

American Psychological Association (2008). Sexual Orientation, Homosexuality, and Bisexuality. Retrieved from http://www.apa.org/helpcenter/sexual-orientation.aspx

Center for American Progress (2014). How to Close the LGBT Healthcare Disparities Gap. Retrieved from http://www.americanprogress.org/issues/lgbt/report/2009/12/21/7048/how-to-close-the-lgbt-health-disparities-gap/

Centers for Disease Control and Prevention (2011). Diagnoses of HIV infection in the United States and Dependent Areas. HIV Surveillance Report, Volume 23. Retrieved from http://www.cdc.gov/hiv/library/reports/surveillance/index.html

Centers for Disease Control and Prevention (2010). Gay and Bisexual Health, Viral Hepatitis. Retrieved from http://www.cdc.gov/msmhealth/viral-hepatitis.htm.

Center for Substance Abuse Treatment (revised 2012). A Provider's Introduction to Substance Abuse Treatment for Lesbian, Gay, Bisexual, and Transgender Individuals Retrieved at http://store.samhsa.gov/shin/content//SMA12-4104/SMA12-4104.pdf

Cheng (2003) as noted in the Pride Institute (2013). Retrieved from http://pride-institute.com/about/why-lgbt-treatment/

Cisgender (n.d.). Oxford Dictionaries. Retrieved from http://www.oxforddictionaries.com/us/definition/american_english/cisgender

Dionne, S.I., (2002). Gay and Lesbian Health Issues. Retrieved from http://health.yahoo.net/galecontent/gay-and-lesbian-health

Eliason M.J. (2010). Identity formation for lesbian, bisexual, and gay persons: Beyond a "minoritizing" view. Journal of Homosexuality. 1996;30(3):31–58.

Grant J., Mottet L.A., & Tanis, J. (2011). Injustice at Every Turn: A Report of the National Transgender Discrimination Survey. Washington: National Center for Transgender Equality and National Gay and 13. Lesbian Task Force, 2011. Available at: www.thetaskforce.org/downloads/reports/reports/ntds_full.pdf

Gates, Gary J. (2011). How many people are lesbian, gay, bisexual and transgender? The Williams Institute on Sexual Orientation and Gender Identity Law and Public Policy at UCLA School of Law. Retrieved from http://williamsinstitute.law.ucla.edu/wp-content/uploads/Gates-How-Many-People-LGBT-Apr-2011.pdf

Healthy People 2020. (2015). "Gay, Lesbian, and Transgender Health." Retrieved from http://www.healthypeople.gov/2020/topicsobjectives2020/overview.aspx?topicid=25

Huckaby, J., PFLAG Organization, personal communication, October 2, 2013.

Institute of Medicine (2001). "The Health of Lesbian, Gay, Bisexual, and Transgender People Building a Foundation for Better Understanding." Retrieved from http://www.ncbi.nlm.nih.gov/books/NBK64806/pdf/TOC.pdf

Lambda Legal (2009). When healthcare isn't caring. When Health Care Isn't Caring. Results from Lambda Legal's Health Care Fairness Survey. http://www.lambdalegal.org/publications/when-health-care-isnt-caring

Leible, A. (2013). Pride Institute, "Why LGBT Treatment?" Retrieved from http://pride-institute.com/about/why-lgbt-treatment/

Poteat, T., German, D., & Kerrigan, D. (2013). Managing uncertainty: A grounded theory of stigma in transgender health care encounters. Social Science and Medicine, 84, pp. 22-29.

Schatz, B., & O'Hanlan, K. (1994). Anti-gay discrimination in medicine: Results of a national survey of lesbian, gay, and bisexual physicians. San Francisco, CA: American Association of Physicians for Human Rights/Gay Lesbian Medical Association.

Xavier J, Honnold, J.A., & Bradford, J. (2007). The Health, Health-Related Needs, and Lifecourse Experiences of Transgender Virginians. Virginia HIV Planning Committee and Virginia Department of Health. Retrieved from www.vdh.virginia.gov/epidemiology/diseaseprevention/documents/pdf/THISFINALREPORTVol1.pdf

Chapter 8:

The Elderly Population and the Consumption of Care

Aly Eisenhardt and Susanne Ninassi

KEY CONCEPTS:

Ageism
Activities of Daily Living
Alzheimer's Disease
Baby Boom
Baby Boomers
Baby Boom Generation
Chronic Disease
Co-Morbidity
Degenerative Illness
Dementia
Dual eligible
Elder abuse
Elder mistreatment
Gerontology
Instrumental Activities of Daily Living
Medicaid
Program of All-Inclusive Care for the Elderly
Sandwich generation

CHAPTER OVERVIEW:

With the baby-boomer population growing older, the elderly population is due to be at an all-time high. Although life expectancy is increasing and overall health for most Americans is improving, inequalities still exist. Healthcare disparities among all minorities, including the elderly, as a defined population are a true concern. Contributing to health disparities among older Americans is that fact that our nation's healthcare professionals still lack the appropriate and specific geriatric training to properly treat this population. Healthcare professionals must understand the specific social, mental, and physical needs of the aging population.

CHAPTER EXPECTATIONS:

Upon reading this chapter, the student will be able to:

- Apply an understanding of ageism and elder abuse, as well as their effects on the elderly population, to real world scenarios.
- Critically analyze the factors that contribute to healthcare disparities among the elderly.
- Characterize the various settings where elderly persons may choose to reside and understand the social, mental and physical effects each environment may have on the individual.
- Analyze the barriers to care for this population.

INTRODUCTION AND HISTORICAL CONTEXT:

The Elderly Population and the Consumption of Care

The 2010 Census recorded that the population of people age 65 and over equaled approximately 40 million or 13% of the total population (U.S. Census Bureau as cited in NCEA, "Statistic Data" n.d.). It is predicted that by 2030, the population will grow to reach more than 19% of the population (AOA, "Profile of Older Americans"2012) and that by 2050, 19 million Americans will be aged 85 or older (U.S. Census Bureau as cited in NCEA, "Statistic Data" n.d.). The enormous growth of the elderly population is being compounded by two main factors: longer life spans and the aging of the baby boomers (CDC, 2013). The "**Baby Boom**," an "explosion" of births that took place after the Second World War ended and American Soldiers came home to their wives (U.S. Census, 2006). The generation born in the post WWII era is consequently often referred to as the **Baby Boomer Generation.**

The growth of the aging population places a larger demand on the already strained American healthcare system. As indicated above, the elderly account for 12% of the U.S. population, but comprise one-third the cost of hospital stays (Weir, Pfuntner & Steiner, 2008). The elderly consume public health, medical, and social services at a greater proportion than younger Americans. The cost of providing healthcare to the elderly is three to five times greater than the cost spent to care for younger adults (Weir, Pfuntner & Steiner, 2008).

The reason for the high healthcare spending among this population is that a large portion of this population suffers from chronic conditions, which are costly to treat and involve long-term healthcare planning and delivery. A **chronic disease** is a disease that can be controlled or treated, but not cured. It is the leading cause of death and disability in the United States today. The CDC (2013) reports a major shift in the leading causes of death for all age groups from 1900 to 2000. The shift is from infectious disease and acute illness to chronic diseases and degenerative illnesses. A **degenerative illness** is an illness or disease that causes deterioration of body tissue or organs and results in loss of function over time. Two out of three older Americans suffer from multiple chronic conditions, or **co-morbidity,** which means to suffer from multiple chronic conditions (CDC, 2013). Treatment for patients with chronic diseases accounts for 66% of U.S. healthcare spending (CDC, 2013).

Although the risk of chronic disease does increase with age, prevention may help delay or eliminate the onset of associated conditions (CDC, 2013). Furthermore, the causes of chronic conditions usually occur early in life. Illness and injury prevention should be a key focus for this population as it is for other populations as well. Prevention is important not only to prolong life, but also to lessen the decline in functioning and maintaining quality of life (Takahashi, 2004). As noted by Schonberg (2008), women ages 80 plus were less likely to be screened for depression, osteoporosis, or counseled about exercise than younger women. However, the same group was more likely to receive counseling about falls and/or incontinence (Schonberg, 2008). It is critical that healthcare professionals understand all issues around geriatric health. Furthermore, the healthcare decision-making should be made in cooperation with elderly patients. For example, whether or not to provide certain types of preventative care is a decision that should not be made based on provider assumptions about older patients and their lifestyles.

WHAT YOU SHOULD KNOW:

Ageism

One must consider why the quality of care for the elderly population is often poor and inefficient. As such, ageism might be one factor and the consideration of it should be discussed. **Ageism** is stereotyping and prejudice against individuals or groups because of their age, especially the elderly (Merriam-Webster, 2013). It is a term used to describe discrimination against seniors, or those over 65 years of age. "Societal norms marginalize seniors, treat them with disrespect, make them feel unwelcome and otherwise generalize as if they were all the same" (ALFA, "Ageism" 2013).

Again, like other forms of discrimination, ageism can be intentional or unintentional. For example, a physician discussing the senior patient's healthcare with the patient's adult child as if the senior was not present in the room exhibits an example of ageism (ALFA, "Ageism" 2013). This type of discrimination robs the elderly "...of choice, independence, dignity and negatively impacts their quality of life" (ALFA, "Ageism" 2013). Although, the behavior of the physician may be unintentionally causing harm, harm is still done.

The presence of ageism in the U.S. healthcare system may lead to a lack in prevention, quality, denials of surgery, and overall substandard healthcare delivery. Older patients are complex and may be on multiple medications, making them susceptible to medication errors. This issue is exacerbated by the lack of geriatric-specific clinical research being conducted, and a shortage of geriatric specialists in the healthcare field (Fiolova, 2009). It is predicted that there will be a shortage of 130,000 physicians across all specialties by the year 2025 (Perlata, 2013). To add to this shortage, there are only approximately 7,000 specialized physicians, who are trained in geriatrics throughout the United States. It is estimated that this is only half of what is needed currently and thus, significantly less than what might be anticipated to fulfill the future medical needs of the growing elderly population (Perlata, 2013).

Cultural competency is the key to ensuring equitable healthcare delivery, regardless of a patient's age. Education should be multi-faceted to include patients, caregivers, provider, and politicians. Recent studies show that the elderly receive less aggressive treatment and medical care than younger patients. Yet seniors are greater consumers of healthcare than the younger population (Shi et al. 2008). The non-elderly consumes nearly three times less than the elderly in overall health care costs (Shi et al. 2008). A contributing factor is longer stays in the hospital for older patients. In fact, the average length of stay (LOS) in the hospital for the elderly patient (65 plus) was almost a full day greater than the rate for patients of all ages. Furthermore, the average LOS increases with age (AOA, 2012).

By providing seamless quality of care, and treating the "whole" patient, regardless of age, healthcare cost may be controlled and the patient experience will be enhanced. The elderly patient should feel empowered to facilitate their healthcare delivery and outcomes within a safe environment.

Living Arrangements

With consideration of the "whole" patient, the social and emotional well being of the patient should be considered. The living environment circumstances of the elderly patient may play a large role in the patient's health and thus, should be a notable factor. The living arrangements for the elderly include living in a non-institutionalized setting with a spouse or another person (i.e. grandchild), living alone, or living in an institutional setting. According to the Administration on Aging, over half, or 57%, of the elderly population in the U.S. (13.2 million or 72% of older men and 10.3 million or 45% of older women) lived with their spouse in a non-institutionalized setting (AOA, "Profile of Older Americans" 2012). During the same year, approximately 11.8 million, or 28%, of all non-institutionalized elderly persons lived alone (AOA, "Profile of Older Americans" 2012).

Elderly requiring some assistance with **Activities Daily Living Activities (ADLs)**, which are basic self-care tasks (i.e., grooming, bathing, dressing, etc.) may choose to live in Assisted Living Communities. Furthermore, some older adults, who need assistance with **Instrumental Activities of Daily Living (IADLs)**, which are complex skills required for independent living (i.e.; managing medications, paying bills, etc.) may also choose to live in Assisted Living Communities. These communities are largely paid for through out-of-pocket expenses and can be very costly. Thus, causing a financial strain on an elderly person, who is in need of some assistance. Alternatively, an independent living setting is for those who require no assistance with ADLs, but who prefer the community setting and access to the convenience of service, such as housekeeping, transportation, meals, etc. Independent living is paid for as a monthly rental and normally requires residents to "buy-into" the facility through the purchase of an apartment or condominium.

Due to the expense of the above-discussed options, many elderly live with their adult children, who become their caregivers. Adult child caregivers of elderly parents are often referred to as the **sandwich generation**, because they are caring for their own children as well as their aging parents. In addition, in 2011, it is estimated 2 million older people lived in a household with a grandchild and about 497,000 of these grandparents had primary responsibility for the care of their grandchildren (AOA, "Profile of Older Americans" 2012). In 2011, only 1.5 million or, 3.6%, of the population 65 and over lived in institutional settings (AOA, "Profile of Older Americans" 2012). Yet, this number increases "...dramatically with age, ranging (in 2011) from 1% for persons 65-74 years to 3% for persons 75-84 years and 11% for persons 85+. In addition, in 2009, approximately 2.7% of the elderly lived in senior housing with at least one supportive service available to their residents" (AOA, "Profile of Older Americans" 2012).

An elderly person in need of greater medical care, may have the option to seek home healthcare, which may be covered in-part through Medicare and/or supplemental insurance. Additionally, those who need 24 hour care may be admitted to a skilled nursing facility. Nursing homes may provide long-term care or acute rehabilitation. The services are often paid for through Medicare and/or Medicaid. Medicaid funding is limited to those in financial need. For this reason, elderly in need of fulltime nursing home care may be forced to "spend-down" their money to prove that there is a "financial need" as well as a medical need for a skilled nursing facility.

The choice of a living arrangement impacts the well being of the elderly (Borsch-Supan et al. 1994). For example, if the elderly person is ill, living alone makes dealing with the illness more difficult; yet living with family eases the situation (Borsch-Supan et al. 1994). Moreover, living arrangements impact the eligibility for government assistance, such as food stamps and supplemental Social Security, as well as demand for social support services such as district nursing and meals-on- wheels (Borsch-Supan et al. 1994). It is expected that one of the main predictors for the selection of living arrangements is health (Borsch-Supan et al. 1994).

Defining the Needs of the Elderly

Although it is well known that older people generally possess a variety of compound and multifaceted social and physical health needs, research notes that 75% of elderly patients have a minimum of one chronic condition and approximately 50% of this population suffers from co-morbidity, possessing at least two chronic conditions (AHQR, 2009). As previously discussed, having multiple medical conditions means managing multiple medications, with some elderly patients being prescribed upwards of 10 different medications per day (AHRQ, 2009). It is easy to understand the margin for error by both the patient and the clinician in these cases.

For the reasons discussed above, elderly patients are often complex and costly to treat. However, if not treated properly, they may become only a statistic in the "revolving door scenario." Take the example of an elderly patient being treated in the Emergency Department (ED) and then sent home with new medications. The patient may have vision problems and the writing on the prescription is small. Did the nurse ask if the patient understood the medication instructions? If not, the patient may take the mediation wrongly and end up back in the ED or worse. Thus, the "revolving door."

As reported by Levy (2013), the following health risks are associated with the aging population:

- Chronic diseases
- Alzheimer's disease and other Dementias
- Arthritis
- Depression
- Psychiatric disorders
- Osteoporosis
- Parkinson's disease
- Urinary incontinence
- Anxiety
- Cancer
- Eye problems
- Diabetes

The elderly population is also at risk for developing dementia. **Dementia** is a term used to describe a range of symptoms related to memory loss and a reduction in cognitive skills. Impairments caused by dementia may affect the following: memory, communication and language, ability to focus and pay attention, reasoning and judgment, and visual perception (Alzheimer's Association, 2013).

Alzheimer's Disease is a specific type of dementia that causes progressive problems with memory, thinking, and behavior. It is the most common dementia-related disease, accounts for the majority of dementia cases. Alzheimer's and dementia are not a part of the normal aging process.

Although among the elderly the risk of illness and disease does increase with age, poor health is not an inevitable consequence of getting older (CDC, "Health Aging," 2011). There are some common side effects of aging that healthcare professionals should be aware of and able to recognize. As the body ages, for example: reaction time is slower, the immune system is weakened, the skin is thinner, and the sense of taste and smell is diminished (Levy, 2013). These body changes impact the overall health and well being of the individual.

Healthcare Costs

Medicare is the insurance utilized by most elderly Americans (Federal Interagency Forum "Older Americans 2012 Key Factors" 2012). It is a federally funded program that provides care for those who are 65 and older. It covers a variety of services, including inpatient hospital care, physician services, hospital outpatient care, home health care, skilled nursing facility care, hospice services, and prescription drugs (Medicaid.gov 2013). Some elderly patients are **dual eligible**, which means they are eligible for both Medicare and Medicaid. Medicaid is a program that provides healthcare services for the poor and disabled. The program is subsidized through both state and federal governments.

More than any other group, the elderly utilize more health care per capita and the "per capita costs are increasing as the "Baby Boom" generation is approaching retirement age" (Federal Interagency Forum "Older Americans 2012 Key Factors" 2012). These costs are impacted by: "demographic" characteristics (e.g. low-income individuals incurred higher health care costs)

- "demographic" characteristics (e.g. low-income individuals incurred higher health care costs)
- health status (e.g. "Individuals with no chronic conditions incurred $5,520 in health care costs on average. Those with five or more conditions incurred $24,658. Average costs among residents of long-term care facilities were $61,318, compared with only $13,150 among community residents.") (Federal Interagency Forum "Older Americans 2012 Key Factors" 2012).

Healthcare costs include the following goods and services (Federal Interagency Forum "Older Americans 2012 Key Factors" 2012):

- inpatient hospital stays,
- physician/outpatient hospital,
- nursing home/long-term institution,
- home healthcare,
- prescription drugs and
- other including short-term institution, hospice and dental.

Of the services listed above, hospital and physician services are the largest components (Federal Interagency Forum "Older Americans 2012 Key Factors" 2012). Long-term care facilities accounted for 12 percent of total costs in 2008. Prescription drugs accounted for 16 percent of health care costs, and average costs per person were $2,834 in 2008 (Federal Interagency Forum "Older Americans 2012 Key Factors" 2012).

Large out-of-pocket expenditures for health care service use have been shown to interfere with access to care. Thus, high out-of pocket costs may ultimately affect health status and quality of life, and leave insufficient resources for other necessities (Federal Interagency Forum "Older Americans 2012 Key Factors" 2012). The older population is burdened with the out of pocket expenditures. Between 1977 and 2009, out of pocket spending for healthcare increased from 83 to 94% for people 65 and over (Federal Interagency Forum "Older Americans 2012 Key Factors" 2012). This is a very real issue that policy makers and healthcare professionals alike should be aware of and should be working together towards a solution.

Healthcare Programs for the Elderly

Recently, with more strain on the healthcare delivery system and costs rising, the government is placing a greater focus on programs that may allow the elderly to "age in place." One such healthcare program for the elderly is the **Program of All-Inclusive Care for the Elderly** (PACE). As part of Medicare and Medicaid, PACE provides a comprehensive long-term service, which entitles the eligible participants to receive needed medical care at home, as opposed to a nursing facility (Medicaid, PACE Programs, 2012). The program benefits are two-fold. Individuals who may otherwise be forced into a dependent living environment are able to receive the same level of care in their homes. Secondly, costly acute-care stays and skilled-nursing stays may be avoided (Wieland et al. 2012).

The PACE program and Pre-PACE programs are now available in approximately 31 states (NPA, "What IS PACE?" 2013). Participation in PACE has shown "an improved care quality, less mortality, preservation of function, fewer unmet assistance needs, greater participant and caregiver satisfaction, less hospital and nursing home (NH) utilization, and lower Medicare costs" (Effects of the Program of All-Inclusive Care for the Elderly on Hospital Use and the Effect of the Program of All-Inclusive Care for the Elderly (PACE) on Quality Final Report cited in Wieland et al. 2012). The programs are showing good outcomes from both cost and health perspectives.

Elder Mistreatment

As the elderly population grows, it is likely the discrimination and abuse against the elderly also may experience an increased incidence. One cannot truly understand the issue of aging and the elderly with considering the reality of "elder mistreatment" (i.e. abuse and neglect). **Elder mistreatment** is defined as "intentional actions that cause harm or create a serious risk of harm (whether or not harm is intended) to a vulnerable elder by a caregiver or other person who stands in a trust relationship to the elder" (NCEA, n.d.). The mistreatment can also be self-inflicted. Mistreatment is not limited to one area of the elderly population, but rather cuts across all including all ethnic backgrounds, men and woman, and social status (NCEA, n.d.).

The abuse is generally divided into six major categories: physical, emotional, sexual, exploitation, neglect, and abandonment (NCEA, "Frequently Asked Questions" n.d.). It is not uncommon for the elderly person to experience multiple forms of abuse at the same occurrence. The number of people experiencing some form of elder abuse is not currently known; yet, it is documented that females experience a higher rate than their male counterparts and "...the older one is the more likely one is to be abused" (NCEA, n.d.). Although, there is no evidence on why this occurs, there is speculation that the older one becomes the more vulnerable one might be due to multiple social, physical, and mental factors.

The scope of abuse among the elderly population is difficult to define. However, a national study that attempted to define the scope of elder abuse noted that the vast majority of abusers, approximately 90%, were family members (The National Elder Abuse Incidence Study: Final Report as cited in NCEA, n.d.). Most often the abusers tend to be adult children, spouses, partners, and others (The National Elder Abuse Incidence Study: Final Report as cited in NCEA, n.d.). Statistics may be inaccurate due to the lack of reporting by victims. Elderly victims may be unwilling or unable to report such crimes due to feeling dependent on family caregivers.

Elder abuse may result in depression, broken bones, sores, bruises, and death (NCEA, "Frequently Asked Questions" n.d.). Because persons experiencing elder abuse are often unable to seek help, friends, family, neighbors, or physicians may be in the best position to recognize and respond to an abusive situation. For this reason, medical professionals must be attuned to recognizing the signs and symptoms of abuse.

Barriers to Seeking Help

Due to the lack of training on detection of abuse, many healthcare professionals may miss the signs of abuse in older Americans (NCEA, n.d.). Signs of abuse may include: depression, withdrawal, and unexplained bodily harm. "The elderly may be reluctant to report abuse themselves because of fear of retaliation, lack of physical and/or cognitive ability to report, or because they don't want to get the abuser, 90% of whom are family members, in trouble." (NCEA, 2013). As detailed in the NCEA (n.d.), the following provides a sampling known about elder abuse:

- "The most recent major studies on incidents reported that 7.6%–10% of study participants experienced abuse in the prior year (Under the Radar: New York State Elder Abuse Prevalence Study and Prevalence and Correlates of Emotional, Physical, Sexual, and Financial Abuse and Potential Neglect in the United States: The National Elder Mistreatment Study, as cited in NCEA, 2012). The study that found an incidence of 1 in 10 adults experiencing abuse did not include financial abuse (The 2004 survey of adult protective services: Abuse of adults 60 years of age and older as cited in NCEA 2013).

- Available data from state Adult Protective Services (APS) agencies show an increasing trend in the reporting of elder abuse.
- Despite the accessibility of APS in all 50 states (whose programs are quite different), as well as mandatory reporting laws for elder abuse in most states, an overwhelming number of cases of abuse, neglect, and exploitation go undetected and untreated each year.
- One study estimated that only 1 in 14 cases of elder abuse ever comes to the attention of authorities (Elder mistreatment: Abuse, neglect and exploitation in an aging America as cited in NCEA, 2013). The New York State Elder Abuse Prevalence Study found that for every case known to programs and agencies, 24 were unknown (Under the Radar: New York State Elder Abuse Prevalence Study as cited in NCEA, 2013).
- Major financial exploitation was self-reported at a rate of 41 per 1,000 surveyed, which was higher than self-reported rates of emotional, physical, and sexual abuse or neglect." (Under the Radar: New York State Elder Abuse Prevalence Study as cited in NCEA, 2013).

Elder abuse may occur in a variety of settings and environments. This includes private homes, institutional settings, and long term care facilities (NCEA, 2013). It should not be assumed that higher incidences of abuse occur in institutional environments, but rather these numbers are more accurately documented. For instance, in 2008, approximately 3.2 million Americans lived in nursing homes (Assisted Living Resident Profile as cited in NCEA, 2013). A sampling of research studies detailing abuse in long-term care facilities include:

- "...of all complaints regarding institutional facilities reported to long term care Ombudsmen were complaints of abuse, neglect, or exploitation (2010 National Ombudsman Reporting System Data Tables as cited in NCEA, 2013).
- In 2000, one study interviewing 2,000 nursing home residents reported that 44% said they had been abused and 95% said they had been neglected or seen another resident neglected (The Silenced Voice Speaks Out: A study of abuse and neglect of nursing home residents as cited by NCEA, 2013).
- A May 2008 study conducted by the U.S. General Accountability Office revealed that state surveys understate problems in licensed facilities: "70% of state surveys miss at least one deficiency and 15% of surveys miss actual harm and immediate jeopardy of a nursing home resident." (Nursing Homes: Federal Monitoring Surveys Demonstrate Continued Understatement of Serious Care Problems and CMS Oversight Weaknesses as cited in NCEA, 2013).

As healthcare professionals, we must understand that elderly people who may become victims of abuse, regardless of the level of abuse, experienced a 300% higher risk of death when compared to those who had not been abused (Elder self-neglect and abuse and mortality risk in a community-dwelling population as cited in NCEA, 2013). Research demonstrates that "...victims have had a significantly higher level of psychological distress and lower perceived self-efficacy than their peers, who were not victimized" (Psychological distress in victims of elder mistreatment: The effects of social support and coping as cited in NCEA, 2013). In addition, older victims of violence have additional health care problems as compared to other older adults (The High Prevalence of Depression and Dementia in Elder Abuse or Neglect as cited in NCEA, 2013). These issues include: increased bone or joint problems, digestive problems, depression or anxiety, chronic pain, high blood pressure, and heart problems (The High Prevalence of Depression and Dementia in Elder Abuse or Neglect as cited in NCEA, 2013).

The fiscal impact of elderly abuse and neglect has a profound effect on our nation (NCEA, 2013). "The direct medical costs associated with violent injuries to older adults are estimated to add over $5.3 billion to the nation's annual health expenditures, and the annual financial loss by victims of elder financial exploitation was estimated to be $2.9 billion in 2009, a 12% increase from 2008" (Prevalence and 3-year Incidence of Abuse Among Postmenopausal Women and The Metlife Study of Elder Financial Abuse: Crimes of Occasion, Desperation and Predation against America's Elders as cited in NCEA, 2013). This is a serious and costly issue.

WRAP-UP:

The elderly population is often complex to manage. They often have one to multiple chronic conditions, take multiple medications, and have various social and mental issues that should be considered. Like all patients, providers should treat the "whole person." The setting in which the elderly reside could also be a factor that may interfere with or facilitate their health and wellbeing. Healthcare professionals should be aware and able to apply their knowledge in order to care for elderly patients with the utmost quality. Along with the responsibility to provide quality and seamless care, comes the responsibility to recognize and report possible signs of abuse and neglect among elderly patients. It is the ethical duty of all who work in healthcare to be able to respond appropriately to possible circumstances where an individual may be at risk for abuse or neglect.

CLASSROOM ACTIVITIES:

The following activities include discussions, scenarios and exercises that can be utilized during or outside of class.

Activity I

Discussion Questions:

1. Explore the idea of "rationing of care." What is meant by rationing care for the elderly?
2. What is meant by the "revolving door" in healthcare? How might care of an elderly patient end up in a "revolving door" scenario?

Activity II: State Acts Explored

Ask students to conduct research and find the abuse prevention act for your state and determine who can petition for relief, what kinds of relief are available etc.

Each student will present a brief summary of the act and its benefits and implications for the elderly.

Activity III: Case Scenarios

1. An 83 year-old retired teacher living in an assisted living facility. She goes to a primary care office for a checkup and overall she is in good health but has lost weight since her last visit. She is with a caregiver from the facility, who is her personal aide for the day. Upon examination, you, as the provider, notice circular bruising around her rib cage. When asked, she tells you that she fell into her dresser in her bedroom. You ask the aide if the facility has a written report of the incident. She says that she is unsure.

   What should you do? Explain why you chose this response.

2. After being away on vacation, Ms. Daniels arrives at her neighbor's home to retrieve her mail. The neighbors, the Rubino family, are very nice. They are a husband and wife, and they care for the wife's elderly father. Upon arriving at the home, she rings the bell, but notices that the door is slightly open. She calls out and cracks the door open a bit. She enters the home and observes that the house was extremely cluttered. Garbage was piled everywhere. The elderly grandfather was dirty, although no symptoms of illness or injury were apparent. The daughter, the owner of the home, was not home. The neighbor departed after five minutes. The neighbor called the state protective agency.

   Did Ms. Daniels do the right thing? Why or why not?

   Would you consider this a form of elder abuse? Why or why not?

3. A 90 year-old nursing home patient with advanced dementia was sent to the local hospital for intestinal issues. The patient was also having difficulty chewing her food, which is often a symptom of late stage dementia. Over the course of 3 days, the patient was treated and then released for transfer back to the skilled nursing facility (SNF).

   The local contract ambulance picked up the patient from the hospital and transferred her back to the SNF during the evening hours when the supervising nurse was not on the premises. Following the facility's policies, the certified nurse's aide (CNA) on shift received and reviewed the patient's paperwork. Prior to signing for the release and acceptance of the patient, she called her supervisor, who is a Registered Nurse. The CNA read over the patient's discharge note, which stated follow-up protocol and discharge instructions and medications. The ambulance transport staff stated that patient was unable to receive dinner, since she was traveling during early evening hours. The staff member told the CNA that the medications provided for the patient needed to be given with food. The medications were provided in liquid form and came with a syringe. The CNA reported all information to the supervisor, who stated that she would visit the patient first thing in the morning and to give dinner and the medications to the patient.

When the CNA was undressing the patient for the evening, she noticed that the patient had what appeared to be a feeding tube coming from her stomach. The CNA did not recall reading about a feeding tube in the discharge paperwork, but since it is not uncommon for advanced dementia patients to have such tubes, she figured that she would ask the supervisor to call the hospital in the morning. She then fed the patient through the tube as well as administered her medications in the same way. In the morning when the supervising nurse rounded on the patient, she noted that the area surrounding the tube was red and inflamed. Upon calling the hospital she was told by the discharge coordinator that the tube was in fact not a feeding tube, but rather a drainage tube. The hospital identified that they did not attach the bulb to the end of the tube. This was an oversight. The patient was transported back to the hospital and treated for an infection caused by the foreign liquid entering the stomach.

1. Who is at fault? Why?
2. If the patient died, does that change the scenario or who is at fault? Why or why not?
3. Do you think something like this could happen? Why or why not? What can be done to prevent episodes like this from occurring?

Activity IV: Elderly Simulation Exercise

Supplies:

- Vaseline
- Clear plastic or glasses
- Dried Beans
- Winter Gloves
- Pill container (Children Proof)
- Tic-tacs
- Earplugs
- Pen and Paper

Preparation for the exercise:

1. Pair students together- one assigned as the “elderly” person, one assigned as the “aide” or helper
2. Lightly smear Vaseline on outside of glasses or plastic
3. Place handful of beans inside elderly persons shoes
4. Place handful of tic-tacs in pill container
5. Have elderly person place earplugs in ears
6. Have elderly person put glasses and gloves on
7. Ask the aide to give all directions to the elderly person in low voice/whisper

Exercise:

1. Have elderly person be led to a chair across the room (or hall)
2. Aide will ask the elderly person to open the pill bottle and take out 3 pills
3. Aide will tell elderly person that they need to write down the following medication instruction: "Take 3 pills 3x daily with food"
4. After they complete Steps 1-3. Have the students "undo" the elderly preparations.
5. Have the pair discuss: how they did?, what was difficult? how did they feel in their roles?
6. Have pair switch and conduct the scenario again.
7. Repeat discussion points.

Activity V: Contemplate the Elderly

Take 5 minutes to write down the first thing that comes to your mind when you think about the elderly. What types of images come to your mind?

Discussion: Are these images stereotypical? Did anyone picture active, healthy people? Why or Why not?

Activity VI: Ageism: posters and presentation

Students are to find pictures from magazines depicting elderly. Discuss the photos you found.

1. How difficult was it to find ads depicting older people? If it was difficult, why might this be?
2. What do the messages and ads imply about being older?
3. What do older people look like in the ads?
4. What does it mean in terms of the media to be a "beautiful" older person?
5. When older people are used in the media, what are the ads about/for?
6. Are the elderly shown in "normal roles" in the ads? Why or why not? What do you think "normal roles" are in terms of the elderly population?

Activity VII: Ageism Writing Assignment

Written Discussion Questions

1. How would you define 'ageism' in the context of health care?
2. In your opinion does ageism exist and if so is it a minor or major issue?
3. From your own experience, provide examples.
4. What can be done to eliminate it and how should it be implemented?

Activity VIII: Senior ERs Assignment

There is a new trend in treating the elderly. Hospitals are investing in the development and implementation of "senior's emergency rooms (ER)." You are an administrator of a 325-bed hospital in your local area. Research the aging demographics in your geographic region and present your position of why the organization should build a senior's ER.

Your organization has decided to move forward with the senior's ER. How should the ER be designed to accommodate this population? What specific needs of this population should be addressed and how does your design accommodate these needs?

Activity IX: Group Case Study and Discussion

The elderly account for nearly 12% of the population in the U.S. and one third of all hospital stays. The aging baby boomers are major consumers of all healthcare services. This growing number of elderly people increases demands on the public health system and on medical and social services.

- In some states, a quarter of the population will be aged 65 and older.
- "The cost of providing health care for an older American is three to five times greater than the cost for someone younger than 65." (Center of Disease Control cited by MedFolio n.d.)
- "By 2030, the nation's health care spending is projected to increase by 25% due to demographic shifts unless improving and preserving the health of older adults is more actively addressed" (MedFolio n.d.).
- Due to the issue of ageism, many elderly adults are denied treatment, surgery, and state of the art, quality care.
- Proper preventative screenings and continuous quality care measures can help reduce many chronic disease issues and frequent hospital stays.

You are heading a committee to establish an elderly community health center in South Florida. Your focus is on disease prevention and population education. Your goal is to treat the elderly in this area.

First look closely at the population in your catchment area. Look at the demographic and health trends for this population. Gather the below necessary information to make informed decisions about your new health care facility.

- What type of facility will it be (community center, service specific, hospital, outpatient, ancillary care)?
- What health care services do you want to offer?
- What services would you not offer? Why?
- Who are the key staff members? Are there additional staff members?
- What other community, state, or federal resources do you need to work in conjunction with to build quality and continuity in health care services?
- What do you think some funding resources would be?
- How would you go about advertising your facility?
- How would you ensure that you are continuously meeting the changing needs of your population?
- What would be the major focuses of the facility?
- What would your payment system be?
- What do you think the barriers would be to maintaining continuity of care for this population?
- Any other issues you foresee in treating this population?
- Would this facility alleviate some of the stressors on other local health care facility, which does not specialize in caring for this population? If so, why and how?

Think about the health risks, beliefs, and culture discussed during class to develop your scenario. Also, search the internet for current community resources.

Activity X: Long-Term Care Interview/Visit

All students will visit a long-term care facility of their choice. Students will interview the administrator of the chosen facility and provide a written feedback paper of the experience. The paper should include: information gathered about the facility (services, level of care, company background), patient population/demographics, staffing, and the administrator's qualifications, as well as any other specific information you gleaned from your interview/tour. Note: If you are having trouble finding a facility please inform the instructor for assistance.

Activity XI: Professional Memo & Presentation

Student selects one long term care issue to research. Assume that a decision maker in healthcare policy (or an organization leader) has asked you to submit a summary of your ideas on this long-term care issue. This will give you a glimpse of their complexity and a basis for some of the class discussions. Write a 2-3 page memo on a topic of your chose.

This assignment requires that you review the literature to discover what is currently known about the selected issue and more importantly to include your insightful innovations on the subject.

You can collaborate with 2-3 other students who have also selected this issue. Each student is to write his/her own memo, but you can brainstorm ideas. This assignment will be graded on how well your paper is supported by references, how specific and concrete your suggestions are, how realistic and innovative your approach is, and style and grammar. Use the APA publishing manual for referencing.

REFERENCES:

Administration on Aging (AOA) (2012), Profile of Older Americans: 2012. Retrieved September 25, 2013 from http://aoa.gov/AoARoot/Aging_Statistics/Profile/index.aspx

Agency for Healthcare Research and Quality (AHRQ), (2009), Elderly Health. Retrieved October 1, 21013 from http://innovations.ahrq.gov/issue.aspx?id=67

Alzheimer's Association (2013). Retrieved from http://www.alz.org/alzheimers_disease_what_is_alzheimers.asp

Assisted Living Federation of America (ALFA) (2013), Ageism. Retrieved October 1, 2013 from http://www.alfa.org/alfa/Ageism.asp

Center for Disease Control and Prevention (CDC) 2011, Healthy Aging, at a Glance Helping People to Live Long and Productive Lives and Enjoy a Good Quality of Life. Retrieved October 1, 2013 from http://www.cdc.gov/chronicdisease/resources/publications/aag/aging.htm

Center for Disease Control and Prevention (CDC) 2013. The State of Aging & Health in America. Retrieved on November 2, 2014 from http://www.cdc.gov/aging/pdf/state-aging-health-in-america-2013.pdf

Federal Interagency Forum on Aging-Related Statistics. Older Americans 2012: Key Indicators of Well-Being. Federal Interagency Forum on Aging-Related Statistics. Washington, DC: U.S. Government Printing Office. June 2012. Retrieved from http://agingstats.gov/agingstatsdotnet/Main_Site/Data/2012_Documents/Docs/EntireChartbook.pdf

Fialova, D. and Graziano, O. (2009). Medication errors in elderly people: contributing factors and future perspectives. British Journal of Clinical Pharmacology: 67(6): 641-645.

Health and Wealth Effects, Advances in the Economics of Aging, National Bureau of Economic Research, 193-216. Retrieved from http://www.nber.org/chapters/c7324.pdf

Levy, M.D., Susan (2013), The Most Common Issues of Aging. Retrieved September 30, 2013 from http://www.agingcare.com/Articles/common-issues-of-aging-102224.htm

MedFolio (n.d.) Statistics on Aging Retrieved October 19, 2013 from http://www.medfoliopillbox.com/statistics-on-aging/

Takahashi, P., Okhravi, H., Lim, L. & Kasten, M. (2004), Preventive Health Care in the Elderly Population: A Guide for Practicing Physicians, Mayo Clinical Proceedings, 79, 416-427

Medicaid.gov (2012), Program of All Inclusive Care for the Elderly PACE. Retrieved September 25, 2013 from http://www.medicaid.gov/Medicaid-CHIP-Program-Information/By-Topics/Long-Term-Services-and-Support/Integrating-Care/Program-of-All-Inclusive-Care-for-the-Elderly-PACE/Program-of-All-Inclusive-Care-for-the-Elderly-PACE.html

Medicaid.gov (2013), Medicaid Benefits. Retrieved October 8, 2013 form http://www.medicaid.gov/Medicaid-CHIP-Program-Information/By-Topics/Benefits/Medicaid-Benefits.html

National Center for Elder Abuse (NCEA)(n.d), Statistics/Data. Retrieved August 28, 2013 from http://www.ncea.aoa.gov/Library/Data/index.aspx

National Center for Elder Abuse (NCEA) (n.d.), Frequently Asked Questions. Retrieved August 28, 2013 from http://www.ncea.aoa.gov/faq/index.aspx

National PACE Association (NPA) 2013, What is PACE?, Retrieved October 1, 2013 from http://www.npaonline.org/website/ article.asp?id=12&title=Who,_What_and_Where_is_PACE?

Perlata (2013), Baby Boomers Aging Adds Strain to Physician Shortage. Medill Reports, Chicago. Retrieved from http://news.medill.northwestern.edu/chicago/news.aspx?id=222236

Schonberg, M. (2008), Preventive Health Care among Older Women in an Academic Primary Care Practice, Women's Health Issues, 18(4), 249–256.

Spector W (AHRQ), Mutter R (AHRQ), Owens P (AHRQ), Limcangco R (SSS). Transitions between Nursing Homes and Hospitals in the Elderly Population, 2009. HCUP Statistical Brief #141. September 2012. Agency for Healthcare Research and Quality, Rockville, MD. Retrieved from http://www.hcup-us.ahrq.gov/reports/statbriefs/sb141.pdf

Vicent, G. K., and Velkoff, V.A., May 2010, The Next Four Decades, the older population in the United States: 2010 to 2050. Retrieved from http://www.aoa.gov/Aging_Statistics/future_growth/DOCS/p25-1138.pdf

Wier, L.M., (Thomson Reuters), Pfuntner, A. (Thomson Reuters), and Steiner, C. (AHRQ). Hospital Utilization among Oldest Adults, 2008. HCUP Statistical Brief #103. December 2010. Agency for Healthcare Research and Quality, Rockville, MD. Retrieved from http://www.hcup-us.ahrq.gov/reports/statbriefs/sb103.pdf

Wieland, D., Kinosian, B., Stallard, E. and Boland, R. (2012), Does Medicaid Pay More to a Program of All-Inclusive Care for the Elderly (PACE) Than for Fee-for-Service Long-term Care? The Journals of Gerontology, 68, 47-55. Retrieved from http://biomedgerontology.oxfordjournals.org/content/68/1/47.short

US Census Bureau, Facts for Featues, January 3, 2006. Retrieved on November 2, 2014 from: http://www.census.gov/Press-Release/www/releases/archives/facts_for_features_special_editions/006105.html

Chapter 9:

Disparities and Special Issues Related to Geography

Amy Dore

KEY CONCEPTS:

Community supported agriculture
Double burden
Low food security
Food deserts
Food security
Food insecurity
Frontier population
Geographic information systems
Health disparity population
Health geography
Health professional shortage area
High food security
Maldistribution
Marginal food security
Medical geography
Medically underserved areas
Medically underserved populations
Metropolitan
Micropolitan
Priority populations
Rural
Rural-urban commuting area
Telehealth
Telemedicine
Urban
Urbanization
Urbanized area
Urbanized Cluster
Very low food security

CHAPTER OVERVIEW:

This chapter introduces the student to the concepts and topics of special issues and health disparities as a result of the geographic area in which the person or population lives. The framework of this chapter focuses on urban and rural populations and the correlating challenges facing these populations. A closer look will provide an explanation of topics within each population such as food deserts in urban areas and maldistribution of services in rural areas. A discussion of the varying ways in which rural (non-metropolitan) and urban (metropolitan) areas are defined will provide the student with a context to better understand these geographic disparities. The importance of this topic will be demonstrated through the lens of a historical context, detailed descriptions of each population, challenges facing each population, next steps to overcome the correlating disparities, and activities and resources for further investigation.

WHY IS THIS IMPORTANT?

In an effort to recognize issues of disparities in health care, Congress charged the Agency for Healthcare and Quality Research (AHRQ) with the task of creating an annual report to track disparities connected to racial factors and socioeconomic factors in priority populations. **Priority populations** include groups with unique health care needs or issues that require special attention (2013). This chapter focuses on the health disparities facing two priority populations with similar, yet unique issues. Urban (metropolitan) health disparities typically stem from factors such as low socioeconomic status, which brings forth disparities for racial and ethnic minority groups in their ability to access health services, adequate housing, limitations in finding and affording healthy, nutritious foods, and safe outlets for recreation (outdoor and built facilities). Rural (non-metropolitan) health disparities are typically connected to similar socioeconomic factors, along with issues connected to typical population characteristics of a rural community and geographic factors such as distance, weather, and terrain. Researching these priority populations to better understand health disparities and their impact on these populations allows for the creation of effective policy initiatives to advocate for improved resources with the intention of eliminating the disparities.

CHAPTER EXPECTATIONS:

Upon reading this chapter, the student will be able to:

- Acknowledge the historical background of health geography and the geographic information systems developed to measure disparities created by geographic limitations and conditions.
- Define the terms "urban" and "rural" and their associated components.
- Synthesize health disparities and special issues related to geography.
- Recognize the unique, yet correlating disparities facing urban and rural populations.
- Understand concepts such as maldistribution of services and food deserts as examples of special issues and health disparities connected to geography.
- Investigate resources, future implications, and the next steps to reduce these disparities.

Broad Street Cholera Pump [Image]. Enemark, Michelle. Retrieved from Atlas Obscura. Web site: http://www.atlasobscura.com/places/broad-street-cholera-pump. Creative Commons Attribution-Share Alike 2.0 Generic license.

INTRODUCTION AND HISTORICAL CONTEXT:

The connection between health and geography and the topic of geographic disparities in health has been studied throughout history. The concept of health geography, also referred to as medical geography, is a sub-discipline of human geography. Health geography is aligned with the study of disease and disease diffusion by using techniques and concepts of geography to investigate health-related issues (Dummer, 2008; Ricketts, 2002). **Health geography** views health from a holistic viewpoint and investigates the social, cultural, and political context for health within a framework of spatial organization. Dummer (2008) explains that health geography includes two distinct paths which supports policy development: 1) the patterns, causes and spread of diseases, and 2) the planning and provision of health services.

The origins of health geography can be traced to the works of Hippocrates (2,500 years ago) with a focus of understanding the relationship between the environment and health. Health geography, in the context we understand today, was introduced in the 18th and 19th century by physicians who strived to connect the relationship between the occurrence of disease and environmental conditions. The most common example can be found in the mapping work completed by Dr. John Snow who is considered by some as the father of modern day epidemiology. Dr. Snow's hand-drawn mapping of cases of cholera, a water-borne disease, pointed to a specific public water pump located on Broad Street in London. History and research has shown that this contaminated water pump killed 500 people in 10 days in 1854 (Black, Renkessler, & Stanestane, 2013). Dr. Snow's discovery, in part, led authorities to remove the pump handle, which assisted in the decline of the epidemic of 1854 (Ricketts, Savitz, Gesler, & Osborne, 1997; Ricketts, 2002). Understanding disease risk factors and how risks (genetic, occupational, lifestyle, environmental) interrelate with the social, built and natural environments all play a key role in the uses of health geography. Furthermore, health geography has become an effective science by providing evidence-based outcomes to assist in making informed decisions and advocating for health policy changes (Dummer, 2008).

Today, various software programs assist in the use of geography in health services research. **Geographic information systems** are computerized systems utilized to collect, store, represent, and manipulate spatial data used to analyze information regarding health events, disease surveillance, health outcomes and health promotion initiatives. Geographic information systems have been vital in public health efforts, but come with some limitations. Basing policy initiatives on incorrect assumptions about people and populations based on aggregated data may result in the misapplication of policies targeting specific populations or geographic locations. Nevertheless, place and geographic setting are known factors and important influences on health. Examples of health geography research include:

- Geographic accessibility of healthy foods (food deserts)
- Analysis of geographic clusters of deaths as a result of breast cancer
- Local and modifiable influences on diet, physical activity, and obesity
- Access to family physicians and hospitals in connection to the use of hospital inpatient services (Dummer, 2008).

Research utilizing health geography has grown to include a focus on health disparities and health inequalities, which assists in policy development. As concluded by Dummer (2008), "health geography recognizes the importance of context, setting, and spatial scale in determining health outcomes."

WHAT YOU SHOULD KNOW:

A **health disparity population** is characterized by "a notable disparity in the overall rate of disease incidence, prevalence, morbidity, mortality, or survival rates in the population as compared to the health status of the general population" (National Institutes of Health, 2002). In comparison to urban populations, rural populations in the U.S. experience critical health challenges and fare worse than other populations on many health measurements (Galambos, 2005).

When considering health disparities, barriers to care, and other health care issues unique to geography we must create a foundation that allows us to clearly understand and recognize the issues. Whether referring to urban (metropolitan) or rural (non-metropolitan) areas, lack of access or shortages of health care services are common themes. Settling on a definition for the concepts of urban and rural might feel like a moving target depending on the reason for the definition (political, scientific, census, etc.). The most common designations recognized by the Federal government are: 1) the Office of Management and Budget and 2) the U.S. Census Bureau. The U.S. Census Bureau defines **rural** as all territory, persons, and housing units not defined as urban. The term **urban** is classified into two types of urban areas:

1. **Urbanized Areas** (UA) = 50,000 or more people
2. **Urban Clusters** (UC) = at least 2,500 and less than 50,000 people (U.S. Census Bureau "Urban and Rural Classification," 2013).

Historically, the definition of urban has been modified to reflect changes in settlement patterns, data use needs, and available technology used in defining urban areas (U.S. Census Bureau "Urban and Rural Areas," 2013).

The Office of Management and Budget (OMB) utilize three designations for counties: 1) metropolitan, 2) micropolitan, or 3) neither.

1. **Metropolitan** (metro) area = a core urban area of 50,000 or more population
2. **Micropolitan** (micro) area = an urban core of at least 10,000 (but less than 50,000) population
3. All counties not part of a metropolitan statistical area are considered **rural** (HRSA "Defining the Rural Population," n.d.).

When considering both sources, the U.S. Department of Health and Human Services make the generalization that the OMB definition as easier to use as it designates all the land and population inside a county as either metro or non-metro, unlike the U.S. Census Bureau, which does not follow city or county boundaries leading to potential difficulties in determining whether a particular area is considered rural or urban (HRSA "Defining the Rural Population," n.d.).

While these are the two most recognized definitions there are many variations. Policy experts recognize the differences in the definitions and the resulting measurement challenges stemming from the two sources. The OMB definition includes rural areas in metropolitan counties, while the Census definition classifies a large portion of suburban areas as rural. These differences bring about a third definition recognized by many from the Office of Rural Health Policy (ORHP), which accepts all non-metro counties as rural and uses a method of determining rurality known as the **rural-urban commuting area** (RUCA). This determination is based on Census data, which assigns a code to each census tract in a RUCA. In all, there are more than 70,000 tracts in the U.S. that meet the definition of a RUCA. Some are quite large and do not account for distance to services and sparse population. As a result, the ORHP designated 132 large RUCA census tracts as rural. These tracts encompass approximately 400 square miles in areas with a population density of no more than 35 people (HRSA "Defining the Rural Population," n.d.). Hart, Larson, & Lishner (2005), conclude that the flexibility shown by RUCAs allows researchers and policy advocates to group RUCAs in a manner that suits specific analytical or policy purposes. Furthermore, RUCAs can identify the rural portions of metropolitan counties and the urban portions of non-metropolitan counties.

When comparing disparities and special issues related to geography, the comparisons are strongly focused on the rural and frontier populations as health disparity populations. Defining the term "frontier" can be just as complex as defining the terms urban and rural. The Rural Assistance Center (RAC) defines a **frontier** area as counties having a population density of six or fewer people per square mile. This definition is limited in its recognition of the composition and vastness of frontier areas. The RAC recommends the following be taken into consideration when classifying an area as frontier, depending on the purpose of the project:

- Population density
- Distance from a population center or specific service
- Travel time to reach a population center or specific service
- Functional connection with other places
- Accessibility of paved roads
- Seasonal changes in access to services (RAC "Frontier Frequently Asked Questions," n.d.).

Approximating the amount of frontier areas in the United States is also complex and depends on how frontier is defined. As an example, in 2011, the National Center for Frontier Communities asked each of the State Offices of Rural Health (SORH) to specify which of their state's counties were considered frontier. As a result, the SORH designated 46% of the land areas of the U.S. as frontier with over 5.6 million people living in these areas as of 2010. Figure 1 illustrates rural (non-metropolitan) and urban (metropolitan) areas as classified by United States Department of Agriculture in 2013.

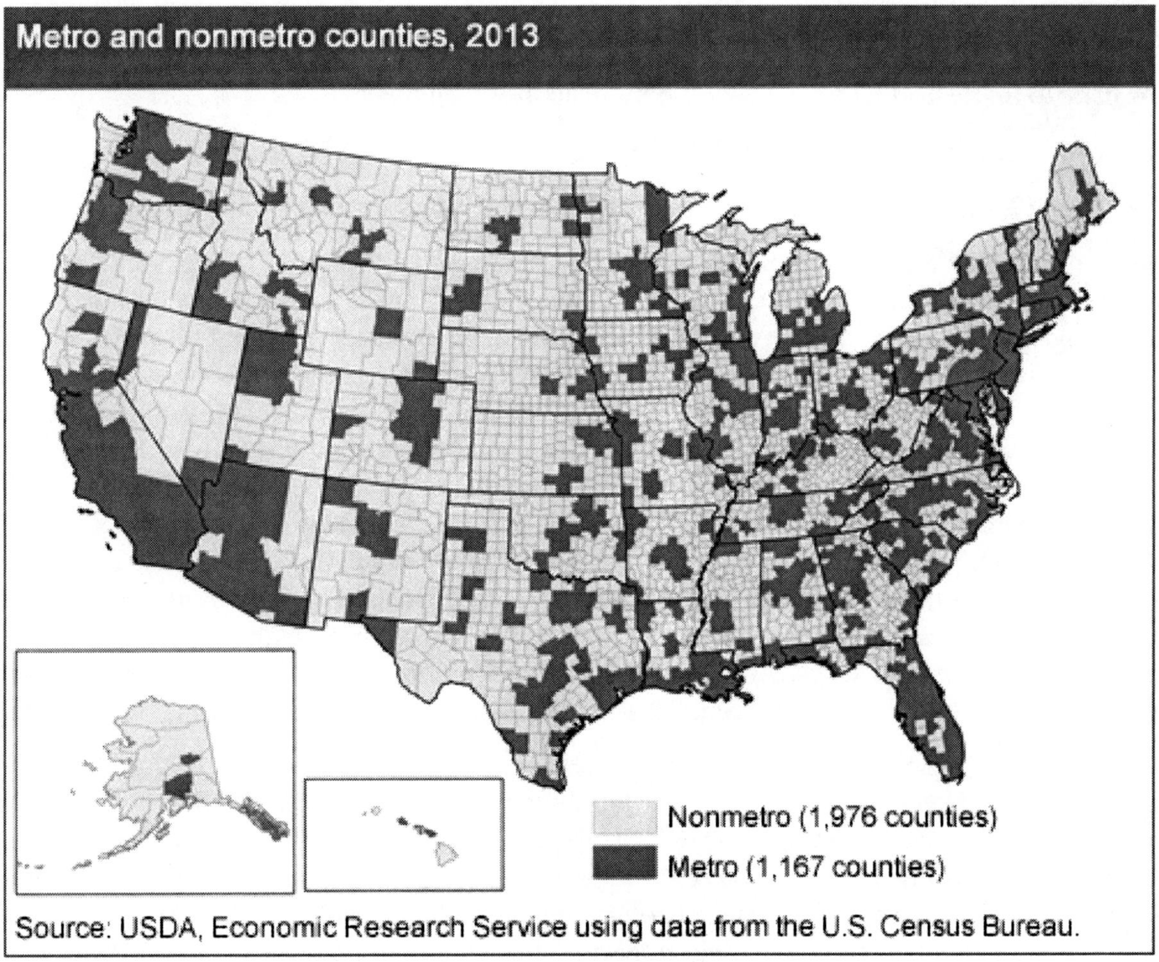

Figure 1. Rural Classifications Overview. (2013, December). United States Department of Agriculture, Economic Research Service. Retrieved from http://www.ers.usda.gov/topics/rural-economy-population/rural-classifications.aspx#.UwAAZRYVCxo

Disparities Unique to Urban Areas

Health disparities unique to urban (metropolitan) areas are typically associated with environmental, behavioral, access, economic, and geographic sources. Several of the issues discussed in this chapter will compare disparities experienced by urban and rural populations. However, there are specific disparities faced by populations living in urban areas that will be reviewed first.

As mentioned in previous chapters, a person's health status is determined by several factors including one's behavior, genetics, social circumstances, environment, and one's access to health care. The conditions a person lives in (homes and neighborhoods), income level, and level of education are also factors that impact health outcomes.

The World Health Organization (WHO) explains that **urbanization**, the demographic transition from rural to urban, as being linked with shifts from an agriculture-focused economy to mass industry, technology, and service. For the first time in history, the majority of the world's population lives in a city, which is a trend expected to continue for the next several decades. Research illustrates the expected demographic shifts:

- One hundred years ago, 2 out of every 10 people lived in an urban setting
- Less than 40% of the global population lived in an urban area in 1990
- As of 2010, more than 50% of all people lived in an urban setting
- By 2030, 6 out of every 10 people will live in a city, and
- By 2050, it is expected that 7 out of every 10 people will live in a city (WHO, 2014).

As of 2012, over 50% of the world's population lived in an urban area (KFF, n.d.). The rapid urbanization of our country (and the world) brings with it changes in the ways in which people live, work, foods they eat, and an increased exposure to a large variety of environmental factors. Additionally, urbanization brings with it a level of modernization. With this modernization comes the assumption that urban populations are healthier than their rural counterparts. As we will see, this is not always the case. Modernization has brought improvements in medical care, technological advances, and shifts from infectious disease to chronic disease. However, researchers are now concerned about a growing trend known as the "**double burden**" of disease, which is exhibited by the presence of both infectious and chronic disease. Rapid urbanization has led to people living in closer proximity to one another, poor living and working conditions, higher rates of crime and violence, the presence of marginalized populations with high risk behaviors (sex workers), and a higher level of psychological stressors that accompany the increased density and diversity of urban areas. Populations with lower socioeconomic status and minority populations are more likely to reside in urban areas. These populations experience barriers to care including poorer quality of care and disproportionate utilization of emergency "safety net" care (Unite, n.d.).

Conditions unique to geography and particular neighborhoods can aggravate health disparities. When compared to neighborhoods predominantly populated by whites, many urban neighborhoods populated by minorities have more fast food outlets, fewer grocery stores, fewer recreational facilities, and are closer in proximity to sources of industrial pollution such as older factories, dump sites, and contaminants such as toxic or radioactive waste. The health effects experienced as a result of pollution and other environmental contaminants have been well documented over time. Blacks and other minorities living in or around low-income or distressed neighborhoods are exposed to higher levels of lead and allergens in their homes, as well as harmful emissions from nearby public transit depots, factories, and dumps (Bahls, 2011). Women and children are the most vulnerable of the urban poor. The urban poor have limited resources available to them, along with substandard information regarding health services and access to health services. Combined with rapid urbanization, these inner-city communities simply cannot keep up (AMSA, "Health Care Delivery: Rural vs. Urban Communities," n.d.).

Air pollution is just one specific example of environmental factors that adversely impact health outcomes. The Colorado Department of Public Health and Environment's 2013 Health Disparities Report (as cited by the American Lung Association, 2001 and Sandberg, 2000) states, "certain populations are disproportionately exposed to air pollution. These groups often live in urban settings, have low socioeconomic status and include a large proportion of racial and ethnic minorities" (Kincheloe, Palacio, Butler, Shupe, & Ward-Hunt, 2013). Individuals at risk for higher exposure to air pollution include those who work outdoors and those who live close to busy roadways. Freeway pollution is connected to an increased incidence of asthma, impaired lung growth, atherosclerosis, low cognitive function, autism, Alzheimer disease, and lower IQ in children with prenatal exposure (Morgan, 2011). A prime example is the "Children's Corridor," a geographic area located along I-70 in the metro-Denver area in which up to 139,000 vehicles travel each day, which is approximately seven times the 20,000 vehicle per day threshold determined to be dangerous. This corridor has been cited as a geographic area associated with very high numbers of at-risk children and is currently the center of a campaign by the Piton Foundation to make the neighborhoods more visible and actionable to the community (The Piton Foundation, 2011; Kincheloe, et.al., 2013).

Access to food is another issue that is typically not considered or not recognized. Approximately 40 percent of the food grown, distributed, made available on grocery shelves and, ultimately, purchased by consumers never gets eaten. This is known as **food waste.** The average American throws away 20 pounds of food a month (PBS "The Lexicon of Sustainability," 2014; NRDC, 2013). **Food security** is defined by the United States Department of Agriculture (USDA) Economic Research Service (ERS) as a household with access by all members, at all times, having the ready availability of nutritionally adequate and safe foods acquired in socially acceptable ways (without resorting to emergency food supplies, scavenging, stealing, or other coping mechanisms). **Food insecurity** is defined as the inadequate or uncertain availability of nutritionally suitable and safe foods or limited or questionable ability to procure acceptable foods in socially acceptable ways. The USDA does not have a measure of hunger or the quantity of hungry people in the United States, yet the USDA's measure of food insecurity does provide information regarding the economic and social contexts that may lead to hunger. However, this does not assess the extent to which hunger actually results (USDA "Food Security in the U.S.," 2013). A household's food security status falls along a continuum recognized from high food security to very low food security. According to the USDA there are four levels that make up the continuum:

FAQ: *The Cost of Food Waste*

- 25% of all freshwater used on U.S.
- 4% of total U.S. oil consumption
- $165 billion per year (> $40 billion from households)
- $750 million per year just to dispose of the wasted food
- 33 million tons of landfill waste (leading to greenhouse gas emissions) (NRDC, 2013).

- **High food security** is when households experience no problems or anxiety about food and consistently have access to adequate food.
- **Marginal food security** is when households experience problems at times and some anxiety about accessing adequate food, yet the quality, variety, and quantity of their food consumption were not substantially condensed.
- **Low food security** describes households with reduced quality, variety, and desirability of their diets. However, the quantity of food intake and normal eating patterns were not markedly interrupted.
- **Very low food security** represents times during the year when eating patterns of one or more household members were disrupted and food consumption was reduced because the household lacked money or other resources for food (USDA "Food Security in the U.S.," 2013).

In addition to food security concerns, residents in urban areas oftentimes face issues related to access of healthy, nutritious foods. A **food desert** is classified as urban neighborhoods and rural towns without ready access to fresh, healthy, and affordable food. The USDA, U.S. Department of Treasury and HHS define a food desert as a census tract with a substantial share of residents who live in low-income areas that have low levels of access to a grocery store or healthy, affordable food retail outlet (USDA "Food Deserts," n.d.). Access to healthy food is a challenge for those living in low-income neighborhoods, communities of color, and rural areas. A study completed in 2009 by the USDA found that approximately 23.5 million people lack access to a grocery store within one mile of their home. In place of grocery stores are often found, in great abundance, convenience stores and fast food restaurants that predominantly sell inexpensive, high-fat, high-sugar, processed foods with few healthy food alternatives. Research shows that, nationally, low-income zip codes have approximately 30 percent more convenience stores, corner markets, and liquor stores (Treuhaft & Karpyn, 2010).

Multiple health concerns are connected to hunger. One in six people in the United States struggle with hunger. In 2012, 49.0 million Americans lived in food insecure households, 15.9 million being children (Feeding America, 2014). According to studies on the topic, hunger – even when experienced in brief periods during childhood and adolescence – can result in outcomes that last a lifetime. The outcomes can include early-onset diabetes, high blood pressure, stunted intellectual growth, cardiovascular disease, and obesity. Even tooth decay in children and early menstruation in girls can be connected to hunger (Kane, 2014). Unemployment is a stronger predictor of food security than poverty. And, food insecurity is more prominent in urban areas than rural households (Feeding America, 2014).

Efforts to reduce waste and increase the availability of food are taking place in the form of political and community-based initiatives. Urban areas are witnessing growth in gardening – at home and in shared urban community plots. Rural residents are benefiting from online **community supported agriculture** (CSAs) in which rural residents can order produce from local farmers. On a national level, during the Obama Administration, First Lady Michelle Obama launched the *Let's Move* initiative. Established in 2010, this initiative is dedicated to solving the problem of obesity in kids – encouraging healthier children who can grow up to live healthier lives. A large component of this initiative is a sub-initiative – the Healthy Food Financing Initiative. This multi-million dollar initiative is a public and private investment (approximately $400 million), which includes the goal of eliminating food deserts (a contributing factor in the obesity epidemic) by 2017 ("You All Took a Stand," 2010). The following goals were established as part of the *Let's Move* initiative to reduce the number of food deserts and, as a result, increase the health of not only children, but also the health of our nation:

- Increase the availability of affordable, health foods in underserved urban and rural communities across the country through a multi-year, multi-agency Healthy Food Financing Initiative.
- Encourage local governments to create incentives that bring supermarkets and grocery stores to underserved neighborhoods and improve transportation routes to health food retailers.
- Encourage food distributors to use their existing distribution chains and systems to bring fresh and healthy foods into underserved communities.
- Increase and encourage the creation and use of direct-to-consumer marketing outlets such as farmers' markets and community supported agriculture subscriptions, therefore, promoting the efforts to provide fruits and vegetables in a variety of settings.
- Promote the formation of regional, city, or county food policy councils to enhance comprehensive food system policy that improve health.
- Institute practices and policies, consistent with the Dietary Guidelines, to promote healthy foods and beverages and reduce or eliminate the availability of calorie-dense, nutrient-poor foods in publicly and privately-managed facilities that service children (hospitals, after-school programs, recreation centers, parks) (Letsmove.gov "White House Task Force...", n.d.).

Disparities Unique to Rural Areas

What is different about rural health care? What types of health disparities do people in rural areas face? A cursory glimpse of available data will show you that, for decades, rural counties accounted for 20-23% of the U.S. population. However, for the first time ever, data shows the rate of population growth for rural communities has slowed. Current data shows that rural counties account for approximately 15 percent (46.2 million people) of the U.S. population, spread across 72 percent of U.S. land area. Between 2010 and 2012, rural counties experienced a decline in population. This decline has been attributed to the housing crisis (2006) along with the recession that began a year later (2007). Additionally, the decline can be attributed to a slowdown in the U.S. population growth (lower birth rates) and dramatically lower immigration rates since 2007 (USDA "Rural America at a Glance," 2012; Cromartie, 2013). While the declines in U.S. birth rate have been seen as one main reason for the population shifts in rural areas, the baby boomers who historically have migrated to a smaller community as they retire are now moving closer to more populated locations. U.S. migration data show that older Americans, who are the most motivated group to live in rural areas, live there until approximately age 74 at which time they move closer to urban areas, in part to be closer to health care services. The oldest of the nation's 76 million baby boomers will turn 74 in 2020, which represents the end of the period in which that group can count in any statistical growth of small towns. Cromartie, a geographer at the U.S. Department of Agriculture, explains, "this period may simply be an interruption in suburbanization, or it could turn out to be the end of a major demographic regime that has transformed small towns and rural areas" (Dreier & Yen, 2013). Whether this is a temporary decline or a hint of the future reality for rural, nonmetropolitan areas, the affects are widespread.

Geographic characteristics distinctive to rural areas also place rural populations at a greater risk for a multitude of diseases, disorders and disparities. Agriculture is the primary industry for most rural areas, along with manufacturing. Rural populations have relatively more elderly residents and children, less educational attainment, higher infant mortality rates, higher unemployment and underemployment, and lower population density with higher percentages of poor, uninsured, and underinsured residents. Dependence on agriculture as a primary industry leaves rural populations more susceptible to economic downturns. Additionally, rural populations and communities experience challenges regarding:

- Accessibility to health care – longer traveling distances, remote locations, hazardous terrain
- Availability of physicians and resources – fewer health care providers with more generalists than specialists
- High closure rates of hospitals
- Higher rates of chronic conditions
- Fewer visits to health care providers
- Less likely to be covered by employer-based health care coverage
- Affordability of health care – continual rising costs of health care combined with lower incomes in rural areas prevent rural residents from the ability to afford acute, chronic and/or preventive health care
- Acceptability of health care – lower patient engagement, differing perspectives from providers on the quality of care, how health is defined and delivered, and a lack of focus on preventive health services (Hart, et. al., 2005; AHRQ "2012 National Healthcare Disparities Report," 2013; AMSA, "Breaking Barriers," n.d.).

Compared to their urban (metropolitan) counterparts, rural residents–especially the elderly–visit primary or ambulatory providers less and are more likely to self-report being in fair or poor health. Rural populations face many obstacles and a combination of factors that create unique health disparities that are significantly different than those in urban areas. The demographics of one rural community can be vastly different from another in that one rural area might have a high population of African Americans, while another community might be comprised of Hispanic migrant workers, non-Hispanic whites, or Native Americans. Additionally, within each of these example populations you will find a variety of racial, ethnic or cultural subpopulations. Even though rural populations can experience greater health care needs than urban residents, research shows that they consume fewer health care resources when compared to urban residents. Economic factors, cultural and social dissimilarities, educational shortcomings, lack of recognition by legislators, and the sheer isolation of living in remote rural areas all create challenging circumstances and barriers in which rural populations must overcome (NRHA "What's Different about Rural Health Care?," n.d.; AMSA "Breaking Barriers," n.d.). One commonality amongst rural communities is the challenges that influence the health status of residents. Population demographic, financial, infrastructure, and staffing challenges for rural hospitals and health care systems include:

- 16.6 percent of the rural population lives in poverty
- Chronic disease is more predominant in rural areas including a higher rate of diabetes mellitus, respiratory infections, obesity, and heart disease
- Approximately half of rural hospitals are critical access hospitals (CAH) with 25 or fewer beds
- Rural hospitals represent half of the total number of hospitals, but represent only 12 percent of spending on hospital care
- Outpatient services represent approximately 56 percent of gross revenue for rural hospitals
- Roughly 60 percent of revenues stem from Medicare and Medicaid, covering nearly 31 percent of the rural population
- Approximately 25 percent of rural residents under the age 25 are uninsured
- Small and rural hospitals and health care systems trail behind urban health centers in exhibiting meaningful use for health information technology
- Small and rural hospitals and health care systems struggle to recruit skilled and experienced health care workers, and
- Insufficient volume for certain medical procedures results in the inability for rural hospitals to meet certain quality standards or have adequate and/or accurate data, which impacts reimbursement (HRET, 2013).

According to the National Association of Community Health Centers (2011), "patients of health centers reflect the underserved communities in which the center is located. Ninety percent of rural health center patients have low incomes (less than 200% of the Federal Poverty Level) while two-thirds are uninsured or insured through Medicaid." As a result, hospitals and providers experience greater dependence on Medicaid and Medicare reimbursement and are particularly vulnerable to policy changes (AHA "Trend Watch," 2011).

As of January 2, 2014, the American Hospital Association reported 1,980 rural community hospitals in the United States (AHA "Fast Facts on U.S. Hospitals," 2014). These hospitals play a vital role in the infrastructure of a small rural town and typically serve as the anchor for a rural region's health-related services and the financial backbone for connective services such as physician practice groups, health clinics, long-term care services, pharmacies, social work and similar types of community outreach programs. Additionally, rural hospitals provide economic stability for their community as the largest or second-largest employer in the community and are unique in their ability to offer highly-skilled jobs typically not present in small rural areas. The economic contribution realized with the presence of a hospital in a rural community highly influences the surrounding local economy. The American Hospital Association credits rural hospitals with job growth and economic stability within a rural community and surrounding areas. For every hospital job in a rural community, approximately 0.32 and 0.77 additional jobs are created in the local economy, spurred by the spending of either hospitals or their employees increasing the attractiveness of a community as a place to live, locate a business, or retire (AHA "Trend Watch," 2011). Figure 2 illustrates the economic impact measure utilized by the Oklahoma Rural Health Works as a method of measuring the unique impact the health sector has on a community's economy. The study can be tailored to varying geographies such as zip code areas, counties, or multiple counties. Demographic data, direct employment, and income data are reported from the health sector. This data is then used to produce "multipliers," which measure the impact of health sector jobs and income on differing industries such as restaurants or retail outlets. When combined, the data and multipliers can show the total economic impact the health care sector has on a local rural community (OKRHW, n.d.).

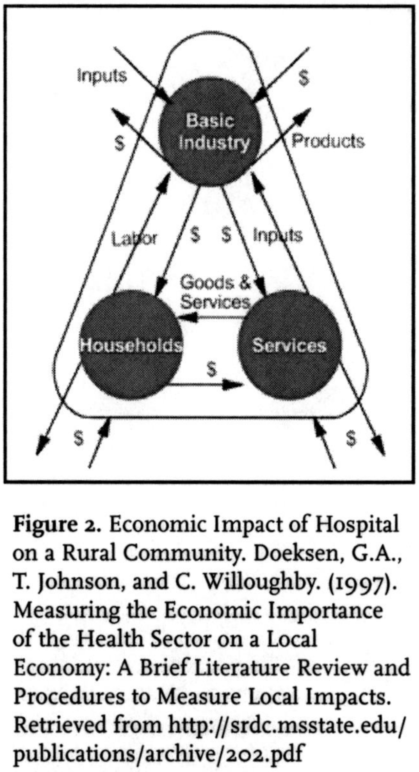

Figure 2. Economic Impact of Hospital on a Rural Community. Doeksen, G.A., T. Johnson, and C. Willoughby. (1997). Measuring the Economic Importance of the Health Sector on a Local Economy: A Brief Literature Review and Procedures to Measure Local Impacts. Retrieved from http://srdc.msstate.edu/publications/archive/202.pdf

Rural hospitals have transformed over time from a focus of inpatient care to outpatient care. This shift requires the ability to adapt to differing needs that bring with it the necessity to provide varying health services that an urban hospital would not necessarily provide (adult day care, assisted living, hospice, and meals on wheels). These services are supported, in essence, out of a sense of community responsibility. The high fixed costs associated with running a hospital make small rural hospitals vulnerable to policy and market changes and reimbursement cuts to Medicare and Medicaid services. These struggles are magnified in light of the Patient Protection and Affordable Care Act of 2010, which is expected to create an influx of new patients who are newly insured. Rural health facilities in general are old (40 years or more), lack sophisticated technology or the ability to update technology, and face an aging workforce that are nearer to retirement when compared to the urban health care workforce. Additionally, rural hospitals have trouble accessing sufficient capital to pay for improvements including the implementation of modern technology such as electronic health records (EHR) (AHA "Trend Watch," 2011).

<1% of rural hospitals have adopted EHR systems that meet the meaningful use required of a certified system (AHA, 2011).

Rural Transportation Issues:

Thomas Ricketts (2002) explains, "one of the most important geographic features that may affect health status and health outcomes, which may contribute to disparities is distance to health care." Residents living in rural areas travel greater distances to access varying points of the health care delivery system. Health care facilities in rural areas are oftentimes small and limited in services they are able to provide. Geographic distance, extreme weather conditions, environmental and climatic obstructions, lack of public transportation, and dangerous roads prohibit rural residents from accessing health care services. Furthermore, timely access to emergency care, response times by emergency medical personnel, and transport times via ambulance to a hospital are notably greater than in urban areas. These difficulties in accessing health care discourage rural patients by increasing patients' emotional and physical stress and, as a result, reducing the likelihood of seeking follow-up care. Motor vehicle accidents that occur in rural areas are more likely to result in death. While one-third of all motor vehicle accidents occur in rural areas, two-thirds of motor vehicle deaths are attributed to accidents that occur on rural roads (Stanford "Healthcare Disparities & Barriers to Healthcare," 2010). The national average response time from motor vehicle accidents to EMS arrival in a rural area was roughly 18 minutes; eight minutes greater than in urban areas (NRHA "What's Different about Rural Health Care?," n.d.).

Many counties and local jurisdictions maintain some form of non-emergency medical transportation (NEMT) services to assist residents in accessing medical care services such as doctor appointments, follow-up care, and rehabilitation therapy. Allocating funds to pay for such transit agencies is challenging, as Medicaid is usually their main funding source. According to AARP (2012), Medicaid spending on transportation far surpasses other federal agencies' transportation costs with expenses estimated at ten times the Federal Transit Administration's specialized transportation allocation. For people with disabilities and the elderly, accessing transportation in rural areas is a major issue. Additional federal agencies that assist in funding human service transportation projects include:

- Department of Education Office of Special Education & Rehabilitative Services
- Department of Health and Human Services Administration for Children and Families
- Administration on Aging
- Center for Medicare and Medicaid Services
- Department of Labor Employment and Training Administration
- Department of Labor Office of Disability Employment Policy
- Department of Transportation Federal Highway Administration
- Social Security Administration Disability Programs (RAC "Transportation," 2014).

Maldistribution of Services

The Merriam-Webster Dictionary defines **maldistribution** as "bad or faulty distribution; undesirable inequality or unevenness of placement or apportionment (population, resources, or wealth) over an area or among members of a group" (2014). A **health professional shortage area** (HPSA) is defined as a geographic region or population group with too few health care providers to provide medical needs for the members living within the correlating area(s) (Ollove, 2014). According to the Health Resources and Services Administration (HRSA) (a division of the U.S. Department of Health and Human Services), HPSAs may be designated as having a shortage of primary medical care, dental, or mental health providers. The shortages may be within urban or rural areas, population groups, or facilities (medical or other public facilities). **Medically underserved areas** (MUAs) can be classified as a whole county or a group of contiguous counties, a group of county or civil divisions, or a group of urban census tracts in which residents experience a shortage of personal health services. **Medically underserved populations** (MUPs) include groups of persons who face economic, cultural, or linguistic barriers to health care (HRSA "Shortage Designation," n.d.).

The American Academy of Family Physicians (AAFP) explains that the United States does not actively regulate the number, type, or geographic distribution of its physician workforce. As a result, health care professionals typically choose where to work based on personal preference and other market forces. This results in an incongruence between the geographic location and the specialty choice of the health workforce that leaves more than 20 million people in the United States living in areas that have a shortage of physicians to meet their basic health care needs. These problems are not restricted to rural areas. Urban communities also suffer from a shortage of medical services (AAFP, n.d.; AMSA "Health Care Delivery," n.d.).

The Agency for Healthcare Research and Quality (AHRQ) noted approximately 209,000 practicing primary care physicians, 56,000 nurse practitioners (NPs), and 30,000 physician assistants (PAs) practicing primary care in the United States as of 2010. Of the nearly 295,000 total providers, 80% practiced in an urban setting while 10% practiced in a large rural area, 5% in a small rural area, and 5% in a remote rural or frontier area. Furthermore, NPs and PAs were more likely than physicians to work in rural areas (AHRQ, 2012).

The below chart illustrates the HPSA designations as defined by the Health Resources and Services Administration (n.d.):

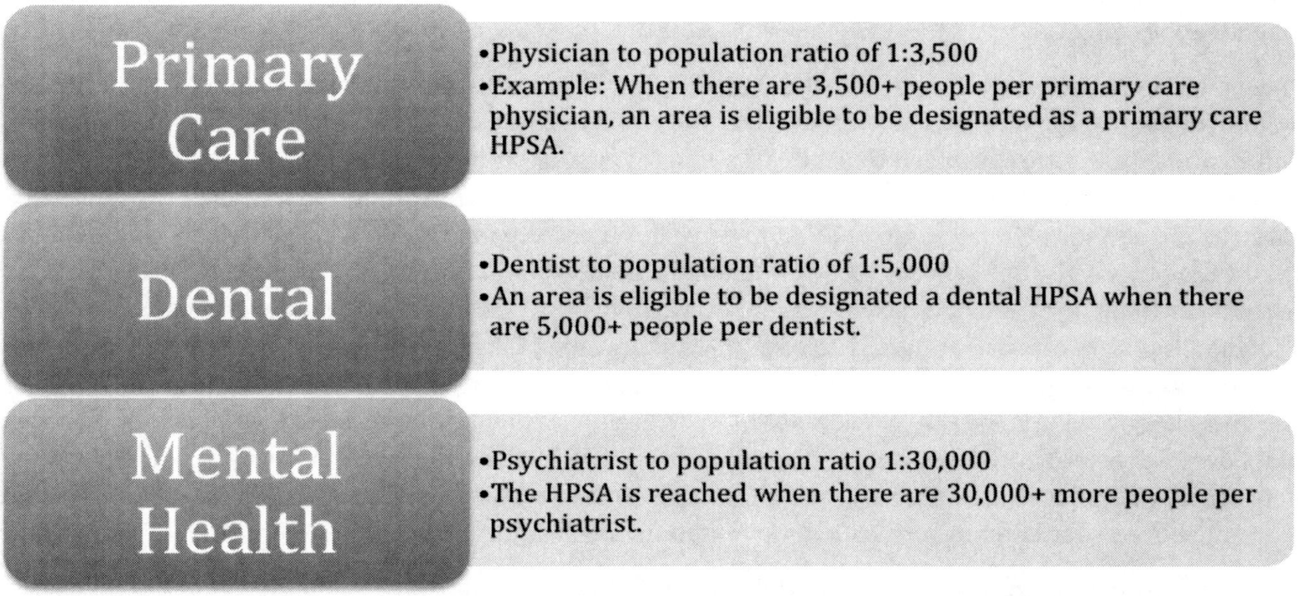

Figure 3. Health Professional Shortage Area Designations. Adapted from: Health Resources and Services Administration, United States Department of Health and Human Services. (n.d.). *Shortage designation: Health professional shortage areas & medically underserved areas/populations.* Retrieved from http://www.hrsa.gov/shortage/

Using the above ratios, as of June 19, 2014, there appears a need in the United States for approximately 8,200 additional primary care physicians, 7,300 additional dentists, and approximately 2,800 more psychiatrists to eliminate the current HPSA designations (HRSA, n.d.). And, as mentioned, HPSAs are not limited to rural areas. While urban residents might live close to concentrations of physicians, such residents might not have access to automobiles, which requires them to find alternate public transportation options that might be difficult to maneuver.

Access to medical specialists is also a challenge in rural areas. Specialist shortages are more pronounced in rural areas than urban areas with 54 specialists per 100,000 rural residents compared to almost two and half times as many specialists per 100,000 urban residents. Examples of specific specialist shortages in rural areas include general surgeons, cardiologists, neurologists, rheumatologists, pediatricians, and obstetricians/gynecologists (AHA "Trend Watch," 2011). According to the Association of American Medical Colleges (AAMC), in the absence of a radical shift, it is estimated there will be a shortage of 45,000 primary care physicians and 46,000 specialists in the United States by the year 2020. One main reason for the primary care shortage stems from the desire of the current generation of medical students to have an acceptable "work-life balance," which takes priority over financial gain. Half of the physicians in training in the United States are women who might prefer a non-traditional, part-time work schedule and prefer to avoid the long work hours and night and weekend calls required of most primary care physicians (Ollove, 2014).

Are there alternatives or solutions to the workforce shortages and access issues? A controversial solution is to allow nurse practitioners, physician assistants, pharmacists and dental aides to complete some of the work typically reserved for physicians and dentists. Several states have already passed legislation to allow such activities while other states are considering similar measures (Ollove, 2014). The most common alternative is telehealth or telemedicine. The HRSA defines **telehealth** as "the use of electronic information and telecommunications technologies to support long-distance clinical health care, patient and professional health-related education, public health and health administration," (HRSA "Telehealth," n.d.). The terms telehealth and telemedicine are oftentimes used interchangeably. While telehealth refers to a broad range of health-related services, **telemedicine** describes direct clinical services (Schwamm, 2014).

One of the largest telehealth providers in the United States, Teladoc, provides an entry point into the healthcare system for people who do not have an established primary care physician, have limited contact with a provider, and/or limited access to a provider. Using this system, patients can connect with a provider by either telephone or Internet access to seek medical help for acute care and minor illnesses with the convenience of around-the-clock access, seven days a week. Uscher-Pines and Mehrotra (2014) analyzed the use of Teladoc and reported that health plans and employers contract with Teladoc primarily to improve access and decrease costs. Teladoc's current per visit rate of $38 makes a health care provider visit with this technology quite affordable. However, with the advantages of a system such as Teladoc, the authors found that users of Teladoc were typically high-end, technologically savvy people who probably have fewer access needs compared to people living in areas characterized by a shortage of primary care providers or those with a socioeconomic disadvantage. Additionally, the rates of follow-up care for Teladoc users are low, compared to patients who visited a physician's office or emergency department (ED). Further research is required to understand whether a system such as Teladoc might be able to improve access for lower-income patients and those living in rural areas (Uscher-Pines & Mehrotra, 2014).

In addition to systems such as Teladoc, health care professionals can provide care to patients with the use of electronic devices that monitor medical conditions, devices that remind patients to take their medications, and other guidance regarding medical conditions. Additional technologies include videoconferencing, store-and-forward imaging, streaming media, and terrestrial and wireless communications. The HRSA is working to increase and improve the use of telehealth to meet the needs of underserved people (urban and rural) by:

- Fostering partnerships within HRSA, and with other Federal agencies, states, and private sector groups to create telehealth projects.
- Administering telehealth grant programs.
- Providing technical assistance.
- Evaluating the use of telehealth technologies and programs.
- Developing telehealth policy initiatives to improve access to quality health services.
- Promoting knowledge exchange about "best telehealth practices" (HRSA "Telehealth", n.d.).

WRAP-UP:

Rural and urban populations experience similar, yet unique challenges as a result of their geographic location. Perspectives of health also differ. Health perceptions of rural and urban populations are a reflection of their health behaviors, health maintenance, and illness treatment. Residents of rural areas value independence and self-reliance and, as a result, are viewed as being highly tolerant of health impairments, seeking treatment for only those conditions that impede daily functioning. Urban populations view health in similar manners, but tend to focus on comfort and life-prolonging aspects of health (AMSA, "Health Care Delivery: Rural vs. Urban Communities," n.d.).

Public awareness of these formidable disparities facing urban and rural communities is just one step in eliminating or, at a minimum, reducing the disparities. For example, whether focusing on underserved urban or rural areas, strategies should be considered such as loan forgiveness, living (housing) allowances, and referral bonuses as methods to recruit and retain physicians, dentists, and medical/dental extenders to practice in these areas. With the encouragement of community members and incentives from governmental sources, convenience-type stores, most commonly found in underserved areas, can revise their current business model to provide fresh, healthy food options more typical of grocery stores. Additionally, with the help of government officials (local and national) and community activists, attention can be drawn and incentives created to bring alternative retail outlets including farmers' markets, public markets, cooperatives, farm community-supported agricultural programs and mobile vendors to areas severally lacking access to healthy, fresh foods (Treuhaft & Karpyn, 2010).

As urbanization continues and the structure of communities evolves, priority populations must be given priority attention by local, state, and national policymakers. The geographic location in which one resides impacts health outcomes. The need to refocus efforts involving our current health care system must be considered, including a renewed focus on community health centers, easy access to user-friendly information on healthy living practices, and the creation of policies to encourage not only healthy living and behavioral changes, but also policies that discourage negative behaviors that have long-term health consequences. To have a healthy nation means the creation of health promotion strategies that benefit all.

RESOURCES:

Agency for Healthcare Research and Quality
http://www.ahrq.gov

Bureau of Primary Health Care (BPHC)
http://bphc.hrsa.gov

Community Food Assessment
http://www.cdc.gov/healthyplaces/healthtopics/healthyfood/community_assessment.htm

Doeksen, G.A., T. Johnson, and C. Willoughby. (1997). Measuring the Economic Importance of the Health Sector on a Local Economy: A Brief Literature Review and Procedures to Measure Local Impacts. Retrieved from http://srdc.msstate.edu/publications/archive/202.pdf

National Health Service Corps
https://nhsc.hrsa.gov

National Resource Center for Human Service Transportation Coordination
http://web1.ctaa.org/webmodules/webarticles/anmviewer.asp?a=23&z=2

National Resources Defense Council
http://www.nrdc.org/living/eatingwell/files/foodwaste_2pgr.pdf

Office of Rural Health Policy
http://www.hrsa.gov/ruralhealth/index.html

Population Reference Bureau
http://www.prb.org/DataFinder.aspx

Robert Wood Johnson Foundation
http://www.rwjf.org

The Urban Institute
www.urban.org

CLASSROOM ACTIVITIES:

Activity #1

Am I Rural? http://ims2.missouri.edu/rac/amirural/

Step 1: Access the above website and familiarize yourself with the website.

Step 2: Create a custom report of rural definitions for your geographic location or the geographic location of a family member or friend.

Step 3: Write a 1-page summary explaining the report results.

Activity #2

USDA ERS – Food Access Research Atlas

http://www.ers.usda.gov/data-products/food-access-research-atlas.aspx

Step 1: Review the webpage. Enter the Food Access Research Atlas link. Review the web links for a better understanding of the atlas. Once you are comfortable with how the atlas works, proceed to Step 2.

Step 2: Utilizing the Food Desert Locator map, enter the zip code where you currently reside or hope to reside in the future. Answer:

1. At what level does the geographic area exhibit low income, low access, and/or low vehicle access?
2. What does this mean for this geographic area regarding health disparities, food access, and access to medical care?

Step 3: Utilizing the Food Desert Locator, enter the zip code of a family member or close friend. Answer:

1. At what level does the geographic area exhibit low income, low access, and/or low vehicle access?
2. What does this mean for this geographic area regarding health disparities, food access, and access to medical care?

Activity #3

Watch the video regarding Food Waste. List and explain five actions you can take to reduce food waste.

http://www.pbs.org/food/features/lexicon-of-sustainability-food-waste/

Activity #4

Pick one rural town and one urban town. Utilizing the resources provided in this chapter, compare and contrast the following:

1. Population size
2. Median income
3. Composition of population (ethnicity, race, etc.)
4. Geography of town
5. Types of businesses and industries operated within the town
6. Types of employment available as a result of these businesses and industries
7. Does this town have a hospital? If yes, how many and size of the hospital(s).
8. Health disparities and other issues related to geography of these two towns
9. Possible areas to improve and suggestions for improvement

Activity #5

In teams of 3-4 have students analyze the following scenario and make recommendations.

Scenario:

You are a team of public health specialists and you just received a substantial grant to improve and promote healthy eating habits in one of Camden, New Jersey's inner city neighborhood. Your team has determined that there is a significant gap in accessibility of healthy foods. There are over 30 fast food restaurants in the neighborhood and several mini-marts, but larger grocery stores are limited and stores with adequate produce are few and far between. The team has decided that in order to promote healthy eating in this location they must first address the issues of accessibility and availability of healthy foods. Often, these foods are more expensive, which is an additional barrier your team must consider. Your team must come up with a project idea that will help to address these issues. Some ideas might be: a co-op garden, a farmers' market, a healthy choice grocery store, a healthy food bank, etc. Once your team has chosen a project, you will present this project idea to the grant "investment team." Develop and present: your project idea, project purpose, a brief plan for promoting the idea and engaging the community, and the anticipated outcome of the project. "Sell your project" to the investment team.

DISCUSSION QUESTIONS:

1. Identify and explain the characteristics of rural and urban populations.
2. Rural and urban populations face distinct health disparities and challenges. In your opinion, which population is worse off? Why?
3. Underserved populations face the issue of finding and retaining medical care providers. Why is this so and what could be done to address the problem?
4. If nothing is done to eradicate health disparities facing urban and rural populations, which issues are likely to worsen over the next several decades?
5. Find one policy initiative, not mentioned in this chapter, promoting the improvement or eradication of health disparities connected to geography. Explain the policy initiative, the population it serves, and its intended goal(s).

REFERENCES:

2012 National Healthcare Disparities Report. June 2013. Agency for Healthcare Research and Quality, Rockville, MD. http://www.ahrq.gov/ research/findings/nhqrdr/nhdr12/index.html

2012 National Healthcare Quality Report: Chapter 10. Access to Health Care. May 2013. *Agency for Healthcare Research and Quality,* Rockville, MD. http://www.ahrq.gov/research/findings/nhqrdr/nhdr12/chap10.html

AARP. (2012). *Meeting older adults' mobility needs: Health care and transportation in rural communities.* Retrieved from http://www.aarp.org/content/dam/aarp/livable-communities/act/transportation/health-care-and-transportation-in-rural-communities-aarp.pdf

American Academy of Family Physicians. (2013, June 20). *Geographic distribution of primary care physicians affects health care, says policy brief.* Retrieved from http://www.aafp.org/news-now/government-medicine/20130620geodistpolicy.html

American Hospital Association. (2014, January). *Fast facts on US hospitals.* Retrieved from http://www.aha.org/research/rc/stat-studies/fast-facts.shtml

American Hospital Association. (2011, April). *Trend watch: The opportunities and challenges for rural hospitals in an era of health reform.* Retrieved from www.aha.org/research/.../11apr-tw-rural.pdf

American Medical Student Association. (n.d.). *Breaking barriers: Barriers to rural health care.* Retrieved from http://www.amsa.org/programs /barriers/rural/barriers.html

American Medical Student Association. (n.d.). *Health care delivery: Rural vs. urban communities.* Retrieved from http://www.amsa.org

Bahls, C. (2011, October 6). Health policy brief: Achieving equity in health. *Health Affairs.* Retrieved from https://www.healthaffairs.org/healthpolicybriefs /brief.php?brief_id=53

Black, A., Renkessler, D. & Stanestane, A. (2013). Broad street cholera pump. *Atlas Obscura.* Retrieved from http://www.atlasobscura.com/places/broad-street-cholera-pump

Bolin, J.N. & Bellamy, G. (n.d.). Rural healthy people 2020 [PowerPoint slides]. Retrieved from http://www.srph.tamhsc.edu/centers/srhrc/images/rhp2020

Corburn, J. (2013, December 27). Taking urban health equity seriously in 2013. *Robert Wood Johnson Foundation, Human Capital* [Blog]. Retrieved from http://www.rwjf.org/en/blogs/human-capital-blog/2012/12/taking_urban_health.html

Cromartie, J. (2013, May 24). How is rural America changing? *Economic Research Service USDA* [PowerPoint slides]. Retrieved from http://www.census.gov /newsroom/cspan/rural_america/20130524_rural_america_slides.pdf

Doeksen, G.A., T. Johnson, and C. Willoughby. (1997). *Measuring the Economic Importance of the Health Sector on a Local Economy: A Brief Literature Review and Procedures to Measure Local Impacts.* Retrieved from http://srdc.msstate.edu/publications/archive/202.pdf

Dreier, H. and Yen, H. (2013, June 13). Rural American posts first-ever loss in population. *Associated Press.* Retrieved from http://bigstory.ap.org/article/census-rural-us-loses-population-first-time

Dummer, T.J. (2008, April 22). Health geography: Supporting public health policy and planning. *Canadian Medical Association Journal,* 178(9). Retrieved from http://www.cmaj.ca/content/178/9/1177.full

Enemark, Michelle. Broad Street Cholera Pump [Image]. Retrieved from Atlas Obscura Web site: http://www.atlasobscura.com/places/broad-street-cholera-pump. Creative Commons Attribution-Share Alike 2.0 Generic license.

Feeding America. (2014). *Hunger in America.* Retrieved from http://feedingamerica. org/hunger-in-america/hunger-facts.aspx

Hart, L.G., Larson, E.H., & Lishner, D.M. (2005, July). Rural definitions for health policy and research. *American Journal of Pubic Health,* 95(7). Retrieved from http://www.ncbi.nlm.nih.gov/pmc/articles/PMC1449333/

Healthcare disparities and barriers to healthcare. (2010). Stanford School of Medicine eCampus Rural Health [Rural Health Fact Sheet]. Retrieved from http://ruralhealth.stanford.edu/health-pros/factsheets/disparities-barriers.html

Health Research & Educational Trust. (2013, June). *The role of small and rural hospitals and care systems in effective population health partnerships.* Chicago, IL: Health Research & Educational Trust. Retrieved from http://www.hpoe.org/ resources/hpoehretaha-guides/1385

Health Resources and Services Administration, United States Department of Health and Human Services. (n.d.). *Shortage designation: Health professional shortage areas & medically underserved areas/populations.* Retrieved from http://www.hrsa.gov/shortage/

Health Resources and Services Administration, United States Department of Health and Human Services. (n.d.). *Telehealth.* Retrieved from http://www.hrsa.gov/ruralhealth/about/telehealth/telehealth.html

Kaiser Family Foundation. (n.d.). *Urban population (Percent of total population living in urban areas).* Retrieved from http://kff.org/global-indicator/urban-population/

Kane, J. (2014, January 24). How stress, money woes contribute to the 'perfect storm' for weight gain. *PBS.org.* Retrieved from http://www.pbs.org/newshour/rundown/why-stress-and-money-woes-may-lead-to-weight-gain/

Kincheloe, J., Palacio, M., Butler, D., Shupe, A., & Ward-Hunt, C.C. (2013). *Health disparities the 2013 report: Exploring health equity in Colorado's 10 winnable battles.* Colorado Department of Public Health and Environment Office of Health Equity. Denver, CO. *Maldistribution.* (2014). Merriam-Webster Dictionary. http://www.merriam- webster.com/dictionary/maldistribution

Morgan, T.E. (2011). Glutamateric Neurons in Rodent Models Respond to Nanoscale Particulate Urban Air Pollutants in Vivo and in Vitro. *Environmental Health Perspectives,* 119(7), 1003.

National Association of Community Health Centers. (2011, November). *Removing barriers to care: Community health centers in rural areas.* Retrieved from https://www.nachc.com/client/documents/Rural%20Fact%20Sheet%20-%20November%202011.pdf

National Institutes of Health. (2002). *Strategic research plan and budget to reduce and ultimately eliminate health disparities, volume 1.* Retrieved from http://www.nimhd.nih.gov/strategicmock/our_programs/strategic/pubs/VolumeI_031003EDrev.pdf

National Resources Defense Council. (2013, March). Your scraps add up: Reducing food waste can save money and resources. Retrieved from http://www.nrdc.org/living/eatingwell/files/foodwaste_2pgr.pdf

National Rural Health Care. (n.d.). *What's different about rural health care?* Retrieved from http://www.ruralhealthweb.org/go/left/about-rural-health

Ollove, M. (2014, January 3). Are there enough doctors for the newly insured? *Kaiser Health News.* Retrieved from http://www.kaiserhealthnews.org/Stories/2014/ January/03/doctor-shortage-primary-care-specialist.aspx

Primary Care Workforce Facts and Stats No. 3. (January 2012). *Agency for HealthcareResearch and Quality,* Rockville, MD. Retrieved from http://www.ahrq.gov/ research/findings/factsheets/primary/pcwork3/index.html

Rural Assistance Center. (n.d.). *Frontier Frequently Asked Questions.* Retrieved from http://www.raconline.org/topics/frontier/faqs

Rural Assistance Center. (2014). *Transportation Frequently Asked Questions.* Retrieved from http://www.raconline.org/topics/transportation/faqs

Ricketts, T.C. (2002, March 13). Geography and disparity in health. Retrieved from http://www.iom.edu/~/media/Files/Activity%20Files/Quality/NHDRGuidance/DisparitiesRicketts.pdf

Ricketts, T.C., Savitz, L.A., Gesler, W.M. & Osborne, D.N. (1997). Using geographic methods to understand health issues. *Agency for Healthcare Research and Quality.* Retrieved from http://archive.ahrq.gov/research/geomap/geomap1.htm

Schwamm, L.H. (2014). Telehealth: Seven strategies to successfully implementdisruptive technology and transform health care. *Health Affairs.* 33(2), 200-206. http://content.healthaffairs.org/content/33/2/200.full.html

The lexicon of sustainability: Know your food [web series episodes]. (2014, February 18). *Public Broadcasting Service.* Retrieved from http://www.pbs.org/food/features/lexicon-of-sustainability-food-waste/

The Piton Foundation. (2011). *What.* Retrieved from The Children's Corridor: http://www.denverchildrenscorridor.org

Treuhaft, S. & Karpyn, A. (2010). The grocery gap: Who has access to healthy food and why it matters. *PolicyLink.* Retrieved from: http://www.policylink.org/site/c.lkIXLbMNJrE/b.5860321/k.89D7/The_Grocery_Gap_Who_Has_Access_to_Healthy_Food_and_Why_It_Matters.htm

Unite for Sight. (n.d.). *Urban versus rural health.* Retrieved from http://www.uniteforsight.org/global-health-university/urban-rural-health

United States Department of Agriculture, Agricultural Marketing Service. (n.d.). *Food Deserts.* Retrieved from http://apps.ams.usda.gov/fooddeserts/foodDeserts.aspx

United States Department of Agriculture, Economic Research Service. (2012, December). *Rural America at a Glance: 2012 Edition.* Retrieved from http://www.ers.usda.gov/publications/eb-economic-brief/eb24.aspx

United States Department of Agriculture, Economic Research Service. (2013, December). *Rural Classifications, Overview.* Retrieved from http://www.ers.usda.gov/topics/rural-economy-population/rural-classifications.aspx#.UwAAZRYVCxo

U.S. Census Bureau. (2013, January). *Urban and Rural Areas.* Retrieved from https://www.census.gov/history/www/programs/geography/urban_and_rural_areas.html

U.S. Census Bureau. (2013, March). *Urban and Rural Classification.* Retrieved from http://www.census.gov/geo/reference/urban-rural.html

U.S. Department of Health and Human Services. (n.d.). *Defining the Rural Population.* Retrieved from http://www.hrsa.gov/ruralhealth/policy/definition_of_rural.html

Uscher-Pines, L. & Mehrotra, A. (2014). Analysis of Teladoc use seems to indicate expanded access to care for patients without prior connection to a provider. *Health Affairs*, 33(2), 258-264. http://content.healthaffairs. org/content/33/2/258.full.html

White House task force on childhood obesity report to the President. (n.d.). *Let's Move: America's Move to Raise a Healthier Generation of Kids.* Retrieved from http://www.letsmove.gov/white-house-task-force-childhood-obesity-report-president

World Health Organization. (2014). *Urban Population Growth.* Retrieved from http://www.who.int/gho/urban_health/situation_trends/urban_population_growth_text/en/

You all took stand. (2010, February 20). *White House Blog.* Message posted to http://www.whitehouse.gov/blog/2010/02/19/you-all-took-a-stand

Chapter 10:

Leading to Quality

Kevin Zeiler

KEY CONCEPTS:

Accident
Adverse Event
Agency for Healthcare Research and Quality (AHRQ)
Baldridge National Quality Act
Benchmarking
Case Management
Continuous Quality Improvement (CQI)
Data Collection
Failure, Modes & Effects Analysis (FMEA)
Fishbone Diagrams
Focus, Analyze, Develop & Execute model (FADE)
Improvement Team
Incident Report
Medical Errors
National Quality Forum (NQF)
Organizational Culture
Patient Safety
Plan, Do, Check & Act (PDCA)
Plan, Do, Study & Act (PDSA)
Quality
Survey
Waste

CHAPTER OVERVIEW:

Health quality is an important aspect for anyone working in the healthcare arena and this chapter addresses the concepts and tools used to measure **quality** within healthcare as they apply to different populations and disparate treatment in the delivery of care. Being able to mitigate the risks involved in **patient safety** as well as reducing **medical errors** will be explored and the ability to apply these techniques to specific patient populations will be explained. In addition, external factors such as legislative acts and accreditation issues will be evaluated, so the reader has a complete understanding of the field and how it is influenced by these forces. Also, the ability to understand the past, apply sound quality measures to the present and prepare for future considerations will provide the present or future manager the ability to work towards embracing quality issues, so that disparate treatment in health care can be eliminated. Finally, performance improvement tools will be looked at, so the aspiring manager will have a better understanding of ways to "close the gap" when dealing with disparate health issues.

WHY IS THIS IMPORTANT?

Quality in healthcare can be broken down very simply to mean that a provider is able to service a patient with the right treatment at the right time and ultimately, achieve the right outcome. By using quality as the benchmark, patients facing health care disparities will be better served and will have the ability to receive the care they need when they need it. Furthermore, quality standards will help to reduce the underuse, overuse and misuse of healthcare services that affect so many in the underserved populations.

CHAPTER EXPECTATIONS:

Upon reading this chapter, the student will be able to:

- Define quality as it applies to healthcare and management responsibilities.
- Measure quality as it applies specifically to a given population.
- Learn to evaluate health care quality data and define quality indicators.
- Redirect organizational goals to address specific health care disparities using quality data.
- Use performance improvement tools for purposes of intervention as it applies to the concepts of underuse, overuse and misuse.
- Understand quality team dynamics and apply them to "best practices" that are used within the industry.
- Recognize internal and external factors that hinder zero error and use this assessment to "close the gap" as it applies to quality standards pertinent to health care disparities.

INTRODUCTION:

The ability to look at factors that contribute to patient safety and the overall health of the individual is tantamount to being able to provide appropriate care. All managers should care about zero error and should therefore, put the patient first. Quality speaks to these issues by addressing patient needs from onset to recovery and beyond. The ability to measure quality and work with the tools of quality will allow managers the ability to better understand specific patient populations and treat them with the best medicine available. Ultimately, care needs to meet the expectations of the individual, be safe, timely, effective and equitable across all patient populations. Quality in healthcare provides the tools to make this a reality.

HISTORICAL CONTEXT:

Most of us look at the medical profession today and generally, feel confident that our providers are well-trained, licensed professionals, but that was not always the case. It was not too long ago that physician training was crude, at best, and hospitals answered to nobody but themselves. The Quality Initiative began with the formation of the American Medical Association (AMA) around 1850 (Western Journal of Medicine, 1994). The AMA began work to help organize and improve healthcare in the United States and thus, improved quality.

Other organizations followed suit and today, we know that there exists multiple organizations that are in charge of accreditation and organizational oversight. Additionally, government at all levels, i.e., federal, state, local, etc., are involved with the industry through legislative acts and other political actions. These organizations were focused on improving care and worked hand-in-hand with all levels of practitioners to ensure that quality care was the priority. Physicians' led the charge by reviewing medical records for errors, so that changes in the form of improved care would occur (Western Journal of Medicine, 1994). This was the standard until the early 1970's when they finally became part of outcome oriented surveys for all accredited facilities.

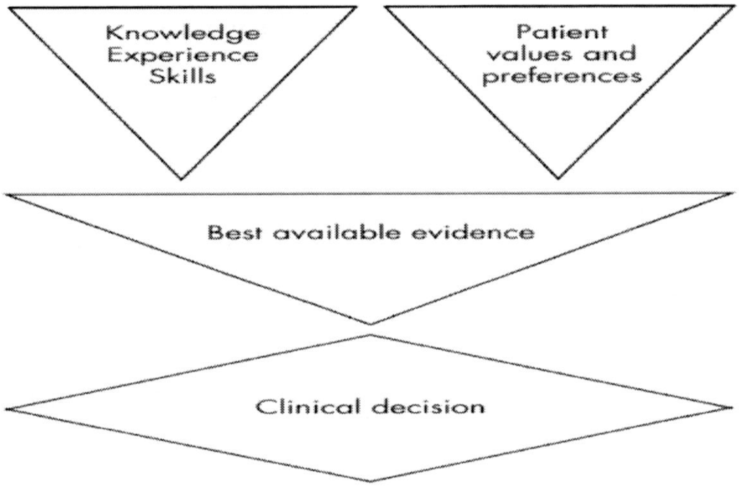

Figure 1: Archives of Disease in Childhood. (2005). *Principles of Evidence Based Medicine.* Retrieved from: http://adc.bmj.com/content/90/8/837.full

Today, modern approaches look at healthcare from an evidence based approach. To accomplish this, organizations use numerous performance measures seen in other industries, but they also add the clinical decision making process, which means that today's quality measures are derived from clinical practice guidelines developed by medical professional groups (Spath, 2009). Figure1 shows the continuum of care using evidence-based medicine.

The above chart illustrates how treatment decisions are made using both input from patients and "best evidence" from treatment modalities. Furthermore, many of the evidence-based measures that are being used to evaluate clinical medicine are in fact mandated by regulatory agencies as well as accrediting bodies (Spath, 2009).

Since we are looking at what is being done for at-risk groups whom often face disparate treatment in health services, models intentionally look at these key factors as well. The following list of performance measures was taken from an academic study that was focused on providing quality care to varying populations. In addition to other measures, the following address at-risk populations:

- Cultural and Linguistic Competence
- Availability of foreign-language written materials
- Availability and ease of use of translation services
- Number and scope of cultural competence training program
- Provider mix reflective of community(ies) served
- Governing board and management staff reflective of community(ies) served (Neil & Nerenz, 2001)

Evidence based medicine is certainly not the only approach, but in healthcare it is the leader when it comes to quality. Since regulatory and accrediting bodies have embraced this technique, it is also the standard that is being utilized today as well. The history of measurment methods in healthcare have led the industry to this point in time, but it is clear that the quest for zero errors will continue forward. Finally, cost and quality have recently merged into a major organizational issue that may be very difficult to contend with. Future quality issues may very well list cost as a determining factor when it comes to patient treatment and outcomes. The continuum chart above (figure 1) does not define cost as a factor, but with the external factors that are influencing health care today, it is only a matter of time before the history of quality in healthcare is rewritten.

WHAT YOU SHOULD KNOW:

The implementation of a well-planned quality management program must be approached, as any other change within an organization would be. Leadership is the first issue that must be addressed in order to make the system work. Therefore, organizational leaders must understand what quality is, where it comes from and expected outcomes.

Quality management, compared to other organizational programs is still in its infancy. For example, it has been a mere twenty years since the AMA has recognized **Medical Quality Management (MQM)** as a specialty (Varkey, 2010). Therefore, leadership must find ways to promote quality to both clinical and administrative personnel in order to achieve the organizational outcomes that are desired. In addition to leadership, healthcare organizations must focus on their own culture, structure, technological capabilities and legal environment (Varkey, 2010). The ability to see the global picture will not only allow the organization to promote change, but it will also allow leadership the ability to see what tools are necessary to implement a quality program that is both effective and accepted by the organization. Furthermore, leadership must lead the charge for changes in quality, especially as it applies to underserved populations that are already facing disparate treatment within the healthcare community. **The National Quality Forum (NQF)** endorses many measures that are a good starting point for leadership to promote a quality program in their institution. The following measures are endorsed by the NQF:

- Make our healthcare system more information rich
- Point to actions physicians, other clinicians, and organizations can take to make healthcare safe and equitable
- Enhance transparency in healthcare
- Ensure accountability of healthcare providers
- Generate data that helps consumers make informed choices about their care (NQF "Who We Are," 2014).

In addition to the quality measures outlined by the NQF, other organizations such as the **Agency for Healthcare Research and Quality (AHRQ)**, have also set standards that establish solid starting points for organizational leaders. These are:

- Make health care safer
- Higher quality
- More accessible
- Equitable
- Affordable (AHRQ "About Us," 2013).

The AHRQ continues by noting that they are also committed to, "working with the U.S. Department of Health and Human Services (HHS) and other partners to make sure that the evidence is understood and used," (AHRQ, 2013). This commitment means that not only is quality improvement focused on making health care quality individual, it also strives to set industry wide standards that will allow providers the tools and research to make solid clinical decisions for best outcomes.

Examples of leadership and reasons for using a health care quality program only answer part of the questions that are necessary for understanding quality issues in health care. What health care quality looks like is another key feature that must be understood in order to fully appreciate the benefits that a quality system will promote within an organization. Defining quality care is certainly not simple, but the following will be used as the basis for quality in healthcare throughout the rest of this chapter. According to the Institute of Medicine (IOM) quality can be defined as, "The degree to which health services for individuals and populations increase the likelihood of desired health outcomes and are consistent with current professional knowledge." (IOM, 2014). As is apparent, this definition works well with the idea that evidence based medicine is leading the charge. Even though this definition seems quite simple, it hides many detailed issues that must be evaluated when looking at quality in healthcare delivery and how quality plays a role with disparate populations. Therefore, for purposes of this chapter, the IOM definition will serve as a basis or launching pad if you will, for understanding this complex area of healthcare and all it entails.

Many look to Managed Care Organizations (MCO's) as a definition of quality of care because of the way they are organized and their goal of reducing costs. For example, using the chart on the right, you will see the techniques used by MCO's to help with care management.

- Contracts with physicians and hospitals to provide comprehensive health services to MCO enrollees.
- Capitation or monthly budgets which shift some financial risk to physicians.
- Utilization review to minimize patient and physician use of services.
- Quality controls to improve clinical services or measured health outcomes.
- Financial incentives for patients to use contracted providers and facilities (American Medical Student Assoc., 1999).

As you can see from the chart to the right these issues speak directly to quality even though they are defined within the bounds of case management. However, case management is a prime example of how existing programs and/or techniques within healthcare can be used to improve quality to all populations. To illustrate, the **Case Management Association of America (CMSA)** defines **case management** as, "... case management is based in the fact that when an individual reaches the optimum level of wellness and functional capability, everyone benefits: the individuals being served, their support systems, the health care delivery systems and the various reimbursement sources, " (CMSA, 2012). Not only does the individual benefit as has been noted earlier in this chapter, but the system as a whole benefits for a plethora of reasons to include financial considerations.

Quality management in health care is certainly a multidimensional area of the industry that cannot be approached from one side. Leadership, management, finance, accounting, economics, clinical, administrative as well as case management techniques, insurance approaches and **organizational culture** must all be included in the quality paradigm. For example, if the organization does not share beliefs and establish norms for operating their business (organizational culture) how will buy-in be achieved? Without buy-in, quality is simply a buzzword that is undefined and unfulfilled within the organization. The ability to bring all of the facets of quality together is the key to turning health disparities around. With quality, inequalities become equalities and the system is better organized for all involved. Ultimately, the ability to instill a culture of acceptance through quality management will define health care in this country and will help to coordinate and organize care for future populations.

Quality Indicators:

Health care quality must be defined, as we noted earlier, by many different variants within healthcare both clinically and administratively. Thus, what are good indicators of quality? One could assume that safety is an obvious choice and this would be a correct assumption, but what else makes good quality indicators? LaVeist (2005) looks at indicators in the realm of cultural competence. In other words, he describes these indicators as those items that, "describe cultural competence as a set of congruent behaviors, attitudes and policies that come together in a system, agency or among professionals and enable effective work in cross-cultural situations," (LaVeist, 2005). However, as LaVeist (2005) continues to note, it is fact that most patients who are racial or ethnic minorities, often see practitioners that do not look like them (LaVeist, 2005). Therefore, using cultural competence as a quality indicator may have its shortcomings. This however may be one of the indicators that organizations may wish to focus on and during the process, build cultural competence into the process.

Ultimately, the goal of health care quality is to achieve better outcomes with fewer errors. The overall goal then will be to accept the fact that multiple factors lead to a positive outcome for the patient. These types of indicators are more indicative of what a good quality outcome may look like.

The patient
- Demographic factors (age, sex, height)
- Lifestyle factors (smoking, alcohol use, weight, diet, physical exercise)
- Psychosocial factors (social status, education)
- Compliance

\+
The illness
- Severity, prognosis
- Comorbidity

\+
The treatment (prevention, diagnostics, care, rehabilitation, therapy and control)
- Competence
- Technical equipment
- Evidence based clinical practice
- Efficacy, accuracy

\+
The organization
- Use of clinical guidelines
- Cooperation
- Delay

= OUTCOME

Figure 2: Quality Indicators. International Journal for Quality in Health Care. (2014). *Defining and classifying clinical indicators for quality improvement.*
Retrieved from: http://www.calidadasistencial.com/images/gestion/biblioteca/63.pdf

As figure 2 illustrates, quality indicators come from several different areas, i.e., the patient, the illness, treatment modalities and the organization itself. Indicators do not have to look the same across the continuum of care, but categories being defined will help to assure that all aspects of care are being considered. It is also easy to see how best practices fit nicely into the treatment category. This is also a good way to "benchmark" or score how the organization is achieving when you look at the organization section of figure 2. In addi tion, figure 2 can help to point out issues that may not be so obvious on first review. These issues often show themselves as underuse, overuse and misuse. Underuse is broadly defined as not providing a service that has a benefit greater than the risk involved, overuse is just as big of a problem because it is often an unproven or even dangerous procedure that is being used and misuse occurs when the best treatment practice is used, but because of errors or other complications, patient outcomes are poor. By watching and understanding the quality indicators, organizations will be in a much better position to provide the best outcomes for patients.

FACT: "Benchmarking stems from a personal and organizational willingness to continuously improve. A vibrant sense of curiosity and a deep respect for learning are keys to successful benchmarking and adoption of best practices," (Spath, 2009).

In addition to the quality indicators, the **Baldridge National Quality Act** takes things a step further. The goal of the **Baldridge Act** is to enhance competition and provide a framework for quality improvement (Buchbinder & Shanks, 2012).

Figure 3 illustrates many of the criteria that have already been discussed throughout this chapter. The chapter opened with leadership, which is clearly illustrated. This is closely followed by the workforce (clinical and administrative staff), strategic business plans and customer (patient) focus. All of these components will combine to provide the best outcome for the patient.

Finally, the Agency for Health Care Research and Quality (AHRQ), the organization charged with making health care safer, notes that quality of care is improving across many indicators, minorities and groups in the lower socio-economic status categories are worsening (Assoc. of American Medical Colleges, 2013). The fact that indicators are being used does show that change is occurring, but quality care is missing the most vulnerable populations. The group continues by noting that most of the data issues stem from the fact that there is poor reporting concerning at-risk populations (Assoc. of American Medical Colleges, 2013). Clearly, indicators are not the only answer to solving issues of quality and safety for those facing healthcare disparities, but it is a place to begin working on these issues and it is also a platform for including better reporting techniques.

Data Evaluation:

What does this all mean? Research indicates that some outcomes are improving, but others are not and overall, minorities and at-risk populations are still losing ground. The goal of evaluating the data is to improve areas where organizations are lacking and ultimately, secure better patient outcomes. As we look at disparities, we report **adverse events** (harmful or undesired effect) and then look at ways to improve safety (prevention of aforementioned events). The goal is to not only cut down on **accidents** and **medical errors**, and ensure that they do not occur, but to ensure that they are addressed properly and do not occur again. As the chapter has pointed out, there are many shortcomings when it comes to **data collection**. For example, the 2013 Colorado Health Disparities Report notes that, "...data are not always available for subpopulations... and due to limitations, the report must often use broad racial and ethnic categories for reporting..." (CDPHE: Office of Health Equity, 2013). This is problematic for users of data and oftentimes means that those most at risk do not receive the quality care they deserve.

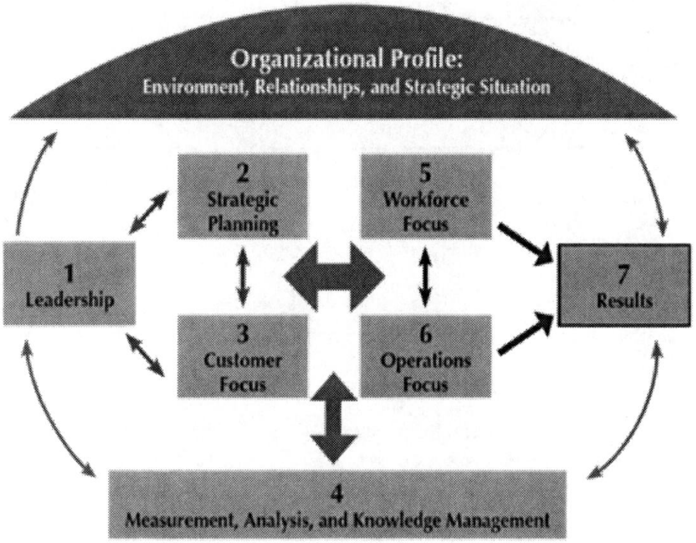

Figure 3. Criteria for Performance Excellence. [Graphic]. This figure is used with permission of the Baldrige Performance Excellence Program. National Institute of Standards and Technology. (2013). Baldridge 2013-2014 Criteria for Performance Excellence. Gaithersburg, MD: U.S. Department of Commerce, National Institute of Standards and Technology. Retrieved from: http://www.nist.gov/baldrige/publications/archive/2013_2014_business_nonprofit_criteria.cfm

Data collection takes place in an ongoing manner and looks at the different variables of interest depending on the improvements that an organization is hoping to achieve. Often, this collection may come in the form of a **survey**, which is sent to different populations for different collection reasons. As an example, patients and family members may receive one to collect information on their stay, how they perceived their care and so on. Also, clinical staff and providers will receive a survey to determine how they perceive the process that goes into providing patient care, systems, training and their overall perception of the system. Clearly, these are two very different types of surveys, but the type of questions being asked and answered help to provide data that can be collected, evaluated and interpreted, so that positive change can be provided to the patient for improved safety and quality of care. Many times data may be collected to determine specific population demographics, i.e., age, gender, race, ethnicity, etc. This data will be used to determine the patient population, so that organizations are better prepared with resources and training on their specific population.

As we will see in the next section of this chapter, there are several different performance improvement tools that can and are used for putting the data that is collected into play. However, the Institute for Healthcare Improvement uses the failure, modes, and effects analysis tool or **FMEA** to look for failures as well as ways to correct them before they become a problem (Institute for Healthcare Improvement, 2014). This tool will continually be used to evaluate the data that is being presented and can constantly change to adapt to new data as well as changes within the organization. Because collecting data is only part of the solution, FMEA takes that data to make it useable in a real world setting.

Additional data is often received from **incident reports**, case studies taken from actual patient contacts and other documented events that occur within healthcare organizations. There also exists a plethora of charts and graphs that are often used to present data, and organizations vary on their utilization of these devices. However, a diagram known as the **fishbone diagram** is often used as a way to measure the cause and effect of a particular issue. These types of diagrams are named after Kaoru Ishikawa who first used them in the 1960's for quality control purposes (Spath, 2009).

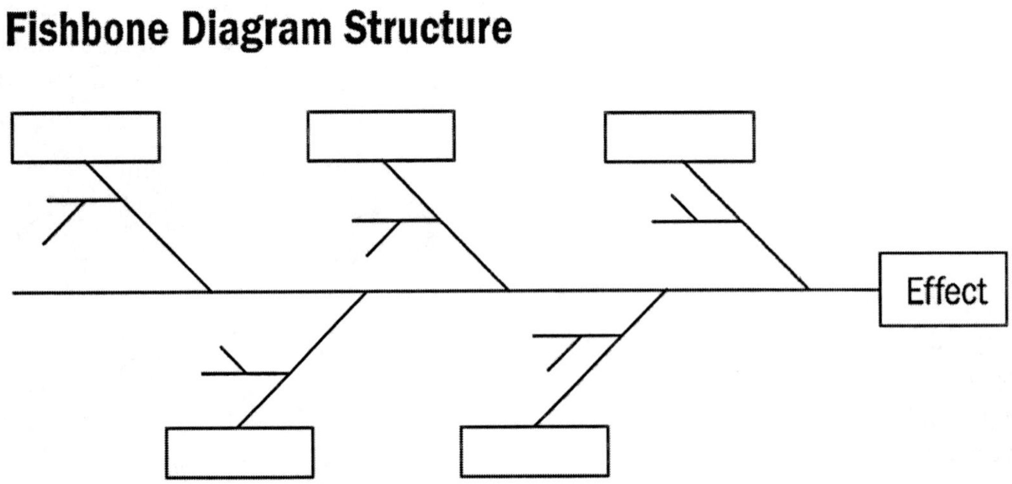

Figure 4: Fishbone Diagram. United States Agency for International Development (USAID). (2011). *Health Care Improvement Project: Cause and Effect Analysis.* Retrieved from: http://pdf.usaid.gov/pdf_docs/Pnadp129.pdf

The above fishbone diagram from the United States Agency for International Development helps to illustrate how a problem can be addressed based on the "cause" and how it affects the health system. An organization can fill in the blanks with any data that is pertinent. For example, the cause may be: external issues, internal problems, regulatory issues and the effect might be prolonged wait times, or unreadable blood lab values. Depending on the data collected, this diagram clearly provides the user a starting point for solving the problem.

Next, the chapter will look at the different performance improvement tools that can be used in conjunction with the data that was collected. As noted in the beginning of this section, the analysis is only as good as the data on which it was based. As we have seen, oftentimes when dealing with racial and ethnic minorities and socioeconomically disadvantaged individuals, the data is often not good enough. Thus, the goal with data acquisition is to collect the best data available and make it pertinent to the patient population that the organization you are working in is representing.

Interventions:

The ability to institute change is without a doubt the number one priority when it comes to decreasing health disparities through quality procedures. The Centers for Medicare and Medicaid (CMS) understand this and have even put together a web page that explains their commitment. The mission of CMS in this battle is to, "reduce and eliminate health disparities for vulnerable minority populations and work towards health equity. This website is dedicated to reporting on the following populations:

- Racial and ethnic minorities
- Low-income groups

- Older adults
- Residents of rural areas and inner cities, and
- Individuals with disabilities and special health care needs," (CMS, 2014).

So, how does an organization like CMS intervene to improve quality? Their organization uses **Quality Improvement Organizations (QIO's)** to establish a process for promoting evidence-based medicine to its partner organizations (CMS, 2014). These programs exist through private contractors to use education as the means for providing the appropriate interventions to promote quality health care. Specifically, the QIO's are mandated to:

- Improve the quality of care for beneficiaries;
- Protecting the integrity of the Medicare Trust Fund by ensuring that Medicare pays only for services and goods that are reasonable and necessary and that are provided in the most appropriate setting; and
- Protecting beneficiaries by expeditiously addressing individual complaints, such as beneficiary complaints; provider-based notice appeals; violations of the Emergency Medical Treatment and Labor Act (EMTALA); and other related responsibilities as articulated in QIO-related law (CMS, 2014).

Not only does this model promote quality and appropriate interventions, it also looks at waste as an item that needs to be eliminated. **Waste** in healthcare refers to numerous items such as **medical errors**, failure of care delivery, medical liability, **accidents**, overtreatment, under treatment and the like (Fleming, 2012). It is these very issues that affect the most vulnerable populations and require immediate intervention to help prevent these types of issues.

Other methods used to address performance improvement include the **PLAN, DO, CHECK and ACT (PDCA)** technique. **PDCA** is defined as a four-step model for carrying out change that continually repeats itself according to the **American Society for Quality** (ASQ, 2004). The procedure for success is based on the following criteria:

Plan–Do–Check–Act Procedure

- **Plan.** Recognize an opportunity and plan a change.
- **Do.** Test the change. Carry out a small-scale study.
- **Check.** Review the test, analyze the results and identify what you've learned.
- **Act.** Take action based on what you learned in the study step: If the change did not work, go through the cycle again with a different plan. If you were successful, incorporate what you learned from the test into wider changes. Use what you learned to plan new improvements, beginning the cycle again (ASQ, 2004).

The motto illustrates the circle that has no end, so those seeking **quality** must always continue the quest for change (ASQ, 2004).

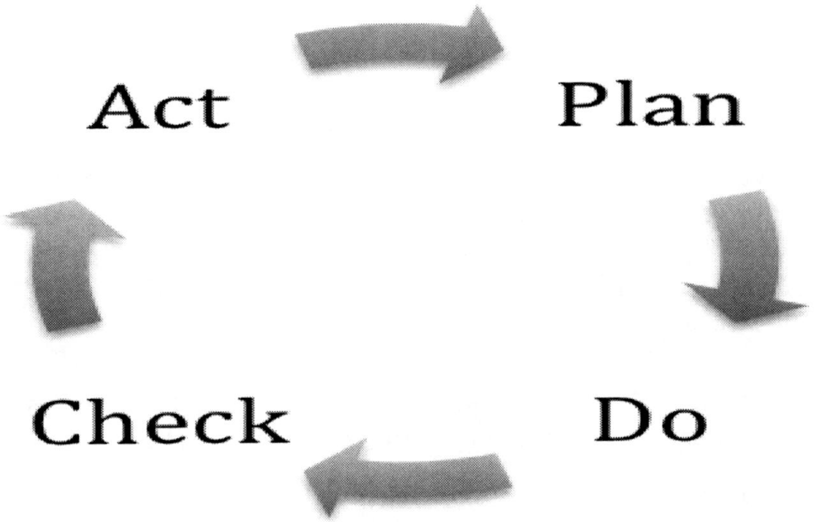

Figure 5: *Plan-Do-Check-Act (PDCA) Cycle.* American Society for Quality (ASQ). (2004). *Plan-Do-Check-Act (PDCA) Cycle.* Retrieved from http://asq.org/learn-about-quality/project-planning-tools/overview/pdca-cycle.html

Another, similar improvement technique that is being used is the **PLAN, DO, STUDY and ACT (PDSA)** approach. This model is also known as the Deming performance improvement model and much like the **PDCA** above, it is used to in a continual process for **continuous quality improvement (CQI)** interventions (Spath, 2009).

One additional model to help illustrate performance improvement is the **FOCUS, ANALYZE, DEVELOP and EXECUTE model (FADE).** The **FADE** model has four distinctive steps and they include:

- **Focus**: Define and verify the process to be improved
- **Analyze**: Collect and analyze data to establish baselines, identify root causes and point toward possible solutions
- **Develop**: Based on the data, develop action plans for improvement, including implementation, communication, and measuring/monitoring
- **Execute**: Implement the action plans, on a pilot basis, and install an ongoing measuring/monitoring (process control) system to ensure success (HRSA, 2014).

The FADE technique specifically addresses the data component for instituting change. Also, the ongoing aspect of this technique is to ensure that the measures being implemented are actually making the desired change or providing the desired outcome.

The above tools are only a few of the options available albeit, they are some of the most popular and most proven. These performance improvement tools are critical to establishing the appropriate interventions based on data collection and the search for positive changes with the quality paradigm.

Closing the Gap:

The previous sections of this chapter have illustrated how quality works within the healthcare industry and how they directly or indirectly affect populations that often face multiple disparities. In many instances, the data indicates that these at-risk populations are not seeing better outcomes and most of the time are seeing worse outcomes. This begs the question, "what can be done to close the gap?" *Healthcare Quality: Vision, Strategy and Tools,* illustrates how numerous reports from the Institute of Medicine outlined the gaps in care that exist, but that there is little being discussed to narrow them (Rawson, et.al., 2008). Not only is this disturbing, but it goes to show that even the most sophisticated performance improvement systems are not doing enough to eliminate disparities. Achieving quality in healthcare is ongoing, as we have discussed, but if data is not accurate, financial considerations are not accounted for and organizations do not fully appreciate the limitations of interventions, the system will not improve. Improving quality within the healthcare arena is the responsibility of all players and anything short of an all-inclusive effort will simply fall short.

Kebede discusses closing the gap in his book; *Global Health Disparities* by stating that global influences play a big role in healthcare today and to ignore them is to ignore healthcare quality (Kebede, 2011). He describes the biggest global trends as food insecurity and obesity, tobacco use, urbanization, climate change and the aging population (Kebede, 2011). Most of us face these issues on the evening news every evening and they often get overlooked if they do not directly affect us. The simple truth is that global issues are now local issues. The quality manager can no longer ignore the fact that problems thousands of miles from where he or she lives will not affect the organization. Building **improvement teams** will be key to dealing with these issues. Groups of individuals working towards reachable goals will lead the way. The world is now global in nature and healthcare is not immune to this idea. Being able to understand not only institutional issues, but also broader, more universal issue understanding is now the norm.

Clearly, there is no simple solution to closing the gap. However, this chapter has provided a wealth of knowledge as it applies to improving quality, so a one-step-at-a-time approach may be the best remedy. Healthcare inequity cannot be allowed to survive, so quality improvement must be approached using any number of tools and evaluated based on the best research available. Closing the gap is certainly possible if these tools are utilized and the informed organization is willing to make the changes necessary.

WRAP-UP:

Health care quality may be easily defined, but as this chapter has illustrated, there are many complex ways that quality is measured and instituted within health care organizations. It is clear that through quality management programs and practices, health care disparities can be better managed and ultimately, the entire health care system is better able to serve the desired population. However, it must be clear that external factors such as legislative actions, economic changes and the general health of the country will always keep health care changing. Quality management must continue to strive to improve patient safety and work to ensure that all patient populations are treated fairly and equitably based on proven medical evidence. Finally, the overarching goal of any plan within the healthcare industry is to provide for best patient outcomes and quality is no different. The ability to deliver equal care for all should remain the goal.

DISCUSSION QUESTIONS:

1. What are quality indicators? How do they apply to race and ethnicity?
2. Define quality based on your reading and understanding of the chapter. Do not use a specific definition as defined in the reading, but instead, use your own words to illustrate the complex field of quality management.
3. Think about the health care organization that you utilize. How can you define quality based on the care you have received? Explain with examples.
4. What is value of care to you? How do providers measure perceived value of care?
5. Is safety quality or is quality safety? Explain.
6. Explain the concept of evidence-based medicine. Is this a good way to determine quality care for all patient populations? Explain your answer.
7. Will quality truly help us to close the gap? Does the gap look different for racial and ethnic minorities? If so, what can be done to work on narrowing the issues that make it different?
8. Explain your thoughts on what quality may look like in the future. What factors, external or internal will play the biggest role in changing the way we define quality?

RESOURCES:

Agency for Healthcare Research and Quality:
http://www.ahrq.gov

National Association for Healthcare Quality:
http://www.nahq.org

National Quality Forum:
http://www.qualityforum.org/Home.aspx

Foundation for Health Care Quality:
http://www.qualityhealth.org

Institute for Healthcare Improvement:
http://www.ihi.org/search/pages/results.aspx?k=quality (Video Library)

Health Information Technology and Quality Improvement (Learning modules)
http://www.hrsa.gov/healthit/toolbox/healthitadoptiontoolbox/qualityimprovement/qualityimprovement.html

Robert Wood Johnson Foundation (Webinar)
http://www.rwjf.org/en/about-rwjf/newsroom/features-and-articles/quality-field-notes/performance-measurement-and-quality-improvement.html

ACTIVITY:

This case study illustrates how mistakes are made because systems are too complex or training has been inadequate.

BLOOD LAB ANALYSIS-WRONG PATIENT, WRONG TIME, WRONG OUTCOME

Billy is a new lab tech at Humpty Dumpty Hospital and because several lab employees have suffered falls and cannot come to work, Billy is being sent to the floor to perform labs on his own. Billy was only privy to the hospital's general orientation program, but has not had a chance to review the blood lab protocols or use the complex laboratory computer system. Nonetheless, Billy feels that this is an opportunity to prove himself, so he tells his manager that he feels comfortable with the system and with the training he has received thus far. Billy grabs his equipment cart, orders for the day and heads out.

Billy draws blood from several patients per the chart defining what labs are to be run and enters them into the computer system. All seems to be going well and Billy is feeling good about his job. As the day gets longer Billy begins to tire and doesn't remember if he entered patient numbers into the system. Because he doesn't want to make mistakes, he goes back in and enters patient numbers once again. Finally, Billy approaches the last patient of the day and draws what he thinks is another routine lab. However, Billy did not see the computer screen that indicated that this patient just recently had surgery on her left arm for an infection and no blood is to be drawn from it. Billy draws from the patient's left arm.

Billy leaves for home feeling that he has done an adequate job and looks forward to the next day.

Questions

1. Explain how Billy got to this point. What could have been done differently to prevent Billy from falling off the wall?
2. What errors can you pick out from the above scenario?
3. Who is to blame for negative outcomes, Billy? Humpty Dumpty Hospital? The patients? Explain.
4. Using your knowledge of health care quality, illustrate what changes you would make as a health care manager to ensure that patient safety is the number one priority for your organization and chart the changes you would make to get there.
5. Mistakes, safeguards, technology, etc., are all issues that must be dealt with and even though it may be impossible to be 100% error free, what can be done to mistake-proof the aforementioned systems?

REFERENCES:

Agency for Healthcare Research and Quality (AHRQ). (2013). *About us: AHRQ Mission and Facts.* Retrieved from: http://www.ahrq.gov/about/index.html

American Medical Student Association. (1999). *Health Care and the Underserved: America's Poor and Managed Care.* Retrieved from: http://www.amsa.org/AMSA/Libraries/Committee_Docs/hlthcareunderserved.sflb.ashx

American Society for Quality (ASQ). (2004). *Plan-Do-Check-Act (PDCA) Cycle.* Retrieved from http://asq.org/learn-about-quality/project-planning-tools/overview/pdca-cycle.html

Archives of Disease in Childhood. (2005). *Principles of Evidence Based Medicine.* Retrieved from: http://adc.bmj.com/content/90/8/837.full

Association of American Medical Colleges (AAMC). (2013). *AHRQ Disparities Report Shows Healthcare Gaps in Quality and Access Persist.* Retrieved from: https://www.aamc.org/advocacy/washhigh/highlights2013/343394/052413ahrqreportshowshealthcare-gapsinqualityandaccesspersistform.html

Buchbinder, S.B., & Shanks, N.H. (2012). *Introduction to Health Care Management. 2nd Edition.* Burlington: Jones & Bartlett.

Case Management Society of America (CMSA). (2012). *What is a Case Manager? Definition of case management.* Retrieved from: http://www.cmsa.org/Home/CMSA/WhatisaCaseManager/tabid/224/Default.aspx

Centers for Medicare and Medicaid Services (CMS). (2014). *Discover the Health Disparities Program.* Retrieved from: http://www.cmspulse.org/about-us/pulse.html

Centers for Medicare and Medicaid Services (CMS). (2014). *About Quality Improvement Organizations.* Retrieved from: http://www.cmspulse.org/about-us/qio/index.html

Colorado Department of Public Health and Environment Office of Health Equity (CDPHE). (2013). *Health Disparities: The 2013 Report.* Retrieved from: http://www.colorado.gov/cs/Satellite?blobcol=urldata&blobheadername1=Content-Disposition&blobheadername2=Content-Type&blobheadervalue1=inline%3B+filename%3D%22Health+Disparities%3A+The+2013+Report.pdf%22&blobheadervalue2=application%2Fpdf&blobkey=id&blobtable=MungoBlobs&blobwhere=1251907510501&ssbinary=true

Fleming, Chris. (2012). *Health Affairs Blog: Health Policy Brief-Reducing Waste in Healthcare.* Retrieved from: http://healthaffairs.org/blog/2012/12/14/health-policy-brief-reducing-waste-in-health-care/

Health Information Technology and Quality Improvement (HRSA). (2014). *What is Quality Improvement?* Retrieved from: http://www.hrsa.gov/healthit/toolbox/HealthITAdoptiontoolbox/QualityImprovement/whatisqi.html

Institute for Healthcare Improvement. (2014). *Failure Modes and Effects Analysis Tool.* Retrieved from: http://app.ihi.org/Workspace/tools/fmea/

Institute of Medicine (IOM). (2013). *Crossing the Quality Chasm: The IOM Healthcare Quality Initiative.* Retrieved from: http://www.iom.edu/Global/News%20Announcements/Crossing-the-Quality-Chasm-The-IOM-Health-Care-Quality-Initiative.aspx

Institute of Medicine (IOM). (2014). *How Far Have We Come in Reducing Health Disparities.* Retrieved from: http://www.nap.edu/openbook.php?record_id=13383&page=1

International Journal for Quality in Health Care. (2014). *Defining and classifying clinical indicators for quality improvement.* Retrieved from: http://www.calidadasistencial.com/images/gestion/biblioteca/63.pdf

Kebede-Francis, E. (2010). *Global Health Disparities. Closing the Gap Through Good Governance.* Burlington: Jones & Bartlett.

LaVeist, T.A. (2005). *Minority Populations & Health. An Introduction to Health Disparities in the United States.* San Francisco: Jossey-Bass.

National Institute of Standards and Technology. (2013). *Baldridge 2013-2014 Criteria for Performance Excellence.* Gaithersburg, MD: U.S. Department of Commerce, National Institute of Standards and Technology. Retrieved from: http://www.nist.gov/baldrige/publications/archive/2013_2014_business_nonprofit_criteria.cfm

National Quality Forum, *National Priorities Partnership.* (Washington, DC). Retrieved from: http://www.qualityforum.org/Setting_Priorities/NPP/National_Priorities_Partnership.aspx

Neil, Nancy & Nerenz, David R. (2001). *Performance Measures for Health Care Services.* Seattle: Center for Health Management Research.

Rawson, E.R., Maulik, S.J., Nash, D.B. & Ransom, S.B. (2008). *The Health Care Quality Book. Vision, Strategy and Tools. 2nd Edition.* Chicago: Health Administration Press.

Spath, P. (2009). *Introduction to Health Care Quality Management.* Chicago: Health Administration Press.

United States Agency for International Development (USAID). (2011). *Health Care Improvement Project: Cause and Effect Analysis.* Retrieved from: http://pdf.usaid.gov/pdf_docs/Pnadp129.pdf

Varkey, P. (2010). *Medical Quality Management: Theory & Practice.* Boston: Jones and Bartlett Publishers.

Western Journal of Medicine. (1994). *A Brief History of Health Care Quality Assessment and Improvement in the United States.* Retrieved from: http://www.ncbi.nlm.nih.gov/pmc/articles/PMC1022402/pdf/westjmed00067-0065.pdf

Chapter 11:

Ethical & Legal Considerations

Kevin Zeiler

KEY CONCEPTS:

Affordable Care Act (ACA)
Beliefs
Beneficence
Bioethics
Compassion
Deontological
Do Not Resuscitate (DNR)
Ethics
Euthanasia
Fairness
Health Policy
Justice
Legislation
Malpractice
Morals
Negligence
Non-maleficence
Precedent
Religion
Social Security Act (SSA)
Statutes
Tort
Utilitarian

CHAPTER OVERVIEW:

An ethical and legal approach to the disparate treatment in the delivery of health services cannot be more complicated and difficult to understand. Ethical studies tell us that health disparities are morally wrong because of social and historical injustice that has taken place, but this is often at odds with current legal principles in the United States. Society speaks of a "right" to this or a right to that, but the question surrounding this right is whether or not we have a legal obligation. Yes, it may be true that the teachings of the great philosophers exhibit manifestations that allow us to see what a moral obligation looks like, but as a society, are these moral obligations what control us or do legal manifestos control the way we function?

The ability to incorporate ethics and law and law and ethics into cohesive, understandable and easy to follow principles is a difficult task to say the least, but by looking at the foundation of both, it is clear that understanding will lead to common sense approaches when discussing health disparities. Furthermore, legal principles are more than not, derived from philosophical underpinnings of society, so the two may not be as far apart as one might think.

This chapter will provide a solid foundation for both the legal system and ethical considerations as they apply to health disparities as well as an historical context to guide the reader to the modern day. Additionally, a search for equity will be undertaken to counter the impact that disparities have on so many populations. Finally, a look at bioethics will be discussed, so that the reader can concentrate on specific medical concerns.

WHY IS THIS IMPORTANT?

Legal and ethical issues affect everything that we, as a society touch. Should I do this or that; is this right or wrong; was it legal? These types of questions are pondered regularly by most individuals and within healthcare, they are just as important. The ability to discern right from wrong is a factor that plays a role in the care of the patient and additionally, the legality of one's actions. As well, many individuals are torn by their own beliefs and values that may conflict with current laws that regulate the delivery of health related services. Ultimately, the ability to understand law and ethics as it pertains to health disparities may very well help to shape a path to more equitable outcomes in the delivery of that care. With understanding and knowledge, the individual will be better prepared to use the tools of morality and the law to work within at-risk populations to react to and reduce disparate treatment in the delivery of healthcare.

CHAPTER EXPECTATIONS:

Upon reading this chapter, the student will be able to:

- Define ethics as it applies to healthcare and management responsibilities.
- Understand legal principles as they apply specifically to a given population.
- Define bioethics and apply its impact on diverse populations.
- Redirect legal principles and moral issues to create a roadmap to health equity.
- Use legal precedent to better understand the law as it applies to populations facing disparate treatment.
- Evaluate cultural issues as they apply to religion, race and communication.
- Understand the history of moral influence and healthcare ethics.

INTRODUCTION:

The ability to understand how law and ethics work together in healthcare is vital to everyone involved with the industry. These concepts affect the daily delivery of healthcare services and no organization can avoid them. Therefore, the ability to understand how ethics and law coexist within this fragile environment is key to being able to successfully operate and deliver high quality, efficient and effective healthcare. Understanding how the law works to regulate the healthcare industry as well as how ethical implications play a role in daily decisions is a critical skill that no one person working within the industry can ignore. The way an organization conducts its daily business is controlled by the decisions of legislatures, judges and local ordinances. Ethical and moral issues are often directed by organizations themselves as well as individuals that utilize the system. Many times, ethical concerns brought forth by those delivering healthcare services may interfere with the delivery of those services and thus, cause a dilemma for managers, legal counsel and the organization itself. Ultimately, the ability to understand the law and how it functions will be a critical component to being able to operate within its bounds. Ethical considerations will be established based on the groundwork laid by the organization as well as the individual. In order to be successful, all parties will need to determine the legal issues that surround their daily work as well as the effects on the organization overall. Finally, the ability to balance law and ethics will continually be a challenge for not only the individual, but the organization as well. This chapter is only the beginning to understanding, as the law is constantly changing and being able to adapt and organize within the bounds of legal and ethical constraints is an ongoing battle.

HISTORICAL CONTEXT:

It has been said that the United States is a country of laws and in healthcare; one doesn't have to venture too far to see that this is true. The biggest argument of recent times surrounds the question of whether healthcare is a right or a privilege. For those that are able to obtain health services this question may seem unimportant, but for those that face disparate treatment within the healthcare system, the questions demand answers. In the long history of healthcare within the U.S., numerous legal and ethical issues have been debated time and time again and the above is merely an example of this. Often times the moral answer is not the same as the legal answer, but because we are a country of laws, we more than not choose the route that keeps our organization safe from litigation. Before we go forward, we must not forget to look at the past to determine what led us to this point and what we can do to change our future course if necessary.

Law:

In the early years, healthcare was often regarded as a personal matter and not a legal matter that the government should become involved with. Even though it was viewed in this manner, laws were still enacted to bring this point home. Even though the law did not view healthcare as a public matter, a law was still necessary to explain and enforce these ideas. It is clear that the law has been used to control most everything that deals with life in America and this includes healthcare. By the late 1920's and 1930's, the healthcare movement in the U.S. was gaining steam and many politicians felt that some form of national healthcare would be necessary to better organize and deliver these services. During this period, the closest that the law came to providing a more organized form of healthcare in the country was the **Social Security Act** of 1935. However, even though this Act fell short of demanding care for all, it was the first substantive piece of legislation to involve the government in the overview of providing benefits to the elderly. The Act states the following:

> The Social Security Act (Act of August 14, 1935) [H. R. 7260]
>
> An act to provide for the general welfare by establishing a system of Federal old-age benefits, and by enabling the several States to make more adequate provision for aged persons, blind persons, dependent and crippled children, maternal and child welfare, public health, and the administration of their unemployment compensation laws; to establish a Social Security Board; to raise revenue; and for other purposes.
>
> Be it enacted by the Senate and House of Representatives of the United States of America in Congress assembled (Social Security, 2014).

World War II brought many changes to the way healthcare was delivered in the U.S. as many new laws were enacted to protect individuals from unscrupulous providers. Furthermore, education standards and requirements also became the norm. It was clear that the delivery of healthcare services was becoming more and more regulated as the system became more sophisticated. Most of these changes have emerged as **statutes**, which are laws that are created by the legislature. However, healthcare law has also been derived from numerous other sources that are present in the rest of the U.S. criminal and civil justice systems. The goal is for **justice** to be served in whatever manner that denotes.

As noted earlier, healthcare law can be further understood when one takes a look at the basic tenets of the foundational laws that exist in the United States. The system of laws begins with the Constitution and grows from there. Issues of tort law, contract law, antitrust, civil procedure and others dictate the ways in which healthcare will be delivered. Also, **precedent** is used extensively in the United States and this is a way to determine how laws will be carried out concerning future cases. Historically, these foundations were utilized and oriented specifically towards healthcare and its delivery. Tort law, for example, is an area of the law that speaks to nearly everything that takes place on a daily basis. A **tort** can be defined as a civil wrong committed against a person or property for which a court provides a remedy in the form of an action for damages (Pozgar, 2012). Within tort law, **negligence** and **malpractice** are sub-categories that those involved with healthcare should pay particular attention to. Negligence is defined as an unintentional commission or omission of an act that a reasonably prudent person would or would not do under the same circumstances (Pozgar, 2012). For example, as it pertains to disparate treatment of individuals, a physician who believes a certain way about a population may not treat them the way he or she would other populations. Specifically, let's say a 19-year-old African American male is delivered to an emergency room for an undisclosed illness. The attending physician believes that all young, African American males are gangsters and will not follow medical direction, so he or she ignores wound care instructions and follow-up care. If the physician would have outlined this type of care as a generally accepted practice of the profession to all other populations and a prudent physician would have done the same, the physician is negligent for not doing so. This clearly illustrates how a bias can get in the way of practicing medicine. Many believe that some bias is inherent, but the inability to look at all people equally or focusing on predisposed stereotypes will lead to unfair treatment of those populations that one has a bias towards. Thus, tort law is used extensively in healthcare to help remedy these types of problems and it has historically been an area that managers and others involved with healthcare need to pay close attention to. Malpractice, on the other hand, can be either a civil or criminal wrong and is defined as an event that occurs when a hospital, doctor or other health care professional, through a negligent act or omission, causes an injury to a patient (ABPLA, 2014). The negligence might be the result of errors in diagnosis, treatment, aftercare or even health management. Even though medical malpractice is difficult to win in a court of law, thousands of cases are presented on an annual basis all around the country.

Historically, the mantra of the physician is to "do no harm." This is best addressed through tort law and summed up best by the concept of **non-malfeasance**. The *Commission for Reproductive Health Standards*, has this to say about non-malfeasance, *"The ethical category of non-Malfeasance represents the doctor's attempt to avoid any act or treatment plan that would harm the patient or violate the patient's trust, and has been popularized in the phrase "first, do no harm." Non-Malfeasance is supported through Confidentiality and Prevention. Confidentiality means maintaining the privacy of patient information, and is the framework in which open, comprehensive doctor-patient communication can take place. Benjamin Franklin's proverb "an ounce of prevention is worth a pound of cure" is a pithy but true commentary on the ethical necessity of Prevention, which comes in two shapes: (1) helping the patient maintain good health to avoid deteriorating conditions and (2) ensuring that all less invasive treatment options are considered before recommending higher-risk measures. It is critically important that the specialist provider of highly invasive treatments uphold Non-Malfeasance by ascertaining that all less-invasive options have been considered by the patient in conjunction with the PCP (for Continuity of Care) before attempting invasive treatment"* (CRHSS, 2014).

The aforementioned definition speaks volumes to just how involved laws have been in healthcare in an historical context. Now, consider **beneficence**, which addresses providing a benefit to others. Even though a physician should not cause harm, some treatments may be potentially harmful, so should they be excluded? What about the benefit? Clearly, from the very utterance of the Hippocratic Oath to follow-up care instructions, laws regulate the way in which providers and healthcare organizations operate. Clearly, these laws do not dictate that individuals should be treated unfairly or differently because of the color of their skin, their racial or ethnic background or their gender. Helping the patient to maintain good health in a safe environment is the goal of laws, rules, policies, regulations and other controlling mechanisms when it comes to healthcare.

Ethics:

The brief legal history above interacts with the ethical considerations that we will look at in an historical context in this section. Law and ethics or ethics and law? The law often incorporates ethical standards to which most in society conform. But laws, like feelings, can move away from what is deemed ethical. Thus, the law and ethics debate is often very difficult for many as they often find conflict between the two even though they often are born of each other. When looking at laws, it is clear that they are often a reflection of the morals and ethics of a country, community or neighborhood. It is ethics that drives laws. A good starting point then, is to define ethics, so we can begin looking at what ethical history has given to healthcare. **Ethics** deserves more than a literal definition, as it is a fluid concept that changes from person to person and from time to time. Therefore, the best way to define ethics is that it is a branch of philosophy concerning moral considerations, but how each person reaches conclusions about those considerations is subjective, meaning the process varies from person to person (Connor & Stanford, 2014). This definition relies on **morals**, which are essentially the individual's beliefs. These beliefs are traditionally shaped by one's upbringing or family life, life events, education, etc. It is clear to see that ethics may be very different for different individuals.

Now that we have defined ethics, let's look at some of the classic principles of ethics study. The American Medical Association (AMA) as early as 1847 codified a code of ethics for practitioners (AMA, 2014). This code was quite extensive and dealt with matters such as social policy, record keeping, practice matters, hospital matter, inter-professional relations and others. These types of ethical codes are mandated for those that practice within the profession and are intended to promote **justice** for patients as well as providers. Justice can be defined in many ways, but for the purpose of this section, justice is synonymous with fairness. Loosely defined, **fairness** definitions range from exactly equal treatment for all to having individuals receive the same treatment they deserve (Buchbinder & Shanks, 2012). We generally assume when we order a meal at a restaurant that we will have to pay for the meal. Therefore, generally speaking, we, as paying customers can assume that we will be treated similarly as it pertains to service, quality, etc. However, in healthcare delivery not everyone pays or is able to pay. Should the uninsured receive the same service for a cardiac condition, as an individual that pays for health insurance every month? What is fair? What is legal? There are no easy answers to the majority of these questions, but ethical principles have worked with legal principles to help find a way to make the system function. To illustrate, numerous legislative acts have made it illegal to not treat an injured person regardless of their ability to pay if they are suffering a life threatening injury or illness. Moral thought and behavior has led to this type of law being enacted.

Where else have ethics been derived from? Many argue that religion is a major factor in determining ethical behavior. However, many feel just the opposite that religious ethics are for religious purposes and not purposes outside the church. What about hospitals with religious affiliations? **Religion**, is defined as:

- The belief in a god or in a group of gods
- An organized system of beliefs, ceremonies, and rules used to worship a god or a group of gods
- An interest, a belief, or an activity that is very important to a person or group (Merriam-Webster, 2014).

Does this not speak to ethics? **Beliefs**, systems, rules, etc., all speak to what we have defined as ethics. Historically, religion has been a driving force not only in healthcare, but in man's everyday life. Other historical thoughts on ethics include **deontological ethics**, which addresses ethics as a duty or right as opposed to a philosophical process. Deontological ethics play a major role in healthcare as it maintains that the individual's rights are most important, so what is best for the individual cannot be precluded by what is best for the greater good (Connor & Stanford, 2014). This speaks to issues of fairness or justice as it applies to all patient populations. It does not matter then what the color of your skin, your age or your racial or ethnic profile is as long as your needs are being addressed. However, we know that this is not always the outcome. Finally, another philosophy that should be addressed is that of utilitarianism. **Utilitarianism** is a belief opposite that of deontology. Utilitarian based ethics believes that ethical dilemmas should error on the side of the majority (Connor & Stanford, 2014). So, if applied to medicine is it in the interest of the greater good to use scarce resources on an individual that cannot pay as opposed to an individual that can?

To conclude the historical perspective, law and ethics have a rich history in every aspect of an individual's life and healthcare is no exception. Nevertheless, both of these areas are often found to be confusing as well as complicated to understand when it comes to making decisions within each ideal. Perhaps nothing is simpler at outlining this section than figure 1. There is law and there is ethics and they coexist and must find ways to work together.

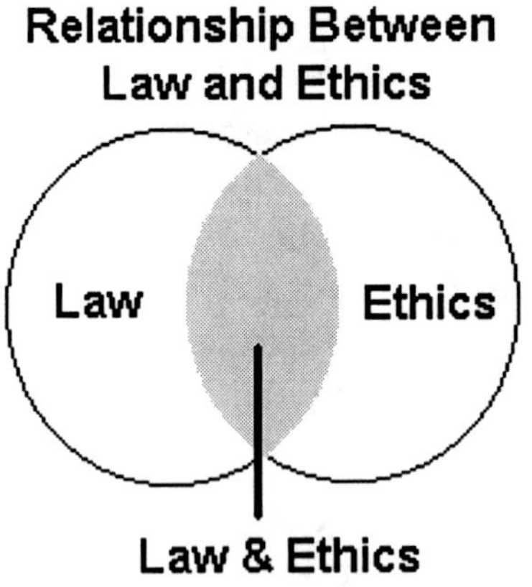

Figure 1: Relationship between law and ethics. Anstead, S.M. (1999). *Law Versus Ethics in Management.* Retrieved from http://ansteadsue.tripod.com/ethics.htm

WHAT YOU SHOULD KNOW:

The preceding sections of this chapter have outlined some of the basic tenants of law and ethics as well as an historical overview, but now we will look at areas within both disciplines that are specific to health disparities. **Legislation** that has been enacted to prevent disparities and ethical issues that speaks to healthcare specifically is a good starting point. No conversation on the topic would be complete without another visit to the past. The past that we will look to is the 1960's when change was occurring for racially segregated populations as well as others who may have found themselves outside of the majority. In 1964, the Civil Rights Act was passed and this Act moved the government from one that supported discrimination to one that set out to enforce policies to dismantle discrimination in health care settings (LaVeist, 2005). This signaled a new beginning as now a law was in place to prevent discrimination, especially racially discriminating practices. Nevertheless, as LaVeist (2005) points out, this did not stop disparities and we are still working to overcome numerous obstacles facing many populations in society today.

In addition to legislative acts like the one mentioned above, public policy is a major driver in reducing health disparities. It is public policy that holds that no one can lawfully cause harm to others or take away from the public good (Pozgar, 2013). Public policy itself does not have the enforcement of law, but by pushing for legislation, public policy takes many legal forms that allow for its function in law. Ethical philosophy leads one to enact sound public policy and a law being created follows this. In this instance, a clear line from ethics to law can be drawn. Other examples of legal changes that have affected health care disparities are the expansion of Medicaid. It is estimated that over $200 billion could be saved if health disparities did not exist and most of this is blamed on a lack of insurance, so by expanding Medicaid, it is hoped that more low income individuals will find a way to afford healthcare services (Perkins, 2012). Additionally, the **Affordable Care Act (ACA)** has done much in recent years to attempt to reduce health disparities. The ACA is not a stand-alone piece of legislation as it relies on states, public health entities as well as the federal government to implement it. The goal is to create an environment to level the playing field, so that all members of society can receive basic health care services.

There is no guarantee that the ACA or any other piece of legislation currently on the table will help to curb the growth of disparate treatment in healthcare delivery, but the law certainly seems to be an avenue that can sway individuals and organizations to make changes. With that being said, what about ethics? If ethical decisions tend to promote new laws, then why aren't more laws being created to reduce disparities and ultimately, eliminate them? The answer is not a simple one. Creating laws is not an easy process that can be done overnight. Furthermore, political powers hold much influence over this process and often times it is political ideals that sway legislation. This is not to say that ethics do not play a role, it merely shows how politics control and influence most aspects of life in America. Clearly issues concerning health disparities are issues that most if not all individuals would like to see remedied. Working to promote new laws that affect the delivery of healthcare will continue long after this text has gone to press and even then, the battle for fairness will continue. Often, our **compassion** for our fellow human beings is merely caught up in politics and disappears without any change being evident. The ability to present bills to our government officials that seek to reduce health disparities and create a system that works to reduce these disparities will certainly be the key as the battle moves forward. Clearly insuring more individuals is the goal of the ACA and that does in fact seem to be a major issue that may help to reduce problems such as access, affordability, etc. However, will this truly reduce disparities or will it create new disparities that were not apparent at the outset? The numbers demonstrate that minorities are less likely to be insured than other groups, but disparities in health come in many forms and therefore, our legislation needs to be multi-dimensional as well.

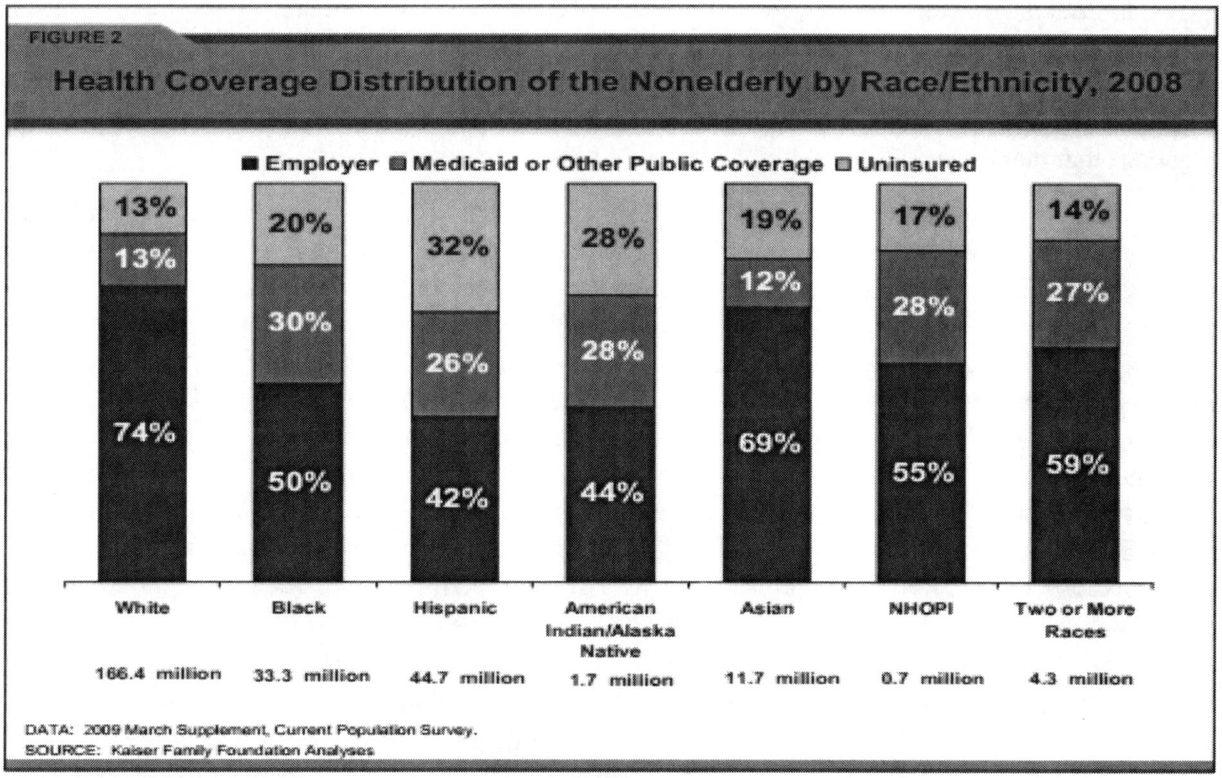

Figure 2: Health coverage distribution. Kaiser Family Foundation (2008).
Health Coverage Distribution of the non-elderly by Race/Ethnicity-2008. Retrieved from http://kff.org

Thus, the law plays a major role in determining what steps can be taken to promote a healthcare system free of disparities, but numerous shortcomings exist within the system. Furthermore, ethics and morality lead the charge to get legislation off the ground, so in tandem, law and ethics work to make changes that may or may not benefit those in need. Remember, just because a law is enacted and changes are mandated, it does not mean that disparities will no longer exist. Legal and ethical considerations are just part of the picture. Next, we will look at specific cultural issues, disparities affecting certain populations and bioethics. Looking at these issues through the lens of law and ethics will provide an insight into how difficult change really is.

Cultural Issues:

Issues surrounding culture have long been discussed when it comes to health disparities in the United States and many believe it is these values that lead to disparate outcomes in health services. Ethics are certainly shaped by cultural values and therefore, it is important for those in healthcare to at least have some understanding of different cultural beliefs or, at the very least, have access to resources that may help when a patient or family member has different beliefs than one's own. Being able to understand different cultures and their values will not only help those at ground zero in healthcare, but it can also help to shape laws that will affect certain populations. Because cultures can be shaped by their value orientations, leaders will be in a better position to understand ethical decisions and respond to moral dilemmas (Johnson, 2009). For example, *Johnson (2009)* points out that most Americans put the individual first when making health decisions, but Japanese emphasize the group dynamic as being most important (Johnson, 2009). It is clear that something that may seem rather simple can have a very broad based impact on any number of people. What if legislation is passed that doesn't allow families to be involved with healthcare decisions prior to surgery? Automatically, certain segments of a population are put at a disadvantage because of this type of policy. Being able to understand culture means being able to understand ethics, values, moral and legal principles. One cannot simply assume that technologies will even the field or that the best practitioners will be able to make outcomes similar for all populations. Being able to complete the puzzle by having all of the pieces is the key to impacting disparate treatment. Who we are affects our daily decisions and laws govern nearly everything we do or touch each day, so we need to make certain that these two realms work in harmony to effectively solve problems.

Other problems that present themselves in the cultural sphere are those, which revolve around location. Providers, managers, etc., need to be cautious about putting everyone in the same cultural basket based on race or ethnicity. For example, African Americans that live in California may have very different cultural values from those that live in the Southeast, so beliefs and perceptions about health care discrimination may be poles apart (Egede, 2006). The list on this topic could go on forever as we could also make this mistake with the Japanese that we mentioned in the previous paragraph. Clearly, this is problematic as it applies to federal law that supersedes state and local statutes. Being able to view individuals as individuals is the best way to make this system work, but in a country of laws, this is not practical or possible. So, the question we must ask is how do we make law and ethics work for the different cultures that are present in the U.S.? There is no easy answer, but there are solutions. Even though groups of individuals within society may all have different values, researchers have found that nations also hold values and ethical priorities in common (Johnson, 2009). This knowledge can be used to look at how a society functions on a global level, so that broad legislation can mandate specific rights, but then allow for individual states, municipalities, healthcare organizations, etc., to enforce different aspects of the legislation as they interpret it for their target population. Look at figure 3 below and notice how the firm looks at its different aspects of evaluation in order to assess and identify its own culture. This same diagram could be used when evaluating patient populations, providers, healthcare organizations and the like. The cultural assessment breaks down each category to interpret the following:

- **Collegiality:** *The manner in which people within a firm deal with each other.*
- **Strategic Focus:** *The degree to which the firm has a clear identity, both to itself and in relation to other firms.*
- **Governance:** *The manner in which the firm deals with its people, and the way that its professionals and staff deal with the firm.*
- **Values:** *The belief systems that represent the collective aspirations of the members of the firm* (Edge, 2014).

Culture is multi-dimensional and cannot be represented by parameters within any population or organization. Culture, much like law and ethics is on the move and is constantly taking on a new look. Understanding, interpreting and legislating culture must do the same to be effective.

Figure 3: Cultural assessment. Wesemann, E. EDGE International. (2014). *The EDGE International Law Firm Cultural Assessment.* Retrieved from http://www.edge.ai/Edge-International-1780902.html

Disparities:

"Disparities" describes a problem; working to create health equity involves tackling the root causes of the problem (CDPHE, 2014). Many organizations, institutions, scholars, etc., are moving towards replacing disparities within the healthcare environment. The above statement speaks to this issue much as wellness speaks to the changes in healthcare itself. Nevertheless, disparities do exist and until they are no longer an issue, they need to be addressed. The following from the *National Conference of State Legislatures* sums up disparities in healthcare:

"Health disparities refer to the gaps in quality of health status and health care that exist. Many factors contribute to disparities including inadequate access to care, quality of care, genetics and personal behaviors. There are other factors that can harm one's health as well. Examples include living in an area that has poor environmental conditions (e.g., violence, bad air quality, and inadequate access to healthy foods), inadequate personal support systems, and illiteracy or limited English proficiency. These factors are often associated with racial and ethnic minority, rural, disabled, and underserved communities" (NCSL, 2014).

The list is exhaustive as can be seen from the above. However, legally, avenues exist to combat disparities as has been noted throughout the chapter, but the key is how? The Civil Rights Act is a starting point and it has done much to change the course of healthcare delivery in the U.S., but it isn't enough. As we have noted earlier, there are many variables that exist when looking at disparities and too often, many issues are more social than health related. So, what approach can an individual, community or government take to extinguish disparities?

Health policy must expand. Proper nutrition, bad air quality, inadequate support systems, etc., are all health policy. **Health policy** then can be best defined as being the policies that help a nation achieve its health goals (WHO, 2014). These policies are derived from the laws that are already in place and those that will be put forth in the future. The policy, again, must be broad based to encompass the many disparities that exist within society. It also must be flexible enough that those charged with carrying out the laws are in a position that allows them to benefit those suffering from disparate treatment in healthcare.

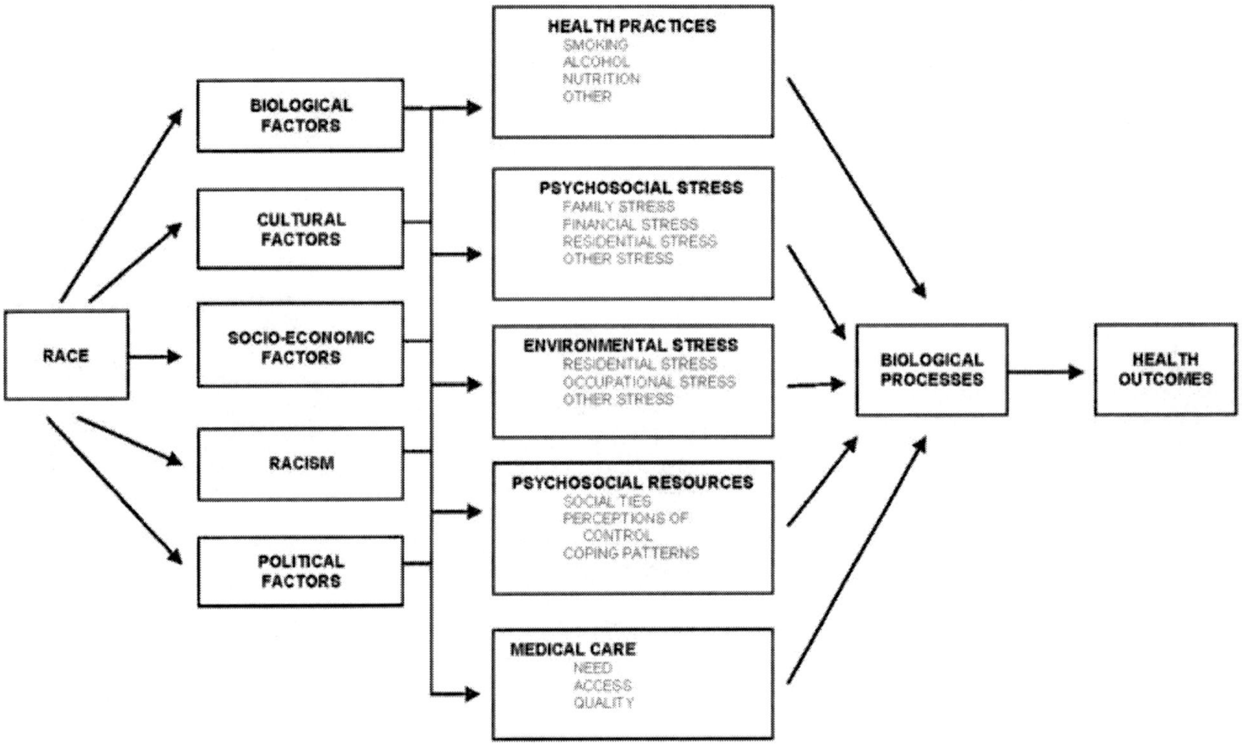

Figure 4: Strategic plan. National Institute of Health (NIH). (2014). *Report from the Strategic Planning Advisory Panel on Health Disparities.* Retrieved from http://www.ninds.nih.gov/about_ninds/plans/NINDS_health_disparities_report.htm

The *National Institute of Health* in the chart above has called for a strategic plan to research health disparities across all disciplines, i.e., social sciences, natural sciences, and others to defeat health disparities within racial and ethnic minority groups (NIH, 2014). This public policy is health policy, but moves across multiple disciplines in order to function. Ethical considerations have created the agenda and policy will put it into play.

Bioethics:

No chapter on law and ethics would be complete without mentioning bioethics. **Bioethics** is "a field of study concerned with the ethics and philosophical implications of certain biological and medical procedures, technologies, and treatments, as organ transplants, genetic engineering, and care of the terminally ill" (Dictonary.com, 2014). From the definition alone it is clear that there are numerous legal and ethical concerns that arise from this discipline. Furthermore, this chapter is also concerned with addressing any disparities of care when it comes to the use of technology, genetics, end of life care, etc. One of the major concerns in this area that affects racial and ethnically diverse populations is the idea that people of color or different ethnic backgrounds are somehow different genetically. LaVeist(2005) notes that, "in most cases this is just speculation...few scientists still believe that biogenetic variation can be adequately described by racial/ethnic groupings which attempt to correspond to biological differences."

The bigger issues in bioethics concerning racial/ethnic minorities comes from items such as end-of-life decisions, **do-not-resuscitate (DNR) orders** and **euthanasia.** With advances in technology, it has been shown that human beings can live much longer lives, but quality of life has not necessarily been associated with the longer period of time. DNR orders, for example, have both ethical and legal implications as the law dictates what can and can't be withheld to include what is an official form and must be respected to what is not. Issues with language and culture can easily cloud these types of decisions. Euthanasia is also a topic that carries legal and ethical concerns in today's world. What treatments are available or may become available in the future? Do those at an economic disadvantage, for example, lose out on opportunities because of their plight? Bioethics speaks to these issues, as does the law. They all play a part in a world where technology is rapidly changing and blurring the lines between life and death.

Leading to Equity:

Healthy People 2020 define health equity as, *"attainment of the highest level of health for all people. Achieving health equity requires valuing everyone equally with focused and ongoing societal efforts to address avoidable inequalities, historical and contemporary injustices, and the elimination of health and health care disparities"* (Health Equity Institute, 2014). The ability to decrease and eventually eliminate health disparities is what legal and ethical considerations are ultimately about. A law is not enacted to create a health disparity; it is enacted to eliminate one. Reaching health equity is the goal of those that promote fairness, justice and sound moral character within healthcare. As the above definition points out, being able to value everyone is the way to achieve this. Therefore, as we have discussed throughout the chapter, the ability to develop laws that benefit not only one person should be the goal. A sound legislature is the key to this being successful and a legislature starts with the people within a society. Sitting back and pretending that nothing is wrong will not achieve equity. We are living in a nation of laws and as such, we need to be actively involved in the process to make it work.

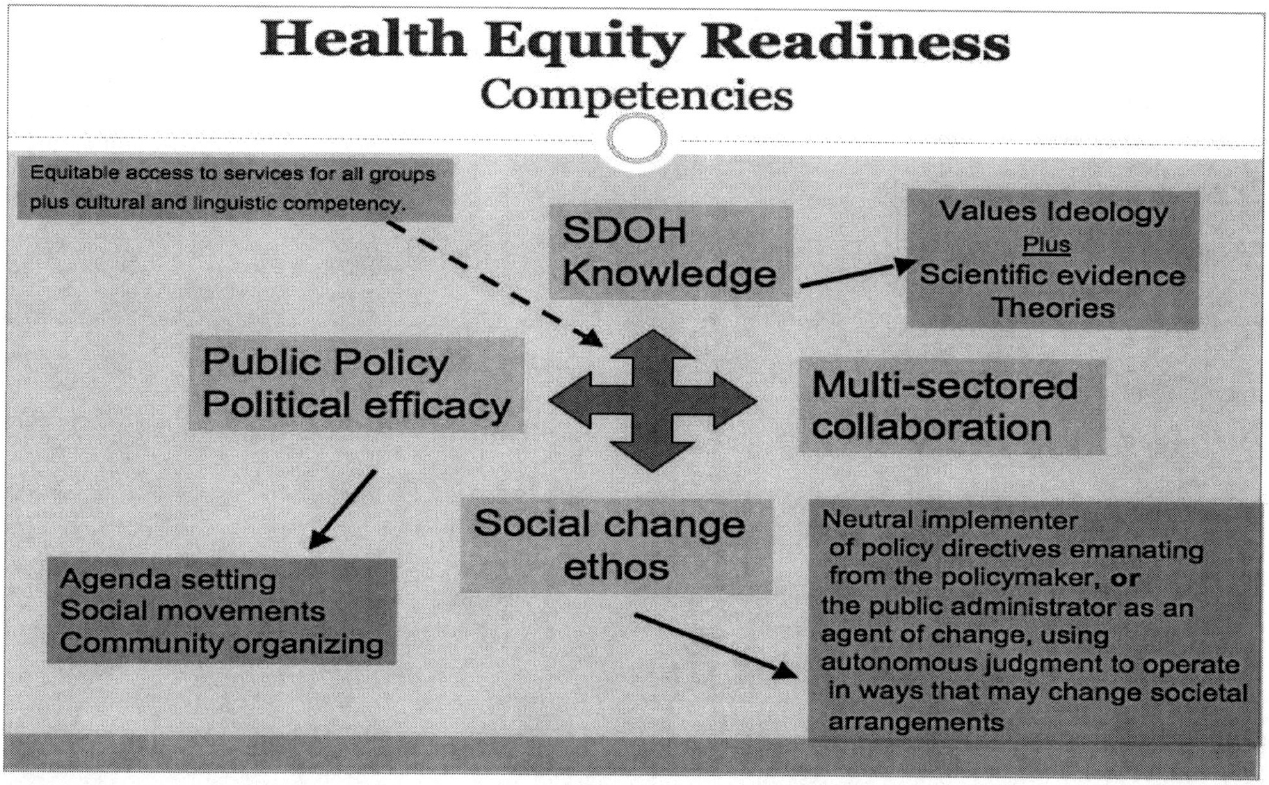

Figure 5: Roadmap to health equity. Andress, L. (2009). *Addressing Health Inequities: Health Equity Readiness in Local Health Systems.* Retrieved from http://www.bridgingthehealthgap. com/uploads/health%20equity%20readiness.pdf

Andress (2009) discusses the roadmap to health equity in figure 5. Notice that it encompasses the entire spectrum of law, policy, values, etc. in order to make the road clear. Furthermore, the social determinants of health (SDOH) knowledge plays a big factor in forming a remedy. The ability to structure legal issues with ethical considerations will make the journey to equity a reality and not merely an idea. Finding value in all people is the starting place.

WRAP-UP:

Law and ethics have been defined in numerous fashions throughout this chapter. Different laws, different avenues for enacting laws as well as ethical considerations based on race and ethnicity have also been brought to light. However, these are not static ideals and as such, they will continue to change with the environment due to changes in human understanding, science, politics and other influences too numerous to mention. The United States does not function without laws, so those interested in healthcare or users of healthcare must be willing to understand and adapt to different laws and how they affect the industry. Additionally, ethics cannot be understood in a silo based on what a population looks like or where they are from. Ethics is broad reaching and needs to be approached as such. There is no one size fits all remedy to solving health disparities through the legal system. Ultimately, the goal must be one of equity in health. Equity for all within healthcare is a broad concept and has no clear definition, but the concept is one that all involved in healthcare can aim to achieve.

DISCUSSION QUESTIONS:

1. Provide several examples of medical/ethical dilemmas. Now, apply them to known issues of disparate treatment in healthcare.
2. Define law and ethics. Do not use a specific definition or define based on your reading, but instead, use your own words to illustrate the complex field of law and ethics.
3. Think about the health care organization that you utilize. Have you experienced any legal or ethical issues specific to healthcare? Explain with examples.
4. Chose one of the ethical beliefs listed in the chapter and apply it to a health disparity. How does this belief provide a remedy for the disparity? How may it do more harm? Explain.
5. Is law ethics or is ethics law? Explain.
6. How should providers work to better address cultural issues in healthcare? Should a moral compass guide them or should the law become involved? Explain your answer.
7. Will the use of law and ethics help to eliminate disparities or will they expand them?
8. Explain your thoughts on how both law and ethics may change in the future. What factors will play the biggest role in changing the way we think morally and what may cause current laws to be changed?
9. What is health equity in your opinion? Discuss ways that you think equity can be achieved.

RESOURCES:

American Society of Law, Medicine and Ethics
http://www.aslme.org

Bioethics.Net
http://www.bioethics.net

Bioethics.com
http://bioethics.com

National Human Genome Research Institute
http://www.genome.gov/page.cfm?pageID=10001618

American Medical Association
http://www.ama-assn.org/ama/pub/physician-resources/medical-ethics/about-ethics-group.page

The Robert Wood Johnson Foundation
http://www.rwjf.org

The Hastings Center
http://www.thehastingscenter.org

The National Center for Ethics in Healthcare
http://www.ethics.va.gov

The Health Equity Institute
http://healthequity.sfsu.edu/content/defining-health-equity

The American Health Lawyers Association
http://www.healthlawyers.org/Pages/Default.aspx

ACTIVITY:

This case study illustrates how misconceptions and preconceived ideas lead to poor patient outcomes.

SPEAK ENGLISH

Mr. Garcia is an elderly gentleman who rarely uses the healthcare system in his community. However, with his advanced age, he has been experiencing a multitude of medical issues that he can no longer ignore. To expand, a friend that ensures he is fed and healthy has become alarmed at the fact that he no longer seems to know where he is and what is going on. His memory seems to have gotten much worse and recently, he only speaks in Spanish even though he has been an English speaker his entire life as well. When the caregiver speaks to him it is as if he does not know or care what she is saying. Since she does not speak Spanish, she is unsure as to what he is saying. Ultimately, she is able to get Mr. Garcia into a vehicle and take him to the emergency room because he is unable to ambulate.

Upon arrival at the hospital, a triage nurse attempts to speak to him, but due to the language barrier, she is unsuccessful. The caregiver requests that a Spanish speaking staff member be assigned and the nurse dismisses her by stating that this is America and he needs to speak English if he wants to be treated. Because of her frustration and inability to discern what is wrong with him, she places him on a bed in the hallway without further evaluation.

Hours pass and the caregiver becomes more concerned because Mr. Garcia is starting to fade in and out of consciousness. The caregiver notifies the nurse and she is still stern with her response and tells her that when he decides to speak English, she will then be able to help him.

Two more hours pass and Mr. Garcia dies. He suffered a hemorrhagic stroke that doctors could have corrected had they saw him even one hour earlier.

QUESTIONS

1. Explain what changes should be instituted at the hospital where Mr. Garcia died.
2. When you review the scenario, what policies may have prevented Mr. Garcia's death? Is the nurse the only one to blame in this scenario? Explain.
3. In a group of 4-6 individuals, work as a legislative body might and develop a law that will prevent this type of issue in the future. Who should be involved in the decision-making? What additional legal legislative actions may be helpful?
4. Where can the hospital go from here? What might a roadmap to equity look like after an incident like this?
5. Explain how this incident will affect the community that Mr. Garcia lived in. What about the Hispanic community?

REFERENCES:

American Board of Professional Liability Attorneys. (2014). *What is Medical Malpractice?* Retrieved from http://www.abpla.org/what-is-malpractice

American Medical Association (AMA). (2014). *History of AMA Ethics.* Retrieved from http://www.ama-assn.org//ama/pub/about-ama/our-history/history-ama-ethics.page

Andress, L. (2009). *Addressing Health Inequities: Health Equity Readiness in Local Health Systems.* Retrieved from http://www.bridgingthehealthgap.com/uploads/health%20equity%20readiness.pdf

Anstead, S.M. (1999). *Law Versus Ethics in Management.* Retrieved from http://ansteadsue.tripod.com/ethics.htm

Buchbinder, S.B., & Shanks, N.H. (2012). *Introduction to Health Care Management. 2nd Edition.* Burlington: Jones & Bartlett.

Colorado Department of Public Health and Environment Office of Health Equity (CDPHE). (2013). *Health Disparities: The 2013 Report.* Retrieved from: http://www.colorado.gov/cs/Satellite/CDPHE-Main/CBON/1251588185631

Commission for Reproductive Health Service Standards (2014). *Non-Malfeasance.* Retrieved from http://www.physiciansforreproductiverights.org/ethics/non-malfeasance/

Connor, V.J. & Stanford, C.C. (2014). *Ethics for Health Professionals.* Sudbury, MA: Jones & Bartlett.

Dictionary.com. (2014). Retrieved from http://dictionary.reference.com/browse/bioethics

EDGE International. (2014). *The EDGE International Law Firm Cultural Assessment.* Retrieved from http://www.edge.ai/Edge-International-1780902.html

Health Equity Institute. (2014). *Defining Health Equity.* Retrieved from http://healthequity.sfsu.edu/content/defining-health-equity

Johnson, C.E. (2009). *Meeting the Ethical Challenges of Leadership: Casting Light or Shadow. 3rd Edition.* Los Angeles: SAGE.

Kaiser Family Foundation (2008). *Health Coverage Distribution of the non-elderly by Race/Ethnicity-2008.* Retrieved from http://kff.org

LaVeist, T.A. (2005). *Minority Populations & Health. An Introduction to Health Disparities in the United States.* San Francisco: Jossey-Bass.

Merriam-Webster Online Dictionary. (2014). Retrieved from http://www.merriam-webster.com/dictionary

National Conference of State Legislatures. (2014). *NCSL Resources on Health Disparities.* Retrieved from http://www.ncsl.org/research/health/health-disparities-laws.aspx

National Institute of Health (NIH). (2014). *Report from the Strategic Planning Advisory Panel on Health Disparities.* Retrieved from http://www.ninds.nih.gov/about_ninds/plans/NINDS_health_disparities_report.htm

Perkins, J. (2012). *50 Reasons Medicaid Expansion Is Good For Your State.* Retrieved from http://www.healthlaw.org/issues/health-disparities/50-reasons-medicaid-expansion-is-good-for-your-state#.UyyUN1zdegd

Pozgar, G.D. (2013). *Legal and Ethical Issues.* Sudbury, MA: Jones & Bartlett.

Pozgar, G.D. (2012). *Legal Aspects of Health Care Administration.* Sudbury, MA: Jones & Bartlett.

Social Security Website. (2014). *The Social Security Act of 1935.* Retrieved from http://www.ssa.gov/history/35act.html

Wesemann, E. with EDGE International. (2014). *The EDGE International Law Firm Cultural Assessment.* Retrieved from http://www.edge.ai/Edge-International 1780902.html

World Health Organization (WHO). (2014). *Health Policy.* Retrieved from http://www.who.int/topics/health_policy/en/

Chapter 12:

Analyzing Health and Healthcare in the Developing World

Uma Keleker & Debasree Das Gupta

KEY CONCEPTS:

Access
Burden of diseases
Curative care
Developing country
Developed country
Female genital mutilation
Fibromyalgia
Gender
Gender-based violence
Gross National Income (GNI)
Health outcome
Health spending
Health systems
High income
Hilots
Infant mortality rate
Lower-income
Lower middle-income
Maternal mortality rate
Millennium Development Goals
Parasitic worms
PhilHealth
Purchasing Power Parity
Schistosomiasis
Sex
Upper middle-income

CHAPTER OVERVIEW:

A combination of high burden of disease and weak health care systems severely limit health governance in the less developed regions of the world. In this chapter, we consider: 1) why health systems often lack adequate capacity to provide necessary health services to its population; and 2) what factors are associated with poor health outcomes in developing countries. In the process of this reflection, we particularly feature the wide disparity in health care and health outcomes that typify and set apart developing countries from developed countries. The descriptive commentary and supporting statistics presented here identify a number of factors that plague health systems in the developing countries. These elements are: (i) low levels of health spending (ii) focus on medical or curative care as opposed to preventive care (iii) shortage of health workers, and (iv) unequal access to and usage of health services in rural areas. In addition, cultural and environmental factors converge with a high burden of disease, as well as considerable variation in health outcomes to further test health systems in developing countries.

WHY IS THIS IMPORTANT?

Health is related to socio-economic development and is thus a crucial component of the agendas of both national and international organizations. While improvements in the health of country's citizens is itself an outcome of interest; it is also arguably a critical input in any attempt to achieve non-health social goals including better education outcomes, empowerment of women, and the eradication of poverty. Understanding what factors contribute to systematic differences in health outcomes across countries is critical if one is interested in designing policies intended to improve the delivery of health care. Performance of the health systems of similar countries might serve as a benchmark for a country's progress that may in turn result in policy experiments and improvement of that country's health system. Tracking of key indicators of interest to health agencies, policy-makers and various other stakeholders might be necessary when making critical decisions pertaining to investments in healthcare.

CHAPTER EXPECTATIONS:

The learning goals are to develop an understanding to:

- Compare and contrast health outcomes, such as life expectancy or infant mortality, among developing countries;
- Evaluate why health outcomes among girls and women are poorer than that in men;
- Review and identify the major institutional challenges faced by the developing countries such as those in financing health care, and in instituting a suitable role for the government; and
- Analyze and appraise some of the most vexing health problems faced by people in the developing world.

INTRODUCTION:

Health is a critical component in human development. It is linked not only to improvements in human welfare through the reduction of morbidity- and mortality-related health outcomes, but also to the realization of such non-health social goals as achieving better education outcomes, empowering women, as well as eradicating hunger and poverty, to name a few. Interplay among a complex web of factors, which include health care in addition to behavioral and aggregate-level socio-environmental conditions, determine the health status of individuals. The role of health in human development is reflected in the eight **Millennium Development Goals** (MDGs) of the United Nations. Originally formulated in 2000 at the United Nations Millennium Summit, all of these goals are related to health, either directly or indirectly (Skolnik, 2012). Components of health care, particularly strength of health systems, are copiously highlighted in the development literature for their pivotal importance in attaining targets under the health-related MDGs (WHO 2010).

A defining feature around health is that **developing countries** differ from **developed countries** on several aspects in health care and health outcomes. While developing countries are defined as those with low or middle levels of Gross National Income (GNI) per capita, developed countries on the other hand are those countries with higher levels of Gross National Income (GNI) per capita where most people enjoy a higher standard of living (World Bank, 2004). **Gross National Income (GNI)** per capita is the dollar value of a country's final income in a year divided by its population, converted to US dollars using Atlas methodology (WHO, 2014).

The different income groups identified based on the 2008 GNI per capita were valid from July 2009 until July 2010. This chapter includes the analysis of countries classified into the following categories–**low income** ($975 or less), **lower-middle income** ($976-3,855), **upper middle income** ($3,856-$11,905) and **high-income countries** ($11,905 or higher) (WTO, 2009).

The discussion of health and related disparity in the developing countries in this chapter is conducted in context to the latest available health indicators published by the World Health Organization (WHO) and the World Bank. This narrative is supplemented with a case study comparing and contrasting health and health care in three countries Uganda (a lower-income country), Philippines (a lower middle-income country) and Peru (higher middle-income country) as well as related specific examples drawn from field visits to these countries. Several dimensions of health care, ranging from access to health care, health infrastructure, and quality of health services, are discussed in this chapter in addition to various health challenges faced by people in the developing world. The rest of this chapter is divided into three parts. In the first part, defining trends that typify health care in the developing countries are presented. This section is followed by a discussion in the next part on major health-related disadvantages that challenge health care delivery in resource-poor countries. In addition, illustrative case studies are included to further illuminate the different themes introduced in the two sections of this chapter.

PART I: CHARACTERISTICS OF HEALTH CARE IN DEVELOPING COUNTRIES

Healthcare Spending

One of the critical elements of a health care system is the amount of money spent on it. Although health spending does not necessarily translate into the desired health outcomes, it is nevertheless an important consideration in the developing world. At the macro level, a country has to determine what proportion of their income needs to be allocated to health care. This decision is influenced by several factors including the economic status, demographic and social factors, political ideology, and health needs of the people. The importance of these factors varies across countries and regions, resulting in different levels of health care spending.

Table 1 shows the disparity in per capita government health spending across the three categories of countries. It is clear from Table 1 that while, on an average, low-income countries spend $81.09 Purchasing Power Parity (PPP), the difference between the highest spending country (Niue) and the lowest spending country (Myanmar) is large. As expected, the level of health care spending goes up as the level of national income increases. On an average, upper-middle-income countries spend more than triple ($577.89 PPP) the amount the lower-middle income countries spend ($188.05 PPP) on health per person. The **Purchasing Power Parity** conversion factor shows how much of a country's currency is needed in that country to buy what $1 would buy in the United States (World Bank, 2004).

The level of health care spending is critical in ensuring the necessary infrastructure, such as the number of hospitals, population-to-physician ratio and the nursing and midwifery personnel. Higher spending, however, does not necessarily ensure whether the existing infrastructure is functional, whether all people have access to them, or whether its use eventually results in the desired health outcomes. These factors instead are most often determined by social, political and economic conditions prevailing in a country.

Low income countries	Country, Region	Per capita government expenditure on health (PPP int $), 2012
Average		**81.09**
Lowest	Myanmar, South East Asia	5.90
Highest	Niue, Western Pacific	1810.7
Lower-middle income countries		
Average		**188.05**
Lowest	Pakistan, Eastern Mediterranean	28.50
Highest	Islamic Republic of Iran, Eastern Mediterranean	630.80
Upper-middle income countries		
Average		**577.89**
Lowest	Fiji, Western Pacific	127.90
Highest	Palau, Western Pacific	1295.00

Table 1. Disparity in health care spending, 2012
Source: World Health Organization (WHO), Retrieved from http://www.who.int/gho/database/en/.

Investment in Health Systems

The World Health Organization defines a **health system** as "the sum total of all the organizations, institutions and resources whose primary purpose is to improve health" (WHO, 2014). Within overall health spending, the amount of resources allocated to the types of health services and the health care infrastructure of a system may vary widely. At the macro level, the general trend is that a large proportion of total health care spending in developing countries is predominantly allocated towards **curative care** (or medical care) and a very small portion is devoted to preventive care. While such spending on seeking medical care is necessary, very little is invested on preventive or health promotion programs that are much more cost-effective (Barnum and Kutzin 1993).

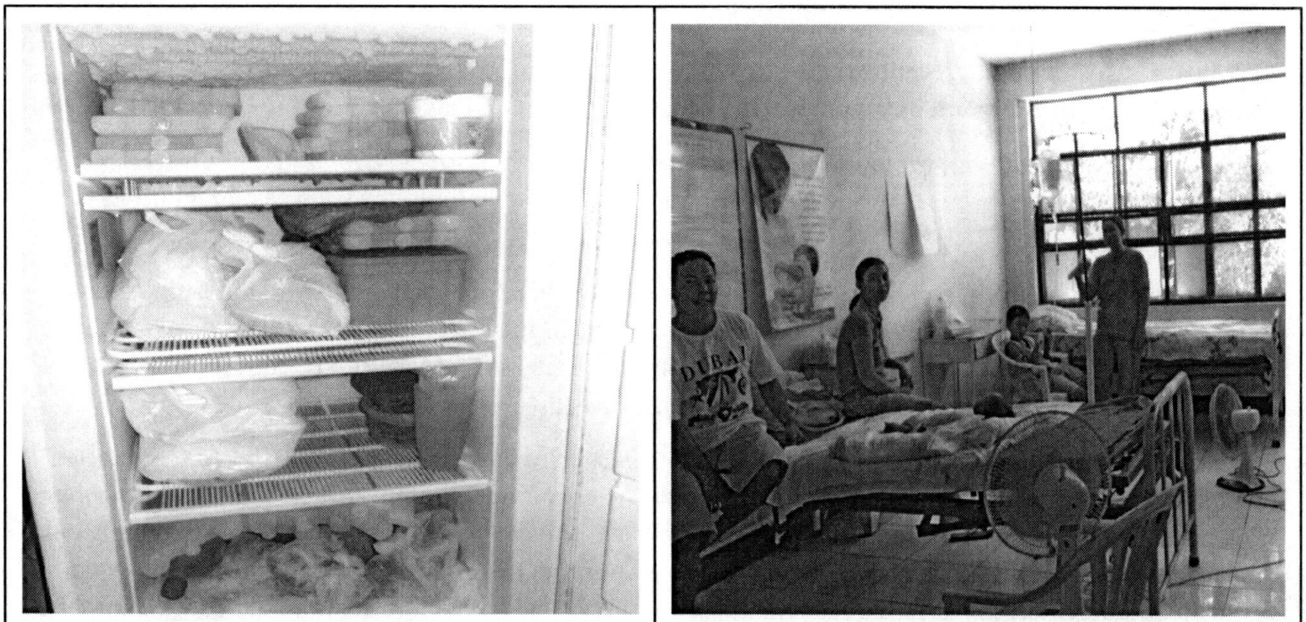

Left-hand side panel: The cold storage was provided by an international non-profit organization to this hospital. Although it was used for the purpose of storing vaccine (the reason it was provided), the employees used it to store their food.	*Right-hand side panel:* This photo is of a district hospital in the Philippines. Since the hospitals did not provide any ceiling fans, the patients carried mobile fans with them to the hospital.

Figure 1: An example of inadequate use or misuse of hospital resources.
Note: The author took these pictures during the field visit to the Philippines.

Next, while the urban metropolitan areas within developing countries are usually better equipped due to better access to capital, the levels of capital spending in the rural areas, in contrast, are largely inadequate resulting in sub-optimal physical infrastructure (See Figure 1). Often, due to the absence of modern medical facilities, people in rural areas have to rely on traditional healers who typically provide primary care. Traditional healers in South Asia including countries such as India, and Bangladesh, may practice a variant of Ayurvedic, Unani, or homeopathic systems of medicine (Khan, 1984). Sometimes, the lack of availability of care may be to the extent that residents of rural areas need to travel long distances to get to the nearest hospital or health facility.

Access to Health Care

The **access**, or the ability of an individual to obtain the necessary care, depends on whether health is viewed as a public good or a market commodity. This varies based on the level of economic development or political will and existing ideology in a country. In most developed and developing countries (with the exception of a few such as the United States), the role government plays in providing health care is vital. Of note are the countries of the former Soviet Union (e.g. Kyrgyzstan, Kazakhstan) that inherited a socialist health system characterized by a wide coverage of health services and little provision of private services. In most other developing countries, a mixture of both private and public provision is available (Makinen et al. 2000). Private health insurance systems, usually made available through the employers or paid by individuals, finance only a small portion of the overall health cost by catering to an endowed small segment of the middle-class population. For instance, in the Philippines, private health insurance coverage ranges from 0.2 percent among households in the lowest wealth quintile to 7 percent among those in the highest wealth quintile households (National Statistics Office and ICF Macro, 2009).

Text Box 1: Investment in preventive care – relevance of health education or promotion initiatives in Peru and Uganda

Health education or health promotion initiatives are examples of cost-effective interventions (Hubley & Gilbert, 2005) that can be effectively used to prevent certain health conditions such as pterygium in Peru or malaria in Uganda.

A pterygium is an eye condition that is widely prevalent in the equatorial belt of the world in Latin America, Africa, and the Middle East. It is a condition that manifests in the form of an external growth on the eye (Coroneo, Girolamo, & Wakefield, 1999). Depending on the size of the growth, this condition can significantly alter one's vision and cause blindness if left untreated.

The development of pterygium in a tropical or sub-tropical climate setting is closely linked to the extent of exposure of the eye to ultraviolet rays. To prevent this condition, wearing sunglasses with ultra-violet protective lens or hats is, therefore, the most cost-effective and convenient option available to the masses (Taylor et al., 2006). While surgery is the most viable option to treat more advanced forms of pterygia, it is not an option readily available to the lower-income masses due to the high cost associated with surgery.

Similarly malaria, which is widespread in sub-Saharan Africa, can be easily prevented through the use of bed nets. However, people need to be educated about the use of bed nets to prevent malaria and other vector-borne diseases that take a huge toll on life in lower-income countries such as Uganda, or Democratic Republic of Congo, etc. (WHO, 2007).

On the public side, a social insurance system, when available, caters to a small section of the population in developing countries including government employees, military, or the indigent people. For instance, **PhilHealth**, the social health insurance system of the Philippines, provides comprehensive health services to Filipinos, including government employees, retirees and pensioners, Overseas Filipino Workers (OFW), as well as marginalized or less privileged sections of the population. Depending on who the beneficiaries are, the costs might be partly or completely borne by the employers (e.g. overseas workers, government (government employees, or indigents) or the individuals themselves (self practicing professionals) (PhilHealth, 2012).

Health care services including inpatient and outpatient care, maternal and childcare, medicines, as well as other services are provided either through government-run hospitals, or through community-based public health centers or clinics. In fact, the delivery of health services offering different levels of care (primary, secondary, and tertiary) is usually organized through a hierarchical network of municipal/district, state/provincial and regional/national-run hospitals or clinics. In the government-run hospitals and health clinics, care is more often than not provided for free. However, a nominal user fee is charged for certain special services such as reserving a bed in a hospital.

Private practitioners or privately run hospitals make up another significant component of the health care system and are particularly concentrated in the urban areas of the developing world. Although the cost of health care received at the private facilities may be substantially higher than the cost of health care received at the public facilities, people nevertheless choose to rely on the widespread network of private providers. While the use of private facilities may be more common among the higher income groups, people from the lower-income sections may also choose to use them partly due to the poor quality of health services offered at government facilities. Evidence provided in the literature corroborates this trend. For example Makinen et al. (2000), noted that the marginalized or less privileged people in Burkina Faso, Paraguay and Thailand tend to spend large portions of their incomes on health. Although this trend may not be solely due to the use of private facilities, it could be one of the contributing factors.

Inequality In The Use Of Health Care Services By Different Socio-Economic Groups:

Makinen et al. (2000) analyzed the distribution of public health services between eight developing or transitioning countries around 1995, and found that in most countries, compared to the poorer sections of the population, the wealthier segments of the population were more likely to receive care or drugs when they were ill. The study finds that spending on health tends to be higher among the richer than the poorer population groups. Makinen et al. (2000) further pointed out usage disparities in health care services among different income quintiles in Indonesia that were also highlighted in a World Bank Report (1993). For example, in Indonesia in 1990, only 12 percent of the government spending on health services was consumed by the poorest 20 percent of the households, while the wealthiest 20 percent were the beneficiaries of 29 percent of the government-funded health care services.

Availability Of Human Resources

Developing countries differ from each other with respect to availability of health workers, specifically physicians, and nurses. As seen in Table 2, the low-income countries in particular have a very low physician-to-people ratio of 1.0303 physicians for every 1000 people. In contrast, upper-middle income countries have a ratio of 1.8883 physicians for every 1000 people. Given this shortage of physicians, nurses and other community health workers, such as midwives, **hilots** or traditional birth attendants, play a critical role in health care provisioning in the developing countries. For instance, in the Philippines, nurses and midwives were the most common providers of pre-natal and post-natal care in 2008, particularly in the rural areas and among lower-income groups (National Statistics Office and ICF Macro, 2009).

Low income countries	**Country, Region**	**Year in which data was available**	**Physicians per 1,000 people**
Average			**0.3422**
Lowest	United Republic of Tanzania, Africa	2006	0.0080
Highest	Niue, Western Pacific	2008	3.0000
Lower-middle income countries			
Average			**1.0303**
Lowest	Lesotho, Europe	2003	0.0490
Highest	Georgia, Europe	2012	4.2360
Upper-middle income countries			
Average			**1.8883**
Lowest	Gabon, Africa	2004	0.2920
Highest	Cuba, Americas	2010	6.7230

Table 2: Physician-to-people ratio *Source: World Health Organization (WHO), Retrieved from http://www.who.int/gho/database/en/.*

PART 2: HEALTH-RELATED DISADVANTAGES IN DEVELOPING COUNTRIES

Burden Of Diseases:

The **burden of diseases** in the developing world varies from the developed world. While people continue to succumb to communicable diseases in the developing as well as the developed world, deaths from infectious diseases take a disproportionately higher toll in the developing world. People still die or suffer from easily treatable or preventable diseases such as malaria, tuberculosis, yellow fever, or typhoid in Africa and parts of Asia, resulting in a compromised quality of life.

Next, while the burden of non-communicable or lifestyle-related diseases such as cardiovascular diseases, mental health disorders or cancer is much higher in the developed part of the world; these diseases have increasingly been on the rise in the developing world, especially among the higher-income groups. For example, specific types of cancer such as mouth cancer are on the rise due to tobacco chewing. This trend is partly explained by changing lifestyle choices and/or higher rates of disease detection in the developing countries (Stevens 2011). (See Table 3 for the estimated number of malaria deaths and deaths resulting from non-communicable diseases).

Low income countries	**Country, Region**	**Estimated number of malaria deaths, 2010**	**Country, Region**	**Percent of non-communicable diseases (NCD) deaths among those less than 70 years, 2012**
Average		**8532.97**		**63.52**
Lowest	[Kyrgyzstan, Tajikistan, Uzbekistan; Europe]	0	Democratic People's Republic of Korea, South East Asia	35.00
Highest	Democratic Republic of Congo, Africa	78,560.00	Sierra Leone, Africa	80.00
Lower-middle income countries				
Average		**10051.42**		**50.74**
Lowest	[Guatemala, Paraguay, Belize; Americas], [Iraq, Eastern Mediterranean, [Azerbaijan, Georgia; Europe]	0.00	Ukraine, Europe	21.00
Highest	Nigeria, Africa	207701.00	[Angola, Nigeria; Africa]	77.00
Upper-middle income countries				
Average		**68.47**		**41.46**
Lowest	[Argentina, Panama, Mexico, Costa Rica; Americas], [Turkey, Bosnia and Herzegovnia; Europe], [Algeria, Africa]	0.00	Bulgaria, Europe	21.00
Highest	Gabon, Africa	589.00	Fiji, Western Pacific	67.00

Table 3. Burden of communicable diseases, 2010 and Burden of non-communicable diseases under age 70, 2012
Source: World Health Organization (WHO), Retrieved from http://www.who.int/gho/database/en/.

Cultural Factors

In addition to the burden of diseases (both communicable and non-communicable), developing countries face additional health challenges owing to the cultural norms and values prevailing in these countries. Because specific cultural beliefs and superstitions may influence perceptions of illnesses, the decision to seek proper and timely medical care as opposed to seeking care from faith healers or not seeking care at all may eventually have an adverse impact on health outcomes. In some cultures people believe that symptoms of many diseases stem from supernatural causes such as offending the gods or being afflicted by the evil eye. For example, malaria is so common in Africa that people just perceive it to be a normal occurrence. **Schistosomiasis**, an affliction widespread in Egypt, is mistakenly referred to as "male menstruation" (Skolnik, 2012, p. 121). **Parasitic worms** borne by a number of freshwater snails cause schistosomiasis in humans when they come in contact with contaminated water. Infection with these parasites affects internal organs including the urinary tract resulting in bloody urine.

Another consequence of misplaced cultural beliefs is gender disparity in health outcomes. Socially constructed gender norms interact with erroneous views around health conditions to create far adverse health outcomes among women than in men. According to the World Bank (2013), "the term '**gender**' refers to the socially-constructed differences between men and women, as distinct from "**sex**", which refers to their biological differences." In developing countries, gender norms impact women through adverse choices across all spheres of socio-cultural (such as pronounced preference for the male child), economic (such as lower female participation in the labor force, or lower provisioning of expenditures on health care for the girl child) life (World Bank, 2013).

The practice of **female genital mutilation** (FGM), "comprises all procedures that involve partial or total removal of the external female genitalia, or other injury to the female genital organs for non-medical reasons" (WHO 2013). It is prevalent widely in Islamic societies, for example, is a non-medical practice that is rooted in cultural beliefs, but is promoted with the misconception of protecting the health of women. Globally, about 140 million girls and women suffer the health consequences of this horrific custom that range from hemorrhage (bleeding) and tetanus or sepsis (bacterial infection) to infertility to increased reproductive and urinary complications (WHO 2013).

Moreover, a culture endemic to gender-dominated communities of the developing world is that women, compared to men, are given a much lower status and are excluded from most household resources and decision making authority. Social practices that are byproducts of these traditions, such as unfavorable nutritional and dietary allocation for girls and women, result in poorer health status among the female population (Lancaster et al. 2006). Indeed, a host of non-communicable and communicable health vulnerabilities in less developed regions of the world, from low birth-weight to susceptibility to infectious diseases such as human immunodeficiency virus/acquired immunodeficiency syndrome (HIV/AIDS), and tuberculosis (TB), are related to poor nutritional intake of women during pregnancy and over their life course (WHO 2013; Katona and Katona-Apte 2008). For example, the incidence of HIV among women in sub-Saharan Africa, about 60 percent of all cases, is among the highest and coincides with high levels of gender inequality and high rates of malnourishment in this region.

Another example is the disease burden of tuberculosis (TB). Reported cases of this treatable, but deadly disease are much higher among socioeconomically backward women in a number of resource-poor nations. Instances of such disparity are evident in the south Asian countries of Pakistan and Bangladesh. Compared to men in Pakistan, reported cases of TB among young females are about 20 – 30% higher, and this male-female difference in disease incidences exists across all age cohorts (Codlin et al. 2011). In the rural parts of Bangladesh, socio-cultural barriers impede treatment-seeking behavior among women with TB largely because of a greater reliance on traditional healers (Ahsan et al. 2004). Poor nutritional status and delayed medical attention accorded to women are, therefore, two of the major factors driving gender disparity in health outcomes.

Indeed, women's health status in developing countries is further aggravated as women seek health services either rarely or when it is already too late. Delayed presentation of symptoms even for routine health events such as childbirth disproportionately affects women's health status. While the topic of maternal death is visited in detail in a later sub-section, another acute health problem that in most cases goes unreported are incidences of domestic and sexual violence against women and girls in developing countries (UNHCR 2003). **Gender-based violence** (GBV) against women has serious long-term health implications, which, for example, could lead to fibromyalgia, or gastrointestinal disorders in women (Rumbold 2008). **Fibromylgia** or FM or FMS is a condition that manifests as chronic and widespread acute pain. Most recent evidence connects GBV to a host of other health and psycho-social impacts. For example, in India, likelihood of HIV prevalence in women who have been victims of sexual and gender based violence is four times higher than those who have not been abused (Silverman et al. 2008). Yet, women seldom receive redress against GBV due to widespread social acceptance of such brutal practices (Rumbold 2008). Table 4 lists various health impacts of sexual and gender based violence against women.

Fatal Outcomes	**Non-fatal Outcomes**		
	Acute Physical	Chronic Physical	Reproductive
Homicide	Injury	Disability	Unwanted pregnancy
Suicide	Shock	Somatic Complaints	Pregnancy-related complications
Maternal Mortality	Disease	Chronic Infections	STIs, including HIV/AIDS
Infant Mortality	Infection	Gastrointestinal problems	Reproductive/sexual disorders
AIDS-related Mortality		Eating/Sleep disorders	
		Alcohol/drug abuse	

Table 4: Various health impacts of sexual and gender based violence against women. United Nations High Commission for Refugees (UNHCR). (2003). Sexual and Gender-Based Violence against Refugees, Returnees and Internally Displaced Persons: Guidelines for Prevention and Response. Retrieved from http://www.refworld.org/docid/3edcd0661.html

Environmental Factors

Another pitfall in the developing countries is adverse environmental conditions that impose a disproportionately high toll on health, particularly among low-income people, in the form of diseases, disability and death. These outcomes are largely attributable to unsafe water, lack of hygiene and sanitation, urban air pollution, and indoor smoke from household use of solid fuels (Skolnik, 2012, p. 141). According to the World Health Organization (WHO) unsafe water and poor sanitation facilities result in the death of an estimated 1.7 million people annually in the developing world, mostly due to diarrheal disease.

Table 5 lists the percent of people with access to safe drinking water and sanitation facilities by income groups of countries in 2012. Not surprisingly, a higher percent of people with access to safe drinking water and sanitation facilities is associated with a higher income level in countries. For instance, the average percentage of people with access to safe drinking water and sanitation facilities in low-income countries in 2012 are 71 and 39 percent respectively. The corresponding figures for upper-middle income countries are 96 and 86 percent respectively.

Low income countries	**Country, Region**	**Percent of people using improved safe drinking water, 2012**	**Country, Region**	**Percent of people using improved sanitation facilities, 2012**
Average		**71.00**		**38.86**
Lowest	Democratic Republic of Congo	46.00	South Sudan, Africa	9.00
Highest	Niue, Western Pacific	99.00	Uzbekistan, Europe	100.00
Lower-middle income countries				
Average		**86.85**		**66.85**
Lowest	Papa New Guinea, Western Pacific	40.00	Congo, Africa	15.00
Highest	Armenia, Europe	100.00	[Maldives, South East Asia] [Turkmenistan, Europe]	99.00
Upper-middle income countries				
Average				**85.75**
Lowest	Dominican Republic, Americas	**95.77**	[Namibia, Africa]	32.00
Highest	Belarus, Europe	81.00	[Bulgaria, Europe] [Palau, Western Pacific]	100.00

Table 5 Disparity in access to safe drinking water/sanitation facilities, 2012
Source: World Health Organization (WHO), Retrieved from http://www.who.int/gho/database/en/.

Health Outcomes

Health outcome is defined as a change in the health status of an individual (or population groups and subgroups) as a result of interventions (such as health policy), and effects of socio-environmental factors and individual lifestyle choices. Poor health outcomes in developing countries continue to persist as one of the biggest challenges to health care. All of the factors, including a disproportionately higher burden of disease, environmental conditions and cultural aspects – as presented above – converge with micro- and macro-level factors to impact health outcomes. Such micro- and macro-level factors, for example, could respectively be an individual's socioeconomic status and the strength of health care systems. A basic indicator of health outcome is life expectancy. Economic advancement accompanied by a rapid diffusion of technology from the developed world helped to bring down the death rate and extend life span in developing countries (Bloom 2012). Such technology diffusion improved living conditions in developing countries through increased access to vaccines, sanitation and safe water. Yet in certain parts of the world, particularly in sub-Saharan Africa, events such as civil war and the heavy burden of HIV/AIDS result in low levels of life expectancy (Hoeffler 2008; WHO 2013). This particular fact comes out clearly through the numbers listed in Table 6 below. The lowest life expectancy for each of the country groupings across the three income levels is consistently in a country in sub-Saharan Africa. Beyond that trend, the statistics in Table 6 also reveal that the higher the level of income per capita in a country, the higher is the life expectancy.

Low income countries	**Country, Region**	**Life expectancy at birth, 2012**
Average		**61.27**
Lowest	Sierra Leone, Africa	46.00
Highest	Vietnam, South East Asia	76.00
Lower-middle income countries		
Average		**68.21**
Lowest	Lesotha, Europe	50.00
Highest	Maldives, South East Asia	77.00
Upper-middle income countries		
Average		**73.78**
Lowest	South Africa, Africa	59.00
Highest	[Chile, Americas] [Lebanon, Eastern Mediterranean]	80.00

Table 6. Disparity in life expectancy across countries, 2012. *Source: World Health Organization (WHO), Retrieved from http://www.who.int/gho/database/en/.*

Two other key indicators of health outcomes, **maternal and infant mortality**, relate to reproductive and child health. While **maternal mortality rate** is the number of women who die during pregnancy and childbirth, per 100,000 live births, **infant mortality** rate is the number of infants dying before reaching one year of age, per 1,000 live births in a given year (World Bank, 2014). Both outcomes are typified by wide inter- and intra-region disparities. In fact, the current burden of maternal mortality in the low- and middle-income countries is 15 times higher than that in high income countries (World Bank 2013). Similarly, infant mortality rate in the more developed regions is one-eighth of the rate prevailing in the developing parts of the world (UN 2011).

The impact of high levels of maternal and child death in the less developed regions of the world is staggering. Consequently, massive resources have been committed worldwide towards reducing the twin burdens through strategies outlined in MDG-4 (reduce child mortality) and MGD-5 (improve maternal health). Such consorted policy efforts have improved maternal and child health in a number of the resource poor nations of the developing world. Yet, in some countries, particularly those in sub-Saharan Africa and South Asia, current levels of maternal and child death continue to remain unacceptably high.

In a majority of the developing countries, the percentage of births that are attended by skilled health staff and the percentage of children who are immunized against vaccine-preventable diseases are low. As a result, a large proportion of the maternal and child death in developing countries are attributable to preventable causes. In Table 7, the levels of maternal mortality ratio (MMR) and the percentage of births attended by skilled health staff are listed.

Income group	Percent (%) of total births attended by skilled health staff, 2007-12	Maternal mortality ratio (per 100,000 live births)*, 2013
Low-income	49	440
Lower middle income	59	240
Upper middle income	97	57

Table 7. Disparity in reproductive health and health care outcomes across countries by income groups
Source: *2013 World Development Indicators, Table 2.17 – Reproductive health. Retrieved from http://wdi.worldbank.org/table/2.17*
*Note: * Model estimates developed by the WHO, UNICEF, UNFPA, and the World Bank.*

In Table 8, infant mortality rate is compared against the percentage of children, ages 12 to 23 months, immunized against the most common diseases. Although a bivariate relation does not provide the full picture, it nevertheless indicates the existence of an inverse relation between the two sets of indicators in each of these tables: (i) the lower the percentage of births attended by skilled health staff, the higher is the MMR in a country; and (ii) the lower the percentage of children immunized against vaccine preventable diseases, the higher is the under-five mortality rate. For example, whereas in Fiji, on average, all births between 2007 and 2012 were attended by skilled health staff, in Sudan, only a quarter of the birth (not shown in the table) occurred in the presence of skilled health staff. Not surprisingly, the estimated MMR in 2013 in Sudan (360 per 100,000 live births) was 6 times higher than that in Fiji (59 per 100,000 live births). Similarly, the under-five mortality rate in Uganda (66 per 1,000 live births) in the same year was four times higher than that in Peru (17 per 1,000 live births).

Income group	Infant mortality (per 1,000 live births), 2013	Under-5 Mortality Rate (per 1,000 live births), 2013
Low income countries	53	76
Lower-middle income countries	44	59
Upper-middle income countries	16	20

Table 8. Disparity in child health and health care outcomes across countries by income groups, 2013
Source: 2013 World Development Indicators, Table 2.16 – Disease prevention coverage and quality; and Table 2.21 Mortality. Retrieved from http://wdi.worldbank.org/table/2.16 and http://wdi.worldbank.org/table/2.21#

WRAP-UP:

In this chapter we visited the major themes characterizing health and health care in developing countries. We grouped these themes under two broad categories corresponding to (i) characteristics of health care and (ii) health-related disadvantages in developing countries. In discussing these topics, the aspect that we particularly highlighted upon was disparity in health care and health-related disadvantages in developing countries. The snapshot that came out of this narrative is: the higher the level of income in a country, the better were the outcomes on the different health and health care indicators we considered. While a finding of such two-way associations is only descriptive in nature, it is the essential first step in an analysis on health, health care, or any other subject.

We also learned that inequities exist not only between the developed countries and their less developed counterparts, but also between countries across the regions of the developing world. Developing countries, which have lower levels of health care and higher levels of health disadvantages invariably, lack a strong health system. Among a number of factors, the two chief reasons behind weak health systems in the developing world are inadequate health funding and insufficient number of skilled health workers. Other significant limiting factors are scant health data and information, and poor institutional capacity, particularly in terms of health governance and health management. These drawbacks are most often exacerbated by irrational government policies, such as deficient health budgets that skew spending towards curative care instead of promotive and preventive care, and urban-biased policies. These inefficiencies reach acute levels in countries that lack social and political stability and/or are mired in civil unrest.

CLASS ACTIVITY:

Students can work in groups for this exercise.

Develop a framework to analyze and report the health status, health services, and health systems of a particular country. And if necessary, compare and contrast that country with another along these dimensions.

- Choose a country and obtain approval from the professor for your country.
- Gather data and list your country's socio-economic, and health indicators.
- List/describe your country's population, health status, risk factors, and access to care
- List/describe your country's health financing, health insurance, and expenditures
- List/describe your country's public health services, ambulatory health services, hospital services, long term care services, and mental health services
- List/describe your country's health technology and health workforce
- List/describe your country's health public policy, health care quality, and health care ethics.

CASE STUDY:

This section presents case studies on three countries: Peru, the Philippines and Uganda. The comparisons have been made using the framework discussed in the previous sections. The three countries differ from each other, not only with respect to their size, but also on their levels of socio-economic development. The Philippines is the largest country with a total population of 93 million, followed by Uganda (33 million) and Peru (29 million). As of 2010, Peru is an upper-middle income country with a per capita income of $4,900 (PPP int. $), the Philippines, a lower-middle income country with a per capita income of $2,060 and Uganda, a low-income country with a per capita income of $550.

One of the key health indicators analyzed across these three countries is life expectancy. Although, for each of these countries, intra-country disparities across geographic regions and different socio-economic groups are wide, people on average lived longer as aggregate income levels increased across the three countries. As of 2012, on an average, Peruvians have a life expectancy of 77 years; Filipinos and Ugandans, in comparison, have a life expectancy of 69 and 57 years respectively.

Although income is not the sole determinant of how long people live or the quality of health services, it is unarguably one of the most important predictors of the quality of health care services in a country (Newhouse, 1977). The bivariate relation between income and average life expectancy do by no means imply causation but is solely descriptive in nature. Similarly, the availability of hospitals, and access to them depends on the economic prosperity of a country.

For a large section of the population in developing countries such as Peru, the Philippines and Uganda, the government is the main provider of health and education services. Therefore, the availability and access to basic health services depends largely on whether the developing country governments recognize the need and invest adequate resources in the health care sector.

As would be expected, government spends the most per person in Peru ($327) (PPP int. $), followed by the Philippines ($76), and then Uganda ($26) (The dollar figures have been rounded up). In terms of health infrastructure, as of 2012, physician-to-population ratio is the highest in the Philippines (1.153 per 1000 people), followed by Peru (1.132) and Uganda (0.117). However, with respect to access to care indicated by the success rate of immunization, and availability of generic medicines, Peru out-performs the Philippines and Uganda.

Despite the fact that a number of the infectious diseases that plague the developing countries are easily preventable or even treatable (for example malaria), HIV-AIDS and malaria continue to take a heavy toll of human lives in the developing world, killing mostly children and young adults (WHO, 2010). Therefore, the performance of these countries in dealing with these two communicable diseases is also listed in the table. As general trends indicate, the Sub-Saharan African region is the worst affected in terms of both these diseases. Peru (the upper-middle income country) does better than the Philippines (the lower-middle income country), while Uganda (low-income country) is the worst performer.

Further, it is conventional knowledge that as a country progresses on the socioeconomic scale, the burden of diseases shifts from communicable to non-communicable diseases explained largely on account of changing lifestyles, or an improved cure/prevention rate of communicable diseases. The three case studies discussed here, however, provide evidence to the contrary. While Uganda, a low-income country has the highest percent of deaths resulting from non-communicable diseases (64%), Peru has the lowest share of deaths (46%). Perhaps, this finding could be explained on account of better access to care in an upper-middle income country like Peru as opposed to Uganda.

INDICATORS	INDICATOR CODE	PERU	PHILIPPINES	UGANDA
Socio-economic and Demographic indicators				
Population, 2010	RS_576	29,076,512	93,260,800	33,424,683
GNI per capita income Atlas method, 2010	RS_576	4,900	2,060	500
Literacy rate among adults >= 15 years	WHS9_85	89.6% (2007)	95.4% (2008)	73.2% (2010)
Health status/Risk factors				
Prevalence of HIV among adults aged 15-49 years (Estimates), 2013	MDG_0000000029	0.3%	No data	7.4%
Estimated number of reported deaths from malaria, 2010	MALARIA003	42	143	17,431
% of Non-communicable deaths (NCD) under 70 years, 2012	NCD_UNDER70	46%	57%	64%
Percentage of children aged less than 5 years underweight, 2011	WHOSIS_000008	4.2%	20.2%	14.1%
Life expectancy, 2012	WHOSIS_000001	77 years	69 years	57 years
Access to care				
Percent of 1 year old children who are immunized against polio, 2011	WHS4_544	91%	80%	82%
Percent of 1 year old children who are immunized against DTP3 (Diphtheria, Tetanus toxoid, and pertussis), 2011	WHS4_100	91%	80%	82%
Median availability of selected generic medicines (%) – Public	MDG_0000000010	61.5% (2005)	15.4% (2005)	20% (2004)
Health care financing/insurance				
Per capita government expenditure on health (PPP int. $), 2012	WHS7_108	$326.70	$76.40	$25.70
Health technology and workforce				
Number of physicians per 1000 people	HRH_26	1.132 (2012)	1.153 (2004)	0.117 (2005)
Number of nursing and midwifery personnel per 1000 people	HRH_26	1.514 (2012)	6 (2004)	1.306 (2005)

Table A.1 Health and socio-economic/demographic indicators across Peru, the Philippines and Uganda

Notes: All the figures have been obtained from the WHO Global Health Observatory Data Repository, for the latest available year. Retrieved from http://www.who.int/gho/database/en/.

DISCUSSION QUESTIONS:

1. How do the countries compare with one another with respect to the socio-economic and health status indicators?
2. Compare and contrast the per capita government expenditure on health to:
   - Health status indicators across the three countries.
   - Available health technology across the three countries.

REFERENCES:

Ahsan, G., Ahmed, J., Singhasivanon, P., Kaewkungwal, J., Okanurak, K., Suwannapong, N., ... & Belayetali, K. (2004). Gender difference in treatment seeking behaviors of tuberculosis cases in rural communities of Bangladesh.

Barnum, H., & Kutzin, J. (1993). *Public hospitals in developing countries: resource use, cost, financing.* Johns Hopkins University Press.

Bloom, D. E. (2012). Population Dynamics in India and Implications for Economic Growth. In C. Ghate (Ed.), *The Oxford Handbook of the Indian Economy.* Oxford: Oxford University Press. Retrieved from http://www.oxfordhandbooks.com/view/10.1093/oxfordhb/9780199734580.001.0001/oxfordhb-9780199734580-e-15.

Codlin, A. J., Khowaja, S., Chen, Z., Rahbar, M. H., Qadeer, E., Ara, I., ... & Khan, A. J. (2011). Gender differences in tuberculosis notification in Pakistan. *The American journal of tropical medicine and hygiene, 85*(3), 514-517.

Coroneo, M. T., Di Girolamo, N., & Wakefield, D. (1999). The pathogenesis of pterygia. *Current opinion in ophthalmology,* 10(4), 282-288.

Hoeffler, A. (2008). Dealing with the Consequences of Violent Conflicts in Africa. Background Paper for the African Development Bank Report. Centre for the Study of African Economies, University of Oxford: Oxford.

Hubley, J., & Gilbert, C. (2006). Eye health promotion and the prevention of blindness in developing countries: critical issues. *British journal of ophthalmology,* 90(3), 279-284.

Lancaster, G., Maitra, P., & Ray, R. (2006). Gender Bias in Nutrient Intake Evidence from Selected Indian States. *South Asia Economic Journal,* 7(2), 255-299.

Katona, P., and Katona-Apte, J. (2008). The Interaction between Nutrition and Infection. *Clinical Infectious Diseases,* 46(10): 1582-1588.

Khan, A. A. M. (1984). Improving Delivery of Health Care in Bangladesh. *Geographical Review,* 100-106.

Makinen, M., Waters, H., Rauch, M., Almagambetova, N., Bitrán, R., Gilson, L., ... & Ram, S. (2000). Inequalities in health care use and expenditures: empirical data from eight developing countries and countries in transition. *Bulletin of the World Health Organization,* 78(1), 55-65.

Newhouse, J. P. (1977). Medical-care expenditure: a cross-national survey. *Journal of human resources,* 115-125.

National Statistics Office [The Philippines] and ICF Macro. 2009. National Demographic and Health Survey 2008. Calverton, Maryland: National Statistics Office and ICF Macro.

PhilHealth. 2012. Accessed online at http://www.philhealth.gov.ph/about_us/.

Rumbold, V. (2008). Sexual and Gender Based Violence in Africa: Literature Review. Population Council: New York.Silverman, J.G., M. Decker, N. Saggurti, D. Balaiah, and A. Raj. (2008). Intimate Partner Violence and HIV Infection Among Married Indian Women. Journal of American Medical association 300(6): 703-710.

Silverman, J.G., M. Decker, N. Saggurti, D. Balaiah, and A. Raj. (2008). Intimate Partner Violence and HIV Infection Among Married Indian Women. Journal of American Medical association 300(6): 703-710.

Skolnik, R. (2012), "Global health 101", Second Edition, Jones and Bartlett Publisher.

Stevens, P. H. I. L. I. P. (2011). The challenge of non-communicable diseases in developing countries: Lessons from HIV and Global Health, Center for Medicine in the Public Interest, New York.

Taylor, S. L., Coates, M. L., Vallejos, Q., Feldman, S. R., Schulz, M. R., Quandt, S. A., ... & Arcury, T. A. (2006). Pterygium among Latino migrant farmworkers in North Carolina. *Archives of environmental & occupational health,* 61(1), 27-32.

The United Nations (UN). (2011). http://esa.un.org/wpp/unpp/panel_indicators.htm.

The WHO Global Malaria Programme. Insecticide-treated mosquito nets: a WHO position statement. Geneva: World Health Organization; 2007.http://www.who.int/malaria/publications/atoz/itnspospaperfinal.pdf.

World Bank. 1993. World Development Report 1993: Investing in Health. New York: Oxford University Press. © World Bank. Accessed at https://openknowledge.worldbank.org/handle/10986/5976 License: CC BY 3.0 IGO.

The World Bank (WB). (2004). *Beyond Economic Growth* Student Book, Accessed online at http://www.worldbank.org/depweb/english/beyond/global/glossary.html.

The World Bank (WB). (2011). Hospital beds. Accessed online at http://data.worldbank.org/indicator/SH.MED.BEDS.ZS.

The World Bank (WB). (2013). "Defining Gender", Accessed at http://web.worldbank.org/WBSITE/EXTERNAL/TOPICS/EXTGENDER/0,,contentMDK:20193040~pagePK:210058~piPK:210062~theSitePK:336868,00.html.

The World Bank (WB). (2014). Accessed online at http://data.worldbank.org/indicator/.

The World Bank (WB). (2014). World Development Indicators. Accessed online at http://wdi.worldbank.org/table/2.21.

The World Health Organization (WHO). (2010). Accelerating progress towards the health-related Millennium Development Goals. WHO/DGO/2010.2, WHO: Geneva.

The World Health Organization (WHO). (2013). Nutrition: Feto-maternal nutrition and low birth weight. Accessed online at http://www.who.int/nutrition/topics/feto_maternal/en/.

The World Health Organization (WHO). (2013). Medical Center: Female genital mutilation. WHO: Geneva. Accessed online at http://www.who.int/mediacentre/factsheets/fs241/en/

The World Health Organization (WHO). (2014). Health systems. Accessed online at http://www.who.int/healthsystems/topics/en/.

The World Health Organization (WHO). (2014). Global Health Observatory Data Repository. Retrieved from http://www.who.int/gho/database/en/.

United Nations High Commission for Refugees (UNHCR). (2003). Sexual and Gender-Based Violence against Refugees, Returnees and Internally Displaced Persons: Guidelines for Prevention and Response. Accessed online at: http://www.refworld.org/docid/3edcd0661.html.

World Trade Indicators. 2009/10. "*WTI Country Classification by Region and Income*". Retrieved from http://siteresources.worldbank.org/INTRANETTRADE/Resources/239054-1261083100072/Country_Classification_by_Region_Income_Dec17.pdf

Chapter 13:

Workforce Challenges and Initiatives

Nancy Sayre

KEY CONCEPTS:

Baby Boomers
Chronic condition
Cultural diversity
Cultural proficiency
Diversity
Generation X
Healthcare workforce development
Inclusive excellence
Millennials
Multigenerational workforce
National CLAS standards
Patient-practitioner concordance
Professionalism
Veterans

CHAPTER OVERVIEW:

In the future, leaders of healthcare organizations will be stressed by enormous workforce challenges. These include hiring and retaining sufficient talented workers to address the growth of the insured population as a result of the Patient Protection and Affordable Care Act and the growing elderly population. These will confront an industry already dealing with accelerating costs, declining reimbursement, an aging workforce, shortages of professionals, burdensome regulations and new performance expectations. Healthcare workforce development is required to recruit, train, and retain competent and diverse healthcare workers in adequate numbers now and into the future to provide care to an increasingly diverse patient population in a society with changing demographics. Healthcare organizations will be able to maintain quality services and respond to new opportunities if they address the critical issue of workforce development.

WHY IS THIS IMPORTANT?

The Patient Protection and Affordable Care Act may change the landscape of healthcare delivery from adding 32 million individuals with newly obtained healthcare coverage, to changing the paradigms around how, where, and by whom, care is given (Robert Wood Johnson Foundation, 2011). The ways that this legislation will affect the workforce and the education and training in preparing future generations of healthcare workers must be addressed, especially given pre-existing workforce challenges. Good planning and practices of human capital management or good healthcare workforce development surround recruiting, training, and retaining competent workers, so that they can continue to provide high quality healthcare services to a diverse patient population. As rates of migration and immigration change the demographics of the aging U.S. patient population, healthcare workers must provide culturally competent care. Healthcare services that are respectful of and responsive to the beliefs, practices and cultural and linguistic needs of all patients can help bring about positive health outcomes and help close the health disparities gap among minority populations.

CHAPTER EXPECTATIONS:

Upon reading this chapter, the student will be able to:

- Identify the factors creating workforce challenges in healthcare organizations
- Analyze best practices for creating and sustaining a positive, talented and diverse healthcare workforce
- Explain the concept of cultural proficiency and related approaches to develop skills and knowledge
- Create management plans for addressing healthcare workforce development strategies for organizations and assessing their value in terms of the individual and organization
- Assess personal and organizational awareness of attitudes and beliefs about culturally diverse or minority populations

WHAT YOU SHOULD KNOW:

Trends in society and the labor force are affecting the nation's ability to deliver quality patient care in healthcare organizations whether a hospital, physician office or other setting. Those trends are explained and are followed by best practices and recommendations for healthcare workforce development.

Demographics and the Changing Patient Population

By 2050, the U.S. population is expected to reach 439 million up from 309 million in 2010 (American Medical Association, 2012). The age of the population is changing, with those aged 65 or older growing at a faster rate than other age groups and comprising the largest segment of the population in the future. By 2030, 78 million boomers will become eligible for Medicare (Robert Wood Johnson Foundation, 2011). As the population grows older, the incidence of chronic diseases will increase. Predictions are that by 2030, 60% of the population age 65 or older will be managing more than one chronic condition (American Medical Association, 2012).

As well as older, the patient population is becoming more racially and ethnically diverse. The U.S. Census projects that by 2050, Hispanic and Asian populations will triple, the black population will double, and the white population will remain the same (Salisbury & Byrd, 2006). Many communities will become increasingly multicultural and some geographic areas in the U.S. have already become majority/minority areas. These shifts in demographics will be reflected in the patient population, and caring for older patients with chronic conditions and diverse patients of varied backgrounds will be the norm.

> **Reminder!** A chronic condition is a disease or symptom that persists over time, typically more than three months. Examples include: diabetes, asthma, and hypertension.

The Aging, Shrinking, and Multi-Generational Healthcare Workforce

By 2016, one-third of the total workforce will be 50 years or older, and an aging workforce poses challenges for the healthcare industry (Harrington & Heidkamp, 2013). According to the 2008 National Sample Survey of Registered Nurses released in September 2010 by the federal Division of Nursing, the average age of the RN population in 2008 was 46 years of age, up from 45.2 in 2000 (U.S. Department of Health and Human Services,

2010). By 2020, nearly half of all registered nurses will be old enough to retire (Harrington, 2013). Nationwide, more than 80% of dentists were over age 45 in 2001 and 40% of practicing physicians are older than 55 years (Harrington, 2013; Robert Wood Johnson Foundation, 2011). If current trends continue, it will be difficult to replace the current workforce as large numbers of older health professionals retire.

By The Numbers!

- By 2030, 78 million boomers will become eligible for Medicare (RWJF, 2011).
- By 2020, nearly half of all registered nurses will be old enough to retire (Harrington & Heidkamp, 2013).
- By 2016, one-third of the total health care workforce will be 50 years or older (Harrington & Heidkamp, 2013).
- By 2010, 94% of all hospital CEOs was white whereas, only 65 % of the population was white (American College of Healthcare Executives, 2010).
- By 2010, Hispanics represented 15% of the U.S. population but 2.8% of physicians (Evans, Johnson, Garman, & Kletke, 2013).
- By 2001, nationwide, more than 80% of dentists were over age 45 and 40% of practicing physicians were older than 55 years (Harrington, 2013; Robert Wood Johnson Foundation, 2011).

To complicate matters, competition for talented individuals is becoming intense as the labor force is shrinking. Economists have pointed out that the employment-to-population ratio has been dropping. Since the early 1960s, labor-force participation among men ages 25 to 64 years has declined which has somewhat been masked by the surge of women in the labor force, but since 2000 even women's participation has been declining (Galston, 2013). The explanations for this trend in the U.S. labor force are myriad, such as tax policies, falling real wages, a shift away from marriage and entitlements. The shrinking labor force is even more acute for clinical positions in healthcare organizations. The shortage of primary care physicians, nurses, dentists and mental health workers has been growing for years and the trend is expected to accelerate. High vacancy rates in hospitals have been reported for multiple positions especially nurses (Evans, Johnson, Garman & Kletke, 2013). This shortage is global in scope with the World Health Organization currently estimating a shortage of 2.4 million physicians, nurses, and midwives (Kuehn, 2007). The shortage of health professionals is exacerbated in rural and remote geographic areas of the United States where there may be too few physicians, dentists and behavioral health professionals. The low population density and long distances make it problematic to find care, particularly primary care. Typically, physicians choose other more lucrative specialties because of their large educational debt.

Presenting an additional challenge, multiple generations of individuals will be mixed in the healthcare workplace. Shaped by the historical, political and social events of the generation in which one was born–work ethic, attitude toward authority, career aspirations, and values all vary. Typically, a generation spans 15 to 20 years and in today's workforce, four distinct generations can include the Veterans or Traditionalists, Baby Boomers, Generation X, and the Millennials or Generation Y. The **Veterans** (1925 to 1945) possess organizational loyalty, and are respectful of authority, supportive of hierarchy, and disciplined in their work habits. The **Baby Boomers** (1946 to 1964) bring wisdom to the workplace, and are known for their strong work ethic because work often defines their self-worth. **Generation X** (1965 to 1980) individuals are self-reliant, resilient, and not afraid of change and value a work-life balance. They tend to have less loyalty to the organization. **Millennials** (1981 to 2000) tend to be more comfortable with technology and multi-culturalism. Knowing the background and perspective of each generation may help bring together employees across the ages and build teams that work together (Murphy, 2007).

Diversity In The Healthcare Workforce

Many groups remain underrepresented in health professions relative to their numbers in the U.S. population. For example, in 2010, Hispanics represented 15% of the U.S. population, but 2.8% of physicians (Evans, 2013). Similarly, African Americans comprised 12% of the population, but only 3.3% of physicians (Evans, 2013). Why is it important that there is **patient-practitioner concordance**, a term that means the patient and practitioner, typically a physician, match in terms of race, ethnicity, gender or sexual orientation? A considerable number of studies have investigated patient-physician concordance. Minority patients tend to receive better interpersonal care from practitioners of their own race or ethnicity and non-English speaking patients experience better interpersonal care, greater medical comprehension, and greater likelihood of keeping follow-up appointments when there is concordance with the language of the provider (U.S. Department of Health and Human Services, Health Resources and Services Administration, Bureau of Health Professions, 2006). The mismatch extends to health care managers as well. In 2010, 94% of all hospital CEOs was white according to the American Hospital Association, whereas, only 65% of the population was white, according to the most recent U.S. Census Bureau data (American College of Healthcare Executives, 2010). Greater racial and ethnic diversity corresponding to the patient population has been associated with enhanced patient care and satisfaction, improved clinical outcomes, and stronger financial performance of healthcare organizations (Witt & Kiefer, 2011).

What is patient-practitioner concordance? It is typically defined as a commonality, or shared identity, between practitioner and patient based on a demographic attribute, such as race, gender, sexual orientation, or age.

Foreign-Born or Internationally-Trained Healthcare Workers

The number of foreign-born healthcare workers in the United States has been on the rise, increasing from 1.5 million to 1.8 million between 2006 and 2010 (McCabe, 2012). Immigrants account for 16% of those employed as healthcare workers in the U.S. with approximately 22% of all aides and 27% of physicians and surgeons (McCabe, 2012). About 6,000 internationally-trained medical graduates complete residency training in the United States each year (Shusterman, 2009). Many of them remain in the United States, often practicing in underserved areas to meet visa requirements. Others may like to stay, but eventually practice elsewhere due to annual visa quotas and immigration restrictions. In some specialties, such as cardiology, internal medicine, psychiatry, and nephrology, foreign trained physicians comprise 30% or more of all active physicians (Shusterman, 2009). In 2010, women accounted for three of every four foreign-born healthcare workers and 40% of them were born in Asia (McCabe, 2012). Although foreign-born healthcare workers may speak English fluently, be naturalized citizens and hold a college degree, differences in values, attitudes and beliefs may surface in the workplace in contrast to those born in the United States.

Healthcare Workforce Policies

Under the Affordable Care Act, a National Health Care Workforce Commission was authorized to be composed of 15 health workforce experts and professionals to do data collection and analysis, and set recommendations to help the nation meet its ever-growing and changing workforce needs. The Commission was designed to examine ways to ensure the number and characteristics of practitioners and primary care and rural practitioners mirrored the changing U.S. demographics. The Commission never began its work and most likely will never be funded. Apart from politics and based on the megatrends mentioned, most would agree that the nation's health care system is in serious need of an integrated, comprehensive, forward-thinking, national health workforce policy. In addition, a team-based approach to healthcare delivery has been called for to increase efficiency and decrease costs of patient care and this will become more common. Recognizing the need to contain spiraling acute care costs, primary care programs will be emphasized and require more primary care practitioners, including physicians, nurse practitioners and physician assistants. For example, "primary-care appointments have leapt 50 percent while the department's staff of primary care doctors has grown by only 9 percent" according to one report of the Veterans Affairs medical system (Oppel & Goodnough, 2014). Sharing responsibility to deliver patient-centered care via shared decision-making and outcomes-driven care will require defined and common goals among teams of providers distributed appropriately in the United States. Healthcare workforce issues may continue to be unresolved in the United States unless policymakers can come to agreement, and leaders can implement bi-partisan solutions appropriate for all.

Role of Leadership in Workforce Development

The future of the healthcare workplace will be different and leaders need to be flexible to adapt to changing circumstances. Leaders must prioritize initiatives to collect metrics about their patient population, analyze the needs of the group, ensure grassroots involvement and set benchmarks for attaining goals related to having a representative workforce through diversity and inclusiveness. Administrators of healthcare organizations must set an example and establish a welcoming culture of openness to all. They must examine the values of the organization; exhibit behaviors, which help set the identity of the organization as an inclusive one; and must be committed to this in the long-term. Resources must be made available to achieve objectives towards a competent, compassionate and diverse workforce as part of the core business. Measurement and accountability should be followed by recognition of success.

The megatrends mentioned here may drive new models of care, necessitating an evaluation of the competencies needed in a healthcare organization. Team-based care and a role for midlevel practitioners may help mitigate the shortage of primary care practitioners in the future. Evidence-based medicine, care coordination, and shared decision-making will be new paradigms and may alter personnel needs. Administrators will need to address these issues with best practices in workforce development to deliver value-based care in the coming years. Ultimately, the goals and related initiatives, and even the supporting culture, rests with the leadership of top administrators and executives of any healthcare organization.

Best Practices for Organizations

Responding to these trends with good business practices is imperative within healthcare organizations. The first step toward developing an effective workforce plan is to conduct a thorough analysis of an organization's workforce situation and data. This analysis should include current demographics, future workplace requirements, and needed competencies. Establishing plans for recruiting, hiring, training, and developing employees will require a strategic workforce plan consistent with the mission, vision, values, and goals of the organization.

Human resource practices are complex and beyond the scope of this chapter, however, establishing a diverse workforce is the focus of recruiting and hiring most related to health equity. Recruiting and retaining diverse employees can enrich the workplace culture, community relations, and the ability to affect the health of the community (American College Healthcare Executives, 2010). The typical mismatch between patients and providers is a compelling rationale to increase the diversity among healthcare workers. **Diversity** can mean any characteristic used to differentiate one individual from another including age, education, race, lifestyle, gender, ethnicity, nationality or sexual orientation. When individuals have varying attitudes, beliefs and values, this is usually referred to as **cultural diversity**. As the patient population changes, diversity initiatives will be paramount to eliminate inequities in the quality and availability of health care for underserved populations. "Increasing racial and ethnic diversity among health professionals is important because evidence indicates that among other benefits, it is associated with improved access to health care for racial and ethnic minority patients, greater patient choice and satisfaction, and better educational experiences for health professions students" (Perez, Hattis & Barnett, 2007). Commonly used in education, the term **inclusive excellence** applies to health care as well; it is recognition of and commitment to an organizational culture that values and engages the rich diversity of employees and patients. Celebrating events such as Cinco de Mayo or Black History Month can raise the level of cultural awareness, and recognizing and perhaps rewarding individuals demonstrating inclusive excellence may set a positive tone.

Training and Retaining–Education for Healthcare Workers

Professionalism is a must for all individuals working in health care. It is easy to identify, but not as simple to teach or instill. Healthcare workers must demonstrate compassion, respect, and empathy and uphold responsibility, and various codes of ethics. Given the variety of settings, individual differences, and many agendas, **professionalism** is a difficult topic but should be based on an obligation to society, a passion for altruism and public service, and a commitment to providing top-notch service to others. Ongoing education for all healthcare workers should address issues such as privacy, confidentiality, bias, sexual harassment, misrepresentation, substance abuse, sleep deprivation, acceptance of gifts, compromising principles, and conflicts of conscience. An example is a hospital workshop offered on creating a more welcoming and safe environment for lesbian, gay, bisexual and transgender individuals. Professionalism can be attained through the acquisition of knowledge and by practicing skills in the real world.

Cultural proficiency is one aspect of professionalism that will be increasingly important as the ethnic and racial profile of the country and patient population shifts. It is defined as policies, behaviors, attitudes and practices that enable individuals and organizations to work effectively in cross-cultural situations. It is the ability to provide appropriate care while meeting the patients' social, cultural, spiritual and linguistic needs. (In the past, cultural proficiency has been termed cultural competency, although because of the potential negative connotation of incompetence, the terminology is evolving). The Joint Commission has published resources to help hospitals integrate communication, cultural competence and patient and family-centered care into organizations (The Joint Commission, 2014).

The goal of training for cultural proficiency should be to reduce health disparities and provide quality care to diverse populations. Best practices include having a broad definition of diversity, establishing ongoing programs, and offering practical yet focused programs with continual assessment and improvement. To promote communication between patients and healthcare workers, the *National Standards for Culturally and Linguistically Appropriate Services in Health and Health Care* (the *National CLAS Standards*) were established in 2005. By providing a blueprint for individuals and organizations, they are intended to promote health equity, improve health care quality, and help eliminate health disparities. Models for cross-cultural communication should be implemented, when addressing differences in ethnicities, races, sexes or ages. Training should include exploring different communication techniques and approaches to conflict and decision-making, but most importantly recognition of the role of respect. Individuals of varying cultures, religions and generations may approach disclosing personal information, completing tasks or learning things in very different ways. To enhance team dynamics, a first step is to create the opportunity to share and learn from each other. Lastly, an evidence-based management approach to training should comprise an assessment of outcomes, satisfaction data, and cost-effectiveness of programs.

Public Policies

Federal, state and local government leaders will need to analyze and project the future needs for healthcare professionals. Medicare, Medicaid and the Department of Veteran Affairs make the largest investment in healthcare workforce development with funding being provided to teaching hospitals. In the future, grants for workforce development may be needed to jumpstart new programs aimed at addressing deficiencies. Minority enrichment programs have been used successfully to increase the number of healthcare providers from underrepresented racial and ethnic populations and other disadvantaged groups (Evans, 2013). Leaders of public agencies and private organizations need to collaborate to ensure a viable health professions pipeline and a competent healthcare workforce. As a component of *Healthy People 2020*, the nation's disease prevention and health promotion agenda, workforce development issues were examined (U.S. Department of Health and Human Services, 2014). It was widely recognized that a diverse and prepared public health workforce is the underpinning of achieving better health and eliminating health disparities in America.

WRAP-UP:

Healthcare workforce development will require acknowledging trends in society that affect employees and patients. Given the shifting demographics in the United States, achieving diversity in the healthcare workforce will help move towards culturally-proficient employees and improve access to preventative and medical services for underserved populations. A competent workforce ready to address challenges and respectfully care for ALL individuals can help address health disparities. One culturally-proficient caregiver at a time can help change the attitudes, values, and beliefs of other workers to help drive the nation towards a place where ALL are welcome at healthcare organizations.

DISCUSSION QUESTIONS:

1. What research should be conducted or data analyzed to ensure that the staff of a large healthcare nonprofit agency matches the client population?
2. What are some predicted impacts on physicians and nurses of an older and more diverse patient population?
3. To promote culturally competent care, what do healthcare workers at different levels of responsibility need to know and do? Or should their knowledge be the same?
4. Should employees be required to participate in cultural proficiency training as a term of their employment? Why or why not?
5. How can an organization document the effectiveness of cultural proficiency programs?
6. How does a manager ensure good communications among healthcare workers when they come from various age groups, countries of origin, religions, and hold different beliefs and values?
7. Are organizations training healthcare professionals for the right skills needed in the future? Why or why not?
8. How should programs and organizations be assessed? What parameters should be evaluated to drive towards success?

ADDITIONAL RESOURCES:

Office of Minority Health United States Department of Health and Human Services
http://minorityhealth.hhs.gov/

U.S. Department of Health and Human Services (n.d.) Foster a 21st Century Health Workforce
http://www.hhs.gov/strategic-plan/health-workforce.html

CLASSROOM ACTIVITIES:

Personal Self-Assessment

Use this tool to heighten your personal awareness of your attitudes and beliefs about culturally diverse or minority populations. Use this scale to rate the following statements.

Ratings:

1. Strongly Agree
2. Agree
3. Neutral
4. Disagree
5. Strongly Disagree

Attitudes and Beliefs	Rating
I respect the culture of my patients and try to learn more about it in order to understand what may affect their health beliefs and understanding of the healthcare system.	
I do not impose my beliefs or values on my patients.	
I believe that other languages are just as important as English.	
I respect my patients' decisions even if they are counter to my ideas or those of most Americans.	
I do not tolerate biased or bigoted comments or behaviors by co-workers.	
I appreciate the difference between communication differences and cultural gaps.	
I understand that health-seeking, decision-making, child-rearing and the role of family members varies by culture.	
I understand that cultural norms can affect communication styles such as eye contact, distance between speakers, humor, and gestures.	
I recognize that limited ability to communicate in English is not a reflection of intelligence.	
I understand that spiritual or religious beliefs may influence my patients' view of wellness or sickness.	
I am open to learning more about other cultures, ethnicities, and life style choices that may impact health and wellness.	

After completing the self-assessment, reflect upon your ratings. Think about: How am I doing? Is this right? Is this enough? Should I go further? What are my next steps? In two to three paragraphs, write about this exercise and your reflections.

Organizational Self-Assessment

Use this tool to heighten the organizational awareness of recommended practices regarding culturally diverse or minority populations. Using the scale, rate your organization according to each statement.

Ratings:

1. Strongly Agree
2. Agree
3. Neutral
4. Disagree
5. Strongly Disagree

Organizational Awareness	Rating
As a management team, we understand the demographics of our current community and the potential impact of future trends and use these in planning.	
As a leadership team, we practice inclusivity, we welcome ALL, and we set a positive example.	
We have inclusive policies and practices that support cultural competence throughout the organization.	
We have a mission, values and strategic goals supportive of ALL.	
We hire, train, and promote employees from all genders, ages, races, sexual orientations, ethnicities, and cultures.	
We are familiar with the U.S. Department of Health and Human Services' Office of Minority Health's National Standards for Culturally and Linguistically Appropriate Services (CLAS) in Health and Health Care.	
We involve our community by soliciting input and have representation by the local population in guiding our actions.	
We conduct data collection and analysis to ensure that effective practices address community needs, language preferences, and socio-cultural factors.	
We invest fiscal resources to support diversity efforts and good workforce management practices.	
Our internal and external communications are respectful of all ages, gender, ethnicities, races, religions, etc. and show our inclusive excellence.	
Our physical space is welcoming to ALL.	

After completing the organizational self-assessment, think upon the ratings. Pick one area that the score might/should be higher. Share with a colleague and brainstorm ideas for improvement.

CASE STUDY:

A major highway passes through a small town in the middle of the United States and has a 23-bed hospital. The town mostly consists of white Americans who have been farming for generations. One summer night, a motor vehicle accident occurred when a car carrying four individuals of Vietnamese descent rolled over due to the driver falling asleep. The driver who was in serious condition was the only one who spoke English. No one at the hospital speaks the language of the victims. The four arrive via ambulance to the Emergency Department. You are the manager on duty at this small hospital. How do you handle this situation?

REFERENCES:

American College of Healthcare Executives (2010). Increasing and sustaining racial/ethnic diversity in healthcare management. Retrieved from http://www.ache.org/policy/minority.cfm

American Hospital Association (2010). Workforce 2015: Strategy trumps shortage. Retrieved from http://www.aha.org/advocacy-issues/workforce/workforce2015.shtml

American Medical Association (2012). Demographics and the health status of the U.S. population: Trends worth watching. Retrieved from *http://www.ama-assn.org/resources/doc/clrpd/demographics-fact-sheet.pdf*

Evans, R.M., Johnson, J.A., Garman, A.N. & Kletke, P. (2013). Meeting the challenge: Career development and targeted enrichment programs insuring a viable pipeline. *Sage Open*. Retrieved from http://sgo.sagepub.com/content/3/2/2158244013484475.full

Galston, W.A. (2013). The incredible shrinking workforce. *The Wall Street Journal*. Retrieved from http://online.wsj.com/news/articles/SB10001424052702303471004579165313972530226

Harrington, L. & Heidkamp, M. (2013, March). The aging workforce: Challenges for the health care industry workforce. The National Technical Assistance and Research Center: Issue brief of the NTAR Leadership Center.

The Joint Commission (2014, July 28). Advancing effective communication, cultural competence, and patient-and family-centered care. Retrieved from http://www.jointcommission.org/Advancing_Effective_Communication/

Kuehn, B.M. (2007). Global shortages of health workers, brain drain stress developing countries. *Journal of American Medical Association*. 298 (16): 1853-1855.

McCabe, K. (2012). Foreign-born health care workers in the United States. Retrieved from http://www.migrationinformation.org/USfocus/display.cfm?id=898

Murphy, S. (2007). Leading a multigeneraltional workforce. Retrieved from http://assets.aarp.org/www.aarp.org_/articles/money/employers/leading_multigenerational_workforce.pdf

Oppel, R.A. & Goodnough, A. (2014, May 29). Doctor shortage is cited in delays at V.A. Hospitals. *The New York Times*. Retrieved from http://www.nytimes.com/2014/05/30/us/doctor-shortages-cited-in-va-hospital-waits.html

Perez T, Hattis P, & Barnett K. (2007, May). Health professions accreditation and diversity: A review of current standards and processes. W.K. Kellogg Foundation. Retrieved from http://www.asph.org/userfiles/Health-Professions-Accreditation-and-Diversity_2007.pdf

Robert Wood Johnson Foundation (2011). Healthcare workforce: Future supply and demand. Washington, D.C.: Alliance for Health Reform. Retrieved from http://www.integration.samhsa.gov/images/res/Workforce,%204.22.pdf

Salisbury, J. & Byrd, S. (2006). Why diversity matters in health care. *CSA Bulletin*. Retrieved from http://www.csahq.org/pdf/bulletin/issue_12/Diversity.pdf

Shusterman, C. (2009, October 8). International medical graduates key to solving the physician shortage. *HealthLeaders Media*. Retrieved from http://www.healthleadersmedia.com/content/PHY-240214/International-Medical-Graduates-Key-to-Solving-the-Physician-Shortage.html

U.S. Department of Health and Human Services, Health Resources and Services Administration, Bureau of Health Professions. (2006, October). The rationale for diversity in the health professions: A review of the evidence. Retrieved from http://bhpr.hrsa.gov/healthworkforce/reports/diversityreviewevidence.pdf

U.S. Department of Health and Human Services, Health Resources and Services Administration. (2010). The registered nurse population: Findings from the 2008 national sample survey of registered nurses. Retrieved from http://bhpr.hrsa.gov/healthworkforce/rnsurveys/rnsurveyfinal.pdf

U.S. Department of Health and Human Services, Health Resources and Services Administration (2014). Public health infrastructure. Retrieved from http://www.healthypeople.gov/2020/topics-objectives/topic/public-health-infrastructure/objectives

Witt & Kiefer (2011). Building the business case: Healthcare diversity leadership: A National survey report. Retrieved from http://www.diversityconnection.org/diversityconnection/membership/Institute-Resource-Center.jsp?fll=S13

Chapter 14:

Trends, Drivers for Change, and Need for Research

Jeffrey Helton

KEY CONCEPTS:

Acute myocardial infarction
American Recovery and Reinvestment Act
Cost effectiveness
Economic incentives
Electronic health record
Employer mandate
Genomic medicine
Health information technology
Individual mandate
Meaningful use
Medicaid
Medical technology
Outcome
Patient experience
Patient portal
Patient Protection and Affordable Care Act
Pay for performance
Process
Structure
Surgical techniques
Telemedicine

CHAPTER OVERVIEW:

The chapter covers important new changes in the health care industry and identifies areas where care to vulnerable populations in the United States may be impacted. Key changes are: increased use of new technologies; expanded use of health information technology applications, provider accountability for quality; the use of quality data to assist consumers in selecting health care providers, and the **Patient Protection and Affordable Care Act of 2010** (commonly referred to as "health reform" or "Obamacare"). Since we do not yet understand how these industry trends have improved (or worsened) disparities in health have improved, further research in these areas will be needed.

WHY IS THIS IMPORTANT?

Health care delivery in the United States is undergoing multiple changes in financing, organization, and accountability. The effect of these changes on the delivery of care to vulnerable populations is as yet undetermined. Will the effects of actions intended to improve our health system reduce currently observed disparities in care? Research in the areas noted here may help us understand where disparities have improved – and where additional work remains.

CHAPTER EXPECTATIONS:

Upon reading this chapter, the reader should be able to describe the following trends, drivers, and areas for further research:

- Access to new medical treatment technology;
- Impacts of the Patient Protection and Accountable Care Act of 2010 (PPACA);
- Impacts of expanded use of health information technology including telemedicine and electronic health records;
- Provider accountability for care including quality of care measures and the relevance of those measures to vulnerable populations; and
- How quality of care data can be used to reduce current disparities in health care.

WHAT YOU SHOULD KNOW:

The health care system in the United States is rapidly changing while the nation itself evolves as well. As you have seen earlier in this text, the needs of different segments of the population are as varied as its origins, orientation, and values. As the health care system changes, its ability to meet the varied needs of an increasingly diverse population could be impacted. How varying health care needs are met in view of major changes expected in the current health care system is yet unknown and fosters a need for greater understanding in the coming years. The reader can use experience, knowledge, and understanding of how health system change will impact the needs of a culturally diverse society to help improve care to all its members. In this chapter, the reader will be introduced to four current health system changes that will likely have an impact on observed disparities in health care services to diverse groups in the United States:

The four areas examined here are:

1. Increased use of new diagnostic and treatment technologies;
2. Expanded use of health information technology applications;
3. Provider accountability for quality in pay for performance programs; and
4. The Patient Protection and Affordable Care Act of 2010

Each of these trends or changes could impact disparities in health care in the United States – for better or worse. We will explore those possibilities – and risks – in this chapter.

Increased use of new technologies

The **medical technology** available to treat and prevent many illnesses has increased significantly in recent years (Lubitz, 2005). Medical technology in this context is usually described as the specific procedures, specialized equipment or tools used to deliver medical care to the sick and injured. The pace of technology advancement seems to be quickening as well.

When considering the potential impact of technology on health disparities, it is not just the ability to treat conditions common to populations suffering disparities that is important. Access to new advances in care is also of interest in measuring any change in currently observed disparities.

In just the past century, there are many areas where technology has improved the efficacy of treating illness or injury. From invention of new drugs, to improvements in prenatal care, refinements in **surgical techniques** (such as use of surgical robots illustrated in Figure 1), to **genomic medicine**, the ability of medical science to treat conditions once considered life threatening is improving quickly.

At the same time, the costs of new technology are also increasing. Unlike many other industries where costs decrease with newer advances, health care demonstrates an opposite pattern – new technology costs more than older technology (Baumol, et al., 2012). In some cases new innovations with higher cost replace lower cost, but adequate technology (CBO, 2008). Much of that increase arises from the research and development costs of new technology. However, the availability of insurance allows new medical care technologies – even those of marginal patient care benefit – to enter the marketplace with little regard to the costs of that innovation (Nyman, 1991).

While new technologies offer the chance to improve health outcomes and health status for much of our population, the fact that they may increase costs could support an argument that advancing technology might actually exacerbate health disparities in coming years. In fact, current health economics principles say that increased technology leads to an increased need for insurance to defray the higher price of a new treatment (Nyman, 1991). Yet we know that lack of access to health insurance resources contributes to many disparities in health care we see in the United States today (Sullivan, 2011).

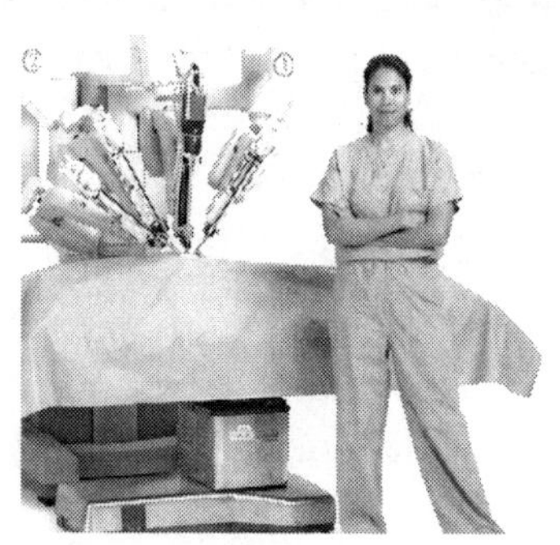

Figure 1.
The DaVinci Surgical Robot
(www.intuitivesurgical.com)

It therefore stands to reason that new treatments would go to areas where there is ample insurance (or general affluence) that can pay the costs of developing and marketing them. In some cases, the need for advanced treatments for cancer or better prenatal care would have the greatest potential benefits for those populations least able to pay for those services. Paradoxically, our current health care system creates strong incentives to provide new treatments where the societal impact may not be as great (Dovidio, et al., 2008).

Is insurance the only means by which vulnerable or underserved populations can access new technology? What advances in health technology come to market that actually reduce the costs per unit of service (**cost effectiveness**), inclusive of its acquisition costs? Are there technologies that produce demonstrable changes in conditions linked to current health disparities such as diabetes, hypertension, asthma, obesity, cancer, and cardiovascular disease? These are among the questions that remain unanswered in terms of the benefit that medical technology could bring to decreasing the current disparities in health care observed in the United States.

New Technologies in Health Care

- Wearable technologies
- 3D Printed tissue and organs
- Optogenetics
- Nanorobots
- Digestible sensors
- Virtual clinical trials

Source: www.referralmd.com

At present, there appear few **economic incentives** to address this problem. Instead, the current fee-for-service payment system only rewards treating illness instead of preventing it. Also, many people who cannot pay are those needing treatment. If people cannot pay, the resources to treat illness tend to go where payments can be obtained, rather than where the services are needed. So a pressing question comes up–Are there new financing mechanisms that would maintain the incentive for innovation while expanding access to new advances in health care?

Related to these questions is the willingness of providers to make new treatments available to the underserved or vulnerable populations currently experiencing disparities in health. Gaddis (2013) raises a poignant question about the availability of a new cardiac care technology that could reduce hospital costs for patients with suspected **acute myocardial infarction** (commonly referred to as "heart attack"). He noted in review of clinical studies of this treatment innovation that it was not always available when needed by patients, due only to the choices of physicians qualified to provide the service. It is an unfortunate reality that some providers may only offer after-hours services to patients with insurance, thus limiting access to new technology to vulnerable and underserved patients. Expanded access to insurance – discussed later in this chapter – may change this dynamic in future years. However, it may also be possible that fees paid under expanded insurance programs will provide inadequate incentive for providers to provide access to new services for all patients. Language barriers may further limit access if insurance programs do not take language into consideration when developing provider networks.

> **What's In It for Me?**
>
> Like manufacturing, health care is a business and like any other business, we do what gets paid for. We call these economic incentives. Health care providers are no different – they do what they get paid to do. Currently, treating illness gets paid (by procedures or treatments) while preventing health does not – since there is no procedure for keeping someone well.

Future consideration should be given to identifying new financing mechanisms that create an optimal level of reimbursement under the current system to create access to new care services for all patients. That examination should also look at what changes occur in the number, types, and frequency of services provided. This can identify what incentives work (or don't work) to address health disparities in our nation. Other opportunities for research may come from identifying patterns among insurers or providers in limiting access to care based on reimbursement issues.

Expanded use of health information technology applications

Since the landmark 2001 National Institutes of Health report, "Crossing the Quality Chasm", health information technology has been viewed as an opportunity to improve care. Among the expected benefits of **health information technology** are better documentation of care, the ability to exchange health information among multiple healthcare providers, sharing health information between providers and their patients, use of clinical decision support to assist providers in better treatment decisions, and use of online reference tools to address difficult clinical problems (Blumenthal & Tavenner, 2010; Chaudry, et al., 2006). Health information technology includes items like the electronic medical records to replace paper patient charts in a physician office or a patient portal to allow patients to view their records over the Internet. While these sorts of technology can help improve patient care and the health of underserved communities, they are expensive–a cost that may not be affordable by providers serving a safety net role in their communities (Gibbons, 2011).

Hing and Burt (2009) found that providers that care for underserved populations are less likely to engage in the use of **electronic health record** ("EHR") technology to care for their patients. While the **American Recovery and Reinvestment Act of 2009** (also known as "ARRA" or the "stimulus act") provided funds to assist safety net providers in acquiring EHR resources, the costs of acquiring, installing and actually operating the systems remain prohibitively high to many providers. The latter of these points – funding ongoing operation and use of EHR software systems–is especially concerning. Despite the high cost to acquire and install this expensive technology, there is at least some subsidy from ARRA for those costs. However there are additional operational costs involved to maintain these systems with code updates, training of staff, and subscription to information exchanges necessary to share patient data in the community. Under ARRA, a provider must "meaningfully use" systems by doing things like checking patient medical histories for allergies to medications or sharing data with other providers in order to qualify for ARRA payments. The costs necessary to meet meaningful use standards are not paid by ARRA subsidies. Those subsidies simply help pay the costs to obtain an EHR. The costs of operating EHR systems must be paid from ongoing operations of a health care provider – something much tougher to do when an organization's clientele are predominantly uninsured or beneficiaries of Medicaid (Butler, et al., 2013). The prospect of changing systems to work with the new ICD-10 diagnosis coding system in 2014 is an example of this prohibitive ongoing cost of maintaining these systems.

To the extent that providers caring for minority and other vulnerable populations have a low rate of adoption of electronic health record systems would have disparities in access to the benefits of that technology otherwise would be available to other populations (Sequist, 2011). Ironically, implementation of EHR in the United States may end up showing that health disparities are worse than we have seen in the past – despite the notion that care should get better. However, use of this technology can gather better data about patient care (where it is used) and may better document the extent to which disparities occur–perhaps identifying new knowledge about disparities. This question will remain a concern as some of this new data is gathered and analyzed. It is also possible that the technology will be unevenly available in a way that parallels existing disparities. Understanding the extent to which these changes actually occur will present an opportunity for future research in health disparities.

In addition to electronic health records, the use of an Internet **patient portal** has been looked at as a tool to assist patients in managing their own health care needs (Gibbons & Casale, 2010). These patient portal technologies provide patients with the ability to directly access their health information and to receive preventive health reminders from their providers. But again, this technology can be expensive and is not covered by the ARRA stimulus program to assist in payment of acquiring electronic health record technology. Sequist (2011) found significant disparities in access to this valuable health care tool where whites were 60% more likely than other minorities to have access to a patient portal tool. In the absence of financial support to providers serving the poor and uninsured for use of patient portals, is another example of a technology with unequal use nationwide – something that will likely further expand observed disparities in health care.

Telemedicine is another example of a health information technology that has the potential to benefit both providers and patients. Telemedicine can allow a provider to expand access to underserved populations or areas such as rural or urban communities that do not have access to a sufficient number of healthcare providers. Implementing telemedicine could thus improve the ability of primary care providers to establish relationships with patients in underserved areas and allow providers in underserved areas to make consultations with specialist physicians such just those at academic medical centers more achievable for people living in medically underserved areas. As with the other technologies discussed here, cost may be a prohibitive factor although the federal government and many commercial insurers are beginning to reimburse telemedicine visits. The significant issue for the poor and underserved populations is the ability of providers who serve a majority of these patients are less likely to be able to pay for a telemedicine program.

Future research is needed to identify the returns on investment for the use of telemedicine (and other health information technologies) to help providers secure capital support to acquire this technology. Expanding access to populations with limited resources to pay – as often seen among underserved populations – does not help fund an investment in telemedicine. ARRA subsidies are also not available to assist in paying for telemedicine, so the challenge becomes finding a way to make a business case for this technology.

In addition, future research may help us identify patterns of lack of equal access and perhaps identify even more contributing factors. Better understanding of the non-cost drivers of disparate adoption of health information technology can direct policy actions to help expand its use in the care of vulnerable populations – perhaps even providing additional support of financial subsidies to providers to acquire such technology.

Provider accountability for quality

There appears a great deal of evidence that racial and ethnic minorities experience poorer health outcomes than do white patients (Sullivan, 2011). Some concerns have been raised in recent research literature suggesting that pay for performance programs may increase disparities in health service access and quality to vulnerable populations (Weissman, et al., 2012). Some authors have suggested that these pay for performance programs could create an incentive for healthcare providers to "cherry pick" patients in order to influence performance scores and maximize reimbursements (Ryan, 2010; Weissman, et al., 2012). Hospital providers serving higher proportions of Medicaid and uninsured patients have demonstrated poorer results on the quality measures that will be used by the Medicare program for pay for performance reimbursements (Helton & Freshman, 2012).

Hospitals and physicians serving high proportions of minority groups and continuing to demonstrate poorer performance quality measures used in **pay for performance** programs over repeated years will find themselves receiving less funding. This poses a significant risk of financial harm to providers serving vulnerable populations. That harm could manifest itself either in closure of a clinic or hospital – which would reduce already limited access to care. The other effect could be cost cutting by organizations in response to reduced payment, resulting in a worsening of care for patients in those organizations (Ryan, 2010; Helton & Freshman, 2012). Either instance could result in an unintended consequence for services to vulnerable populations that increase our existing problems with disparities in care.

Current pay for performance programs are supposed to statistically adjust for cost or risk of severe illness or comorbidities that may exist with patients in vulnerable populations. However, those statistical risk adjustment models are still in their infancy and may not completely identify and control for the risks of health issues common for racial and ethnic minority patients. Since pay for performance programs are becoming tied to reimbursement for providers, the lack of a reasonable control for the risk of serving minority patients could cause potential financial harm to providers serving these populations. Since there is evidence that care to the poor has been associated with poorer outcomes and poor outcomes could result in lost revenues, there is a strong incentive for providers to attempt to direct these patients away or "game" the performance system (Chien, 2011). Because there are potential gaps in the statistical risk adjustment in pay for performance programs, providers may mistakenly perceive that minority patients have greater risks due to issues such as poor prior healthcare or assumptions of a history of noncompliance with medical recommendations. So, providers may find it in their financial interest to limit access to minority patients in order to avoid the risk of lost revenues from pay for performance programs (Ryan, 2010; Chien, 2011; Weissman, et al., 2012).

Evidence supporting this concern is so far fairly limited and represents a significant opportunity for future research. A study by Weissman and colleagues (2012) suggested that pay for performance programs in percutaneous coronary angioplasty (PTCA) did not reduce access to care. However, it did note that providers serving a higher proportion of minority patients did demonstrate poorer performance on PTCA quality measures. A prior study of Medicare pay for performance measures by Ryan in 2010 had a similar finding. Much is it not yet known about the actual long-term consequences of the current pay for performance programs on access to care by vulnerable populations or the extent to which such programs increase existing disparities in care. But currently available research suggests that the actual quality of care received by vulnerable populations is comparable to other persons.

Tell me more:
Pay for Performance

Pay for performance programs provide bonuses to providers for meeting or exceeding quality targets based on these types of goals

Process – How things get done

Outcome – Results of treatments

Patient Experience – How patients feel about their care

Structure – About the resources and staff involved in care

As long as there is a risk to a provider of lost reimbursements for quality–and performance on those quality measures can be influenced by patient population selections–the risk exists that future programs could have an unintended consequence of limiting access to care for minority and ethnic populations. Providers could either find ways to "cherry pick" patients or they could not participate in pay for performance programs. However, in so doing they could potentially limit the reimbursements they collect and possibly impact their ability to provide good quality care to their patients. This question will merit additional future study, once these programs have been in effect for longer periods of time, allowing more data to come into analysis.

One other area of concern on the potential impact of pay for performance plans in addressing health disparities comes from the design of such plans. If a plan seeks only to improve documentation of care processes but does nothing to incentivize changes in the way care is provided, then existing problems in the care of vulnerable populations are not likely to get much better. The care would be better documented, but not necessarily better from a clinical standpoint. Also the incentives in a pay for performance program focused on elderly or wealthier patient populations may not address improvement in the health issues of minority or ethnic patients. A "one size fits all" approach to performance incentives may in fact widen the disparities we see in our current system simply by encouraging caregivers to focus on the needs of patients with a pay for performance reimbursement system and pay less attention to the needs of more vulnerable populations. Further research in the area of developing pay for performance incentives relevant to health disparities is needed.

The Patient Protection and Affordable Care Act of 2010

Much has been said about the relationship between a patient having health insurance and health disparities (Williams 2011). Uninsured persons are much less likely to have a regular source of healthcare services and tend to have higher rates of mortality and chronic disease such as diabetes type pretension and asthma. Current low-income insurance programs (generally known as "**Medicaid**") provide insurance coverage only to select few persons based on a limited scope of medical needs such as pregnancy or long-term care. These public insurance programs while valuable to meet those specific needs, are limited in their ability to serve the large number of poor or low-income minority families. Approximately 80% of the population without insurance is a member of a working family. However many of those people work in jobs that do not offer health insurance. For others, the cost of health insurance is prohibitively high. Public health insurance programs are valuable for meeting specific needs but have a great deal to do to provide coverage for other needy populations (Williams, 2011).

Tell me more:
What's in the ACA?

The Patient Protection and Affordable Care Act of 2010 makes several changes in the U.S. Health Care system including:

Expand access to health insurance – create large marketplaces for insurers to compete for patients and expand state Medicaid programs

Change rules for health insurance plans – requires a minimum level of coverage for preventive health services, makes insurance available to persons with prior serious health conditions, requires insurers to spend a minimum amount of premiums on health care, allows parents to keep insurance on children to age 26, and prevents insurers from terminating coverage.

Individual mandate – persons are required to have health insurance or pay a tax penalty.

Employer mandate – employers of more than 50 persons to provide health insurance benefits to employees or pay a penalty fee.

Source: Adapted from: Williams, R. (2011). The Good, the Bad, and the Ugly: Overview of the Health Reform Law and Its Impact on Health Care Disparities. In R.A. Williams (ed.), Healthcare Disparities at the Crossroads with Healthcare Reform, New York: Springer Science+Business Media.

The **Patient Protection and Affordable Care Act of 2010** ("ACA") was intended to expand insurance coverage to all the persons in the United States beginning in 2014. A part of this program was an expansion of existing state Medicaid programs to permit them to cover all adults with incomes up to 133% of the federal poverty level. Initial estimates suggest that as many as 16 million additional low-income persons will be covered by Medicaid. Expansion of the Medicaid program, coupled with expansion of private insurance coverage through Federal mandates is expected to significantly improve the proportion of people with access to health insurance in the United States. With that greater access to health insurance, it is expected that many health disparities related to access to care could be reduced or eliminated (Williams, 2011). However, the ACA is not just aimed at health insurance needs. The Act also provides for resources to increase the number of providers serving ethnic communities and Native American/Alaskan Native populations; improve the health literacy in vulnerable populations; and increase the health care workforce in underserved communities (Williams, 2011).

The broad scope of this legislation poses a great challenge to the government to implement its multiple provisions. Not only is there a challenge from getting the law implemented, but also once that is done, maintaining the programs will be a challenge. With over $100 billion in funding required from the Federal government from 2010-2019, the Act will represent a significant obligation (Aaron, 2010). A concern with respect to the influence the Act can have on health disparities will be the ability of the United States government to fund its ongoing operation. The current environment of conflict and partisan disagreement in Congress could indeed place some provisions of the Act at jeopardy of being closed down, should legislative priorities change. The future of the Act and its intended improvements in access to health care services for the underserved in the United States will require a ongoing monitoring and advocacy to keep funding available. At the same time, great opportunities will exist to monitor the effectiveness of interventions put into place by the Act to improve or eliminate some health disparities in the United States. Insights from this research could perhaps offer some guidance to the legislative priority setting process when Congress sets future funding levels for programs created by the Act.

WRAP-UP:

The delivery of health care services in the United States is undergoing many significant changes, some of which have the potential to reduce existing health disparities. Expansion of new medical technologies (both diagnostic and information), pay for performance, and health reforms under the 2010 Patient Protection and Affordable Care Act all have potential benefit to vulnerable populations in this country. However, all are such new interventions in the current health care system that little is known about the impact (positive or negative) that these changes can have on the health care system. The need for research to better understand the changes in health disparities in the United States will be valuable not only in identifying areas of improvement, but in a time of legislative partisan conflict it may well guide the Congressional priority setting process.

DISCUSSION QUESTIONS:

1. Pay for performance programs are intended to improve services provided to patients. Is this true for the medically underserved and vulnerable populations? Why or why not?
2. New technology is constantly being added to the United States' health care system, yet it may not be reducing health disparities. Why would this be happening? What ideas might improve this situation?
3. How can health information technology reduce health disparities? What barriers exist to the use of this technology by providers that serve vulnerable populations?

WEB RESOURCES:

More information on current issues in health disparities from the Kaiser Family Foundation:
http://kff.org/disparities-policy/

Information on health information technology:
http://www.healthit.gov/

Information on the Patient Protection and Accountable Care Act and health disparities:
http://www.urban.org/health_policy/vulnerable_populations/

REFERENCES:

Aaron, H. (2010) The midterm elections-high stakes for health policy. New England Journal of Medicine 363 (18), 1685-1687.

Ash A. (2008). Measuring quality. Medical Care, 46(2), 105-8.

Baoumol, W. (2012). The Cost Disease: Why Computers Get Cheaper and Health Care Doesn't. New Haven, CT: Yale University Press.

Bau, I. (2011). The Potential of Health Information and Communications Technologies to Reduce Health Care Disparities. National Civic Review 10, 15-18.

Blumenthal,D. & Tavenner, M. (2010). The "Meaningful Use" Regulation for Electronic Health Records. The New England Journal of Medicine 363 (6), 501-504.

Butler, M., Harootunian, G., & Johnson, W. (2013). Are Low Income Patients Receiving the Benefits of Electronic Health Records? A Statewide Survey. Health Informatics Journal, 19 (2), 91-100.

Casey, D. (2012). Reducing Health Care Disparities: Next Steps Require Better Evidence. American Journal of Medical Quality, 27 (4), 273-274.

Chaudry, B., Wang, J., Wu, S., Maglione, M., Mojica, W., & Roth, E. (2006). Systematic review: Impact of Health information technology on quality, efficiency, and costs of medical care. Annals of Internal Medicine, 144, 742-752.

Chien, A. (2011). The Potential Impact of Performance Incentive Programs on Racial Disparities in Health Care. In R.A. Williams (ed.), Healthcare Disparities at the Crossroads with Healthcare Reform, New York: Springer Science+Business Media.

Congressional Budget Office. (2008). Technological Change and the Growth of Health Care Spending. Washington, DC: Congressional Budget Office.

Dovidio J., Penner L., Albrecht, T., Norton, W., Gaertner, S., & Shelton, J. (2008). Disparities and Distrust: The Implications of Psychological Processes for Understanding Racial Disparities in Health and Health Care. Social Science and Medicine, 67(3), 478–86.

Gaddis, G. (2013). Physicians Who Cause Health Care Outcomes Disparities. Academic Emergency Medicine, 307-308.

Gibbons, M. & Casale, C. (2010). Reducing Disparities in Health Care Quality: The Role of Health IT in Underresourced Settings. Medical Care Research and Review, 67 (5), 155-162.

Helton, J. & Freshman, B. (2012) Does Serving the Poor Reduce Hospital Quality? An Assessment of Cross-Sectional Data – 2006-2009. American Journal of Management, 12 (2), 40-49.

Hing, E. & Burt, C. (2009). Are There Patient Disparities When Electronic Health Records Are Adopted? Journal of Health Care for the Poor and Underserved, 20 (2), 473-488.

Kaiser Family Foundation. (2012). Focus on Health Care Disparities: Key Facts. Retrieved May 15, 2013, from http://kff.org/disparities-policy/issue-brief/disparities-in-health-and-health-care-five-key-questions-and-answers/

Kaiser Family Foundation. (2013). Health Coverage by Race and Ethnicity: The Potential Impact of the Affordable Care Act. Retrieved May 15, 2013, from http://kff.org/disparities-policy/issue-brief/health-coverage-by-race-and-ethnicity-the-potential-impact-of-the-affordable-care-act/

Kaiser Family Foundation. (2007). Snapshots: How Changes in Medical Technology Affect Health Care Costs. Retrieved May 15, 2013, from Kaiser Family Foundation: http://kff.org/health-costs/issue-brief/snapshots-how-changes-in-medical-technology-affect/

Li, C. & West-Strum, D. (2010). Patient Panel of Underserved Populations and Adoption of Electronic Medical Record Systems by Office-Based Physicians. HSR: Health Services Research, 45 (4), 964-984.

Lubitz, J. (2005). Health, Technology, And Medical Care Spending. Health Affairs, 24 (2), 81-85.

Nyman, J. (1991). Costs, Technology, and Insurance in the Health Care Sector. Journal of Policy Analysis and Management, 10 (1), 106-111.

Sequist, T. (2011). Health Information Technology and Disparities in Quality of Care. Journal of General Internal Medicine, 26 (10), 1084–5.

Smedley, B., Stith, A. & Nelson, A. (2003). Unequal treatment: confronting ethnic and racial disparities in health care. Washington, DC: The National Academic Press.

Sogie-Thomas, B. (2007). Pay for Performance and its Potential Impact on American Healthcare. Journal of the National Medical Association 99 (2), 128.

Snowden, A., Kunerth, V., Carlson, A., McRae, J., & Vetta, E. (2012). Addressing Health Care Disparities Using Public Reporting. American Journal of Medical Quality, 27 (4), 275-281.

Sullivan, L. (2011). An Overview of the US Healthcare System and US Health Disparities at the Beginning of the Twenty-First Century. In R.A. Williams (ed.), Healthcare Disparities at the Crossroads with Healthcare Reform, New York: Springer Science+Business Media.

Weissman, J., Hasnain-Wynia, R., Weinick, R., Kang, R., Vogeli, C., Iezzoni, L., and Landrum, M. (2012). Journal of Health Care for the Poor and Underserved 23: 1, 144-160.

Williams, R. (2011). The Good, the Bad, and the Ugly: Overview of the Health Reform Law and Its Impact on Health Care Disparities. In R.A. Williams (ed.), Healthcare Disparities at the Crossroads with Healthcare Reform, New York: Springer Science+Business Media.

Index:

Cultural Learning in Healthcare: Recognizing & Navigating Differences

CPSIA information can be obtained
at www.ICGtesting.com
Printed in the USA
FFOW02n1849150117
31335FF